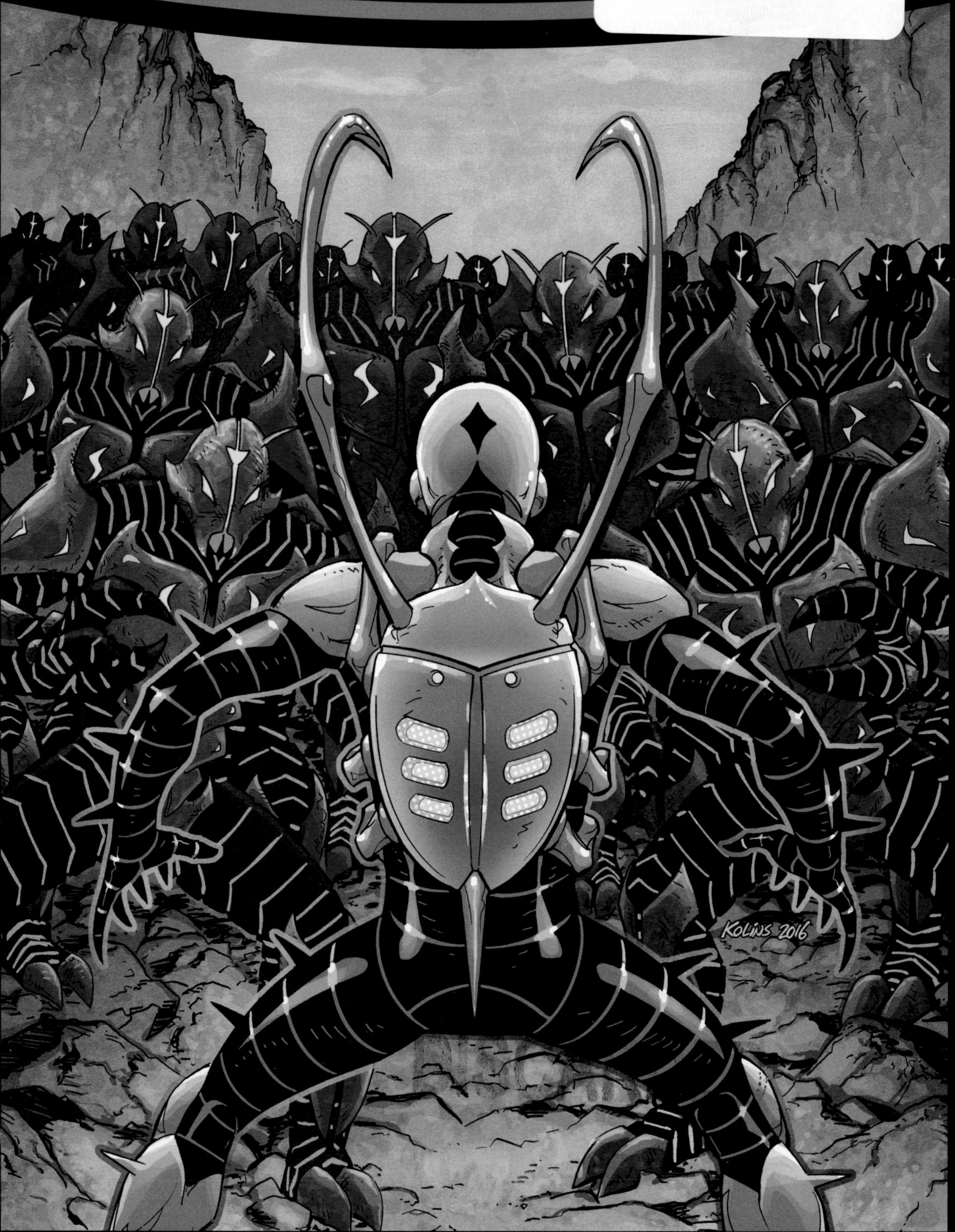
KOLINS 2016

BLUE BEETLE

VOL. 1 THE MORE THINGS CHANGE

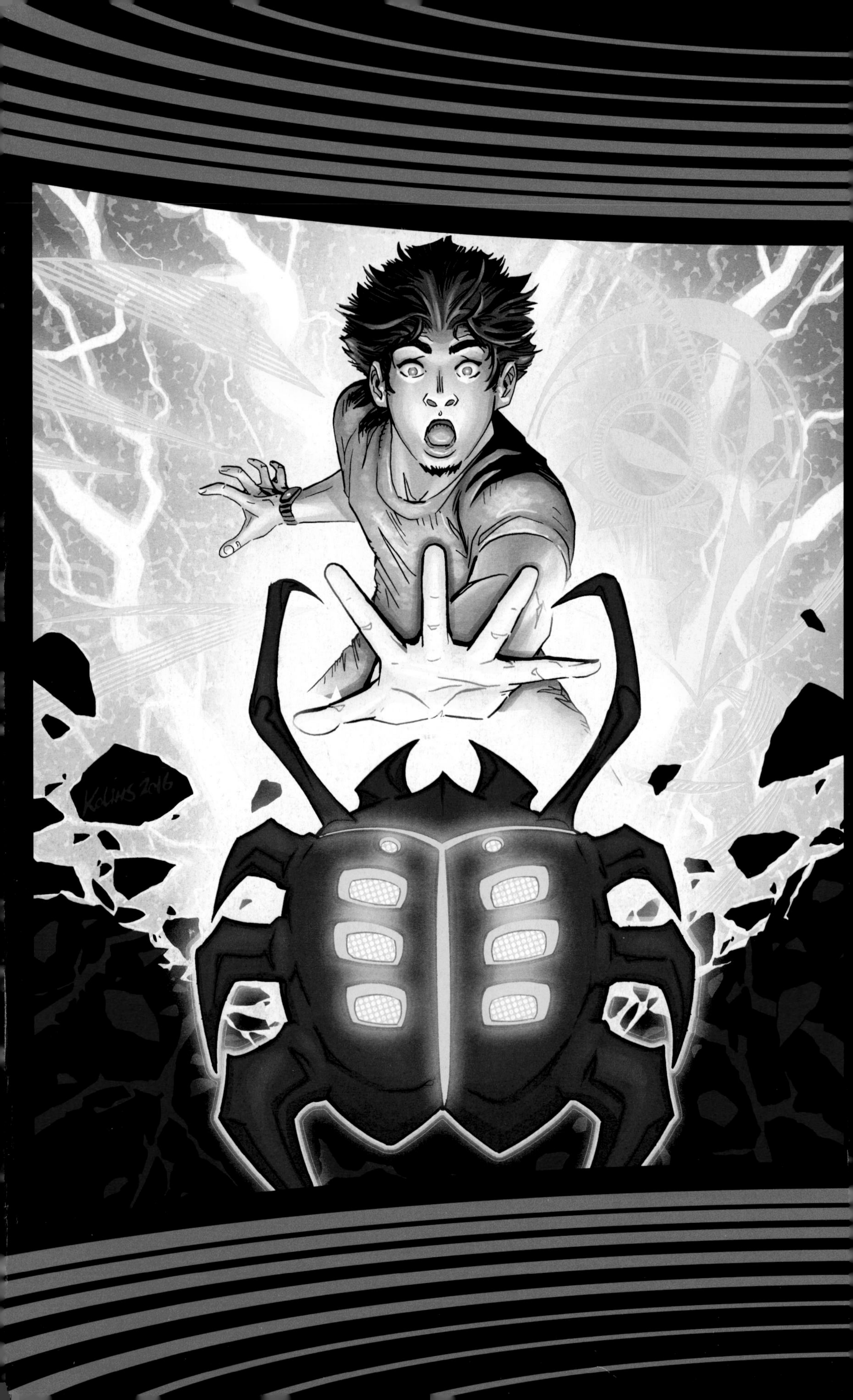

BLUE BEETLE

VOL. 1 THE MORE THINGS CHANGE

KEITH GIFFEN * **SCOTT KOLINS**
story

KEITH GIFFEN
script

SCOTT KOLINS
art

ROMULO FAJARDO JR.
colorist

JOSH REED
letterer

SCOTT KOLINS
series and collection cover artist

Winona Public Library
151 W 5th St
Winona, MN 55987

JIM CHADWICK DAVID WOHL Editors - Original Series ● ROB LEVIN SUSIE ESPARZA Assistant Editors - Original Series
JEB WOODARD Group Editor - Collected Editions ● ERIKA ROTHBERG Editor - Collected Edition
STEVE COOK Design Director - Books ● DAMIAN RYLAND Publication Design

BOB HARRAS Senior VP - Editor-in-Chief, DC Comics

DIANE NELSON President ● DAN DiDIO Publisher ● JIM LEE Publisher ● GEOFF JOHNS President & Chief Creative Officer
AMIT DESAI Executive VP - Business & Marketing Strategy, Direct to Consumer & Global Franchise Management
SAM ADES Senior VP - Direct to Consumer ● BOBBIE CHASE VP - Talent Development
MARK CHIARELLO Senior VP - Art, Design & Collected Editions ● JOHN CUNNINGHAM Senior VP - Sales & Trade Marketing
ANNE DePIES Senior VP - Business Strategy, Finance & Administration ● DON FALLETTI VP - Manufacturing Operations
LAWRENCE GANEM VP - Editorial Administration & Talent Relations ● ALISON GILL Senior VP - Manufacturing & Operations
HANK KANALZ Senior VP - Editorial Strategy & Administration ● JAY KOGAN VP - Legal Affairs
THOMAS LOFTUS VP - Business Affairs ● JACK MAHAN VP - Business Affairs
NICK J. NAPOLITANO VP - Manufacturing Administration ● EDDIE SCANNELL VP - Consumer Marketing
COURTNEY SIMMONS Senior VP - Publicity & Communications
JIM (SKI) SOKOLOWSKI VP - Comic Book Specialty Sales & Trade Marketing
NANCY SPEARS VP - Mass, Book, Digital Sales & Trade Marketing

BLUE BEETLE VOL. 1: THE MORE THINGS CHANGE

Published by DC Comics. Compilation and all new material Copyright © 2017 DC Comics. All Rights Reserved. Originally published in single magazine form
in BLUE BEETLE: REBIRTH 1, BLUE BEETLE 1-5. Copyright © 2016, 2017 DC Comics. All Rights Reserved. All characters, their distinctive likenesses and related
elements featured in this publication are trademarks of DC Comics. The stories, characters and incidents featured in this publication are entirely fictional.
DC Comics does not read or accept unsolicited submissions of ideas, stories or artwork.

DC Comics, 2900 West Alameda Ave., Burbank, CA 91505
Printed by LSC Communications, Salem, VA, USA. 4/7/17. First Printing.
ISBN: 978-1-4012-6868-8

Library of Congress Cataloging-in-Publication Data is available.

PEFC Certified

Printed on paper from
sustainably managed
forests, controlled
sources

PEFC/29-31-337   www.pefc.org

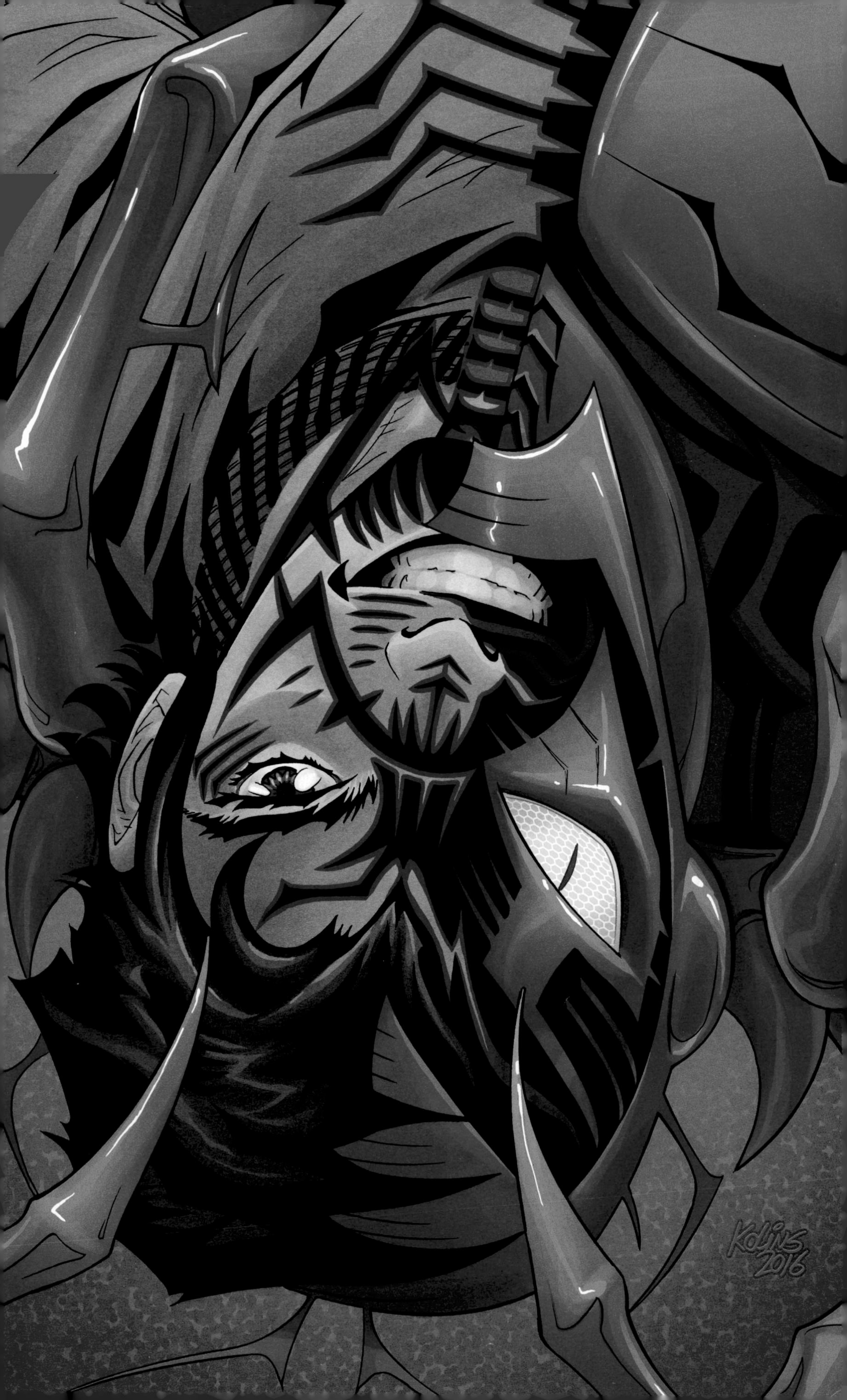
Kolins
2016

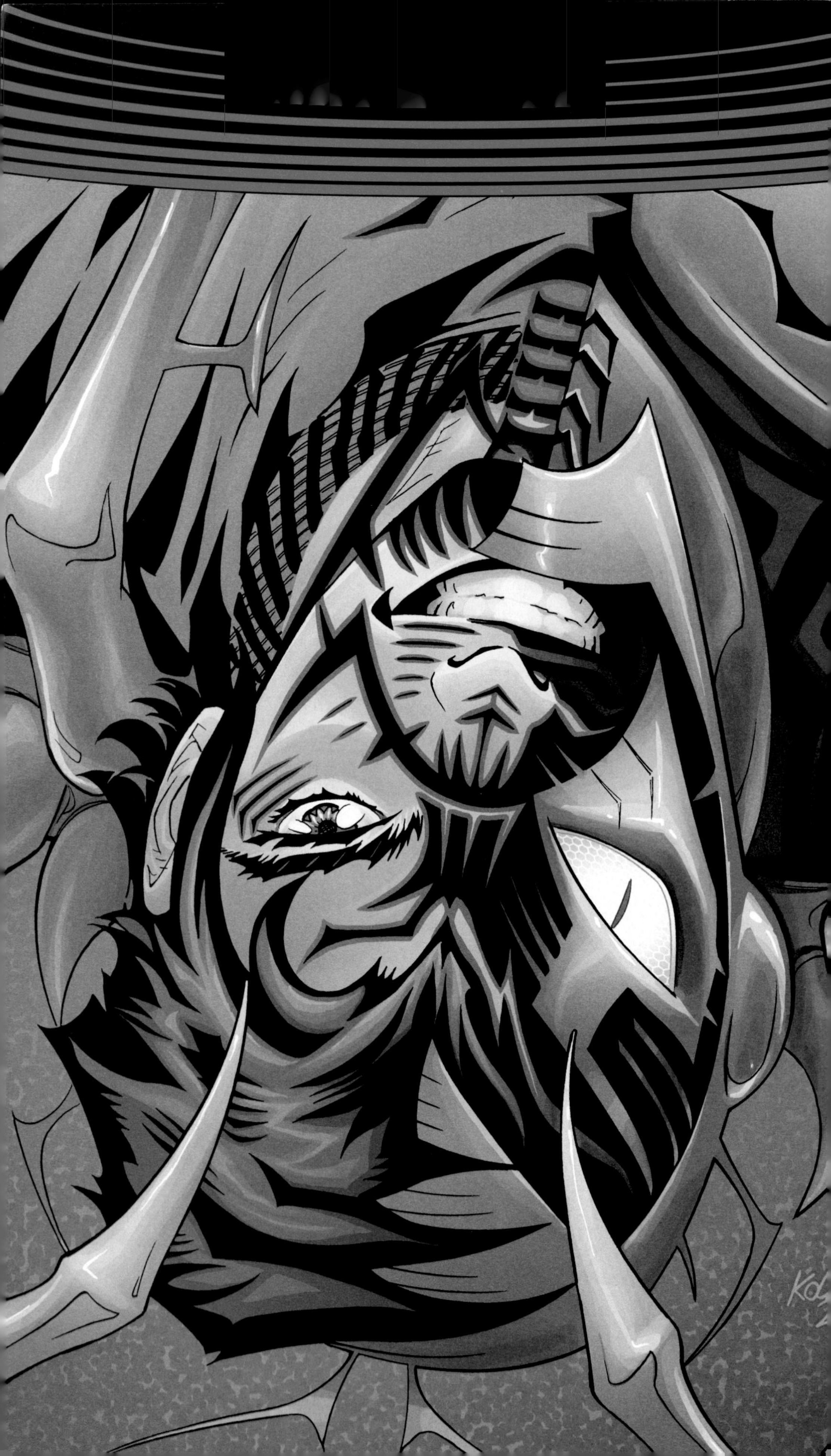

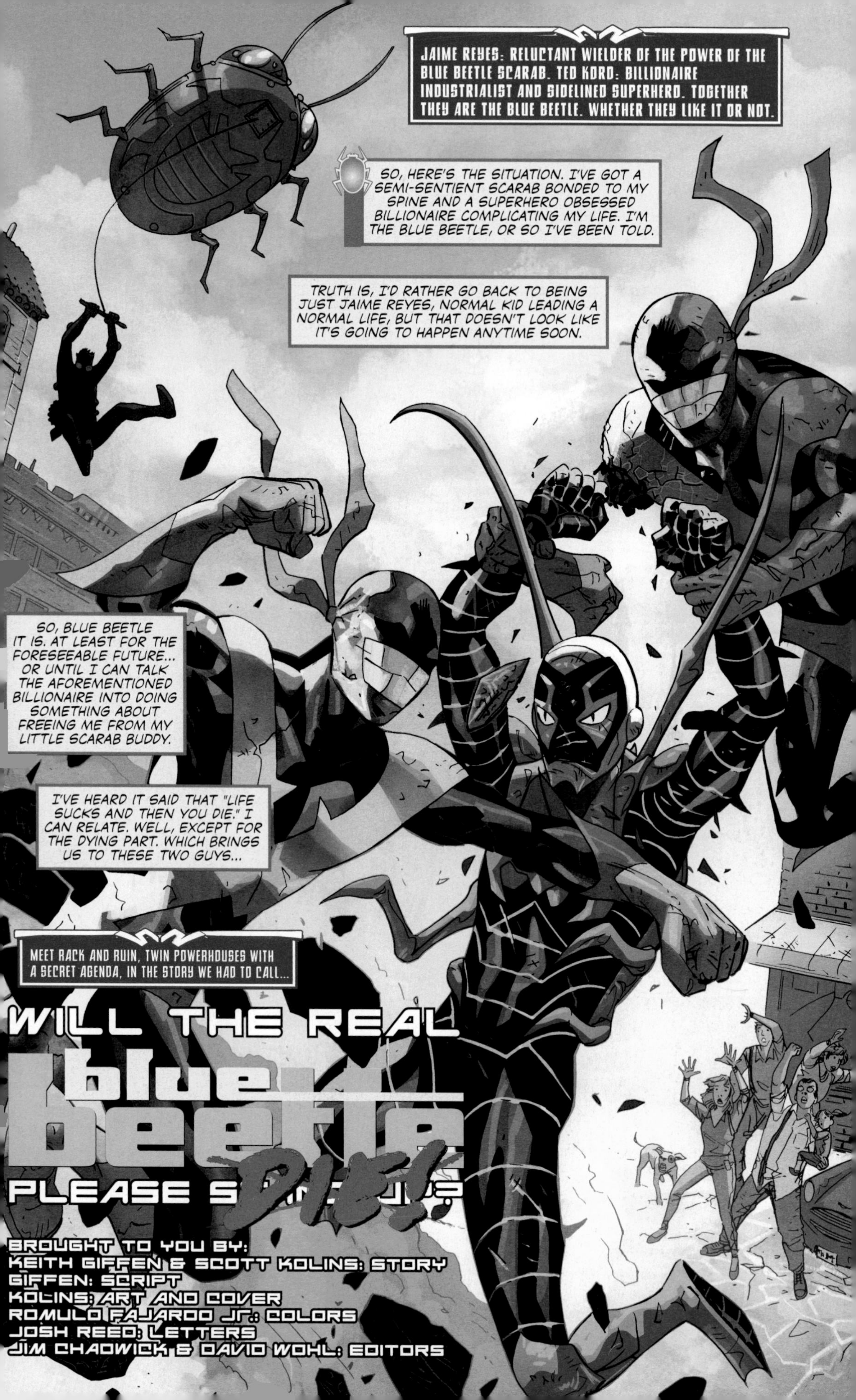
JAIME REYES: RELUCTANT WIELDER OF THE POWER OF THE BLUE BEETLE SCARAB. TED KORD: BILLIONAIRE INDUSTRIALIST AND SIDELINED SUPERHERO. TOGETHER THEY ARE THE BLUE BEETLE. WHETHER THEY LIKE IT OR NOT.
SO, HERE'S THE SITUATION. I'VE GOT A SEMI-SENTIENT SCARAB BONDED TO MY SPINE AND A SUPERHERO OBSESSED BILLIONAIRE COMPLICATING MY LIFE. I'M THE BLUE BEETLE, OR SO I'VE BEEN TOLD.
TRUTH IS, I'D RATHER GO BACK TO BEING JUST JAIME REYES, NORMAL KID LEADING A NORMAL LIFE, BUT THAT DOESN'T LOOK LIKE IT'S GOING TO HAPPEN ANYTIME SOON.
SO, BLUE BEETLE IT IS. AT LEAST FOR THE FORESEEABLE FUTURE... OR UNTIL I CAN TALK THE AFOREMENTIONED BILLIONAIRE INTO DOING SOMETHING ABOUT FREEING ME FROM MY LITTLE SCARAB BUDDY.
I'VE HEARD IT SAID THAT "LIFE SUCKS AND THEN YOU DIE." I CAN RELATE. WELL, EXCEPT FOR THE DYING PART. WHICH BRINGS US TO THESE TWO GUYS...
MEET RACK AND RUIN, TWIN POWERHOUSES WITH A SECRET AGENDA, IN THE STORY WE HAD TO CALL...
WILL THE REAL
blue beetle
PLEASE S
DIE!
BROUGHT TO YOU BY:
KEITH GIFFEN & SCOTT KOLINS: STORY
GIFFEN: SCRIPT
KOLINS: ART AND COVER
ROMULO FAJARDO JR.: COLORS
JOSH REED: LETTERS
JIM CHADWICK & DAVID WOHL: EDITORS

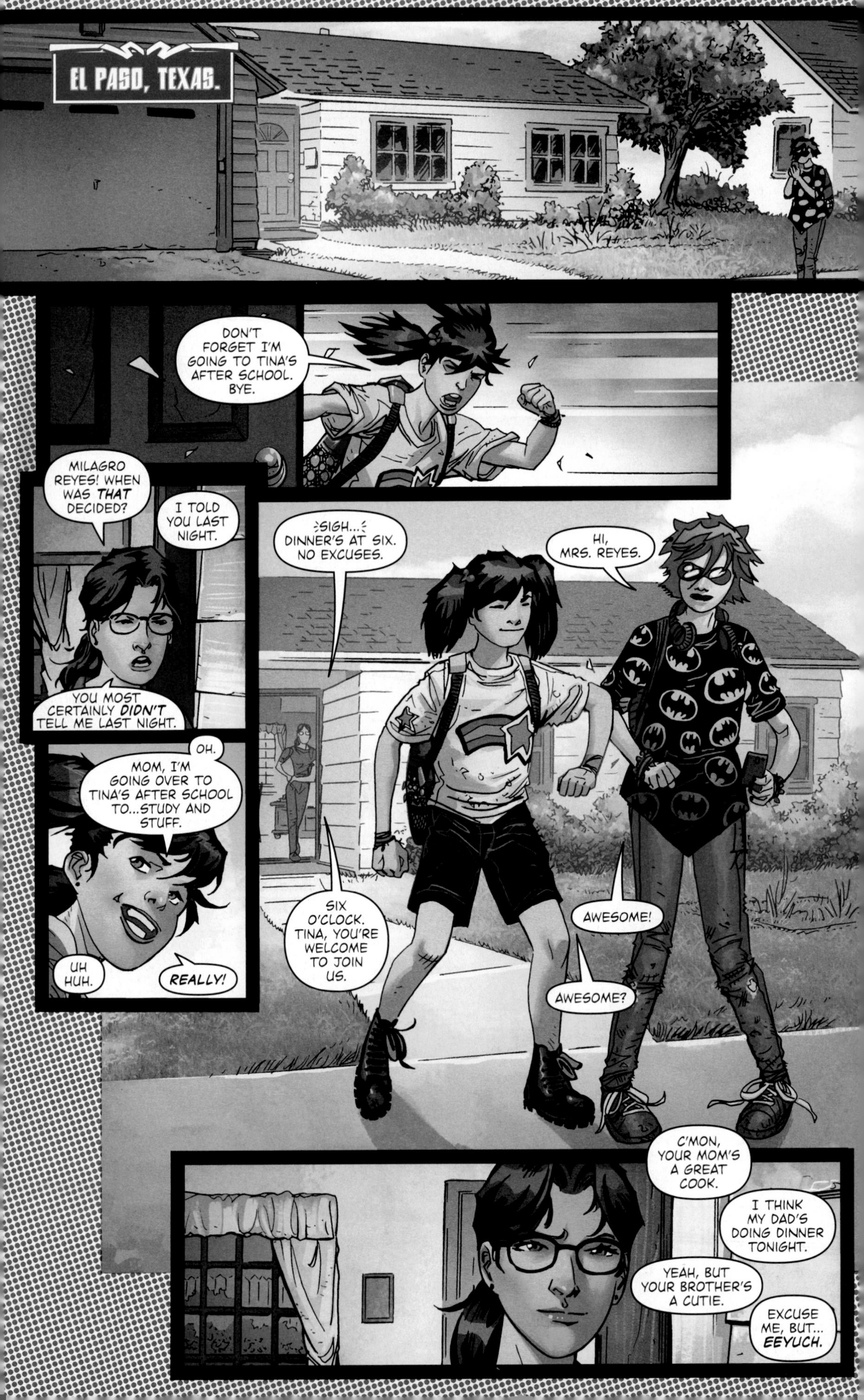
EL PASO, TEXAS.
DON'T FORGET I'M GOING TO TINA'S AFTER SCHOOL. BYE.
MILAGRO REYES! WHEN WAS THAT DECIDED?
I TOLD YOU LAST NIGHT.
YOU MOST CERTAINLY DIDN'T TELL ME LAST NIGHT.
OH.
MOM, I'M GOING OVER TO TINA'S AFTER SCHOOL TO...STUDY AND STUFF.
UH HUH.
REALLY!
SIGH... DINNER'S AT SIX. NO EXCUSES.
HI, MRS. REYES.
SIX O'CLOCK. TINA, YOU'RE WELCOME TO JOIN US.
AWESOME!
AWESOME?
C'MON, YOUR MOM'S A GREAT COOK.
I THINK MY DAD'S DOING DINNER TONIGHT.
YEAH, BUT YOUR BROTHER'S A CUTIE.
EXCUSE ME, BUT... EEYUCH.

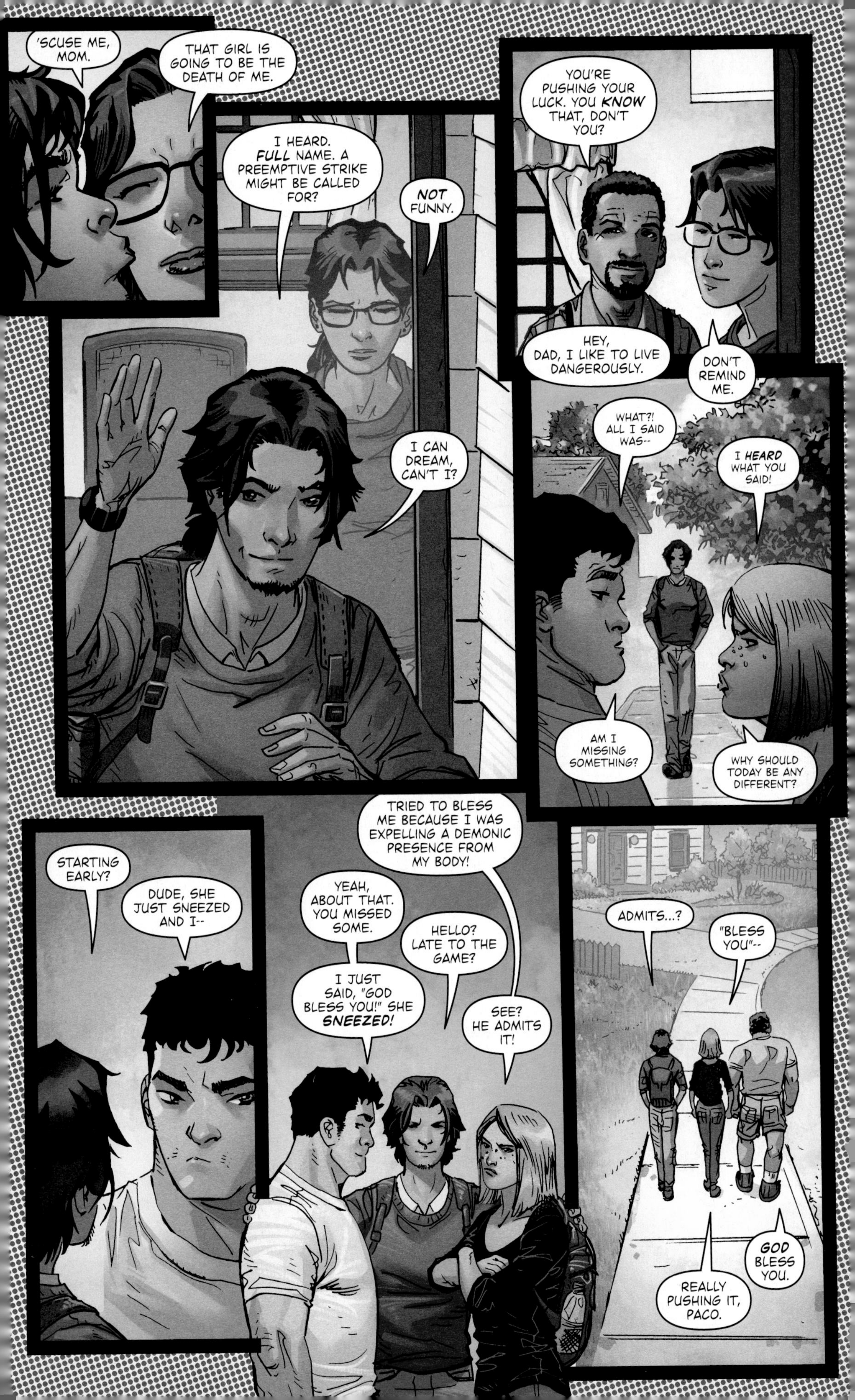
'SCUSE ME, MOM.
THAT GIRL IS GOING TO BE THE DEATH OF ME.
I HEARD. **FULL** NAME. A PREEMPTIVE STRIKE MIGHT BE CALLED FOR?
NOT FUNNY.
I CAN DREAM, CAN'T I?
YOU'RE PUSHING YOUR LUCK. YOU **KNOW** THAT, DON'T YOU?
HEY, DAD, I LIKE TO LIVE DANGEROUSLY.
DON'T REMIND ME.
WHAT?! ALL I SAID WAS--
I **HEARD** WHAT YOU SAID!
AM I MISSING SOMETHING?
WHY SHOULD TODAY BE ANY DIFFERENT?
STARTING EARLY?
DUDE, SHE JUST SNEEZED AND I--
TRIED TO BLESS ME BECAUSE I WAS EXPELLING A DEMONIC PRESENCE FROM MY BODY!
YEAH, ABOUT THAT. YOU MISSED SOME.
HELLO? LATE TO THE GAME?
I JUST SAID, "GOD BLESS YOU!" SHE **SNEEZED!**
SEE? HE ADMITS IT!
ADMITS...?
"BLESS YOU"--
GOD BLESS YOU.
REALLY PUSHING IT, PACO.

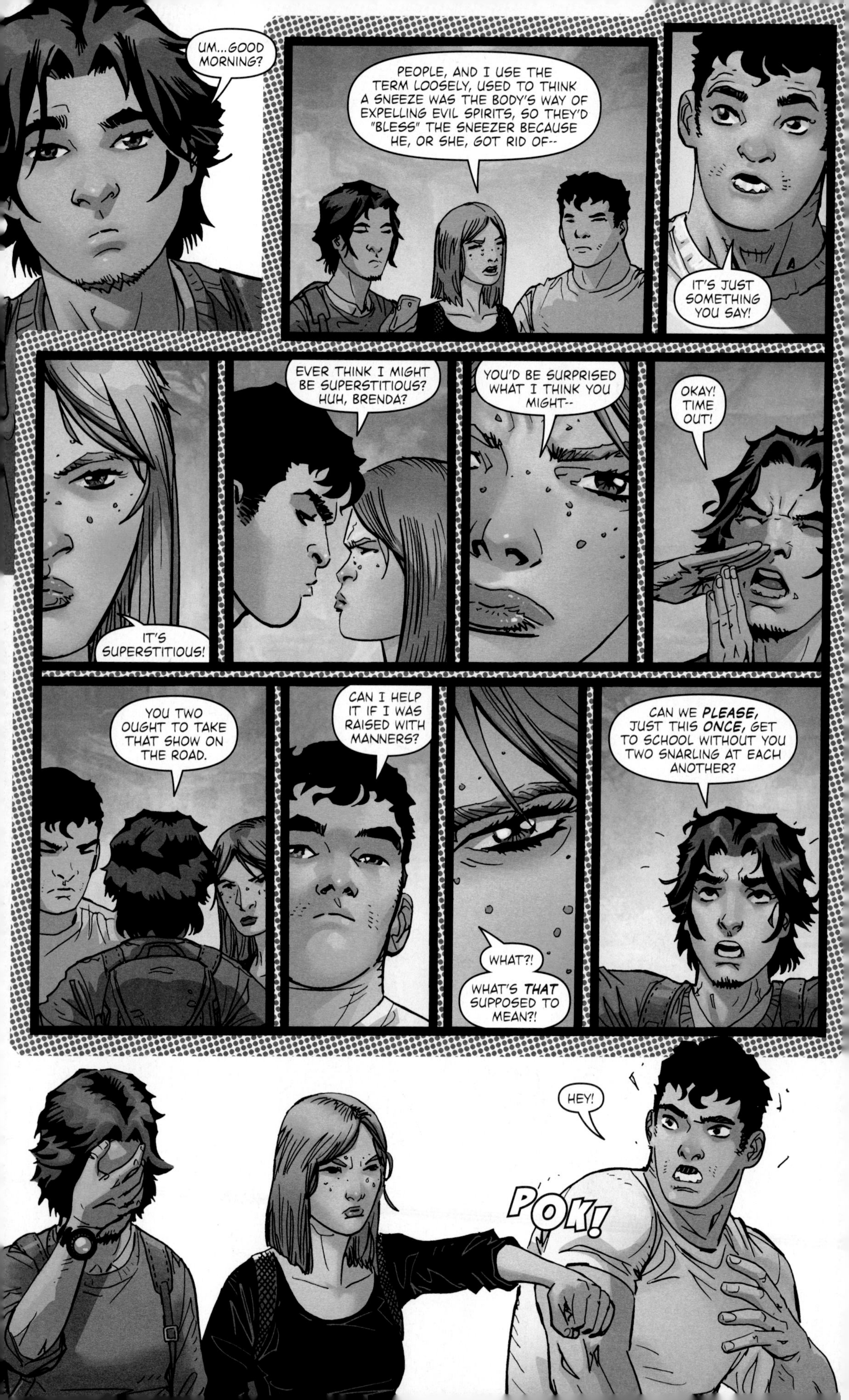
UM...GOOD MORNING?
PEOPLE, AND I USE THE TERM LOOSELY, USED TO THINK A SNEEZE WAS THE BODY'S WAY OF EXPELLING EVIL SPIRITS, SO THEY'D "BLESS" THE SNEEZER BECAUSE HE, OR SHE, GOT RID OF--
IT'S JUST SOMETHING YOU SAY!
IT'S SUPERSTITIOUS!
EVER THINK I MIGHT BE SUPERSTITIOUS? HUH, BRENDA?
YOU'D BE SURPRISED WHAT I THINK YOU MIGHT--
OKAY! TIME OUT!
YOU TWO OUGHT TO TAKE THAT SHOW ON THE ROAD.
CAN I HELP IT IF I WAS RAISED WITH MANNERS?
WHAT?!
WHAT'S **THAT** SUPPOSED TO MEAN?!
CAN WE **PLEASE,** JUST THIS **ONCE,** GET TO SCHOOL WITHOUT YOU TWO SNARLING AT EACH ANOTHER?
HEY!
POK!

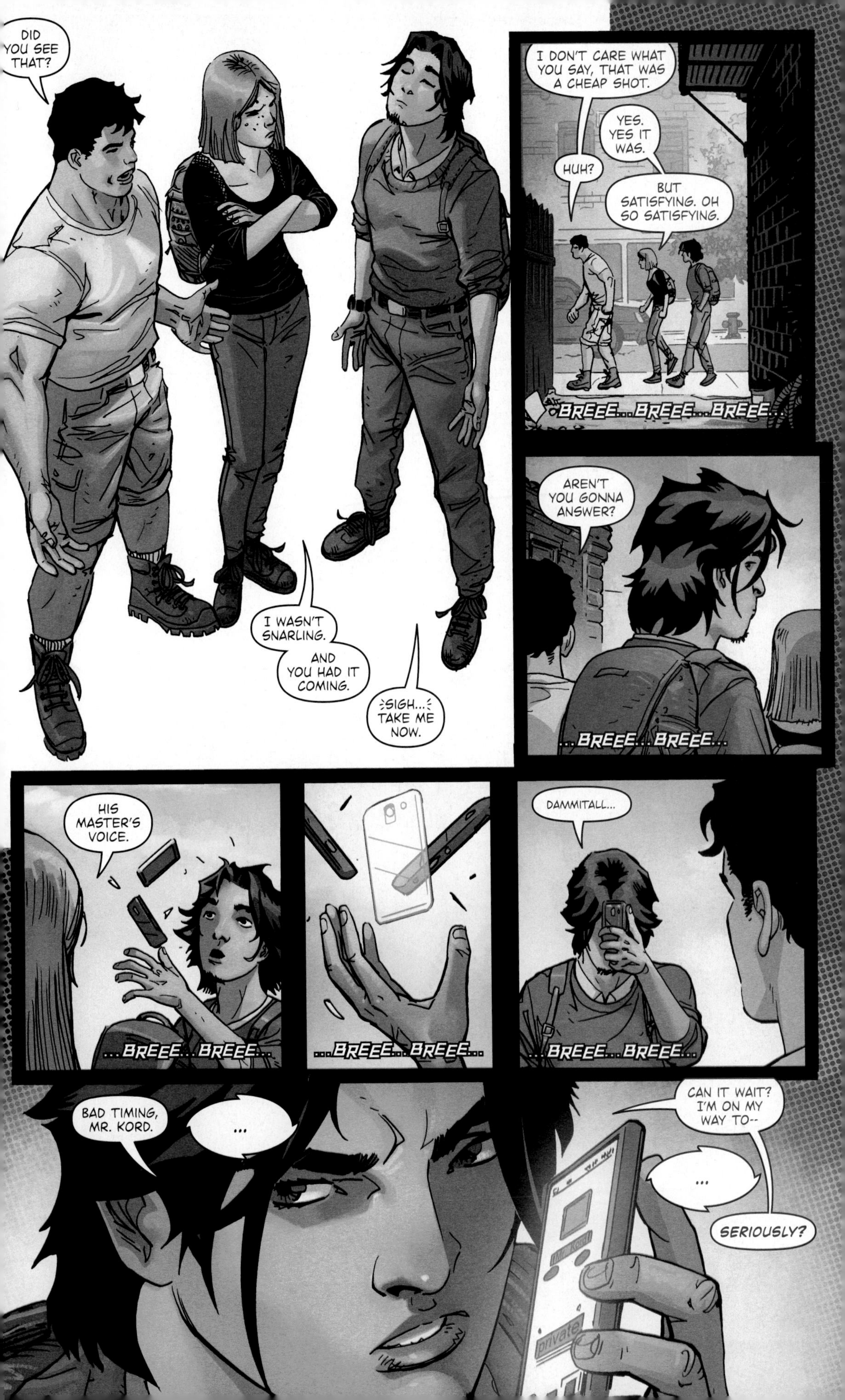
DID YOU SEE THAT?
I WASN'T SNARLING.
AND YOU HAD IT COMING.
SIGH... TAKE ME NOW.
I DON'T CARE WHAT YOU SAY, THAT WAS A CHEAP SHOT.
YES. YES IT WAS.
HUH?
BUT SATISFYING. OH SO SATISFYING.
BREEE...BREEE...BREEE...
AREN'T YOU GONNA ANSWER?
...BREEE...BREEE...
HIS MASTER'S VOICE.
...BREEE...BREEE...
...BREEE...BREEE...
DAMMITALL...
...BREEE...BREEE...
BAD TIMING, MR. KORD.
...
CAN IT WAIT? I'M ON MY WAY TO--
...
SERIOUSLY?
private

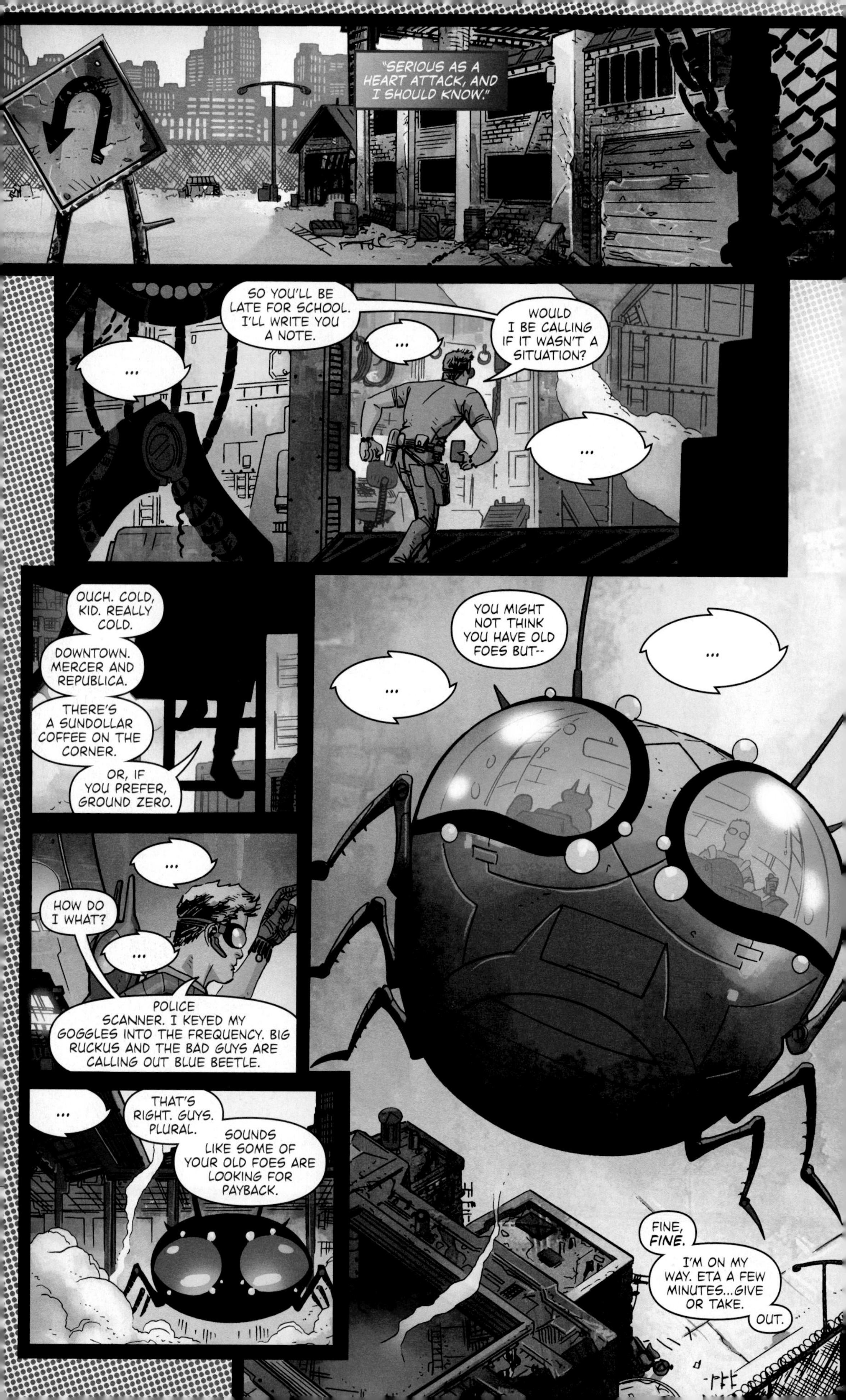
"SERIOUS AS A HEART ATTACK, AND I SHOULD KNOW."
...
SO YOU'LL BE LATE FOR SCHOOL. I'LL WRITE YOU A NOTE.
...
WOULD I BE CALLING IF IT WASN'T A SITUATION?
...
OUCH. COLD, KID. REALLY COLD.
DOWNTOWN. MERCER AND REPUBLICA.
THERE'S A SUNDOLLAR COFFEE ON THE CORNER.
OR, IF YOU PREFER, GROUND ZERO.
...
HOW DO I WHAT?
...
POLICE SCANNER. I KEYED MY GOGGLES INTO THE FREQUENCY. BIG RUCKUS AND THE BAD GUYS ARE CALLING OUT BLUE BEETLE.
...
THAT'S RIGHT. GUYS. PLURAL.
SOUNDS LIKE SOME OF YOUR OLD FOES ARE LOOKING FOR PAYBACK.
...
YOU MIGHT NOT THINK YOU HAVE OLD FOES BUT--
...
FINE, **FINE.**
I'M ON MY WAY. ETA A FEW MINUTES...GIVE OR TAKE.
OUT.

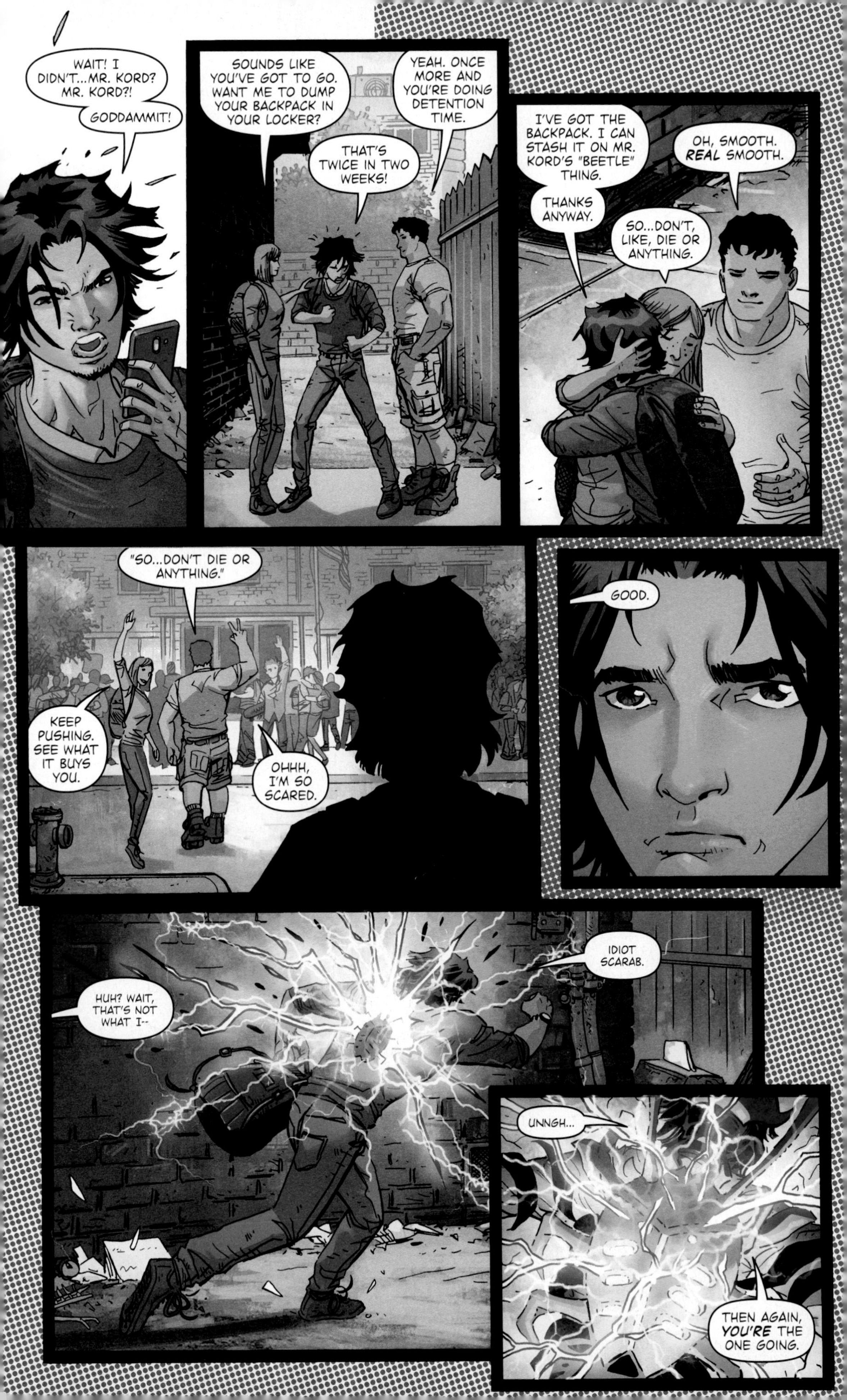
WAIT! I DIDN'T...MR. KORD? MR. KORD?!
GODDAMMIT!
SOUNDS LIKE YOU'VE GOT TO GO. WANT ME TO DUMP YOUR BACKPACK IN YOUR LOCKER?
YEAH. ONCE MORE AND YOU'RE DOING DETENTION TIME.
THAT'S TWICE IN TWO WEEKS!
I'VE GOT THE BACKPACK. I CAN STASH IT ON MR. KORD'S "BEETLE" THING.
OH, SMOOTH. **REAL** SMOOTH.
THANKS ANYWAY.
SO...DON'T, LIKE, DIE OR ANYTHING.
"SO...DON'T DIE OR ANYTHING."
KEEP PUSHING. SEE WHAT IT BUYS YOU.
OHHH, I'M SO SCARED.
GOOD.
IDIOT SCARAB.
HUH? WAIT, THAT'S NOT WHAT I--
UNNGH...
THEN AGAIN, ***YOU'RE*** THE ONE GOING.

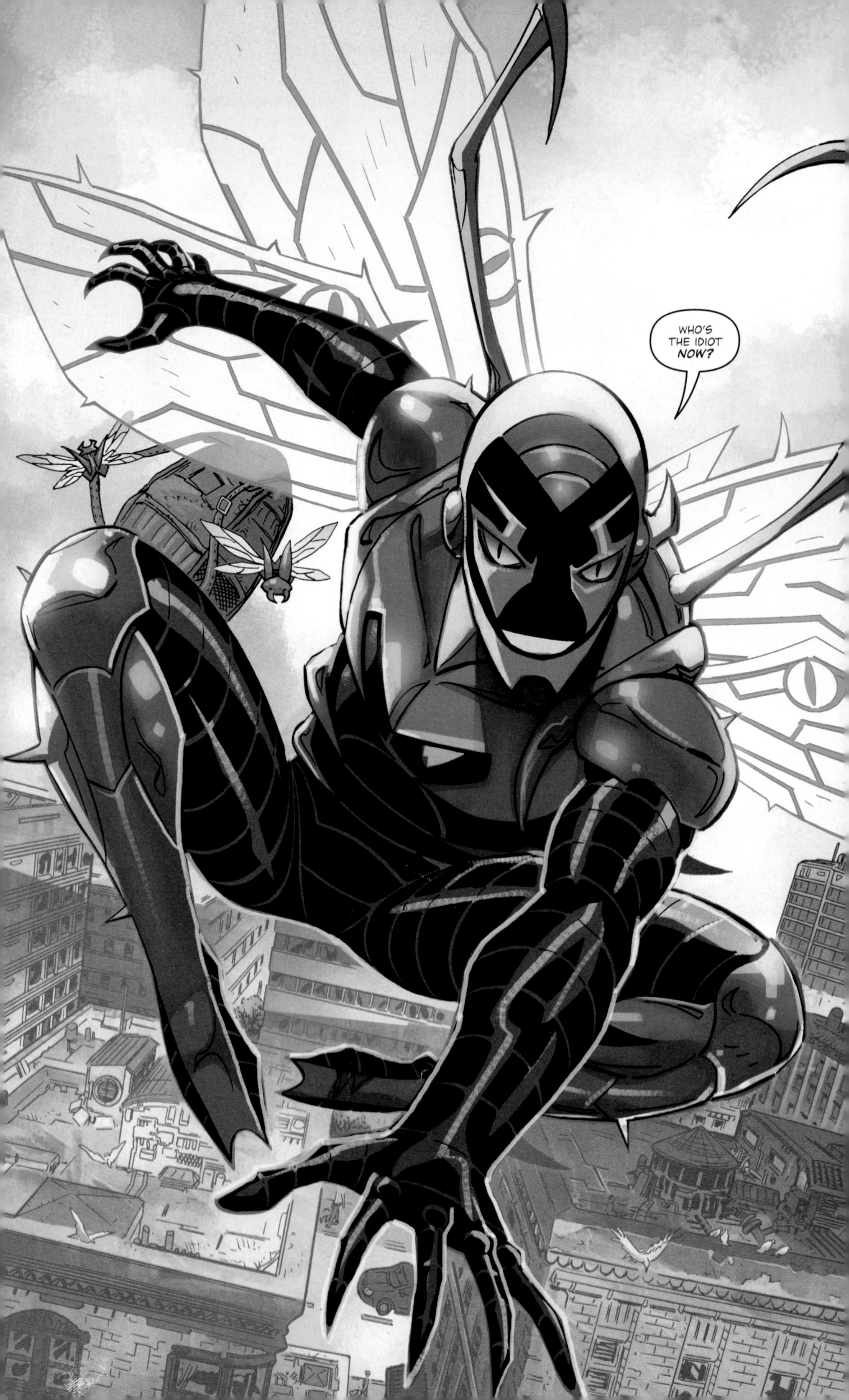
WHO'S THE IDIOT NOW?

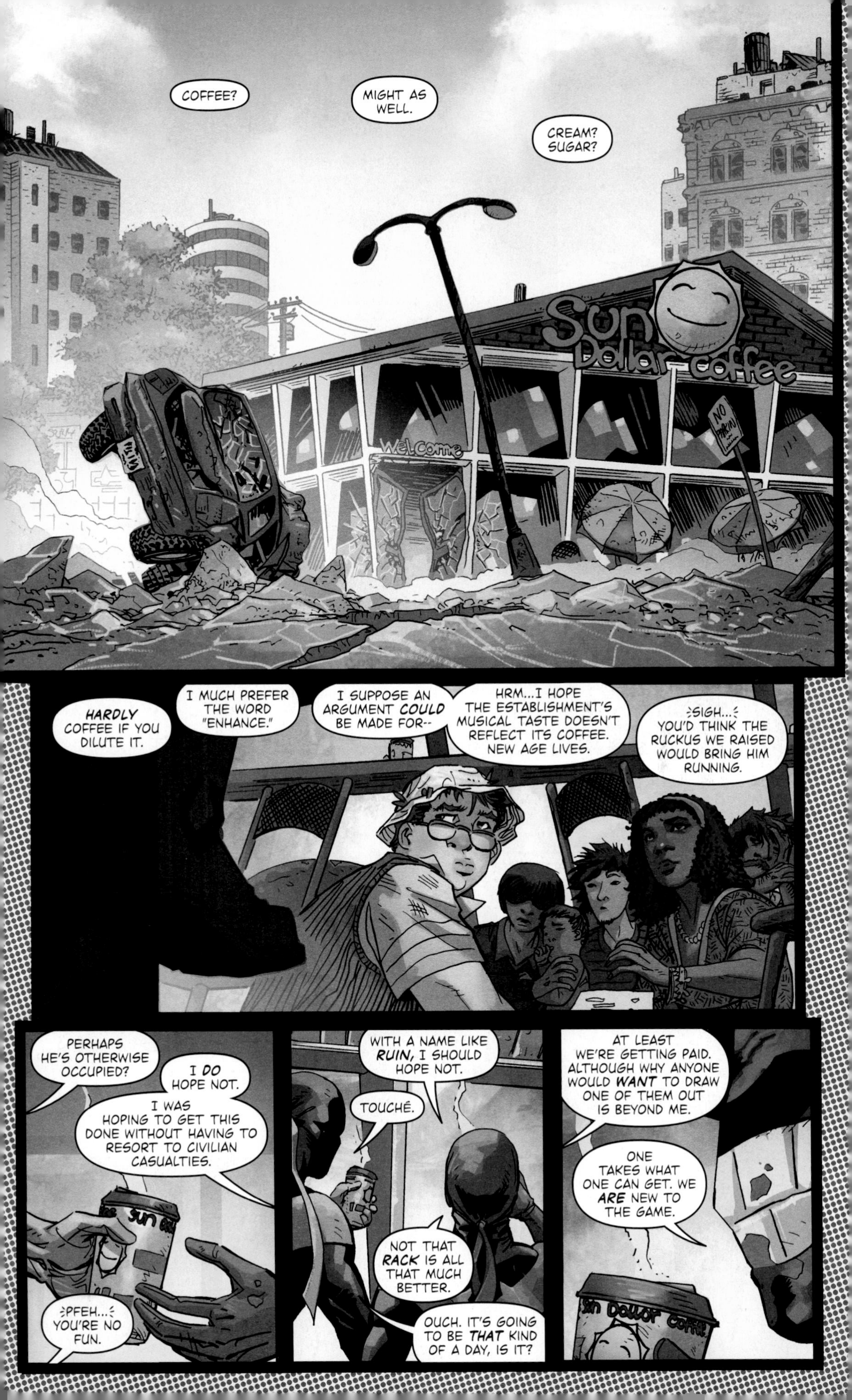
COFFEE?
MIGHT AS WELL.
CREAM? SUGAR?
Sun Dollar coffee
Welcome
HARDLY COFFEE IF YOU DILUTE IT.
I MUCH PREFER THE WORD "ENHANCE."
I SUPPOSE AN ARGUMENT COULD BE MADE FOR--
HRM...I HOPE THE ESTABLISHMENT'S MUSICAL TASTE DOESN'T REFLECT ITS COFFEE. NEW AGE LIVES.
SIGH... YOU'D THINK THE RUCKUS WE RAISED WOULD BRING HIM RUNNING.
PERHAPS HE'S OTHERWISE OCCUPIED?
I DO HOPE NOT.
I WAS HOPING TO GET THIS DONE WITHOUT HAVING TO RESORT TO CIVILIAN CASUALTIES.
PFEH... YOU'RE NO FUN.
WITH A NAME LIKE RUIN, I SHOULD HOPE NOT.
TOUCHÉ.
NOT THAT RACK IS ALL THAT MUCH BETTER.
OUCH. IT'S GOING TO BE THAT KIND OF A DAY, IS IT?
AT LEAST WE'RE GETTING PAID. ALTHOUGH WHY ANYONE WOULD WANT TO DRAW ONE OF THEM OUT IS BEYOND ME.
ONE TAKES WHAT ONE CAN GET. WE ARE NEW TO THE GAME.

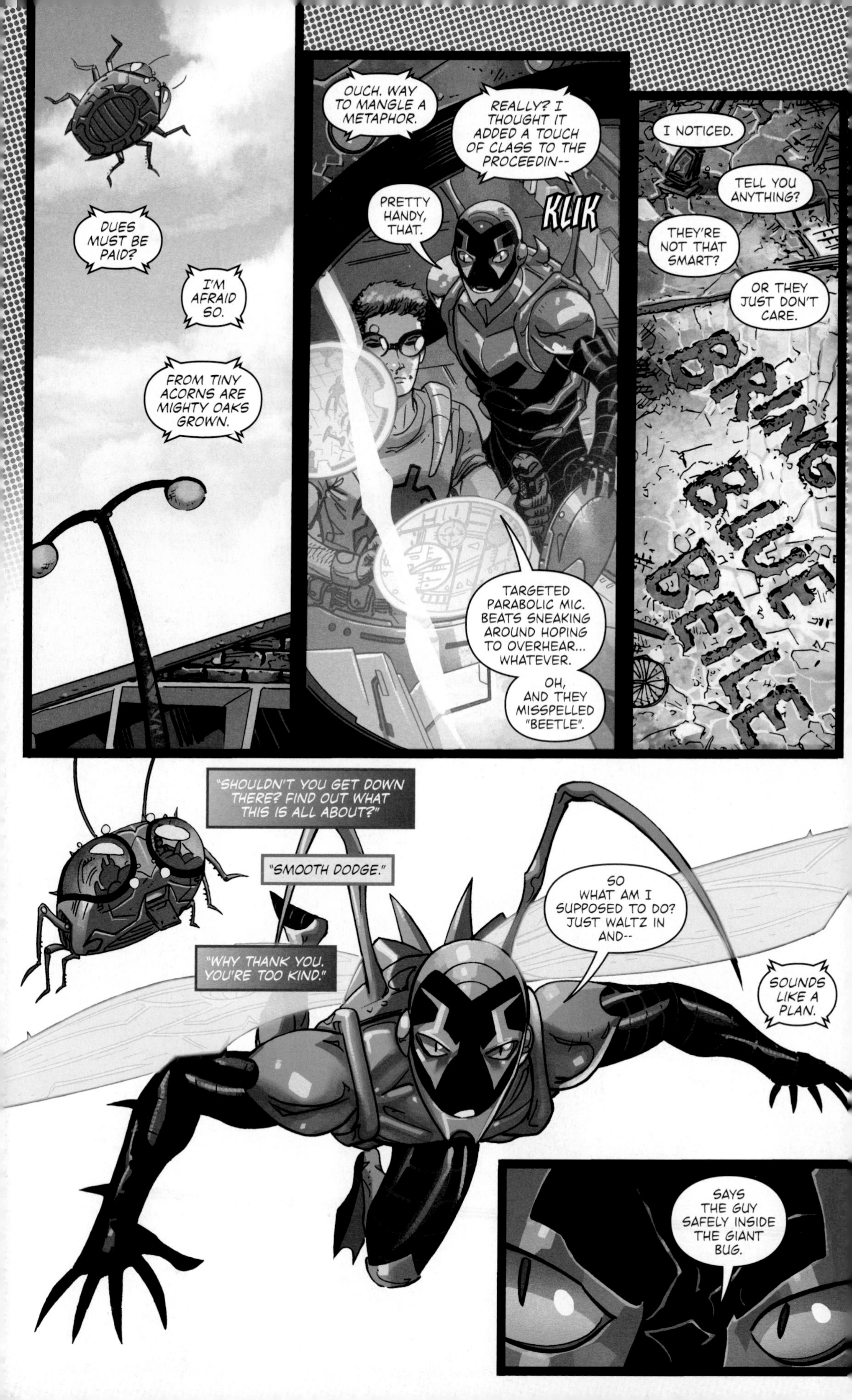

DUES MUST BE PAID?
I'M AFRAID SO.
FROM TINY ACORNS ARE MIGHTY OAKS GROWN.
OUCH. WAY TO MANGLE A METAPHOR.
REALLY? I THOUGHT IT ADDED A TOUCH OF CLASS TO THE PROCEEDIN--
KLIK
PRETTY HANDY, THAT.
TARGETED PARABOLIC MIC. BEATS SNEAKING AROUND HOPING TO OVERHEAR... WHATEVER.
OH, AND THEY MISSPELLED "BEETLE".
I NOTICED.
TELL YOU ANYTHING?
THEY'RE NOT THAT SMART?
OR THEY JUST DON'T CARE.
BRING BLUE BEETLE
"SHOULDN'T YOU GET DOWN THERE? FIND OUT WHAT THIS IS ALL ABOUT?"
"SMOOTH DODGE."
"WHY THANK YOU. YOU'RE TOO KIND."
SO WHAT AM I SUPPOSED TO DO? JUST WALTZ IN AND--
SOUNDS LIKE A PLAN.
SAYS THE GUY SAFELY INSIDE THE GIANT BUG.

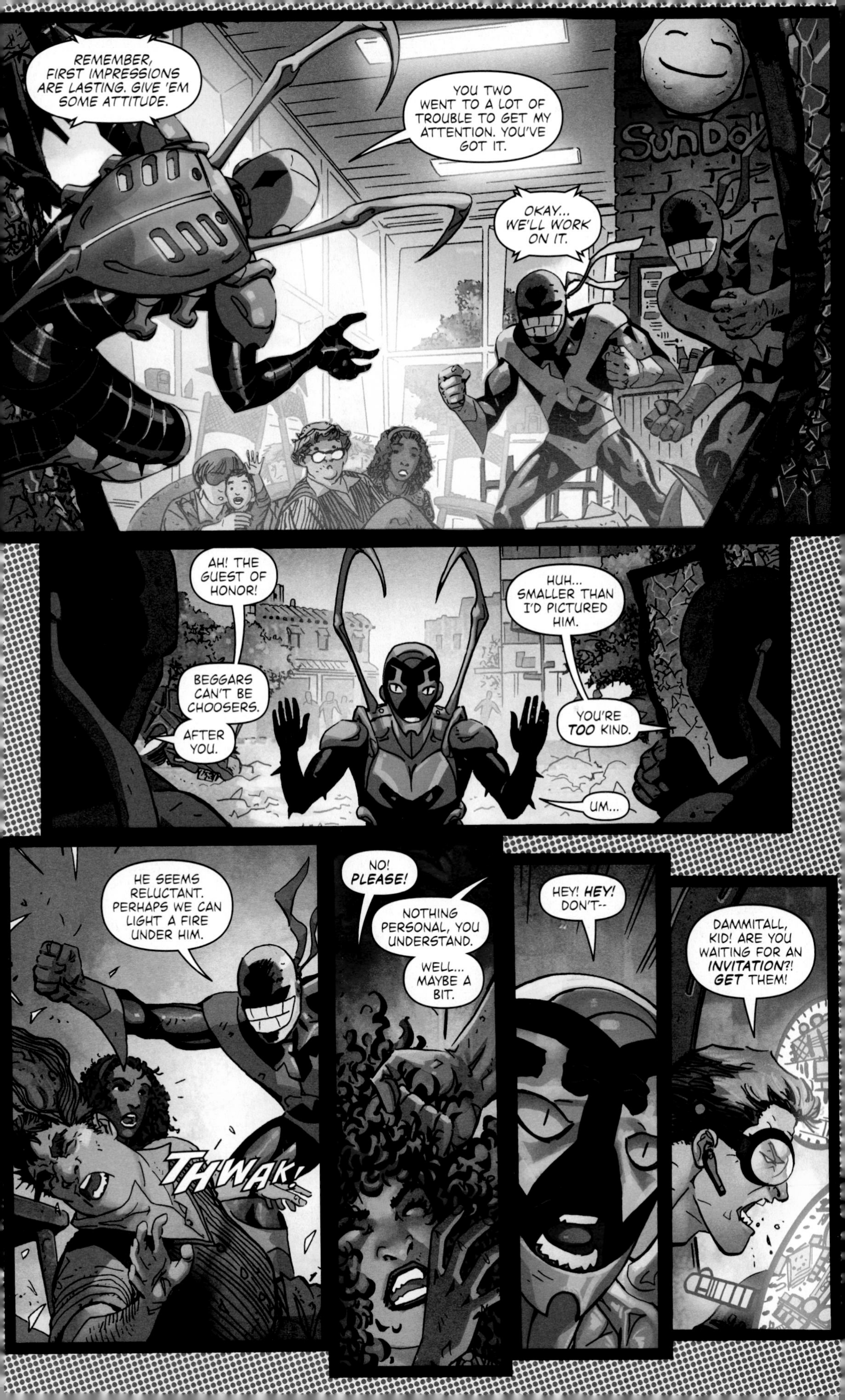
REMEMBER, FIRST IMPRESSIONS ARE LASTING. GIVE 'EM SOME ATTITUDE.
YOU TWO WENT TO A LOT OF TROUBLE TO GET MY ATTENTION. YOU'VE GOT IT.
OKAY... WE'LL WORK ON IT.
SunDo
AH! THE GUEST OF HONOR!
HUH... SMALLER THAN I'D PICTURED HIM.
BEGGARS CAN'T BE CHOOSERS.
AFTER YOU.
YOU'RE TOO KIND.
UM...
HE SEEMS RELUCTANT. PERHAPS WE CAN LIGHT A FIRE UNDER HIM.
THWAK!
NO! PLEASE!
NOTHING PERSONAL, YOU UNDERSTAND.
WELL... MAYBE A BIT.
HEY! HEY! DON'T--
DAMMITALL, KID! ARE YOU WAITING FOR AN INVITATION?! GET THEM!

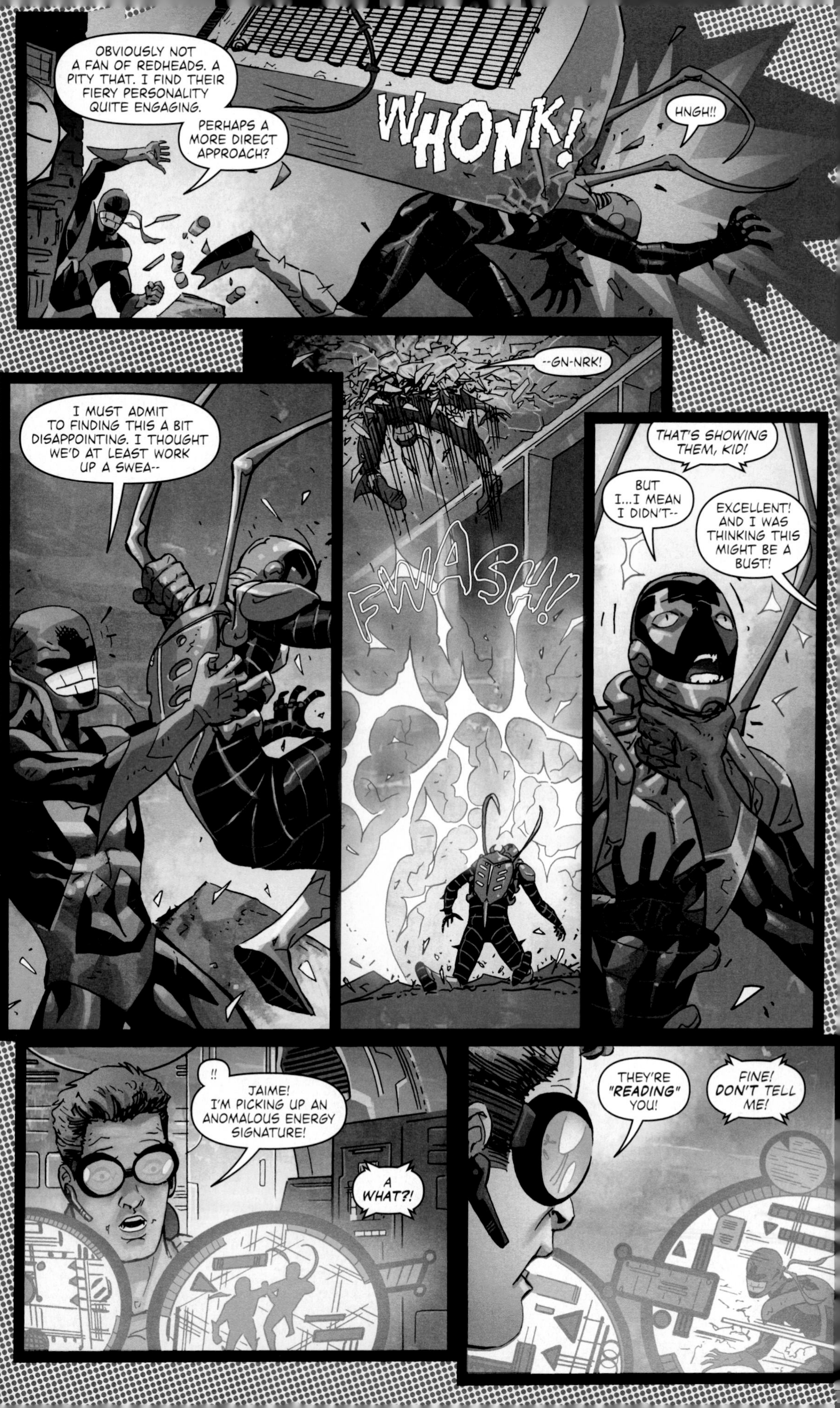
OBVIOUSLY NOT A FAN OF REDHEADS. A PITY THAT. I FIND THEIR FIERY PERSONALITY QUITE ENGAGING.
PERHAPS A MORE DIRECT APPROACH?
WHONK!
HNGH!!
--GN-NRK!
I MUST ADMIT TO FINDING THIS A BIT DISAPPOINTING. I THOUGHT WE'D AT LEAST WORK UP A SWEA--
FWASH!!
THAT'S SHOWING THEM, KID!
BUT I...I MEAN I DIDN'T--
EXCELLENT! AND I WAS THINKING THIS MIGHT BE A BUST!
!!
JAIME! I'M PICKING UP AN ANOMALOUS ENERGY SIGNATURE!
A WHAT?!
THEY'RE "READING" YOU!
FINE! DON'T TELL ME!

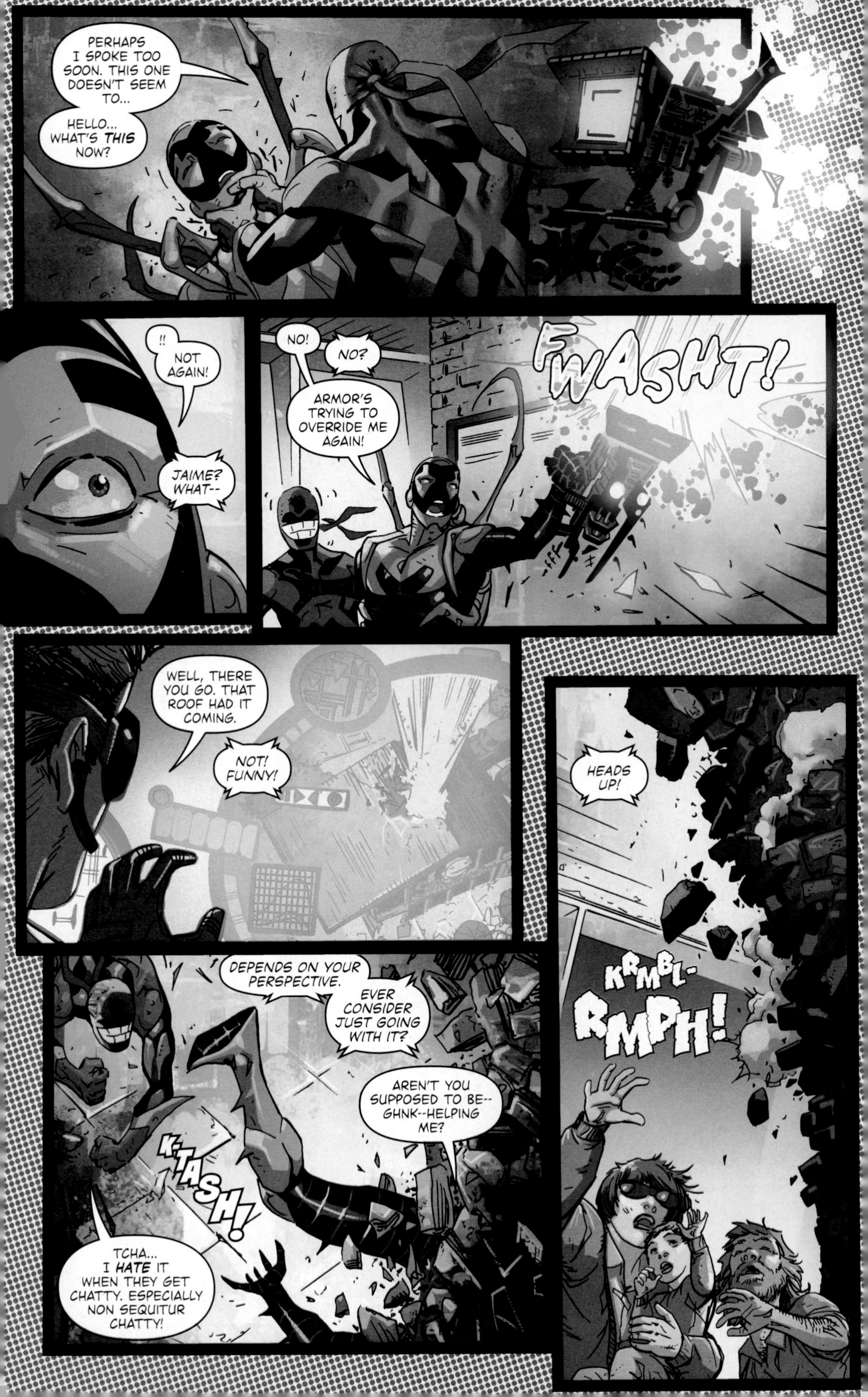
PERHAPS I SPOKE TOO SOON. THIS ONE DOESN'T SEEM TO...
HELLO... WHAT'S **THIS** NOW?
!! NOT AGAIN!
JAIME? WHAT--
NO!
NO?
ARMOR'S TRYING TO OVERRIDE ME AGAIN!
FWASHT!
WELL, THERE YOU GO. THAT ROOF HAD IT COMING.
NOT! FUNNY!
HEADS UP!
KRMBL-RMPH!
DEPENDS ON YOUR PERSPECTIVE.
EVER CONSIDER JUST GOING WITH IT?
AREN'T YOU SUPPOSED TO BE--GHNK--HELPING ME?
K-TASH!
TCHA... I ***HATE*** IT WHEN THEY GET CHATTY. ESPECIALLY NON SEQUITUR CHATTY!

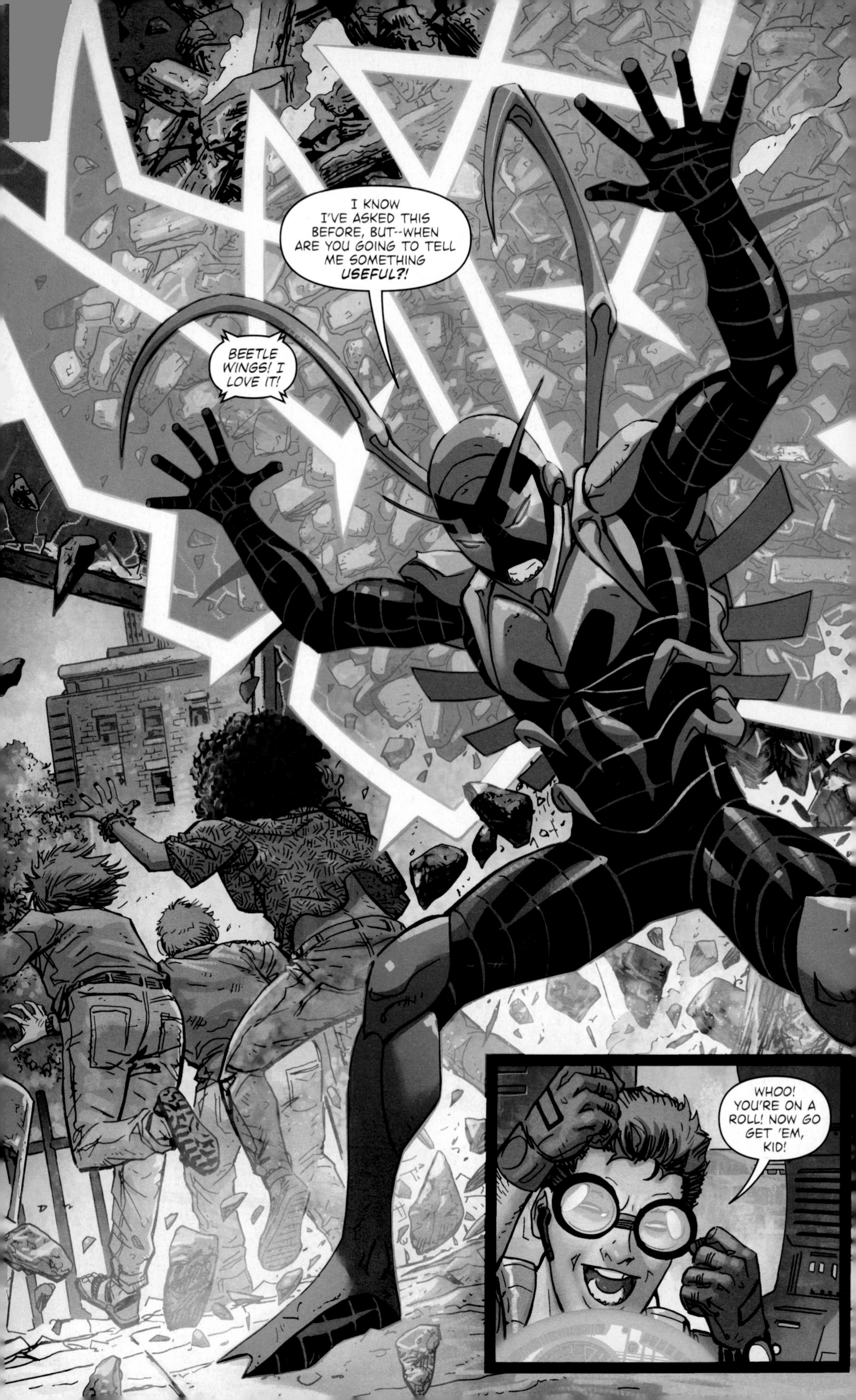
I KNOW I'VE ASKED THIS BEFORE, BUT--WHEN ARE YOU GOING TO TELL ME SOMETHING USEFUL?!
BEETLE WINGS! I LOVE IT!
WHOO! YOU'RE ON A ROLL! NOW GO GET 'EM, KID!

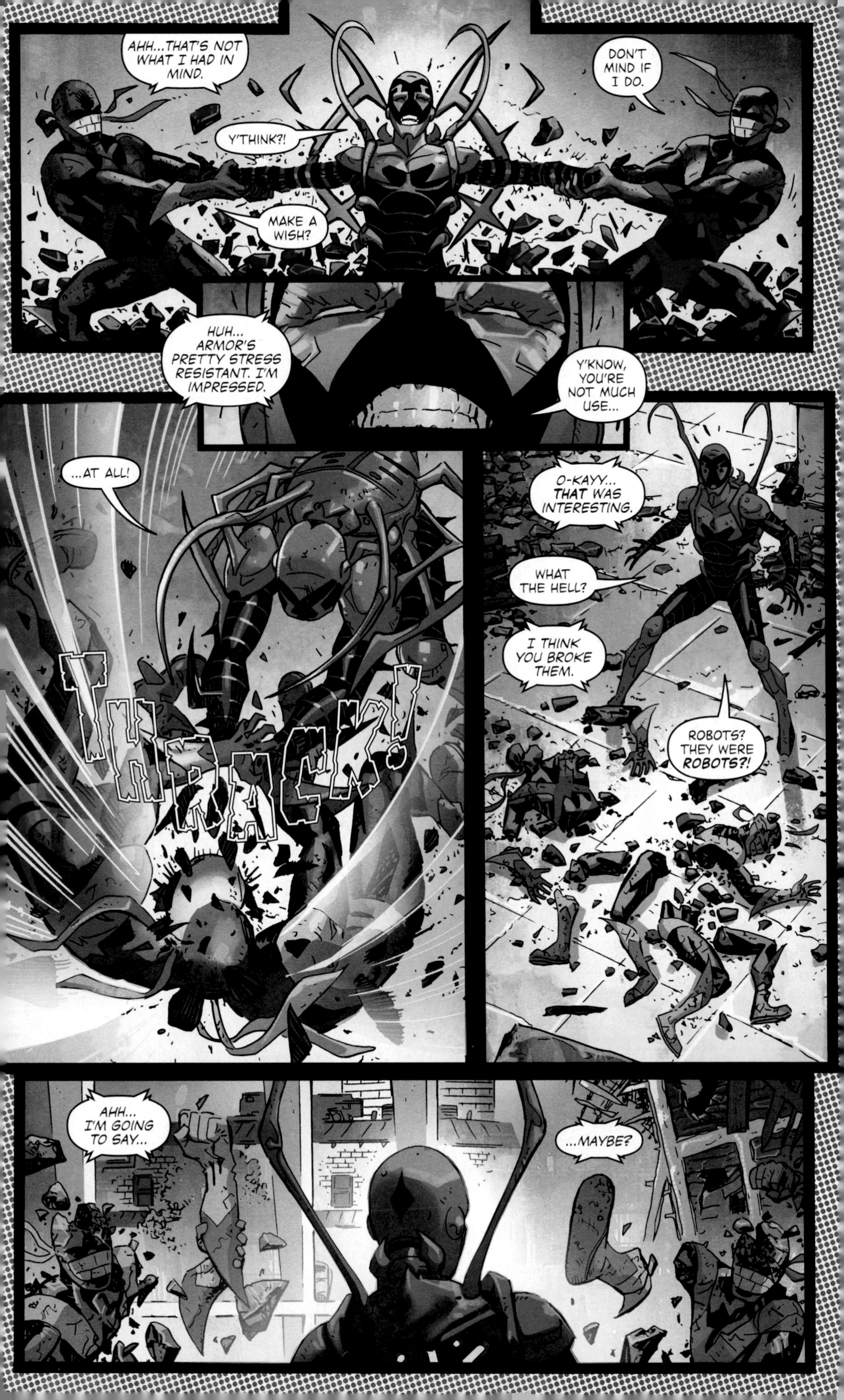
AHH...THAT'S NOT WHAT I HAD IN MIND.
DON'T MIND IF I DO.
Y'THINK?!
MAKE A WISH?
HUH... ARMOR'S PRETTY STRESS RESISTANT. I'M IMPRESSED.
Y'KNOW, YOU'RE NOT MUCH USE...
...AT ALL!
THRACK!
O-KAYY... THAT WAS INTERESTING.
WHAT THE HELL?
I THINK YOU BROKE THEM.
ROBOTS? THEY WERE ROBOTS?!
AHH... I'M GOING TO SAY...
...MAYBE?

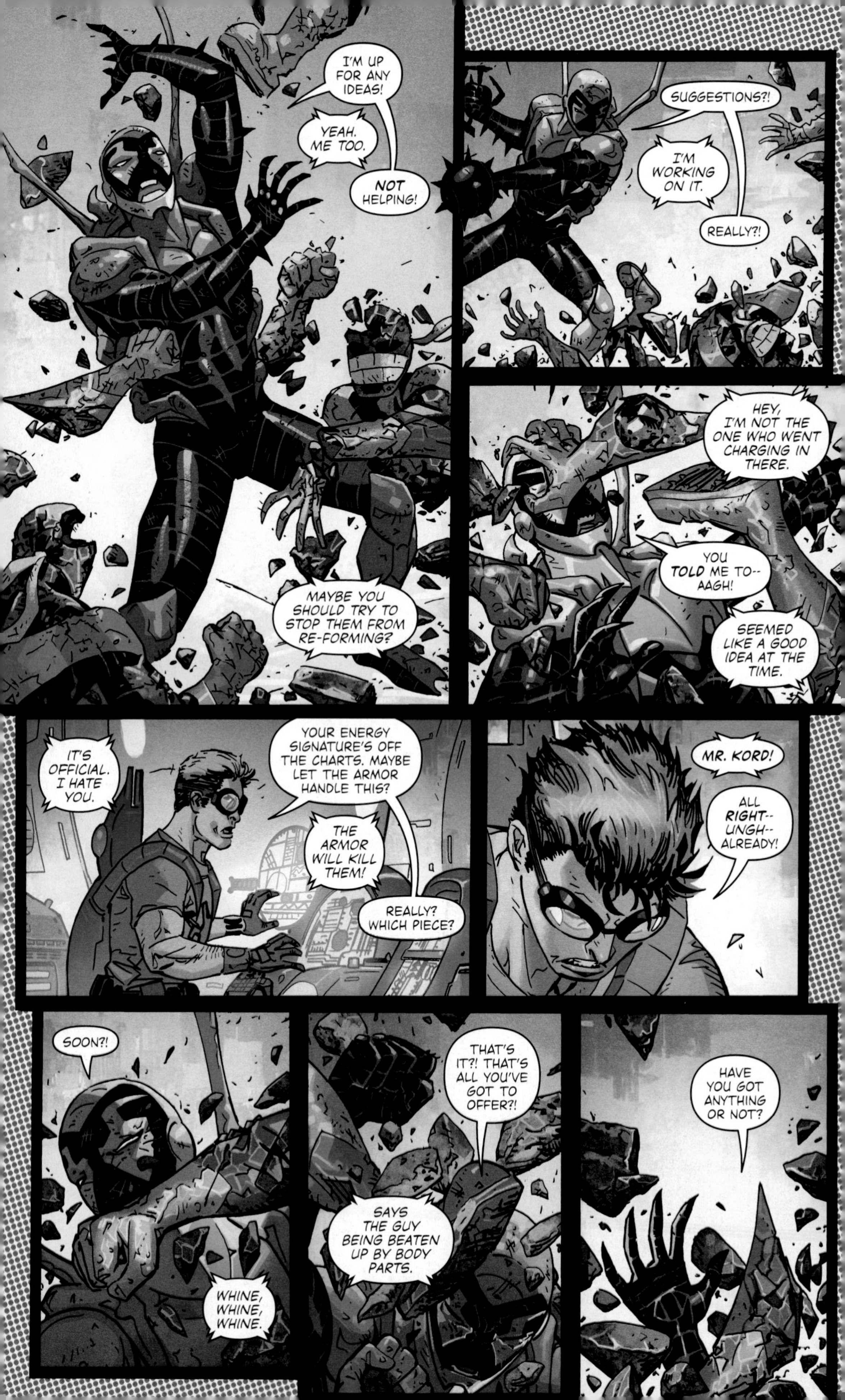
I'M UP FOR ANY IDEAS!
YEAH. ME TOO.
NOT HELPING!
MAYBE YOU SHOULD TRY TO STOP THEM FROM RE-FORMING?
SUGGESTIONS?!
I'M WORKING ON IT.
REALLY?!
HEY, I'M NOT THE ONE WHO WENT CHARGING IN THERE.
YOU TOLD ME TO-- AAGH!
SEEMED LIKE A GOOD IDEA AT THE TIME.
IT'S OFFICIAL. I HATE YOU.
YOUR ENERGY SIGNATURE'S OFF THE CHARTS. MAYBE LET THE ARMOR HANDLE THIS?
THE ARMOR WILL KILL THEM!
REALLY? WHICH PIECE?
MR. KORD!
ALL RIGHT-- UNGH-- ALREADY!
SOON?!
WHINE, WHINE, WHINE.
THAT'S IT?! THAT'S ALL YOU'VE GOT TO OFFER?!
SAYS THE GUY BEING BEATEN UP BY BODY PARTS.
HAVE YOU GOT ANYTHING OR NOT?

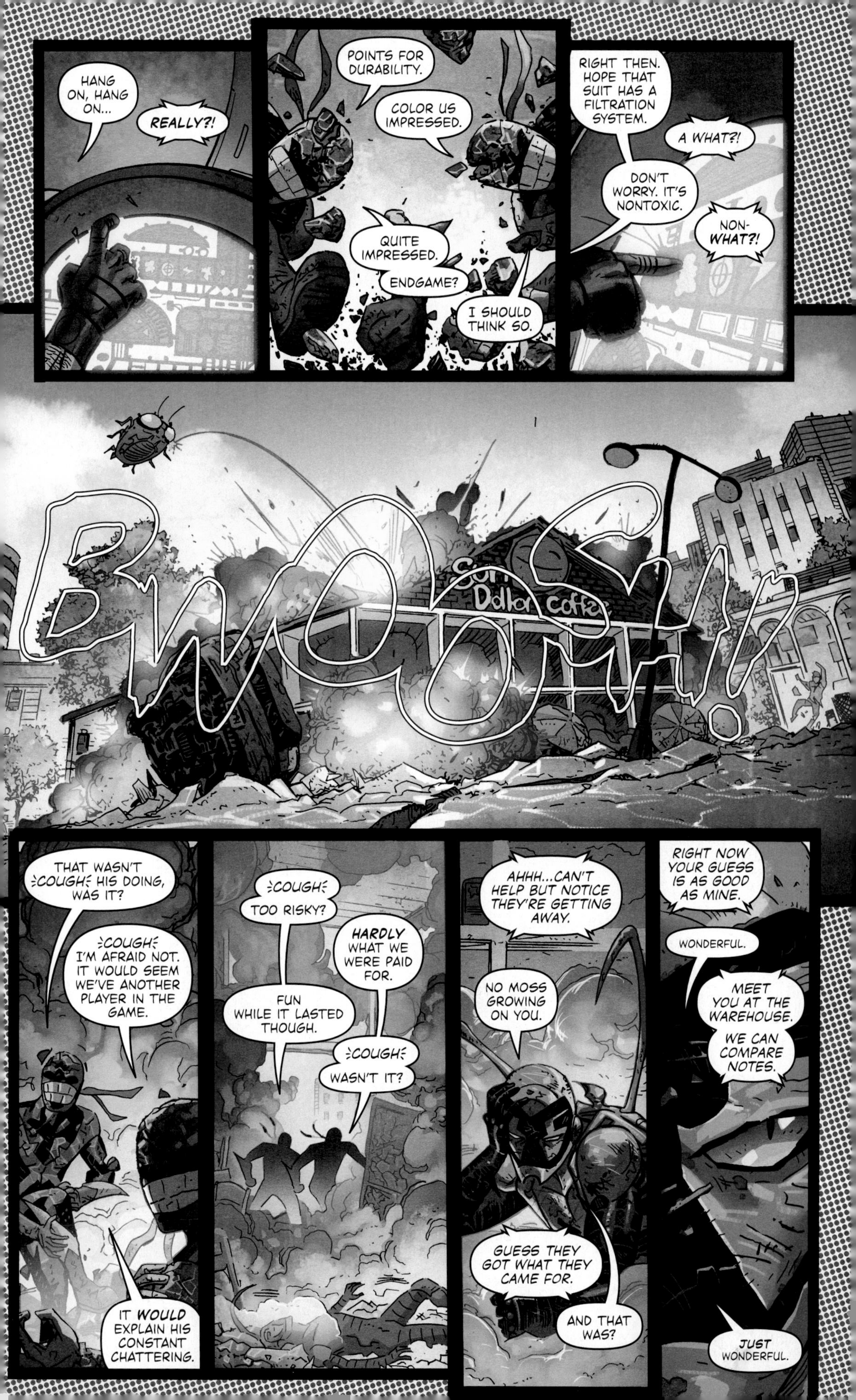
HANG ON, HANG ON...
REALLY?!
POINTS FOR DURABILITY.
COLOR US IMPRESSED.
QUITE IMPRESSED.
ENDGAME?
I SHOULD THINK SO.
RIGHT THEN. HOPE THAT SUIT HAS A FILTRATION SYSTEM.
A WHAT?!
DON'T WORRY. IT'S NONTOXIC.
NON-WHAT?!
BWOOSHH!!
THAT WASN'T *COUGH* HIS DOING, WAS IT?
COUGH I'M AFRAID NOT. IT WOULD SEEM WE'VE ANOTHER PLAYER IN THE GAME.
IT WOULD EXPLAIN HIS CONSTANT CHATTERING.
COUGH
TOO RISKY?
HARDLY WHAT WE WERE PAID FOR.
FUN WHILE IT LASTED THOUGH.
COUGH
WASN'T IT?
AHHH...CAN'T HELP BUT NOTICE THEY'RE GETTING AWAY.
NO MOSS GROWING ON YOU.
GUESS THEY GOT WHAT THEY CAME FOR.
AND THAT WAS?
RIGHT NOW YOUR GUESS IS AS GOOD AS MINE.
WONDERFUL.
MEET YOU AT THE WAREHOUSE.
WE CAN COMPARE NOTES.
JUST WONDERFUL.

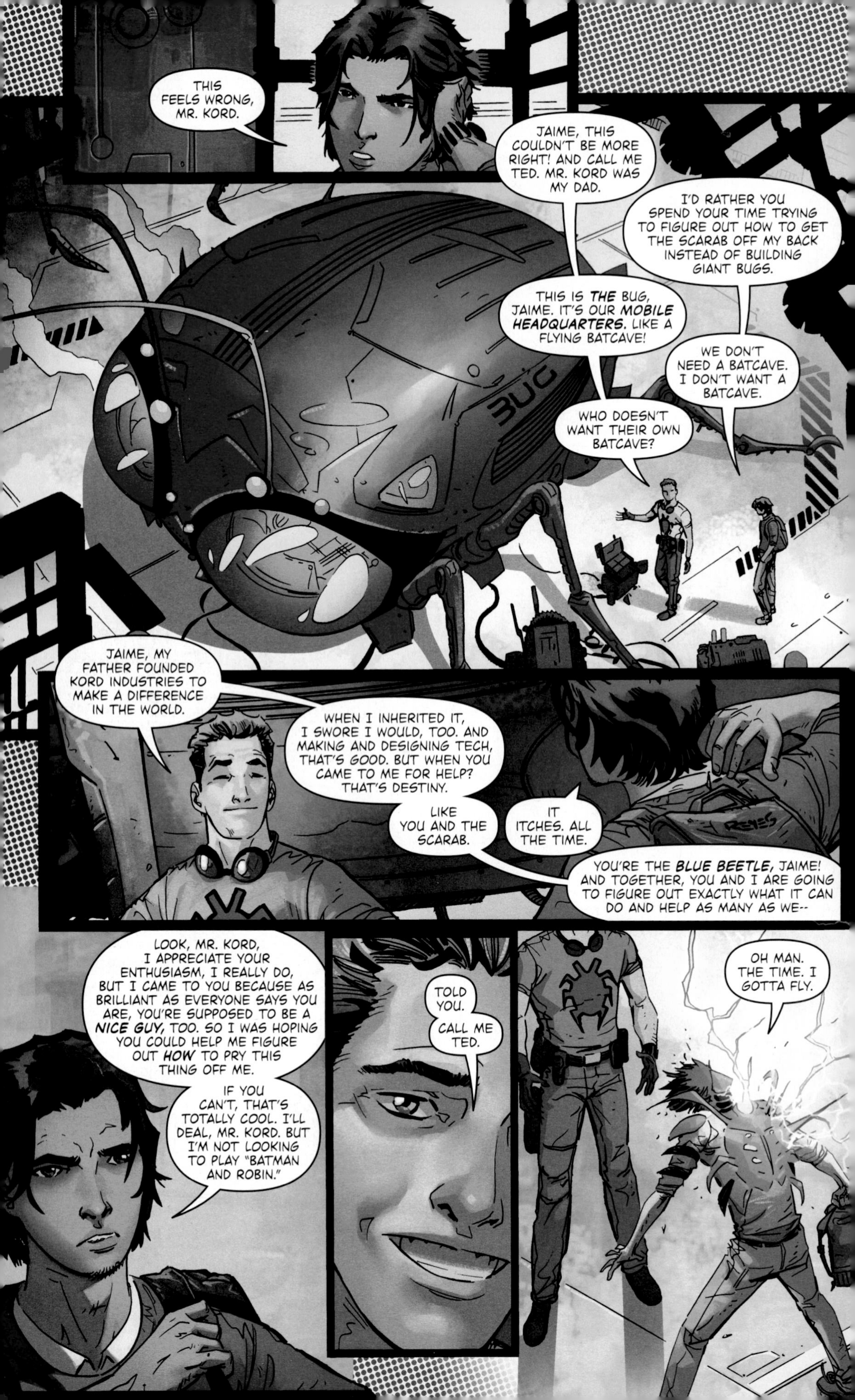
THIS FEELS WRONG, MR. KORD.
JAIME, THIS COULDN'T BE MORE RIGHT! AND CALL ME TED. MR. KORD WAS MY DAD.
I'D RATHER YOU SPEND YOUR TIME TRYING TO FIGURE OUT HOW TO GET THE SCARAB OFF MY BACK INSTEAD OF BUILDING GIANT BUGS.
THIS IS **THE** BUG, JAIME. IT'S OUR **MOBILE HEADQUARTERS.** LIKE A FLYING BATCAVE!
WE DON'T NEED A BATCAVE. I DON'T WANT A BATCAVE.
WHO DOESN'T WANT THEIR OWN BATCAVE?
BUG
JAIME, MY FATHER FOUNDED KORD INDUSTRIES TO MAKE A DIFFERENCE IN THE WORLD.
WHEN I INHERITED IT, I SWORE I WOULD, TOO. AND MAKING AND DESIGNING TECH, THAT'S GOOD. BUT WHEN YOU CAME TO ME FOR HELP? THAT'S DESTINY.
LIKE YOU AND THE SCARAB.
IT ITCHES. ALL THE TIME.
REYES
YOU'RE THE **BLUE BEETLE,** JAIME! AND TOGETHER, YOU AND I ARE GOING TO FIGURE OUT EXACTLY WHAT IT CAN DO AND HELP AS MANY AS WE--
LOOK, MR. KORD, I APPRECIATE YOUR ENTHUSIASM, I REALLY DO, BUT I CAME TO YOU BECAUSE AS BRILLIANT AS EVERYONE SAYS YOU ARE, YOU'RE SUPPOSED TO BE A **NICE GUY,** TOO. SO I WAS HOPING YOU COULD HELP ME FIGURE OUT **HOW** TO PRY THIS THING OFF ME.
IF YOU CAN'T, THAT'S TOTALLY COOL. I'LL DEAL, MR. KORD. BUT I'M NOT LOOKING TO PLAY "BATMAN AND ROBIN."
TOLD YOU.
CALL ME TED.
OH MAN. THE TIME. I GOTTA FLY.

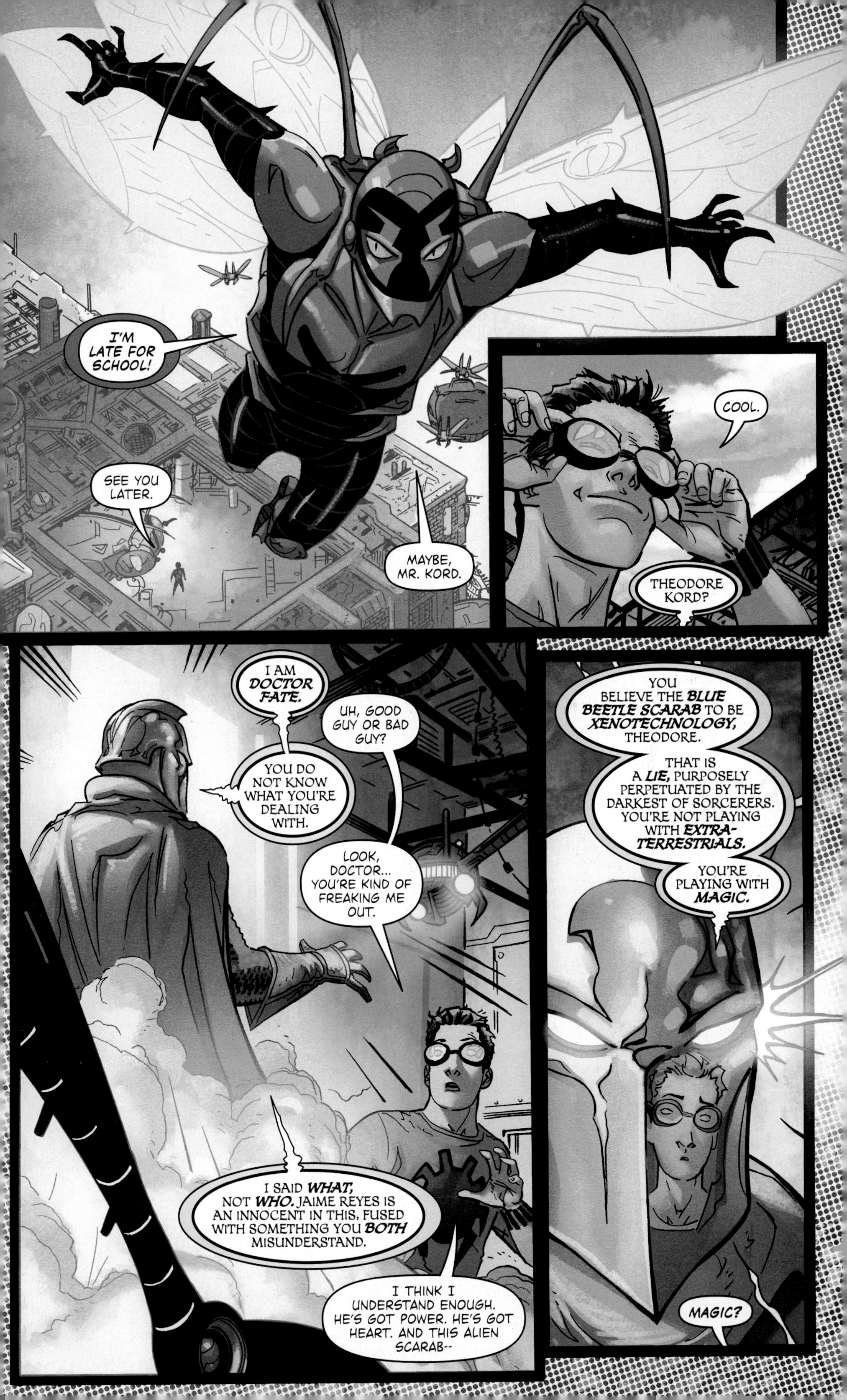
I'M LATE FOR SCHOOL!
SEE YOU LATER.
MAYBE, MR. KORD.
COOL.
THEODORE KORD?
I AM DOCTOR FATE.
UH, GOOD GUY OR BAD GUY?
YOU DO NOT KNOW WHAT YOU'RE DEALING WITH.
LOOK, DOCTOR... YOU'RE KIND OF FREAKING ME OUT.
I SAID WHAT, NOT WHO. JAIME REYES IS AN INNOCENT IN THIS, FUSED WITH SOMETHING YOU BOTH MISUNDERSTAND.
I THINK I UNDERSTAND ENOUGH. HE'S GOT POWER. HE'S GOT HEART. AND THIS ALIEN SCARAB--
YOU BELIEVE THE BLUE BEETLE SCARAB TO BE XENOTECHNOLOGY, THEODORE.
THAT IS A LIE, PURPOSELY PERPETUATED BY THE DARKEST OF SORCERERS. YOU'RE NOT PLAYING WITH EXTRA-TERRESTRIALS.
YOU'RE PLAYING WITH MAGIC.
MAGIC?

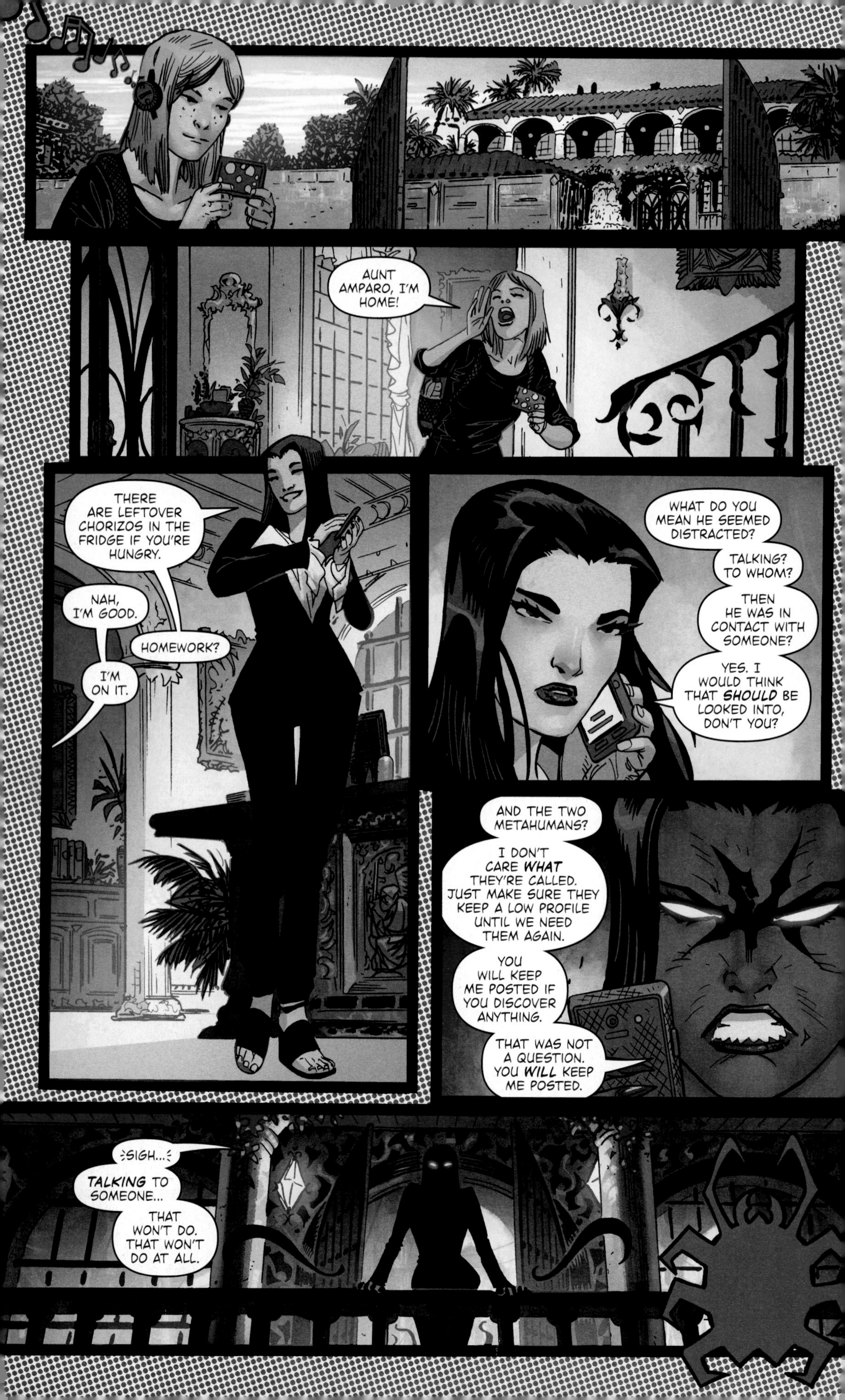
AUNT AMPARO, I'M HOME!
THERE ARE LEFTOVER CHORIZOS IN THE FRIDGE IF YOU'RE HUNGRY.
NAH, I'M GOOD.
HOMEWORK?
I'M ON IT.
WHAT DO YOU MEAN HE SEEMED DISTRACTED?
TALKING? TO WHOM?
THEN HE WAS IN CONTACT WITH SOMEONE?
YES. I WOULD THINK THAT SHOULD BE LOOKED INTO, DON'T YOU?
AND THE TWO METAHUMANS?
I DON'T CARE WHAT THEY'RE CALLED. JUST MAKE SURE THEY KEEP A LOW PROFILE UNTIL WE NEED THEM AGAIN.
YOU WILL KEEP ME POSTED IF YOU DISCOVER ANYTHING.
THAT WAS NOT A QUESTION. YOU WILL KEEP ME POSTED.
SIGH...
TALKING TO SOMEONE...
THAT WON'T DO. THAT WON'T DO AT ALL.

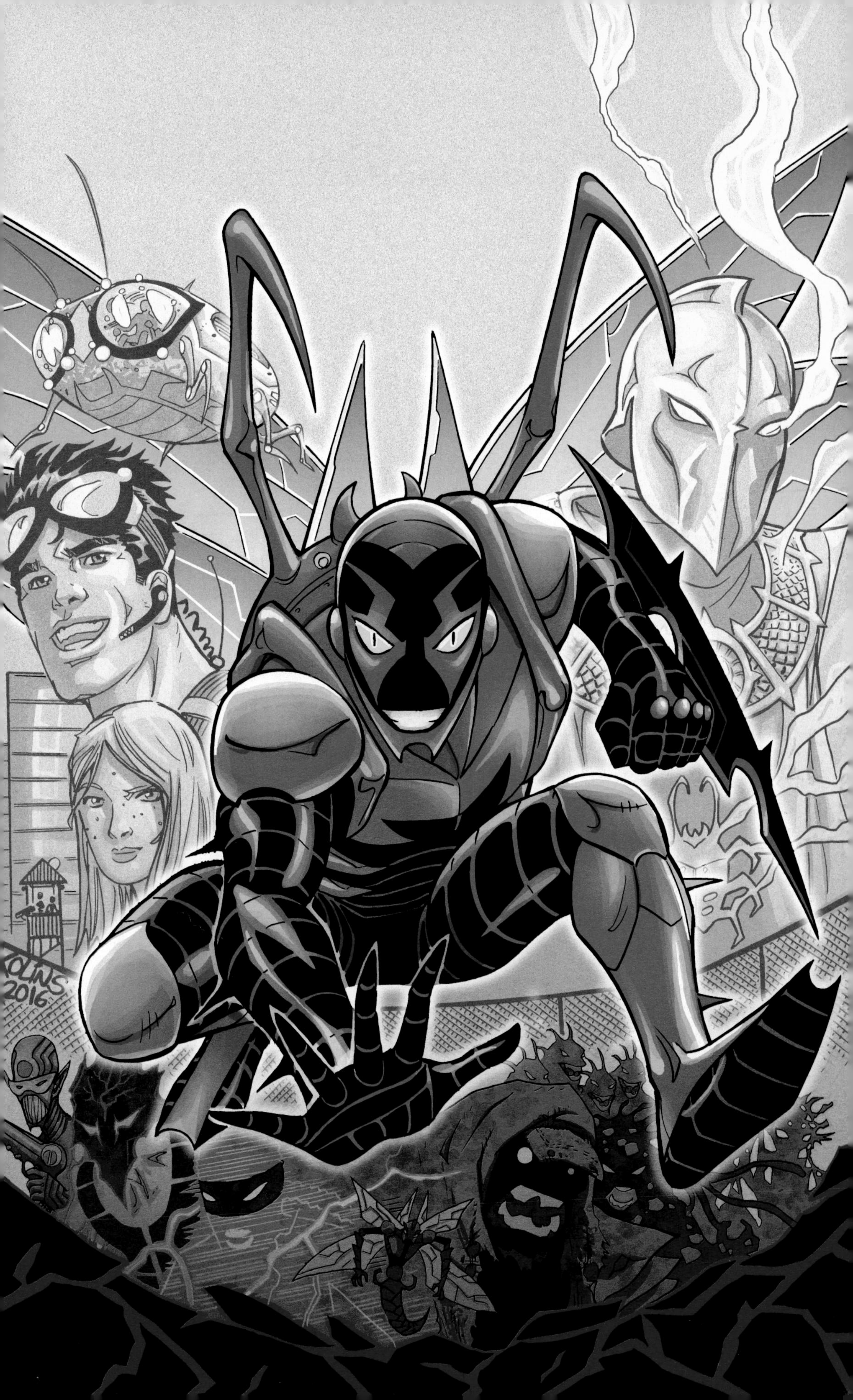

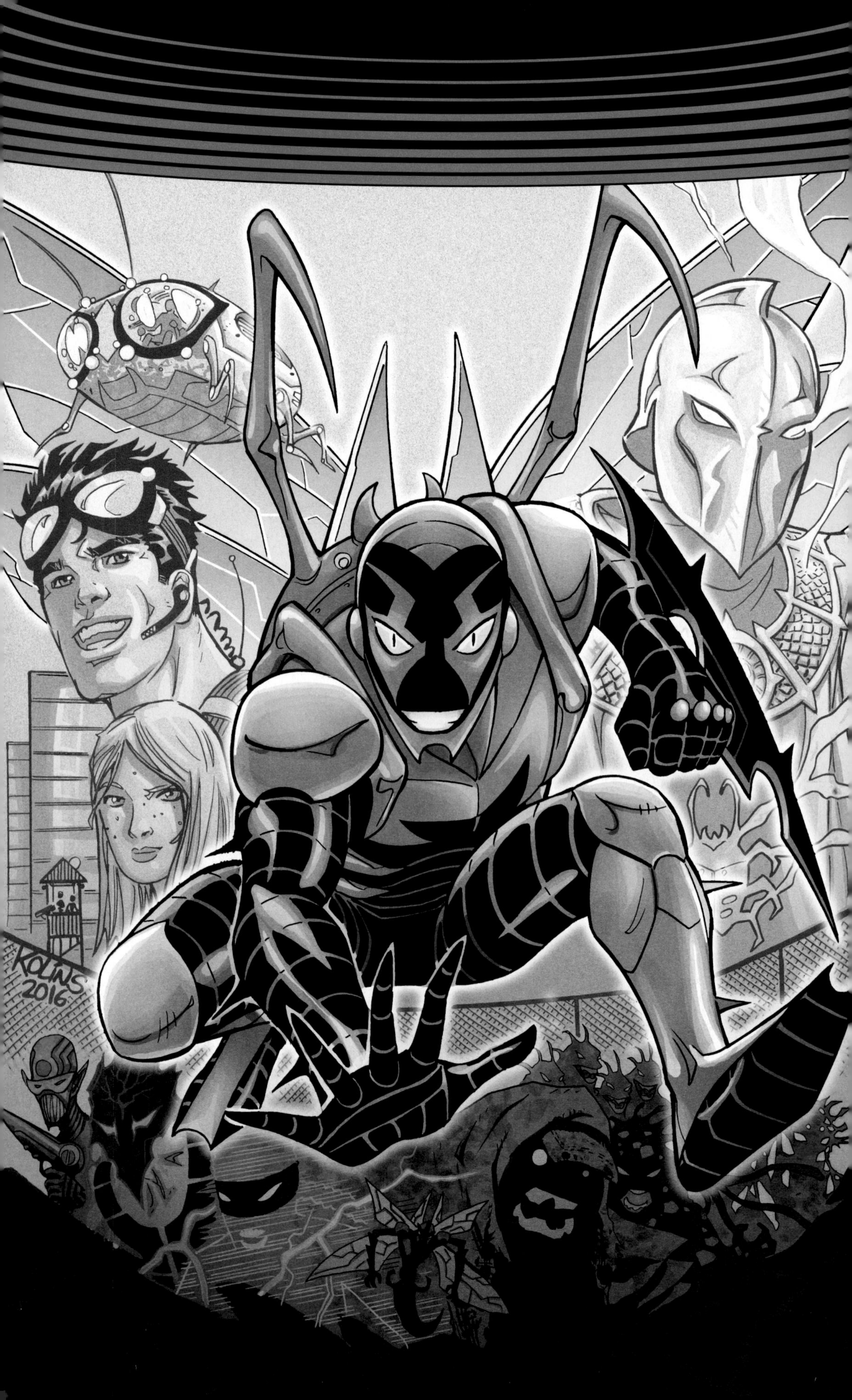
KOLINS
2016

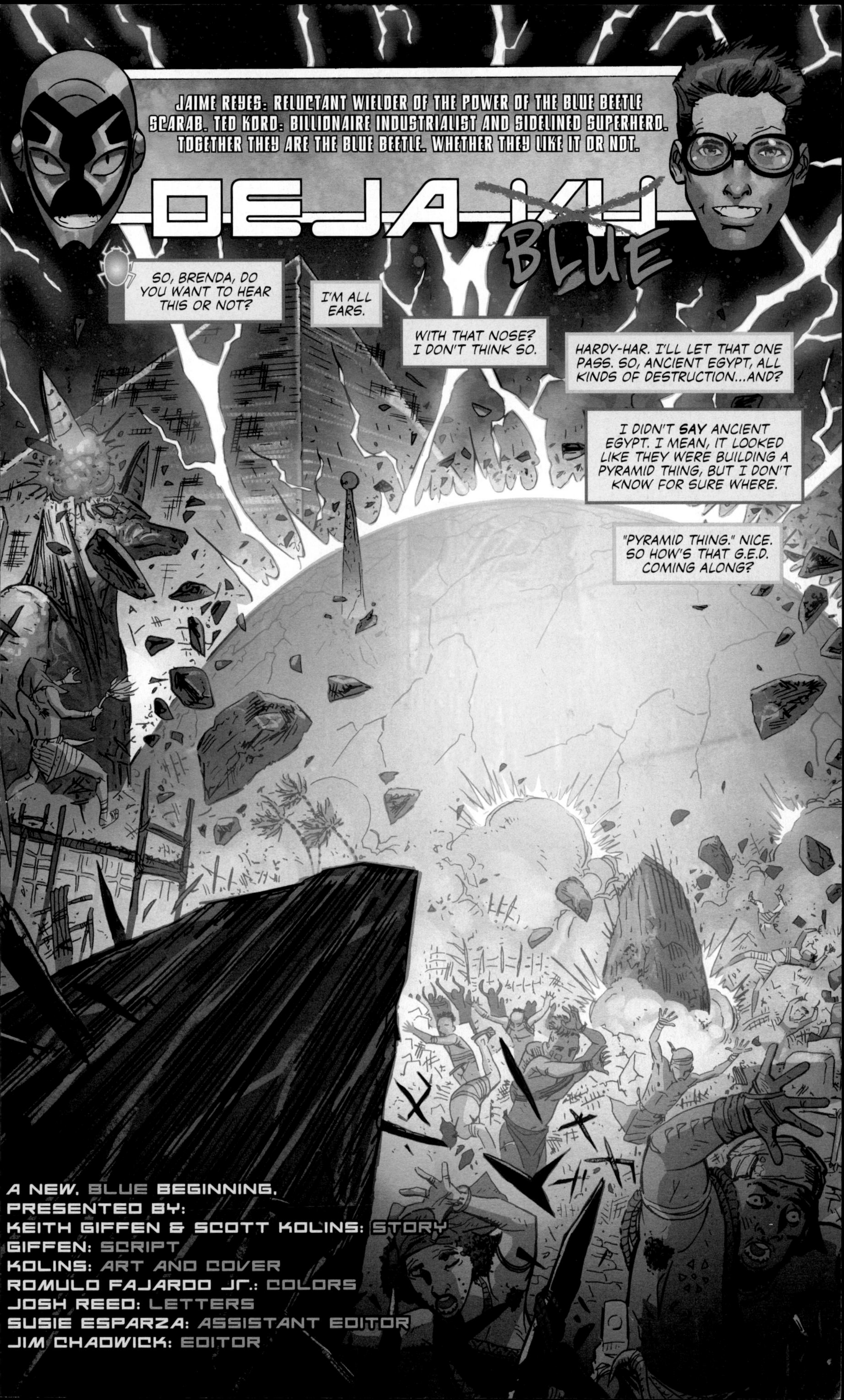
JAIME REYES: RELUCTANT WIELDER OF THE POWER OF THE BLUE BEETLE SCARAB. TED KORD: BILLIONAIRE INDUSTRIALIST AND SIDELINED SUPERHERO. TOGETHER THEY ARE THE BLUE BEETLE. WHETHER THEY LIKE IT OR NOT.
DEJA ~~VU~~ BLUE
SO, BRENDA, DO YOU WANT TO HEAR THIS OR NOT?
I'M ALL EARS.
WITH THAT NOSE? I DON'T THINK SO.
HARDY-HAR. I'LL LET THAT ONE PASS. SO, ANCIENT EGYPT, ALL KINDS OF DESTRUCTION...AND?
I DIDN'T **SAY** ANCIENT EGYPT. I MEAN, IT LOOKED LIKE THEY WERE BUILDING A PYRAMID THING, BUT I DON'T KNOW FOR SURE WHERE.
"PYRAMID THING." NICE. SO HOW'S THAT G.E.D. COMING ALONG?
A NEW, BLUE BEGINNING, PRESENTED BY:
KEITH GIFFEN & SCOTT KOLINS: STORY
GIFFEN: SCRIPT
KOLINS: ART AND COVER
ROMULO FAJARDO JR.: COLORS
JOSH REED: LETTERS
SUSIE ESPARZA: ASSISTANT EDITOR
JIM CHADWICK: EDITOR

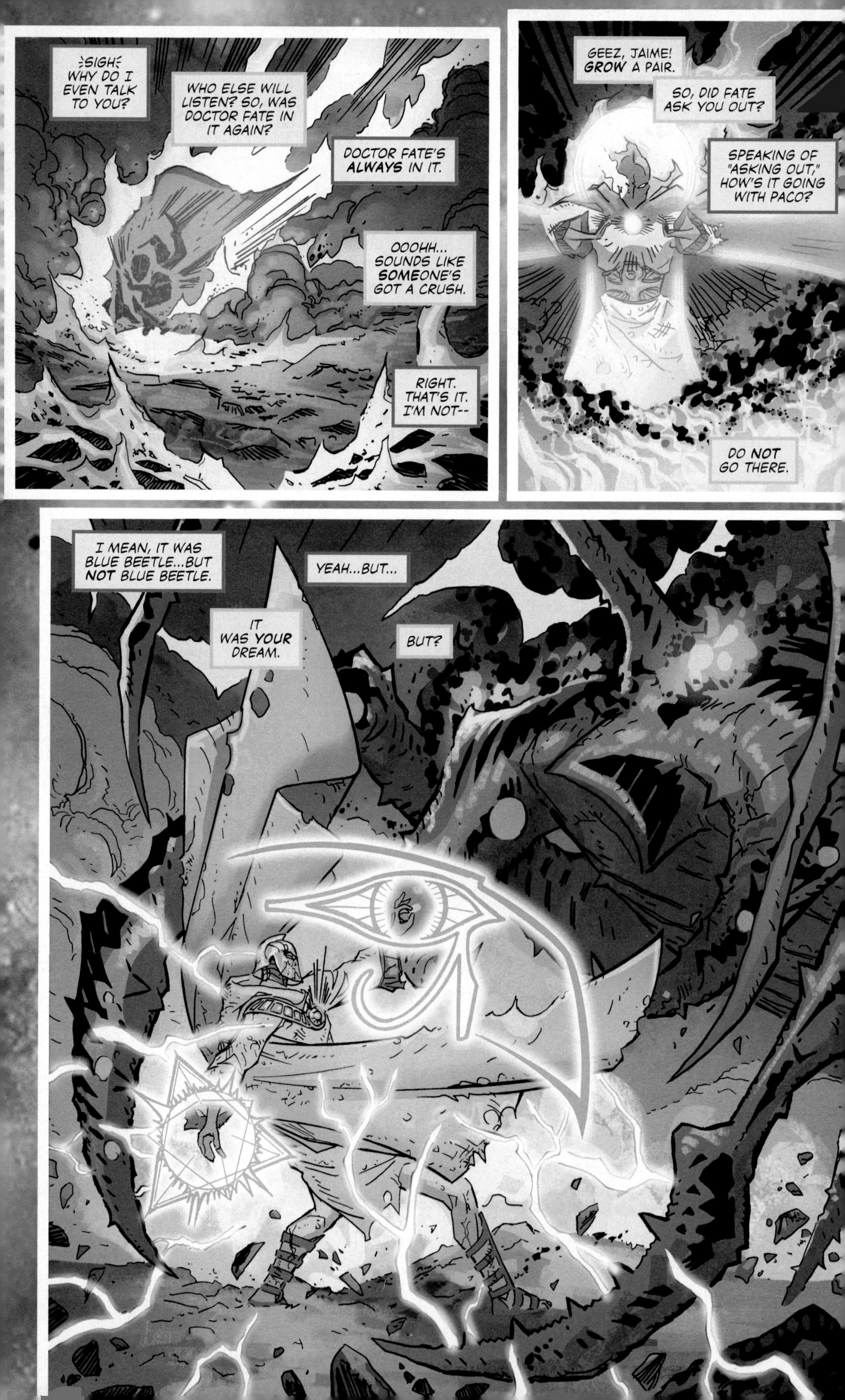

⁝SIGH⁝ WHY DO I EVEN TALK TO YOU?
WHO ELSE WILL LISTEN? SO, WAS DOCTOR FATE IN IT AGAIN?
DOCTOR FATE'S **ALWAYS** IN IT.
OOOHH... SOUNDS LIKE **SOME**ONE'S GOT A CRUSH.
RIGHT. THAT'S IT. I'M NOT--
GEEZ, JAIME! **GROW** A PAIR.
SO, DID FATE ASK YOU OUT?
SPEAKING OF "ASKING OUT," HOW'S IT GOING WITH PACO?
DO **NOT** GO THERE.
I MEAN, IT WAS BLUE BEETLE...BUT **NOT** BLUE BEETLE.
YEAH...BUT...
IT WAS **YOUR** DREAM.
BUT?

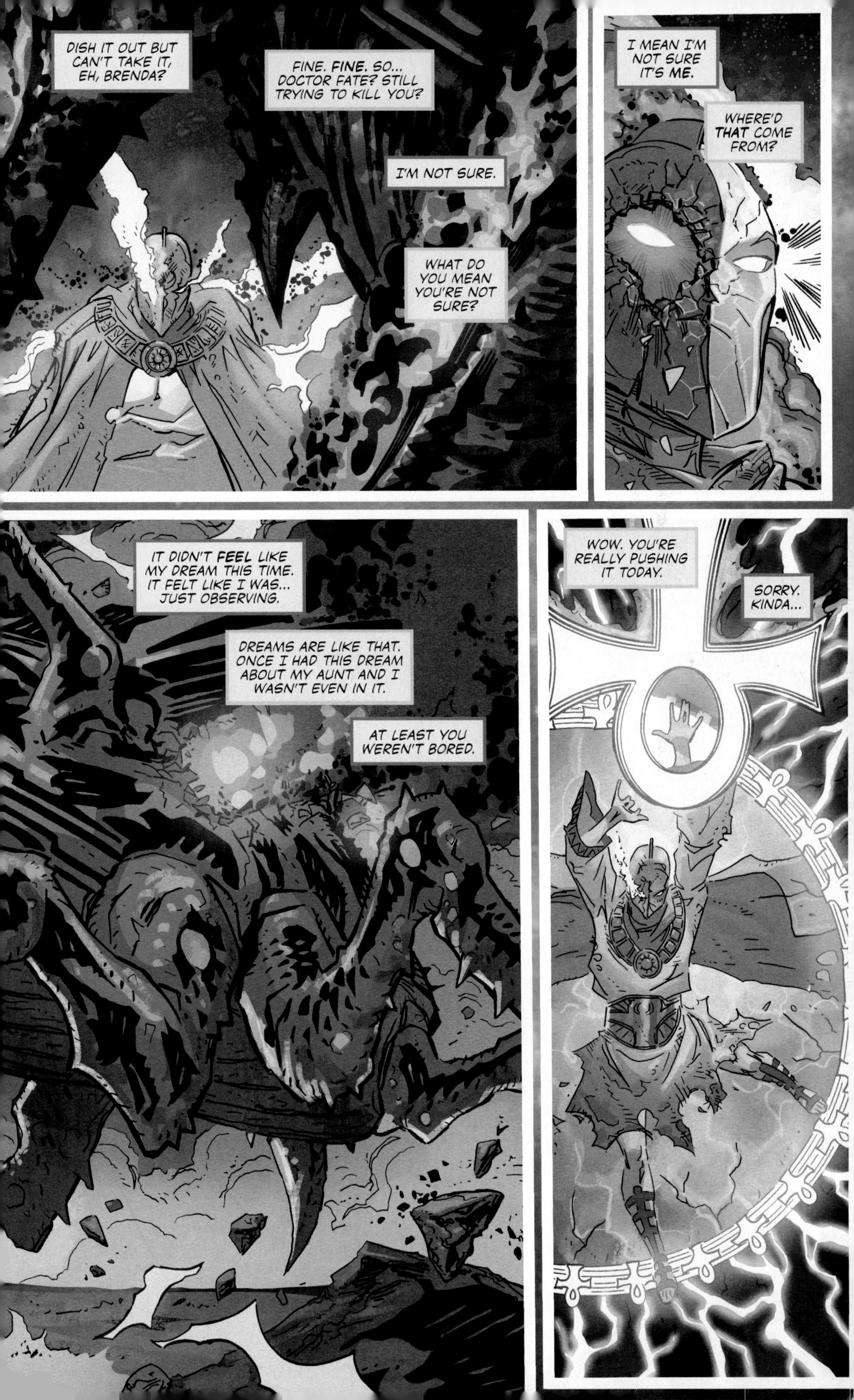
DISH IT OUT BUT CAN'T TAKE IT, EH, BRENDA?
FINE. **FINE.** SO... DOCTOR FATE? STILL TRYING TO KILL YOU?
I'M NOT SURE.
WHAT DO YOU MEAN YOU'RE NOT SURE?
I MEAN I'M NOT SURE IT'S **ME.**
WHERE'D **THAT** COME FROM?
IT DIDN'T **FEEL** LIKE MY DREAM THIS TIME. IT FELT LIKE I WAS... JUST OBSERVING.
DREAMS ARE LIKE THAT. ONCE I HAD THIS DREAM ABOUT MY AUNT AND I WASN'T EVEN IN IT.
AT LEAST YOU WEREN'T BORED.
WOW. YOU'RE REALLY PUSHING IT TODAY.
SORRY. KINDA...

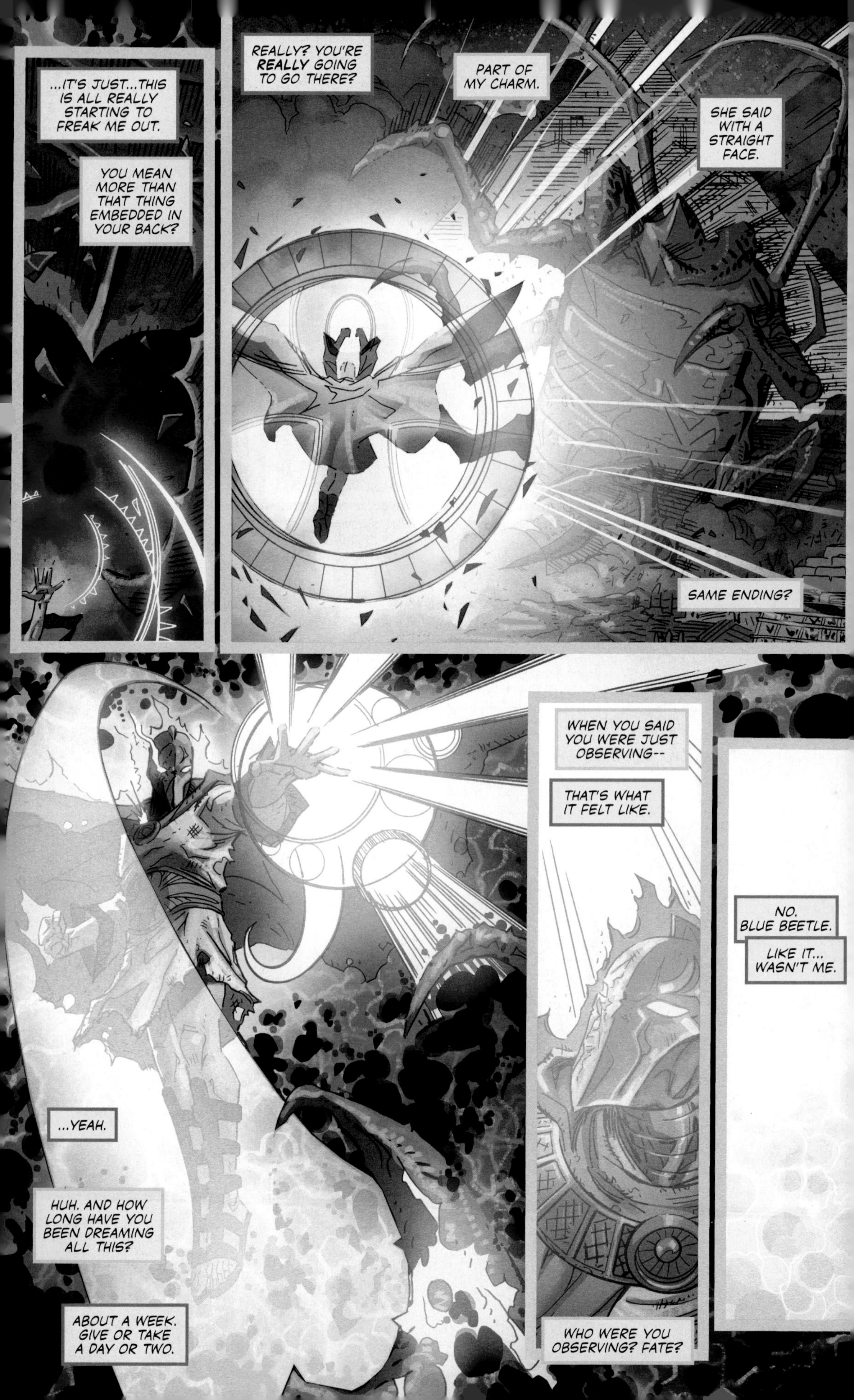
...IT'S JUST...THIS IS ALL REALLY STARTING TO FREAK ME OUT.
YOU MEAN MORE THAN THAT THING EMBEDDED IN YOUR BACK?
REALLY? YOU'RE REALLY GOING TO GO THERE?
PART OF MY CHARM.
SHE SAID WITH A STRAIGHT FACE.
SAME ENDING?
...YEAH.
HUH. AND HOW LONG HAVE YOU BEEN DREAMING ALL THIS?
ABOUT A WEEK. GIVE OR TAKE A DAY OR TWO.
WHEN YOU SAID YOU WERE JUST OBSERVING--
THAT'S WHAT IT FELT LIKE.
WHO WERE YOU OBSERVING? FATE?
NO. BLUE BEETLE.
LIKE IT... WASN'T ME.

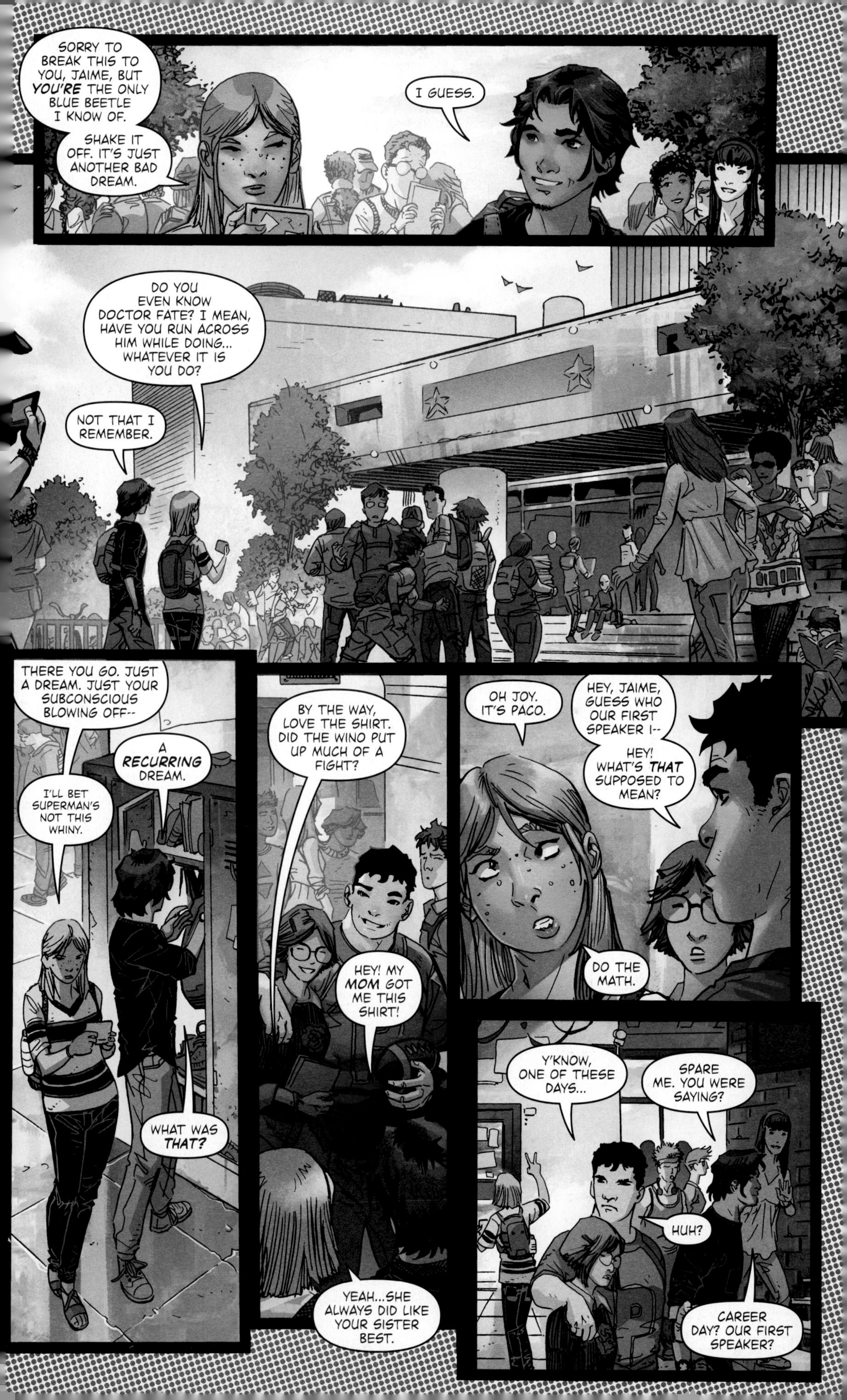
SORRY TO BREAK THIS TO YOU, JAIME, BUT YOU'RE THE ONLY BLUE BEETLE I KNOW OF.
SHAKE IT OFF. IT'S JUST ANOTHER BAD DREAM.
I GUESS.
DO YOU EVEN KNOW DOCTOR FATE? I MEAN, HAVE YOU RUN ACROSS HIM WHILE DOING... WHATEVER IT IS YOU DO?
NOT THAT I REMEMBER.
THERE YOU GO. JUST A DREAM. JUST YOUR SUBCONSCIOUS BLOWING OFF--
A RECURRING DREAM.
I'LL BET SUPERMAN'S NOT THIS WHINY.
WHAT WAS THAT?
BY THE WAY, LOVE THE SHIRT. DID THE WINO PUT UP MUCH OF A FIGHT?
HEY! MY MOM GOT ME THIS SHIRT!
YEAH...SHE ALWAYS DID LIKE YOUR SISTER BEST.
OH JOY. IT'S PACO.
HEY, JAIME, GUESS WHO OUR FIRST SPEAKER I--
HEY! WHAT'S THAT SUPPOSED TO MEAN?
DO THE MATH.
Y'KNOW, ONE OF THESE DAYS...
SPARE ME. YOU WERE SAYING?
HUH?
CAREER DAY? OUR FIRST SPEAKER?

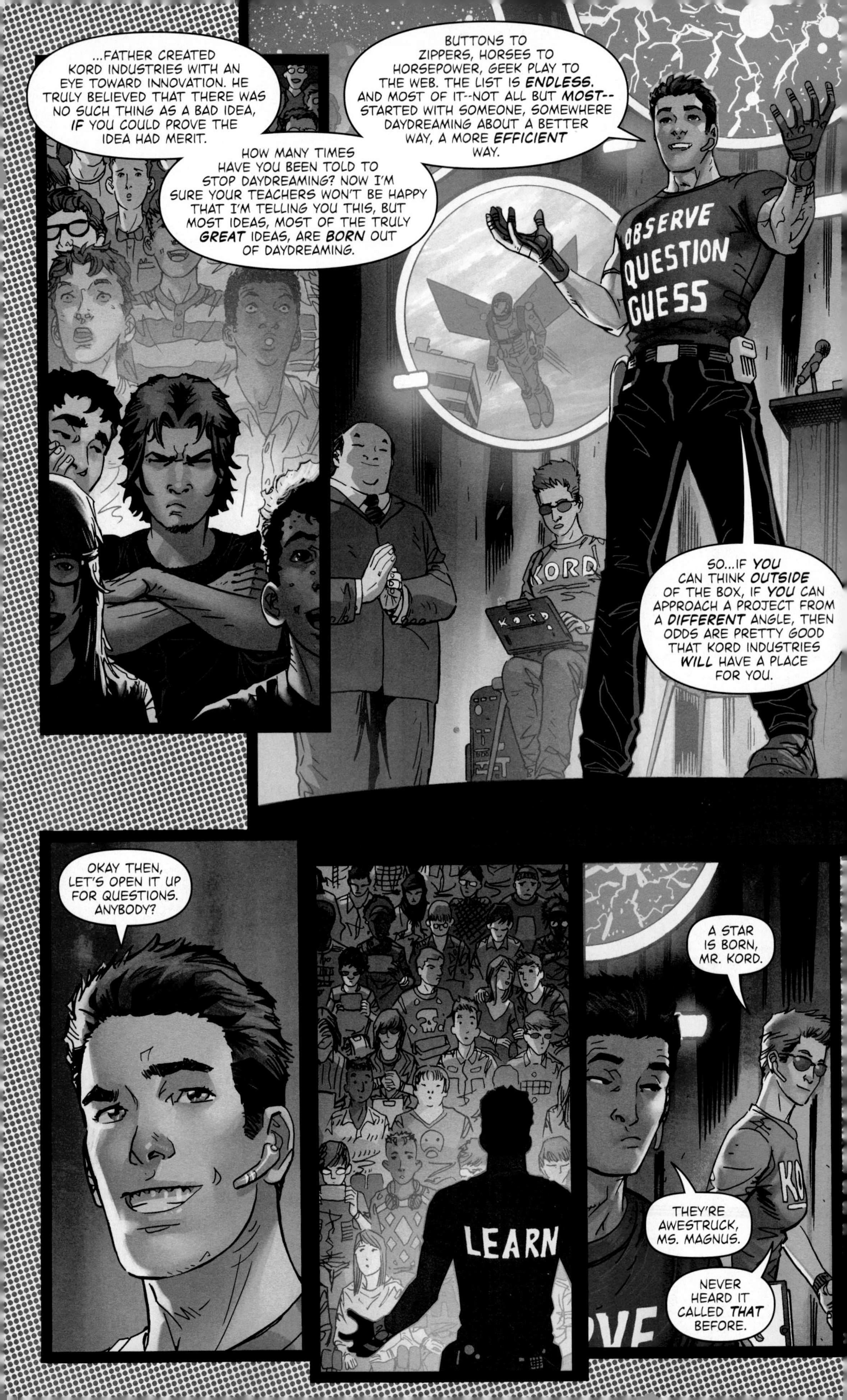
...FATHER CREATED KORD INDUSTRIES WITH AN EYE TOWARD INNOVATION. HE TRULY BELIEVED THAT THERE WAS NO SUCH THING AS A BAD IDEA, *IF* YOU COULD PROVE THE IDEA HAD MERIT.
HOW MANY TIMES HAVE YOU BEEN TOLD TO STOP DAYDREAMING? NOW I'M SURE YOUR TEACHERS WON'T BE HAPPY THAT I'M TELLING YOU THIS, BUT MOST IDEAS, MOST OF THE TRULY *GREAT* IDEAS, ARE *BORN* OUT OF DAYDREAMING.
BUTTONS TO ZIPPERS, HORSES TO HORSEPOWER, GEEK PLAY TO THE WEB. THE LIST IS *ENDLESS.* AND MOST OF IT--NOT ALL BUT *MOST*--STARTED WITH SOMEONE, SOMEWHERE DAYDREAMING ABOUT A BETTER WAY, A MORE *EFFICIENT* WAY.
OBSERVE QUESTION GUESS
KORD
SO...IF *YOU* CAN THINK *OUTSIDE* OF THE BOX, IF *YOU* CAN APPROACH A PROJECT FROM A *DIFFERENT* ANGLE, THEN ODDS ARE PRETTY GOOD THAT KORD INDUSTRIES *WILL* HAVE A PLACE FOR YOU.
OKAY THEN, LET'S OPEN IT UP FOR QUESTIONS. ANYBODY?
LEARN
A STAR IS BORN, MR. KORD.
THEY'RE AWESTRUCK, MS. MAGNUS.
NEVER HEARD IT CALLED *THAT* BEFORE.

BRRRRI-IINGG

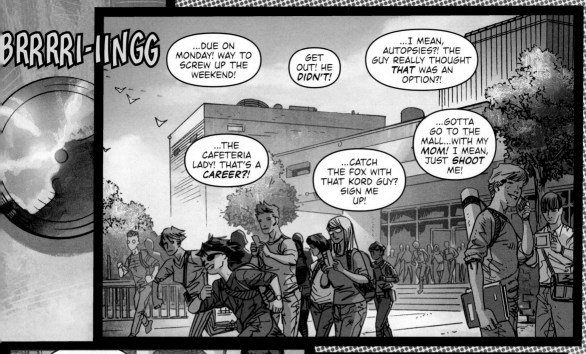

...DUE ON MONDAY! WAY TO SCREW UP THE WEEKEND!

GET OUT! HE *DIDN'T*!

...I MEAN, AUTOPSIES?! THE GUY REALLY THOUGHT *THAT* WAS AN OPTION?!

...THE CAFETERIA LADY! THAT'S A *CAREER*?!

...CATCH THE FOX WITH THAT KORD GUY? SIGN ME UP!

...GOTTA GO TO THE MALL...WITH MY *MOM*! I MEAN, JUST *SHOOT* ME!

I'M JUST WONDERING WHY THEY BOTHER?

HUH?

NOT EVERYONE'S GOING TO GO INTO THE FAST FOOD INDUSTRY.

"YOU WANT FRIES WITH THAT?"

WHAT'S *THAT* SUPPOSED TO MEAN?

DO THE MATH.

CAN WE, MAYBE, GET THROUGH A DAY WITHOUT THE TWO OF YOU SNIPING AT EACH OTHER?

NO.

≥SIGH≤

DOESN'T LOOK THAT WAY.

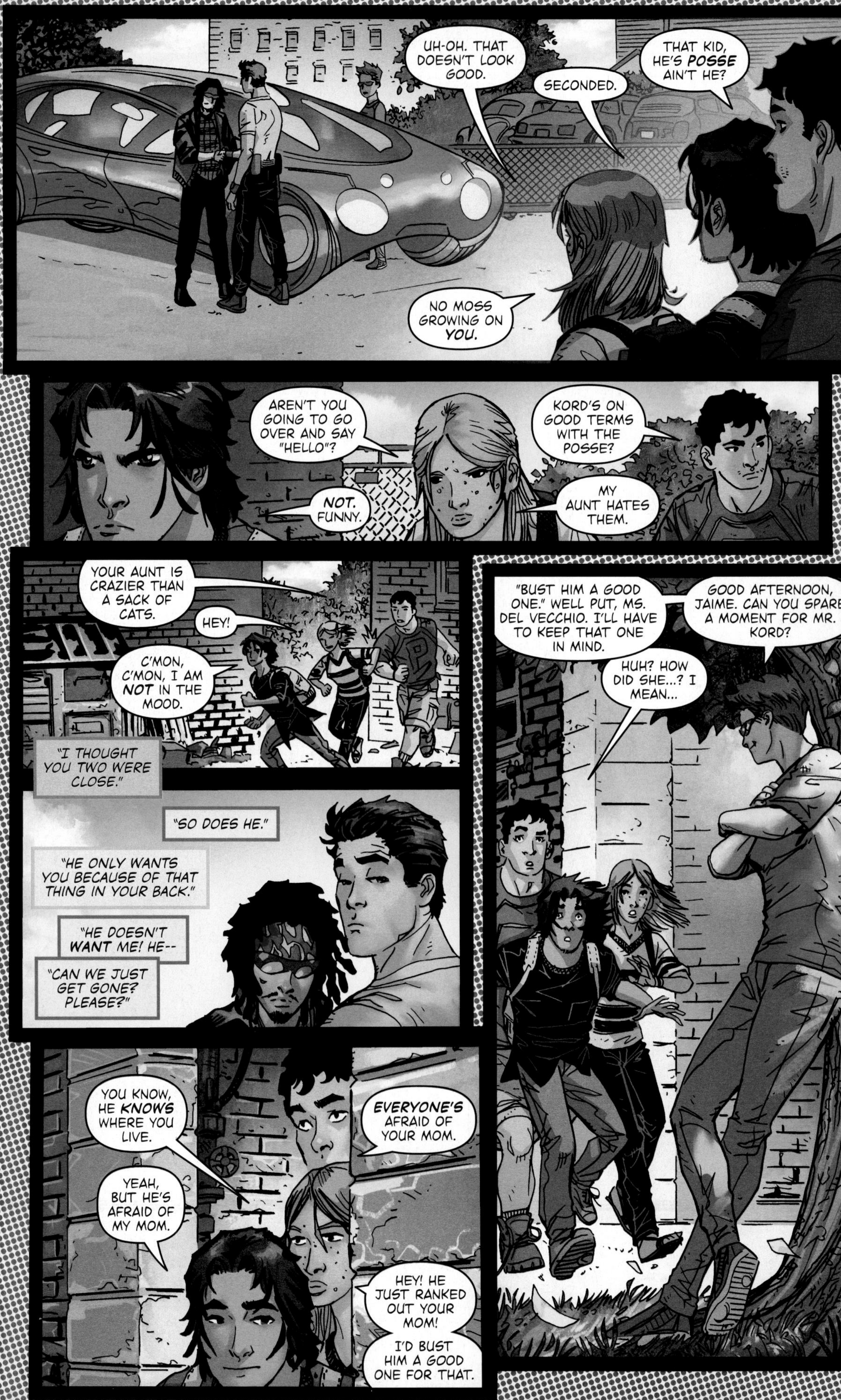
UH-OH. THAT DOESN'T LOOK GOOD.
SECONDED.
THAT KID, HE'S POSSE AIN'T HE?
NO MOSS GROWING ON YOU.
AREN'T YOU GOING TO GO OVER AND SAY "HELLO"?
NOT. FUNNY.
KORD'S ON GOOD TERMS WITH THE POSSE?
MY AUNT HATES THEM.
YOUR AUNT IS CRAZIER THAN A SACK OF CATS.
HEY!
C'MON, C'MON, I AM NOT IN THE MOOD.
"I THOUGHT YOU TWO WERE CLOSE."
"SO DOES HE."
"HE ONLY WANTS YOU BECAUSE OF THAT THING IN YOUR BACK."
"HE DOESN'T WANT ME! HE--
"CAN WE JUST GET GONE? PLEASE?"
YOU KNOW, HE KNOWS WHERE YOU LIVE.
YEAH, BUT HE'S AFRAID OF MY MOM.
EVERYONE'S AFRAID OF YOUR MOM.
HEY! HE JUST RANKED OUT YOUR MOM!
I'D BUST HIM A GOOD ONE FOR THAT.
"BUST HIM A GOOD ONE." WELL PUT, MS. DEL VECCHIO. I'LL HAVE TO KEEP THAT ONE IN MIND.
GOOD AFTERNOON, JAIME. CAN YOU SPARE A MOMENT FOR MR. KORD?
HUH? HOW DID SHE...? I MEAN...

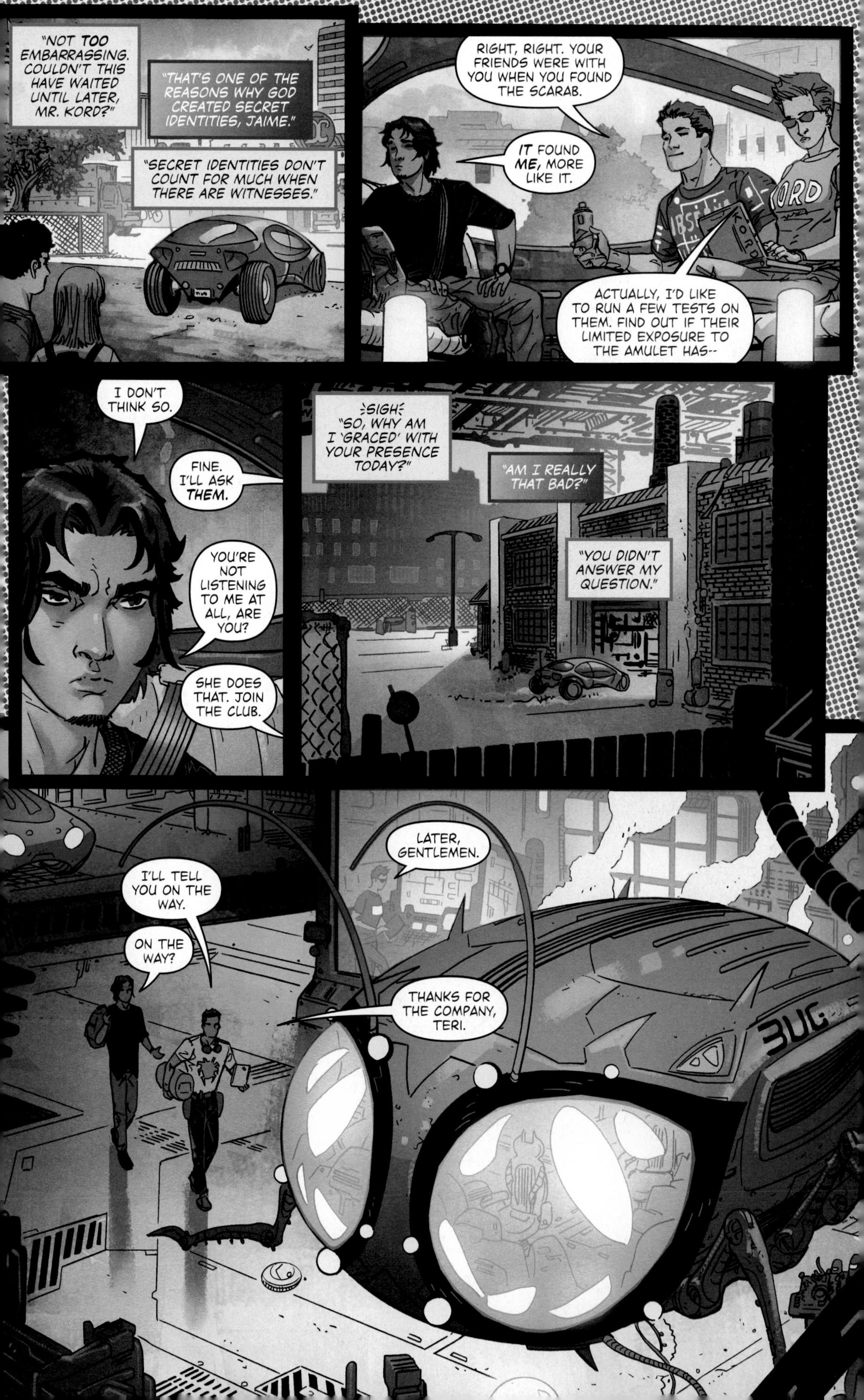
"NOT TOO EMBARRASSING. COULDN'T THIS HAVE WAITED UNTIL LATER, MR. KORD?"
"THAT'S ONE OF THE REASONS WHY GOD CREATED SECRET IDENTITIES, JAIME."
"SECRET IDENTITIES DON'T COUNT FOR MUCH WHEN THERE ARE WITNESSES."
RIGHT, RIGHT. YOUR FRIENDS WERE WITH YOU WHEN YOU FOUND THE SCARAB.
IT FOUND ME, MORE LIKE IT.
ACTUALLY, I'D LIKE TO RUN A FEW TESTS ON THEM. FIND OUT IF THEIR LIMITED EXPOSURE TO THE AMULET HAS--
I DON'T THINK SO.
FINE. I'LL ASK THEM.
YOU'RE NOT LISTENING TO ME AT ALL, ARE YOU?
SHE DOES THAT. JOIN THE CLUB.
SIGH "SO, WHY AM I 'GRACED' WITH YOUR PRESENCE TODAY?"
"AM I REALLY THAT BAD?"
"YOU DIDN'T ANSWER MY QUESTION."
I'LL TELL YOU ON THE WAY.
ON THE WAY?
LATER, GENTLEMEN.
THANKS FOR THE COMPANY, TERI.
BUG

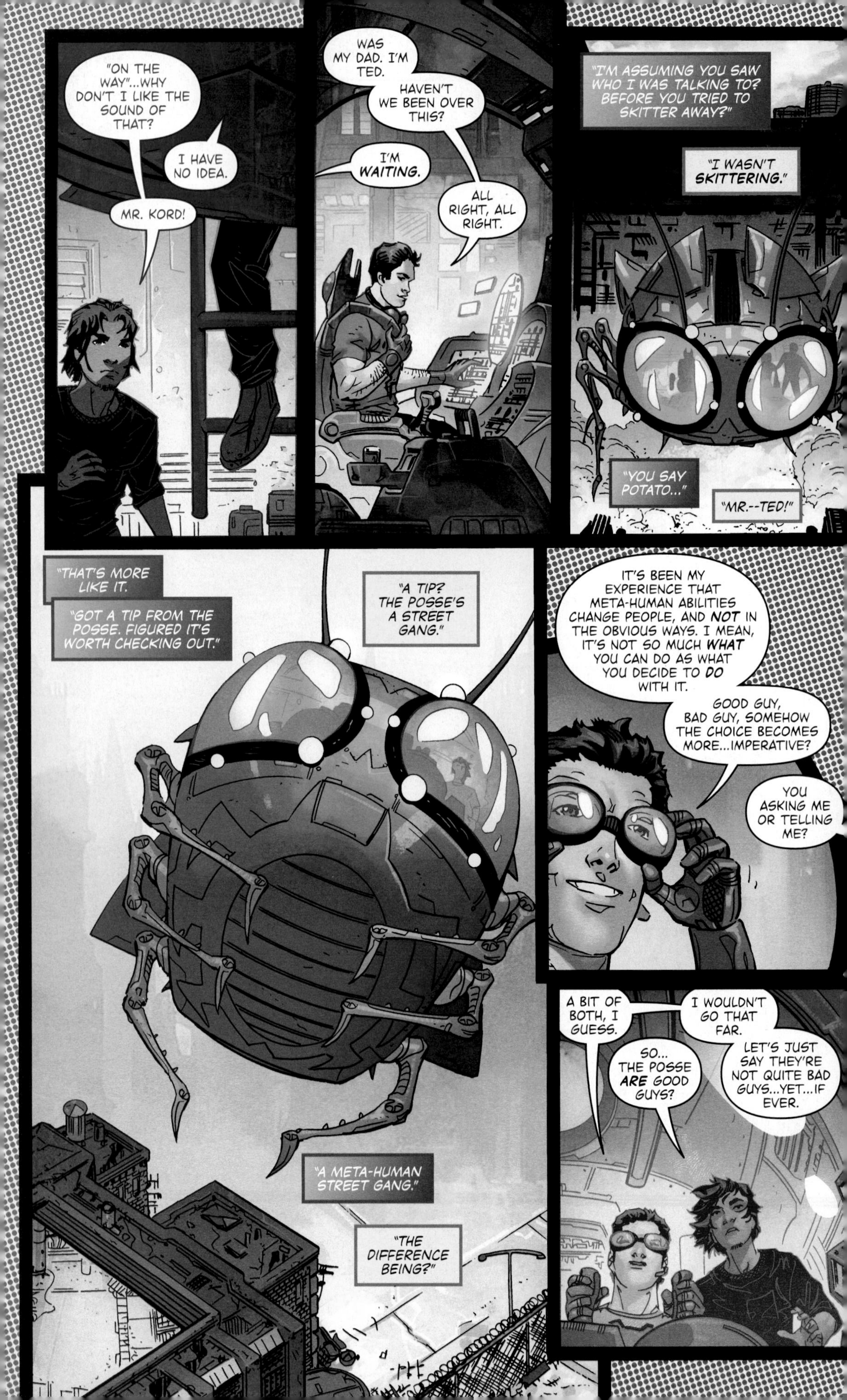
"ON THE WAY"...WHY DON'T I LIKE THE SOUND OF THAT?
I HAVE NO IDEA.
MR. KORD!
WAS MY DAD. I'M TED.
HAVEN'T WE BEEN OVER THIS?
I'M WAITING.
ALL RIGHT, ALL RIGHT.
"I'M ASSUMING YOU SAW WHO I WAS TALKING TO? BEFORE YOU TRIED TO SKITTER AWAY?"
"I WASN'T SKITTERING."
"YOU SAY POTATO..."
"MR.--TED!"
"THAT'S MORE LIKE IT.
"GOT A TIP FROM THE POSSE. FIGURED IT'S WORTH CHECKING OUT."
"A TIP? THE POSSE'S A STREET GANG."
"A META-HUMAN STREET GANG."
"THE DIFFERENCE BEING?"
IT'S BEEN MY EXPERIENCE THAT META-HUMAN ABILITIES CHANGE PEOPLE, AND NOT IN THE OBVIOUS WAYS. I MEAN, IT'S NOT SO MUCH WHAT YOU CAN DO AS WHAT YOU DECIDE TO DO WITH IT.
GOOD GUY, BAD GUY, SOMEHOW THE CHOICE BECOMES MORE...IMPERATIVE?
YOU ASKING ME OR TELLING ME?
A BIT OF BOTH, I GUESS.
SO... THE POSSE ARE GOOD GUYS?
I WOULDN'T GO THAT FAR.
LET'S JUST SAY THEY'RE NOT QUITE BAD GUYS...YET...IF EVER.

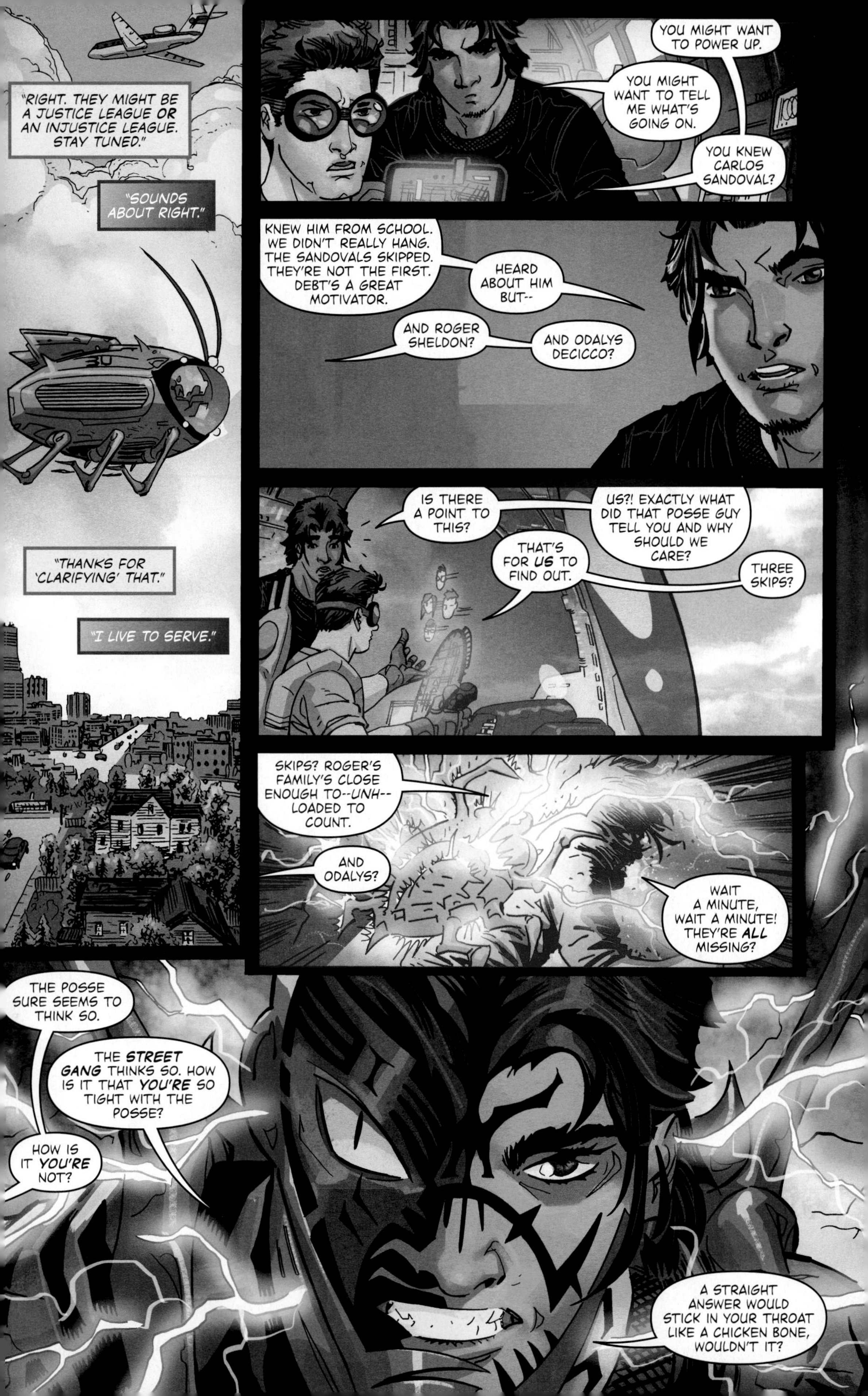
"RIGHT. THEY MIGHT BE A JUSTICE LEAGUE OR AN INJUSTICE LEAGUE. STAY TUNED."
"SOUNDS ABOUT RIGHT."
"THANKS FOR 'CLARIFYING' THAT."
"I LIVE TO SERVE."
YOU MIGHT WANT TO POWER UP.
YOU MIGHT WANT TO TELL ME WHAT'S GOING ON.
YOU KNEW CARLOS SANDOVAL?
KNEW HIM FROM SCHOOL. WE DIDN'T REALLY HANG. THE SANDOVALS SKIPPED. THEY'RE NOT THE FIRST. DEBT'S A GREAT MOTIVATOR.
HEARD ABOUT HIM BUT--
AND ROGER SHELDON?
AND ODALYS DECICCO?
IS THERE A POINT TO THIS?
US?! EXACTLY WHAT DID THAT POSSE GUY TELL YOU AND WHY SHOULD WE CARE?
THAT'S FOR US TO FIND OUT.
THREE SKIPS?
SKIPS? ROGER'S FAMILY'S CLOSE ENOUGH TO--UNH--LOADED TO COUNT.
AND ODALYS?
WAIT A MINUTE, WAIT A MINUTE! THEY'RE ALL MISSING?
THE POSSE SURE SEEMS TO THINK SO.
THE STREET GANG THINKS SO. HOW IS IT THAT YOU'RE SO TIGHT WITH THE POSSE?
HOW IS IT YOU'RE NOT?
A STRAIGHT ANSWER WOULD STICK IN YOUR THROAT LIKE A CHICKEN BONE, WOULDN'T IT?

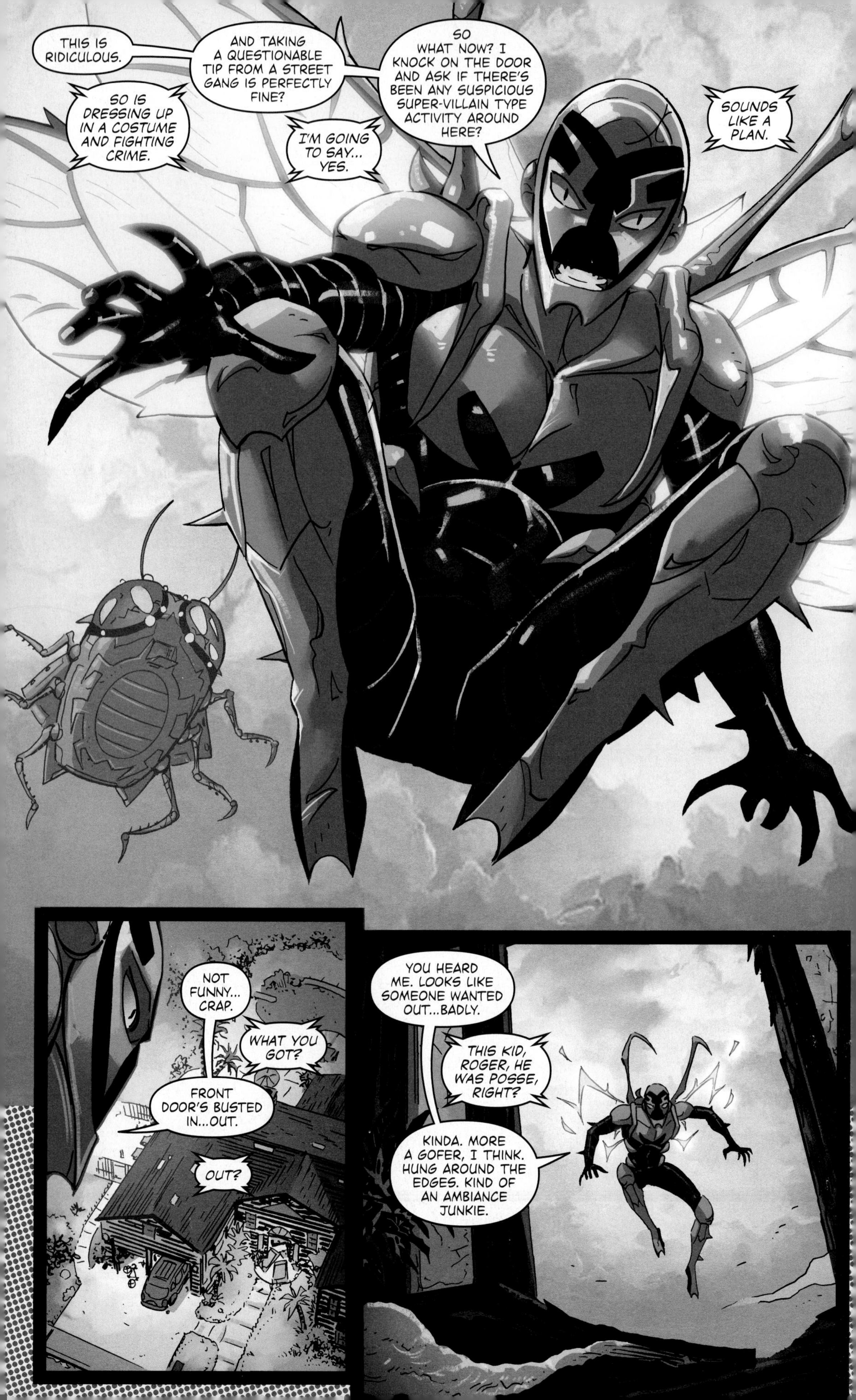
THIS IS RIDICULOUS.
AND TAKING A QUESTIONABLE TIP FROM A STREET GANG IS PERFECTLY FINE?
SO IS DRESSING UP IN A COSTUME AND FIGHTING CRIME.
I'M GOING TO SAY... YES.
SO WHAT NOW? I KNOCK ON THE DOOR AND ASK IF THERE'S BEEN ANY SUSPICIOUS SUPER-VILLAIN TYPE ACTIVITY AROUND HERE?
SOUNDS LIKE A PLAN.
NOT FUNNY... CRAP.
WHAT YOU GOT?
FRONT DOOR'S BUSTED IN...OUT.
OUT?
YOU HEARD ME. LOOKS LIKE SOMEONE WANTED OUT...BADLY.
THIS KID, ROGER, HE WAS POSSE, RIGHT?
KINDA. MORE A GOFER, I THINK. HUNG AROUND THE EDGES. KIND OF AN AMBIANCE JUNKIE.

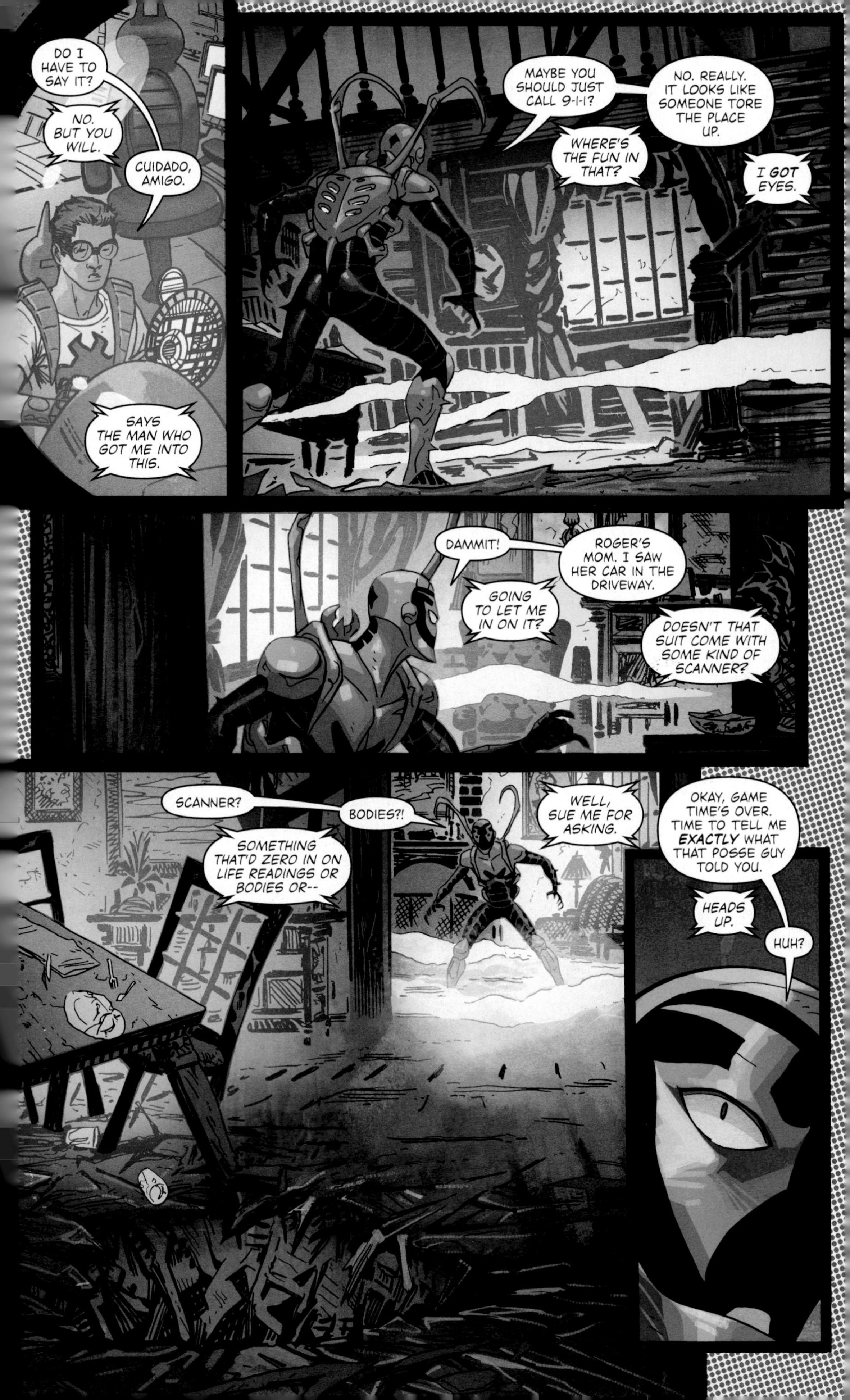
DO I HAVE TO SAY IT?
NO. BUT YOU WILL.
CUIDADO, AMIGO.
SAYS THE MAN WHO GOT ME INTO THIS.
MAYBE YOU SHOULD JUST CALL 9-1-1?
WHERE'S THE FUN IN THAT?
NO. REALLY. IT LOOKS LIKE SOMEONE TORE THE PLACE UP.
I GOT EYES.
DAMMIT!
GOING TO LET ME IN ON IT?
ROGER'S MOM. I SAW HER CAR IN THE DRIVEWAY.
DOESN'T THAT SUIT COME WITH SOME KIND OF SCANNER?
SCANNER?
SOMETHING THAT'D ZERO IN ON LIFE READINGS OR BODIES OR--
BODIES?!
WELL, SUE ME FOR ASKING.
OKAY, GAME TIME'S OVER. TIME TO TELL ME EXACTLY WHAT THAT POSSE GUY TOLD YOU.
HEADS UP.
HUH?

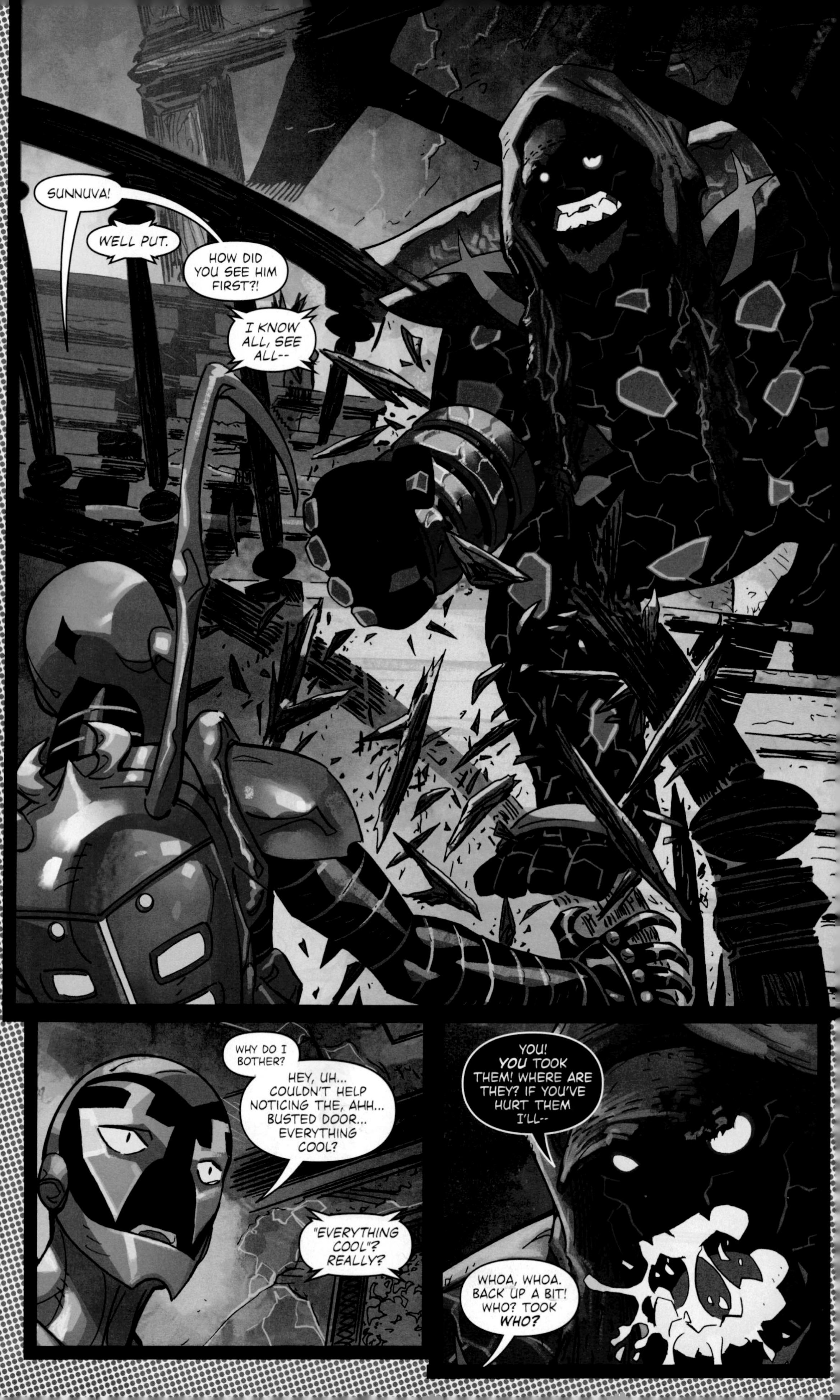
SUNNUVA!
WELL PUT.
HOW DID YOU SEE HIM FIRST?!
I KNOW ALL, SEE ALL--
WHY DO I BOTHER?
HEY, UH... COULDN'T HELP NOTICING THE, AHH... BUSTED DOOR... EVERYTHING COOL?
"EVERYTHING COOL"? REALLY?
YOU! YOU TOOK THEM! WHERE ARE THEY? IF YOU'VE HURT THEM I'LL--
WHOA, WHOA. BACK UP A BIT! WHO? TOOK WHO?

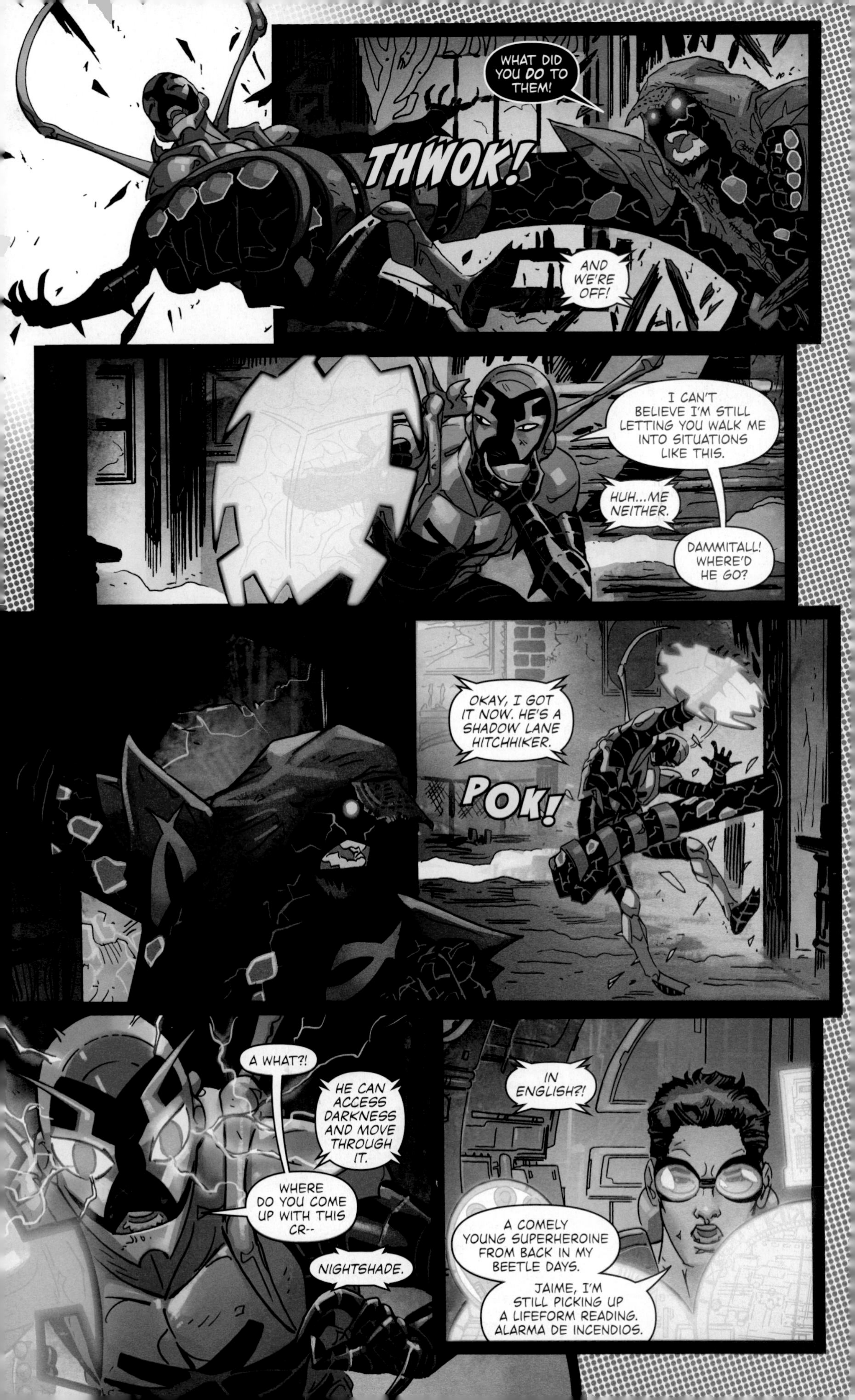
WHAT DID YOU DO TO THEM!
THWOK!
AND WE'RE OFF!
I CAN'T BELIEVE I'M STILL LETTING YOU WALK ME INTO SITUATIONS LIKE THIS.
HUH...ME NEITHER.
DAMMITALL! WHERE'D HE GO?
OKAY, I GOT IT NOW. HE'S A SHADOW LANE HITCHHIKER.
POK!
A WHAT?!
HE CAN ACCESS DARKNESS AND MOVE THROUGH IT.
WHERE DO YOU COME UP WITH THIS CR--
NIGHTSHADE.
IN ENGLISH?!
A COMELY YOUNG SUPERHEROINE FROM BACK IN MY BEETLE DAYS.
JAIME, I'M STILL PICKING UP A LIFEFORM READING. ALARMA DE INCENDIOS.

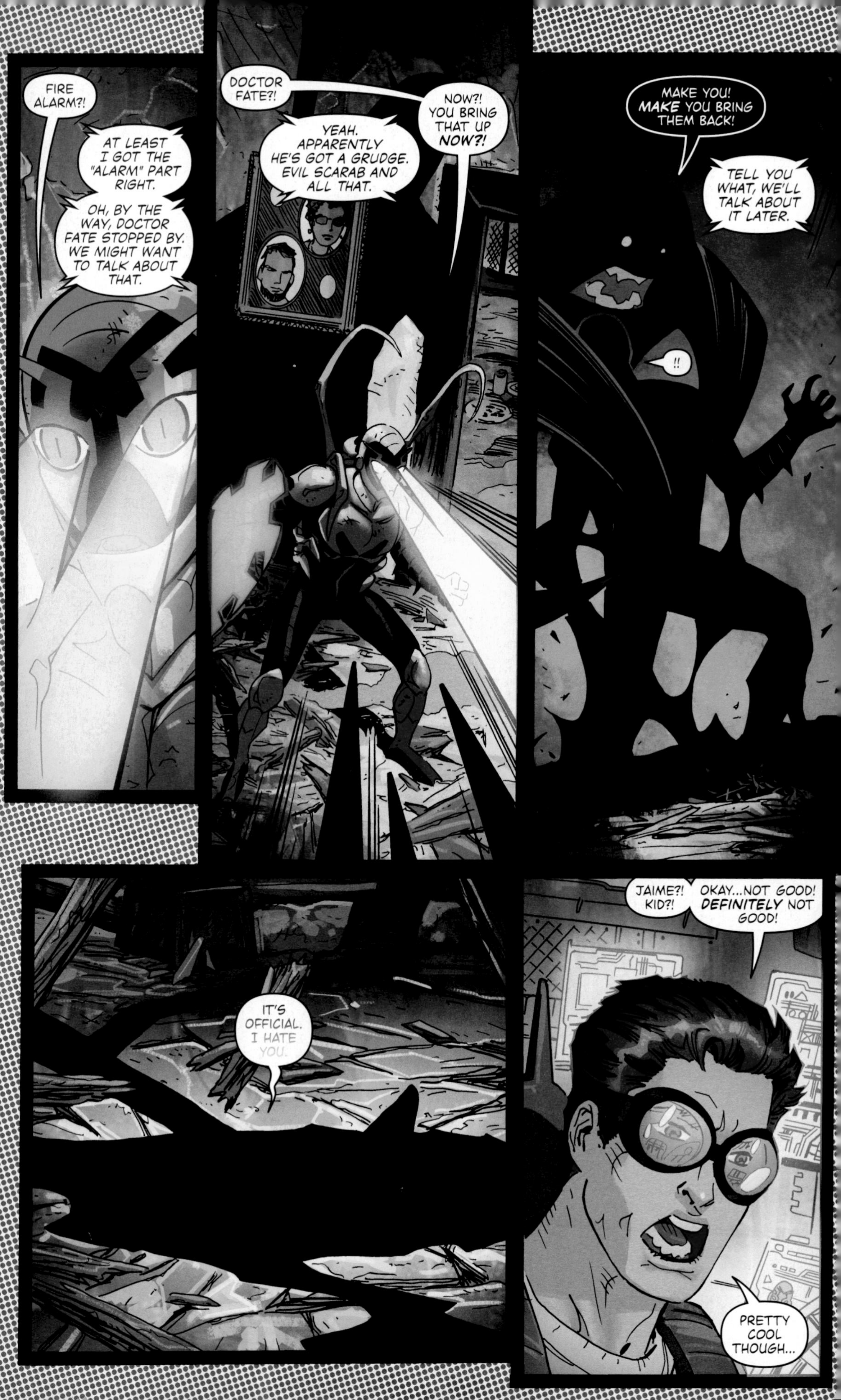
FIRE ALARM?!
AT LEAST I GOT THE "ALARM" PART RIGHT.
OH, BY THE WAY, DOCTOR FATE STOPPED BY. WE MIGHT WANT TO TALK ABOUT THAT.
DOCTOR FATE?!
YEAH. APPARENTLY HE'S GOT A GRUDGE. EVIL SCARAB AND ALL THAT.
NOW?! YOU BRING THAT UP NOW?!
MAKE YOU! MAKE YOU BRING THEM BACK!
TELL YOU WHAT, WE'LL TALK ABOUT IT LATER.
!!
IT'S OFFICIAL. I HATE YOU.
JAIME?! KID?!
OKAY...NOT GOOD! DEFINITELY NOT GOOD!
PRETTY COOL THOUGH...

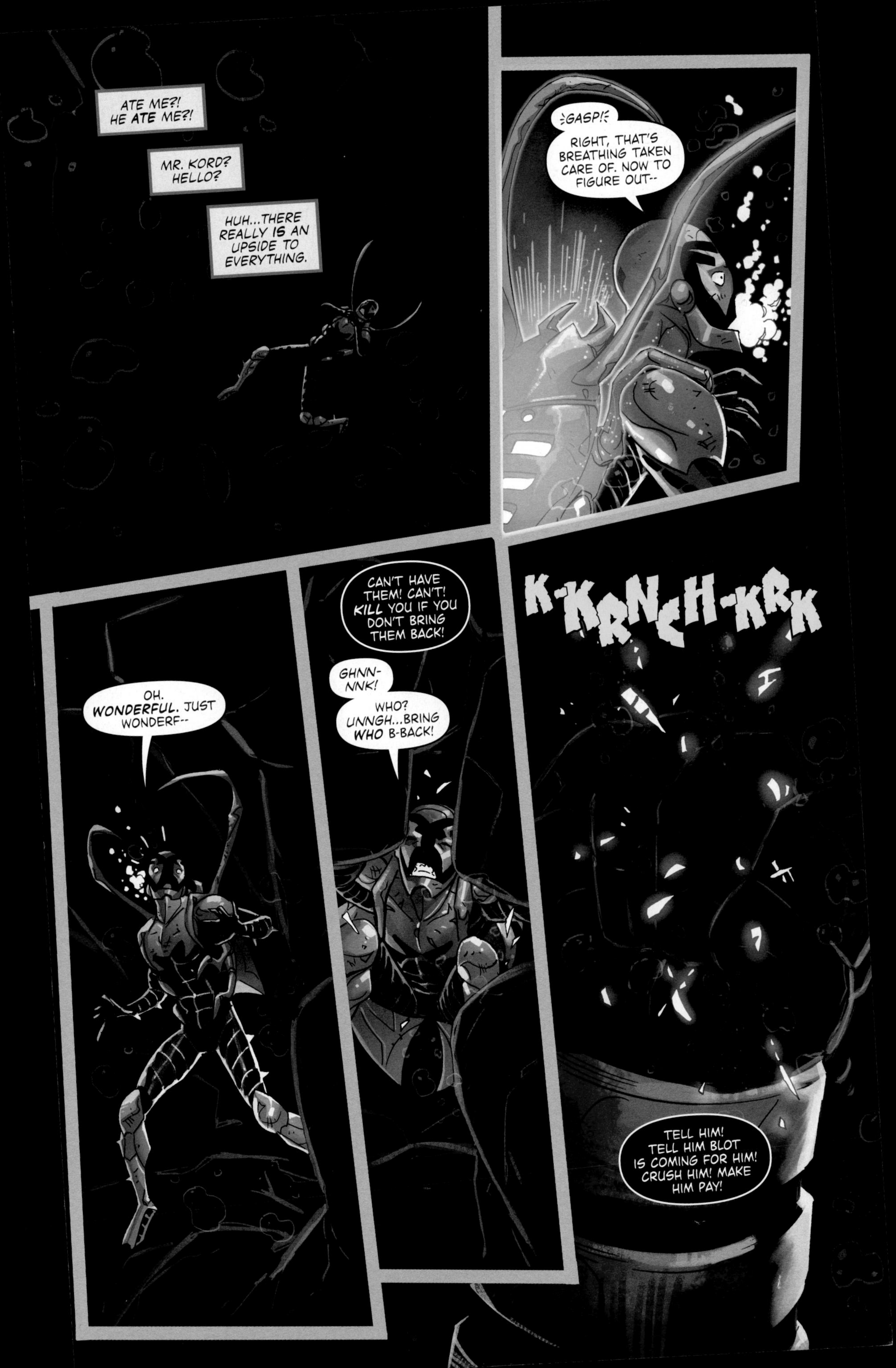
ATE ME?! HE ATE ME?!
MR. KORD? HELLO?
HUH...THERE REALLY IS AN UPSIDE TO EVERYTHING.
GASP!
RIGHT, THAT'S BREATHING TAKEN CARE OF. NOW TO FIGURE OUT--
OH. WONDERFUL. JUST WONDERF--
CAN'T HAVE THEM! CAN'T! KILL YOU IF YOU DON'T BRING THEM BACK!
GHNN-NNK!
WHO? UNNGH...BRING WHO B-BACK!
K-KRNCH-KRK
TELL HIM! TELL HIM BLOT IS COMING FOR HIM! CRUSH HIM! MAKE HIM PAY!

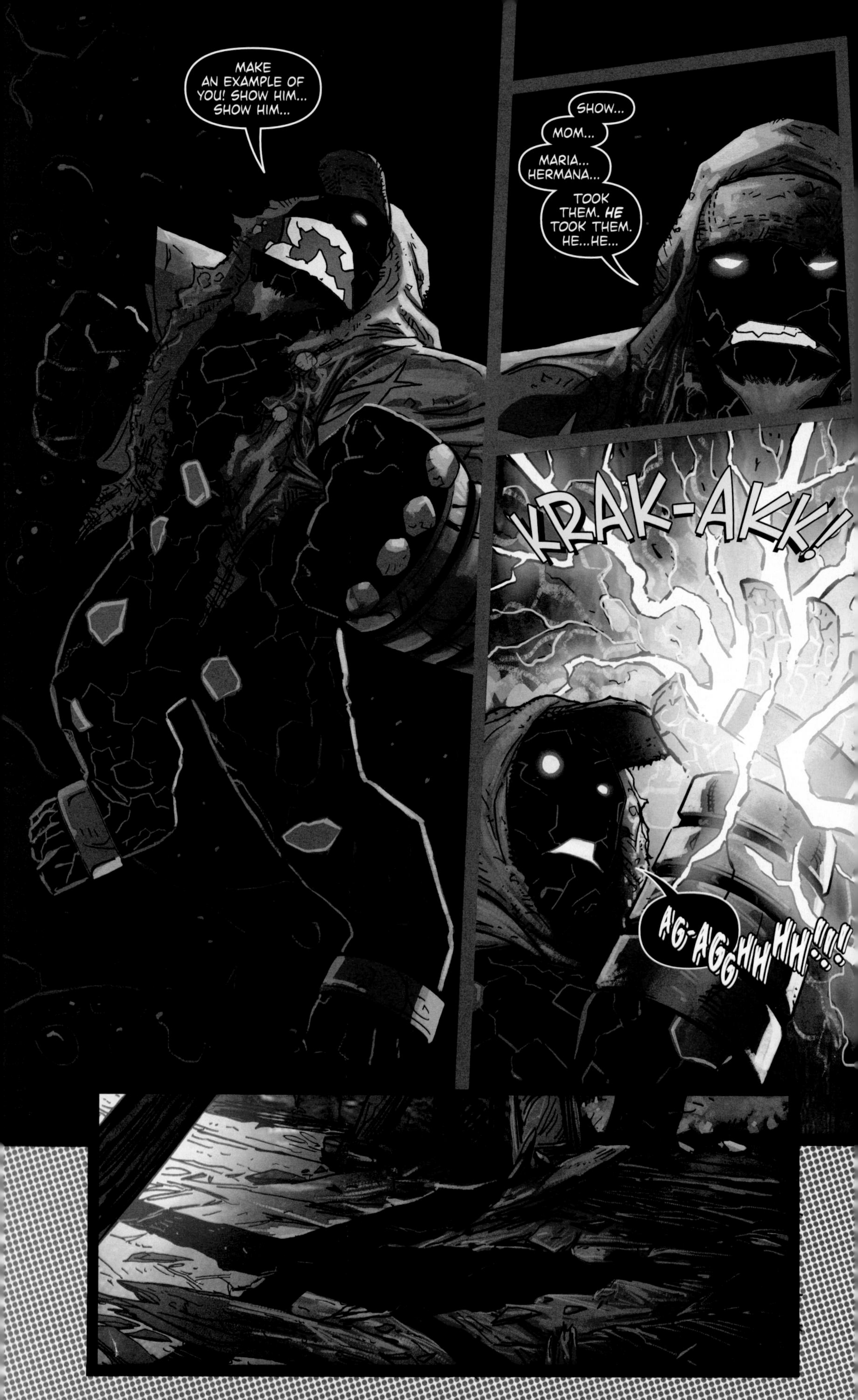
MAKE AN EXAMPLE OF YOU! SHOW HIM... SHOW HIM...
SHOW...
MOM...
MARIA... HERMANA...
TOOK THEM. HE TOOK THEM. HE...HE...
KRAK-AKK!
AG-AGGHHHH!!!!

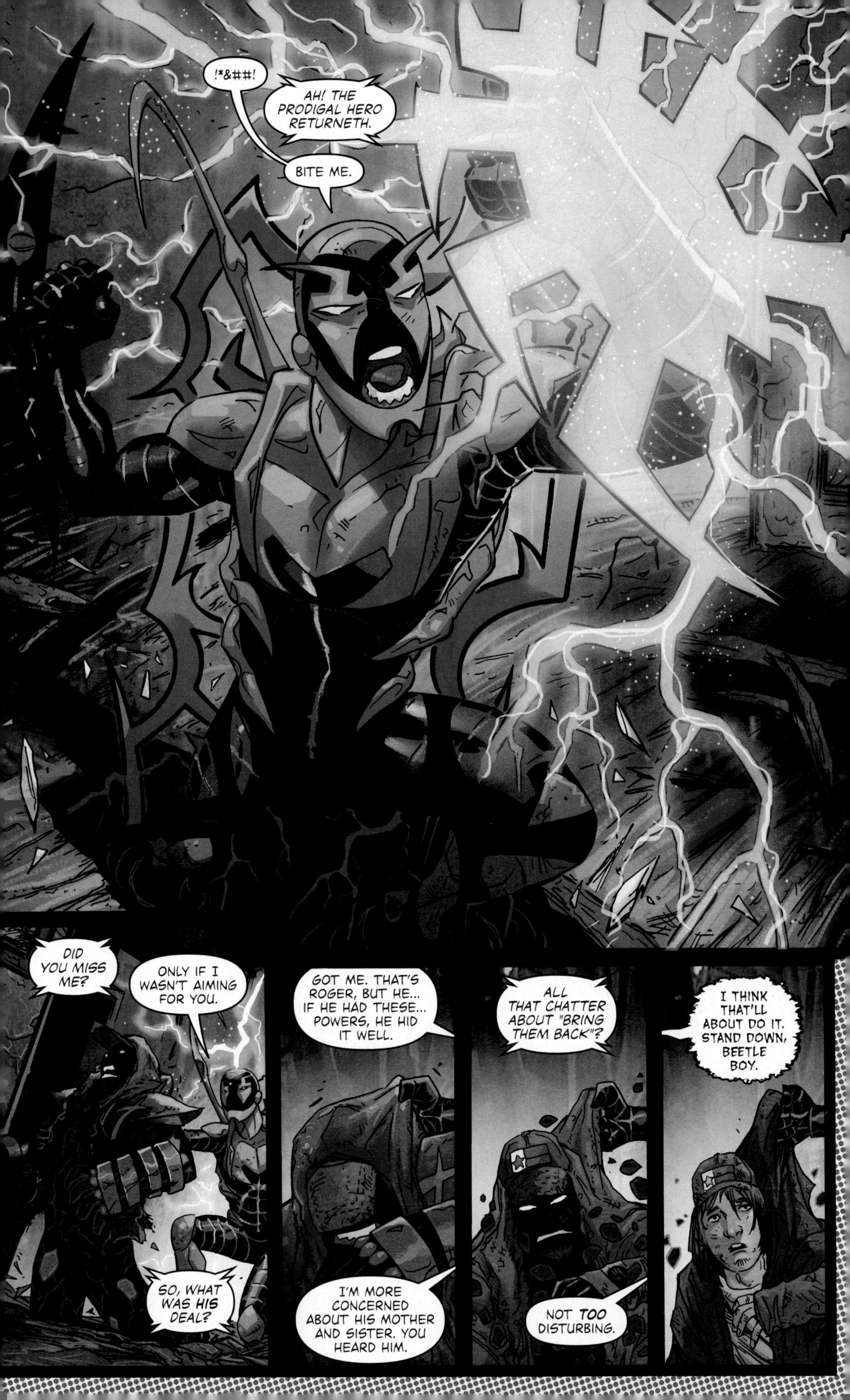

!*&##!
AH! THE PRODIGAL HERO RETURNETH.
BITE ME.
DID YOU MISS ME?
ONLY IF I WASN'T AIMING FOR YOU.
SO, WHAT WAS **HIS** DEAL?
GOT ME. THAT'S ROGER, BUT HE... IF HE HAD THESE... POWERS, HE HID IT WELL.
I'M MORE CONCERNED ABOUT HIS MOTHER AND SISTER. YOU HEARD HIM.
ALL THAT CHATTER ABOUT "BRING THEM BACK"?
NOT **TOO** DISTURBING.
I THINK THAT'LL ABOUT DO IT. STAND DOWN, BEETLE BOY.

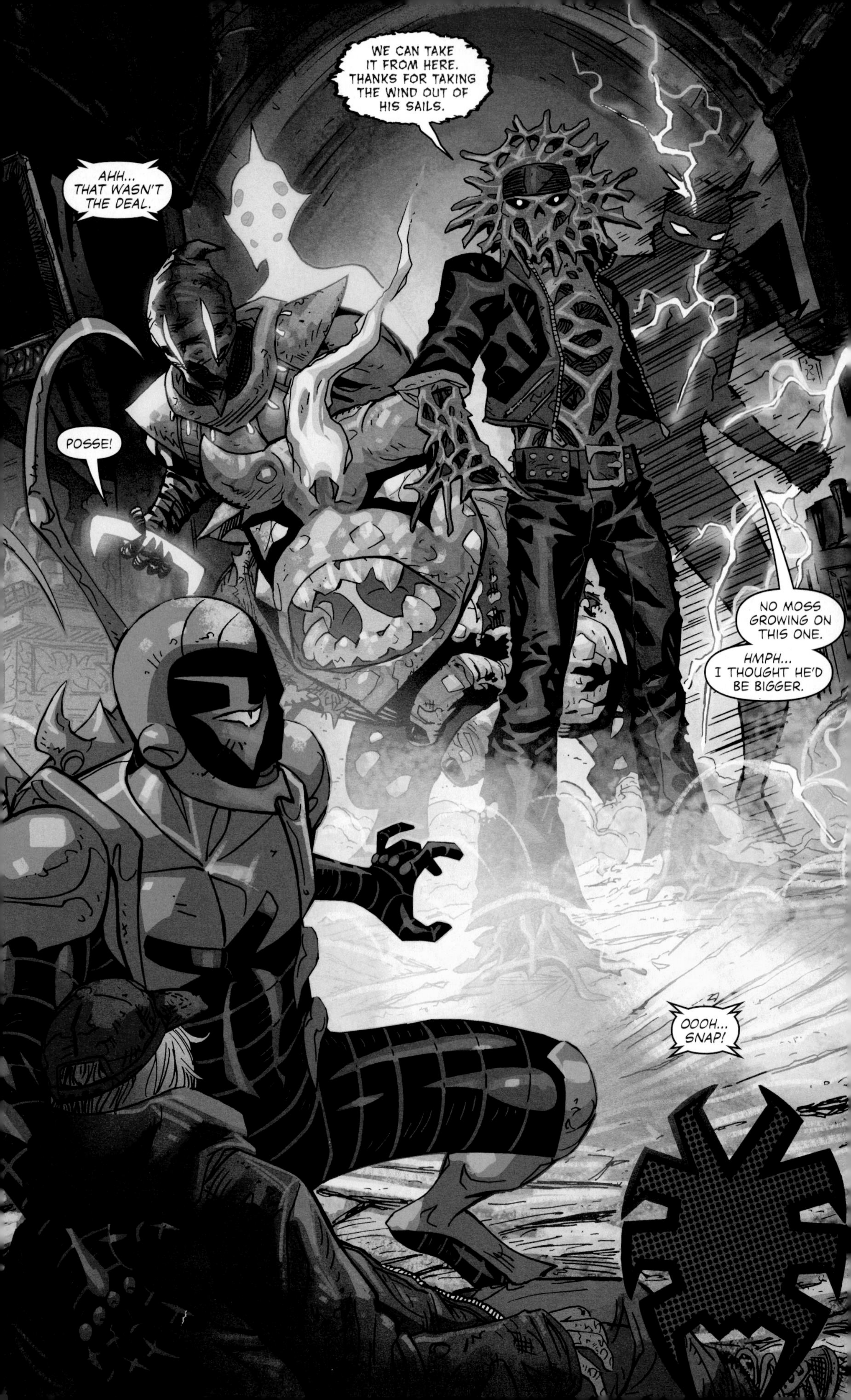
WE CAN TAKE IT FROM HERE. THANKS FOR TAKING THE WIND OUT OF HIS SAILS.
AHH... THAT WASN'T THE DEAL.
POSSE!
NO MOSS GROWING ON THIS ONE.
HMPH... I THOUGHT HE'D BE BIGGER.
OOOH... SNAP!

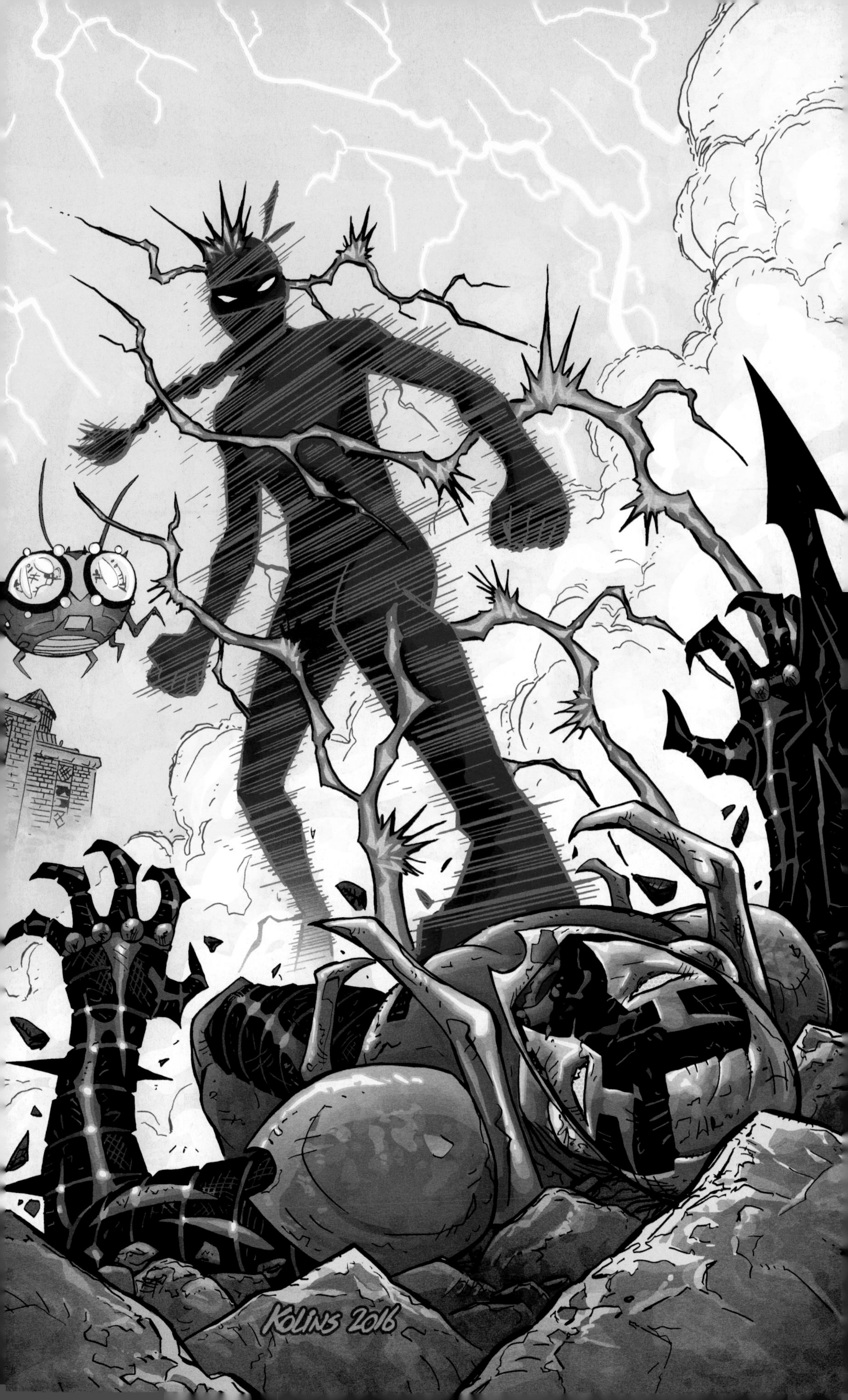
KOLINS 2016

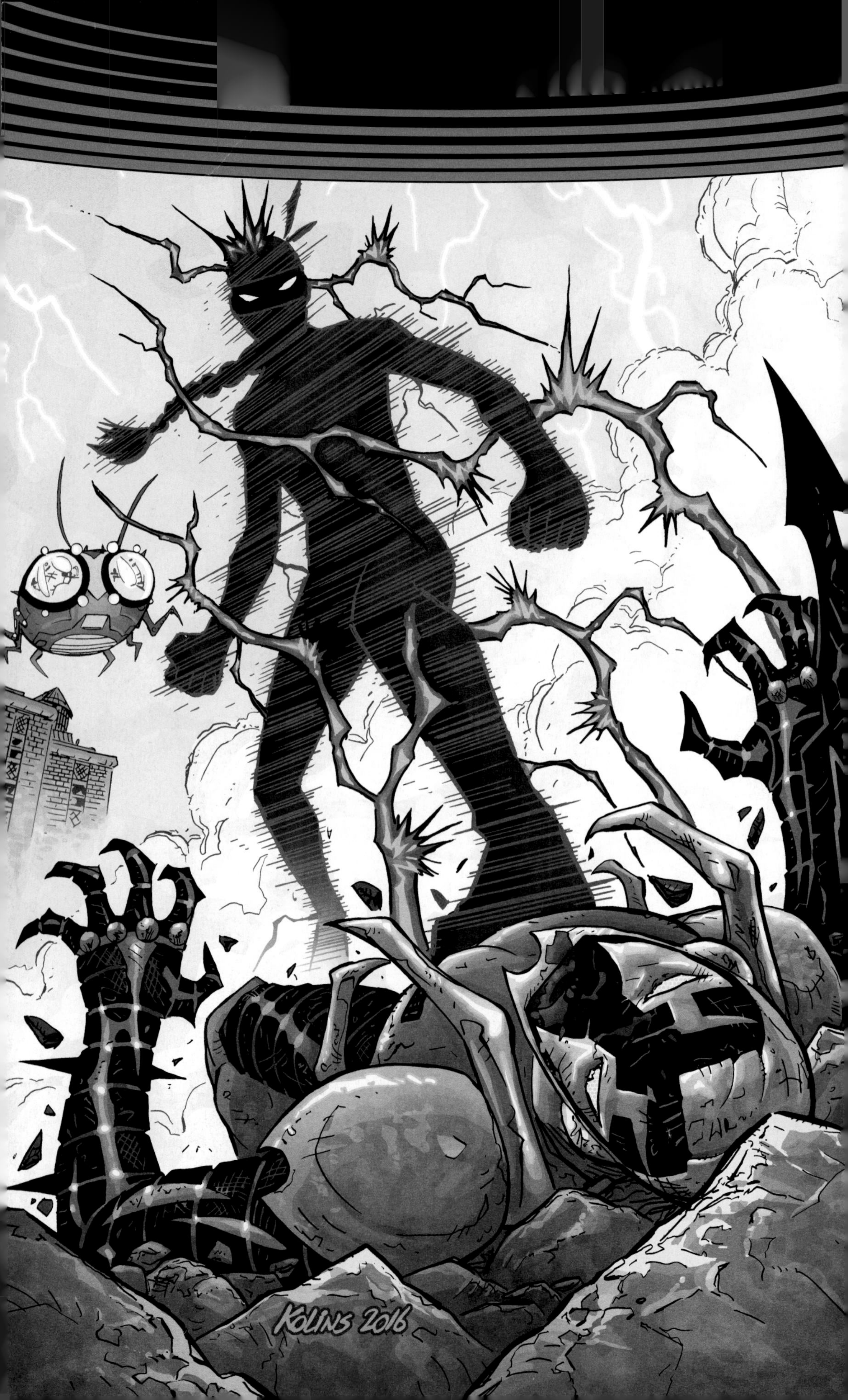
KOLINS 2016

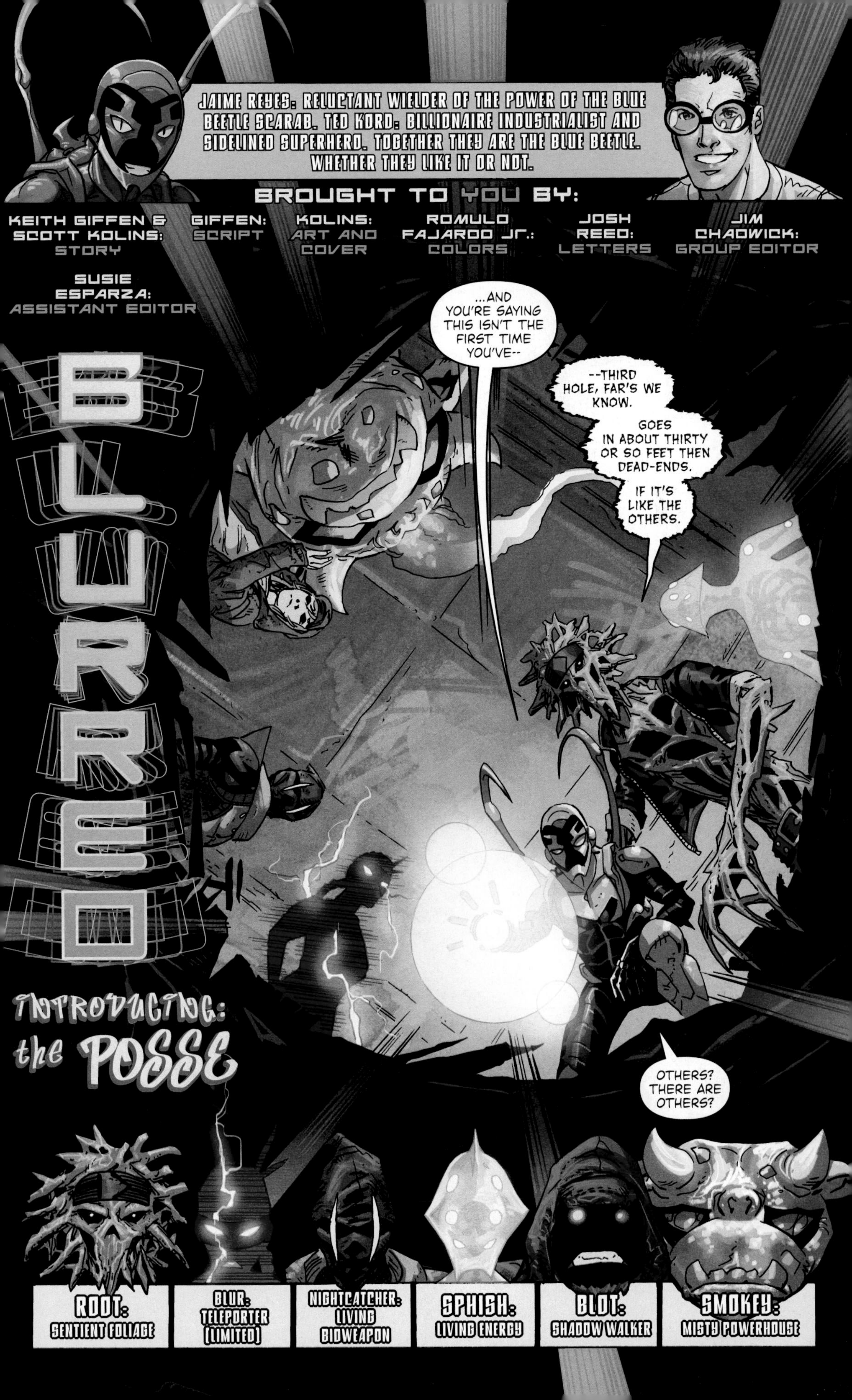
JAIME REYES: RELUCTANT WIELDER OF THE POWER OF THE BLUE BEETLE SCARAB. TED KORD: BILLIONAIRE INDUSTRIALIST AND SIDELINED SUPERHERO. TOGETHER THEY ARE THE BLUE BEETLE. WHETHER THEY LIKE IT OR NOT.
BROUGHT TO YOU BY:
KEITH GIFFEN & SCOTT KOLINS: STORY
GIFFEN: SCRIPT
KOLINS: ART AND COVER
ROMULO FAJARDO JR.: COLORS
JOSH REED: LETTERS
JIM CHADWICK: GROUP EDITOR
SUSIE ESPARZA: ASSISTANT EDITOR
BLURRED
...AND YOU'RE SAYING THIS ISN'T THE FIRST TIME YOU'VE--
--THIRD HOLE, FAR'S WE KNOW.
GOES IN ABOUT THIRTY OR SO FEET THEN DEAD-ENDS.
IF IT'S LIKE THE OTHERS.
INTRODUCING: the POSSE
OTHERS? THERE ARE OTHERS?
ROOT: SENTIENT FOLIAGE
BLUR: TELEPORTER (LIMITED)
NIGHTCATCHER: LIVING BIOWEAPON
SPHISH: LIVING ENERGY
BLOT: SHADOW WALKER
SMOKEY: MISTY POWERHOUSE

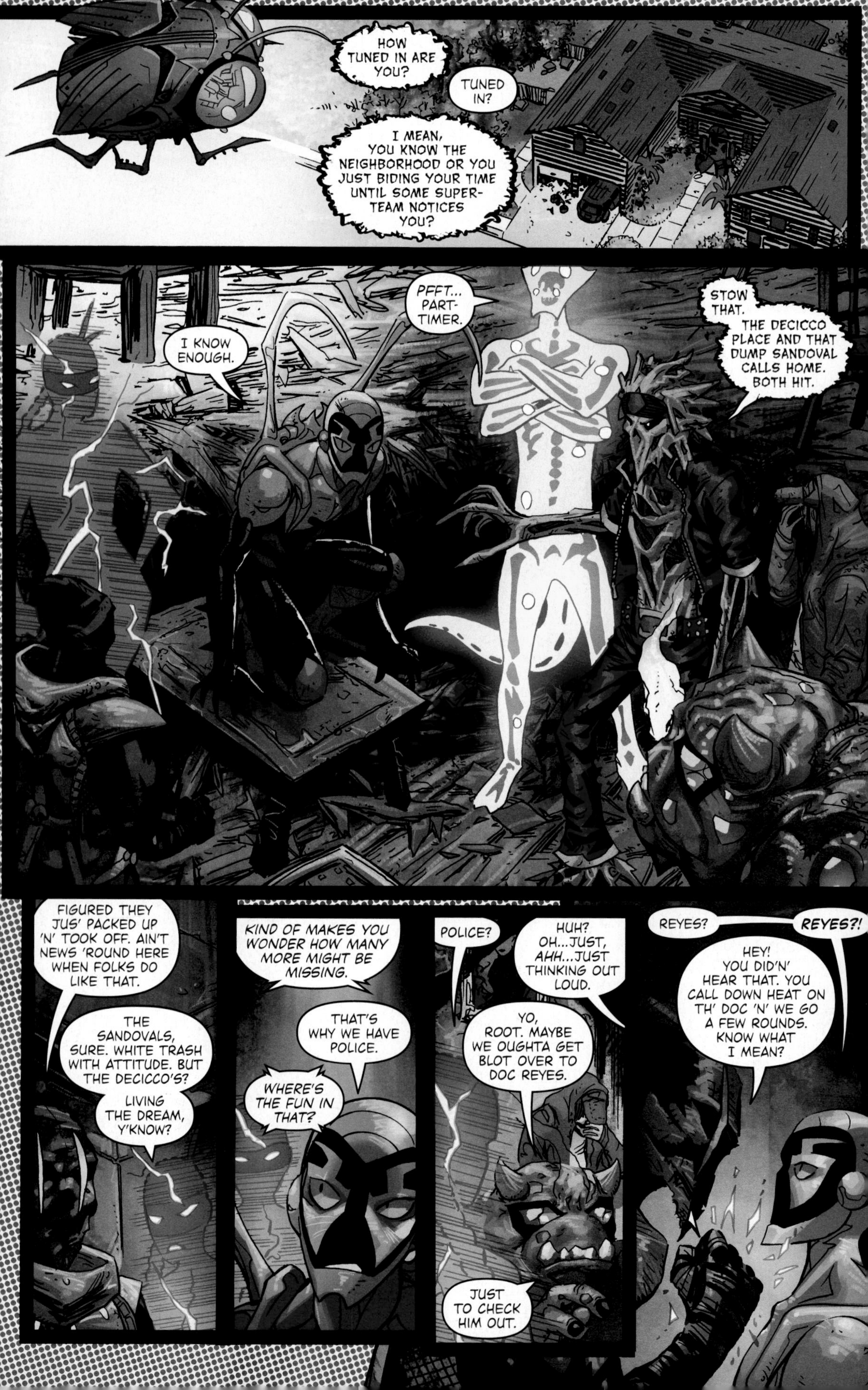
HOW TUNED IN ARE YOU?
TUNED IN?
I MEAN, YOU KNOW THE NEIGHBORHOOD OR YOU JUST BIDING YOUR TIME UNTIL SOME SUPER-TEAM NOTICES YOU?
I KNOW ENOUGH.
PFFT... PART-TIMER.
STOW THAT.
THE DECICCO PLACE AND THAT DUMP SANDOVAL CALLS HOME. BOTH HIT.
FIGURED THEY JUS' PACKED UP 'N' TOOK OFF. AIN'T NEWS 'ROUND HERE WHEN FOLKS DO LIKE THAT.
THE SANDOVALS, SURE. WHITE TRASH WITH ATTITUDE. BUT THE DECICCO'S?
LIVING THE DREAM, Y'KNOW?
KIND OF MAKES YOU WONDER HOW MANY MORE MIGHT BE MISSING.
THAT'S WHY WE HAVE POLICE.
WHERE'S THE FUN IN THAT?
POLICE?
HUH? OH...JUST, AHH...JUST THINKING OUT LOUD.
YO, ROOT. MAYBE WE OUGHTA GET BLOT OVER TO DOC REYES.
JUST TO CHECK HIM OUT.
REYES?
REYES?!
HEY! YOU DID'N' HEAR THAT. YOU CALL DOWN HEAT ON TH' DOC 'N' WE GO A FEW ROUNDS. KNOW WHAT I MEAN?

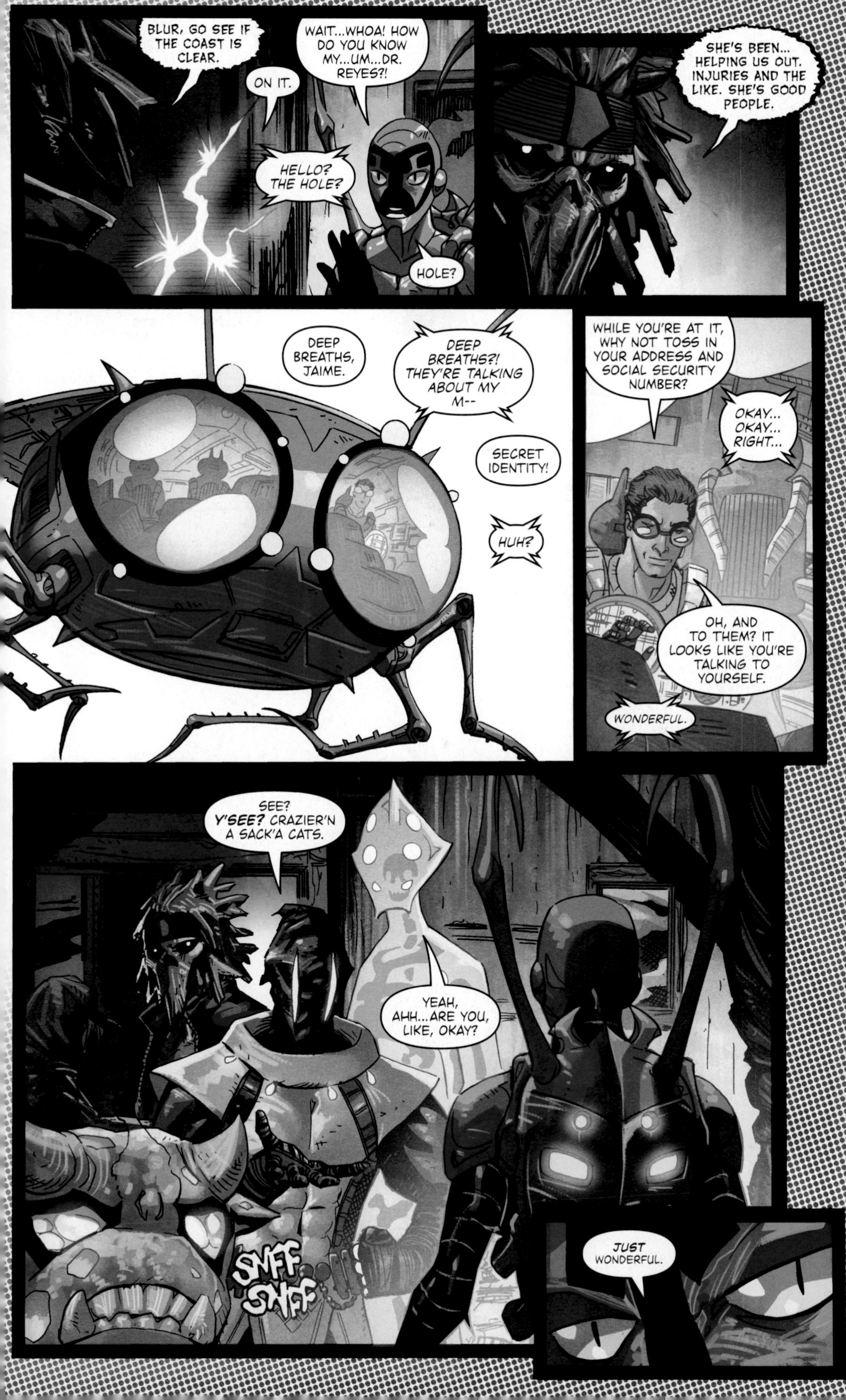
BLUR, GO SEE IF THE COAST IS CLEAR.
ON IT.
WAIT...WHOA! HOW DO YOU KNOW MY...UM...DR. REYES?!
HELLO? THE HOLE?
HOLE?
SHE'S BEEN... HELPING US OUT. INJURIES AND THE LIKE. SHE'S GOOD PEOPLE.
DEEP BREATHS, JAIME.
DEEP BREATHS?! THEY'RE TALKING ABOUT MY M--
SECRET IDENTITY!
HUH?
WHILE YOU'RE AT IT, WHY NOT TOSS IN YOUR ADDRESS AND SOCIAL SECURITY NUMBER?
OKAY... OKAY... RIGHT...
OH, AND TO THEM? IT LOOKS LIKE YOU'RE TALKING TO YOURSELF.
WONDERFUL.
SEE? Y'SEE? CRAZIER'N A SACK'A CATS.
YEAH, AHH...ARE YOU, LIKE, OKAY?
SNIFF SNIFF
JUST WONDERFUL.

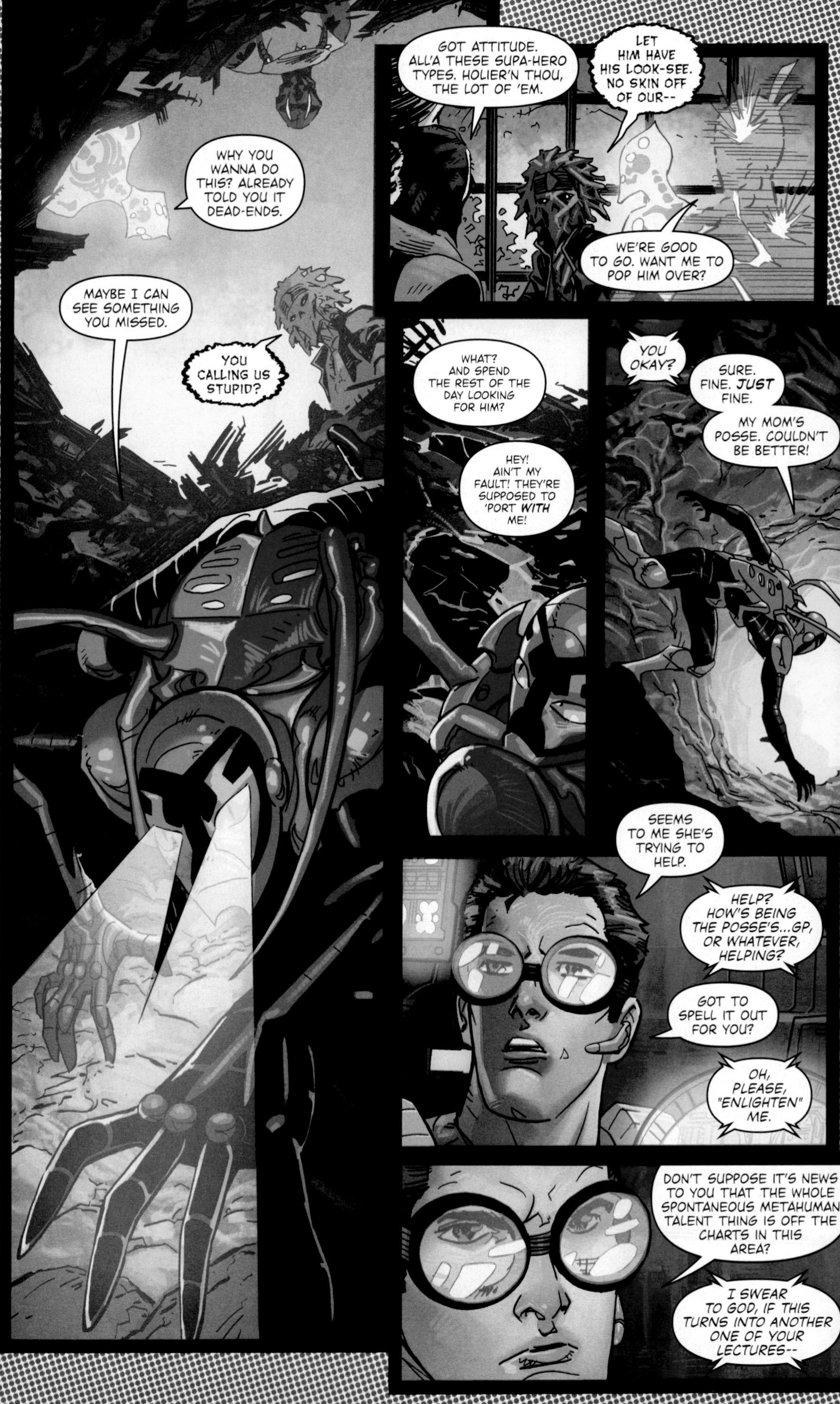

WHY YOU WANNA DO THIS? ALREADY TOLD YOU IT DEAD-ENDS.
MAYBE I CAN SEE SOMETHING YOU MISSED.
YOU CALLING US STUPID?
GOT ATTITUDE. ALL'A THESE SUPA-HERO TYPES. HOLIER'N THOU, THE LOT OF 'EM.
LET HIM HAVE HIS LOOK-SEE. NO SKIN OFF OF OUR--
WE'RE GOOD TO GO. WANT ME TO POP HIM OVER?
WHAT? AND SPEND THE REST OF THE DAY LOOKING FOR HIM?
HEY! AIN'T MY FAULT! THEY'RE SUPPOSED TO 'PORT WITH ME!
YOU OKAY?
SURE. FINE. JUST FINE.
MY MOM'S POSSE. COULDN'T BE BETTER!
SEEMS TO ME SHE'S TRYING TO HELP.
HELP? HOW'S BEING THE POSSE'S...GP, OR WHATEVER, HELPING?
GOT TO SPELL IT OUT FOR YOU?
OH, PLEASE, "ENLIGHTEN" ME.
DON'T SUPPOSE IT'S NEWS TO YOU THAT THE WHOLE SPONTANEOUS METAHUMAN TALENT THING IS OFF THE CHARTS IN THIS AREA?
I SWEAR TO GOD, IF THIS TURNS INTO ANOTHER ONE OF YOUR LECTURES--

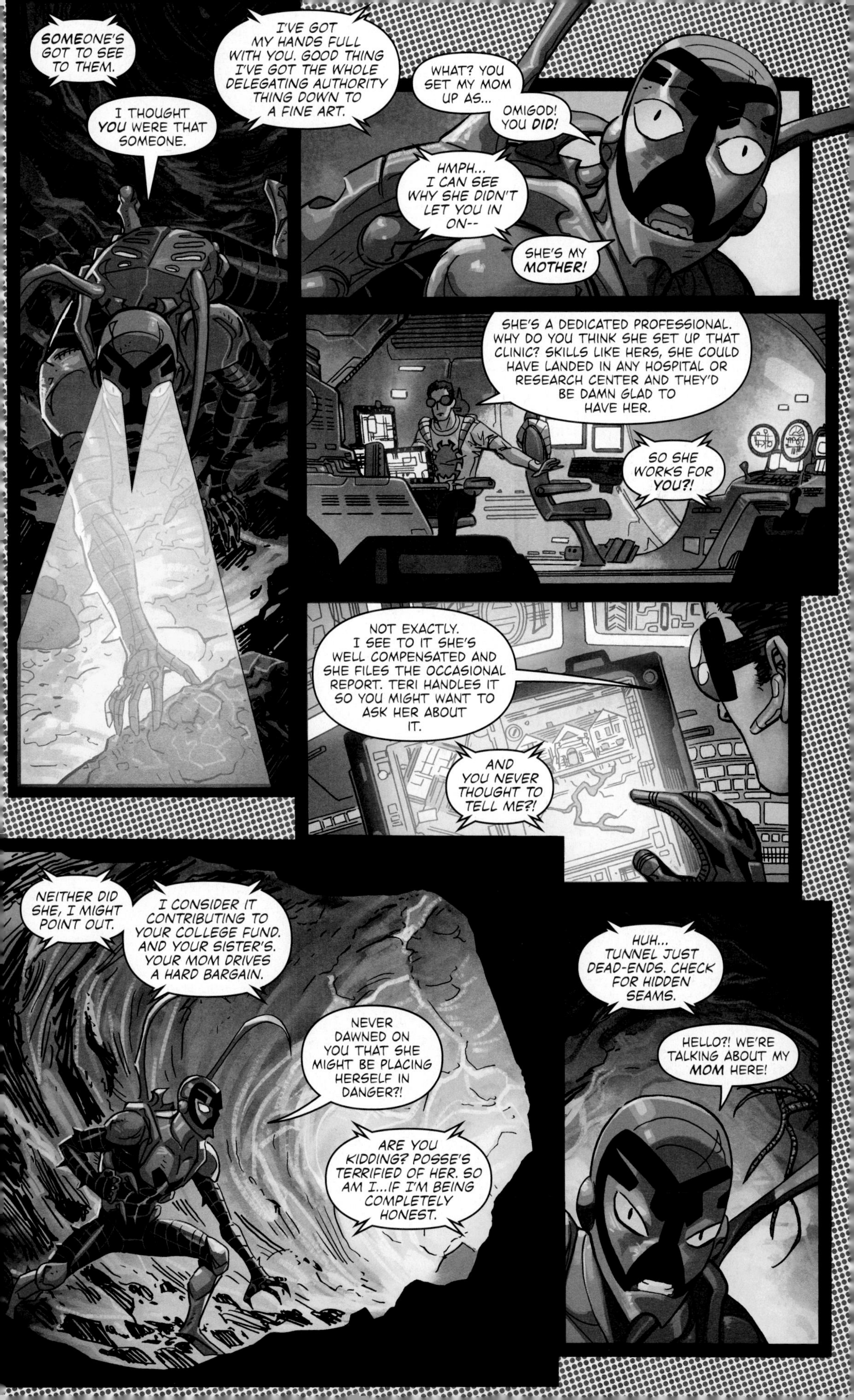
SOMEONE'S GOT TO SEE TO THEM.
I THOUGHT YOU WERE THAT SOMEONE.
I'VE GOT MY HANDS FULL WITH YOU. GOOD THING I'VE GOT THE WHOLE DELEGATING AUTHORITY THING DOWN TO A FINE ART.
WHAT? YOU SET MY MOM UP AS...
OMIGOD! YOU DID!
HMPH... I CAN SEE WHY SHE DIDN'T LET YOU IN ON--
SHE'S MY MOTHER!
SHE'S A DEDICATED PROFESSIONAL. WHY DO YOU THINK SHE SET UP THAT CLINIC? SKILLS LIKE HERS, SHE COULD HAVE LANDED IN ANY HOSPITAL OR RESEARCH CENTER AND THEY'D BE DAMN GLAD TO HAVE HER.
SO SHE WORKS FOR YOU?!
NOT EXACTLY. I SEE TO IT SHE'S WELL COMPENSATED AND SHE FILES THE OCCASIONAL REPORT. TERI HANDLES IT SO YOU MIGHT WANT TO ASK HER ABOUT IT.
AND YOU NEVER THOUGHT TO TELL ME?!
NEITHER DID SHE, I MIGHT POINT OUT.
I CONSIDER IT CONTRIBUTING TO YOUR COLLEGE FUND. AND YOUR SISTER'S. YOUR MOM DRIVES A HARD BARGAIN.
NEVER DAWNED ON YOU THAT SHE MIGHT BE PLACING HERSELF IN DANGER?!
ARE YOU KIDDING? POSSE'S TERRIFIED OF HER. SO AM I...IF I'M BEING COMPLETELY HONEST.
HUH... TUNNEL JUST DEAD-ENDS. CHECK FOR HIDDEN SEAMS.
HELLO?! WE'RE TALKING ABOUT MY MOM HERE!

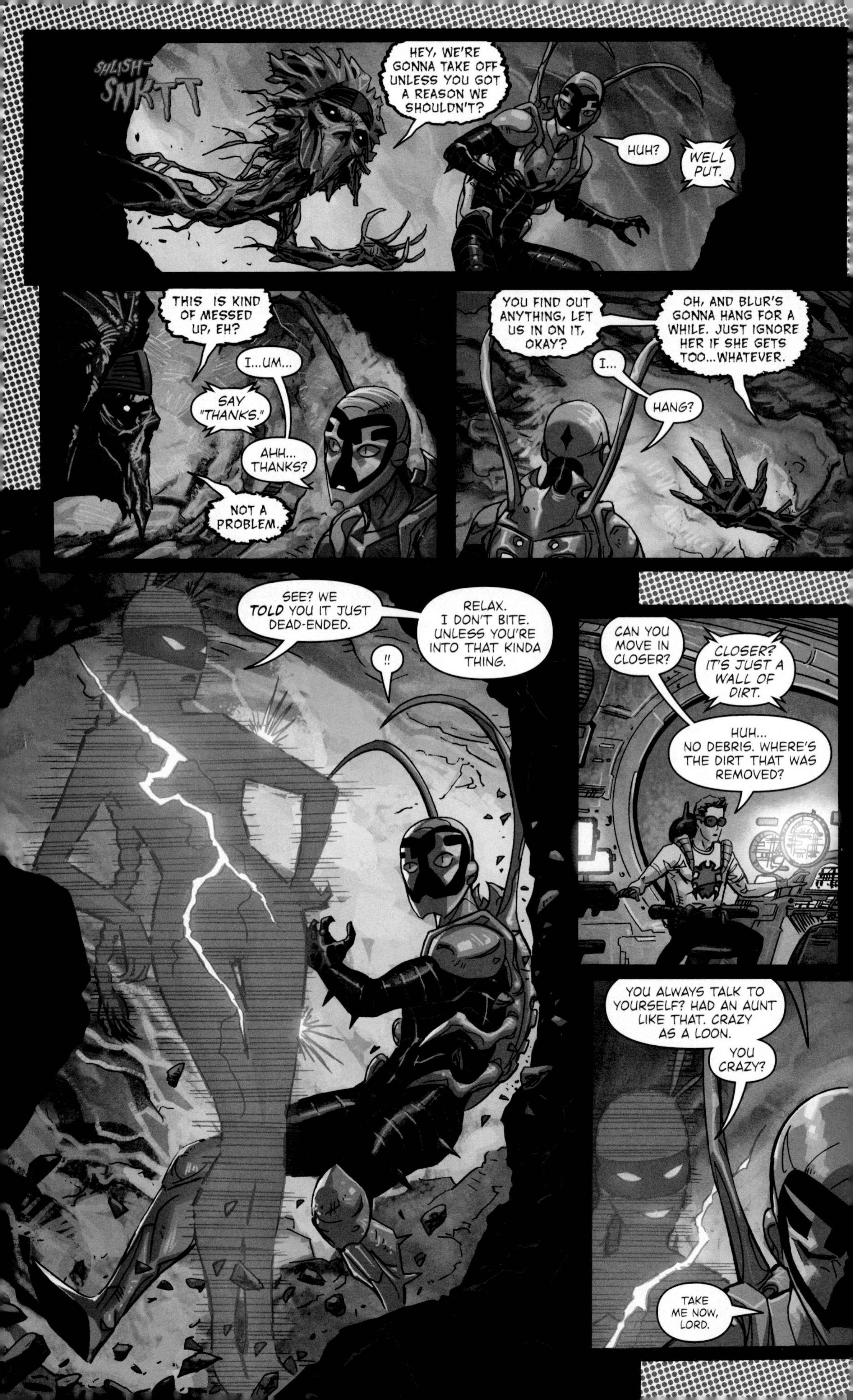
SHLISH-
SNKTT
HEY, WE'RE GONNA TAKE OFF UNLESS YOU GOT A REASON WE SHOULDN'T?
HUH?
WELL PUT.
THIS IS KIND OF MESSED UP, EH?
I...UM...
SAY "THANKS."
AHH... THANKS?
NOT A PROBLEM.
YOU FIND OUT ANYTHING, LET US IN ON IT, OKAY?
OH, AND BLUR'S GONNA HANG FOR A WHILE. JUST IGNORE HER IF SHE GETS TOO...WHATEVER.
I...
HANG?
SEE? WE TOLD YOU IT JUST DEAD-ENDED.
RELAX. I DON'T BITE. UNLESS YOU'RE INTO THAT KINDA THING.
!!
CAN YOU MOVE IN CLOSER?
CLOSER? IT'S JUST A WALL OF DIRT.
HUH... NO DEBRIS. WHERE'S THE DIRT THAT WAS REMOVED?
YOU ALWAYS TALK TO YOURSELF? HAD AN AUNT LIKE THAT. CRAZY AS A LOON.
YOU CRAZY?
TAKE ME NOW, LORD.

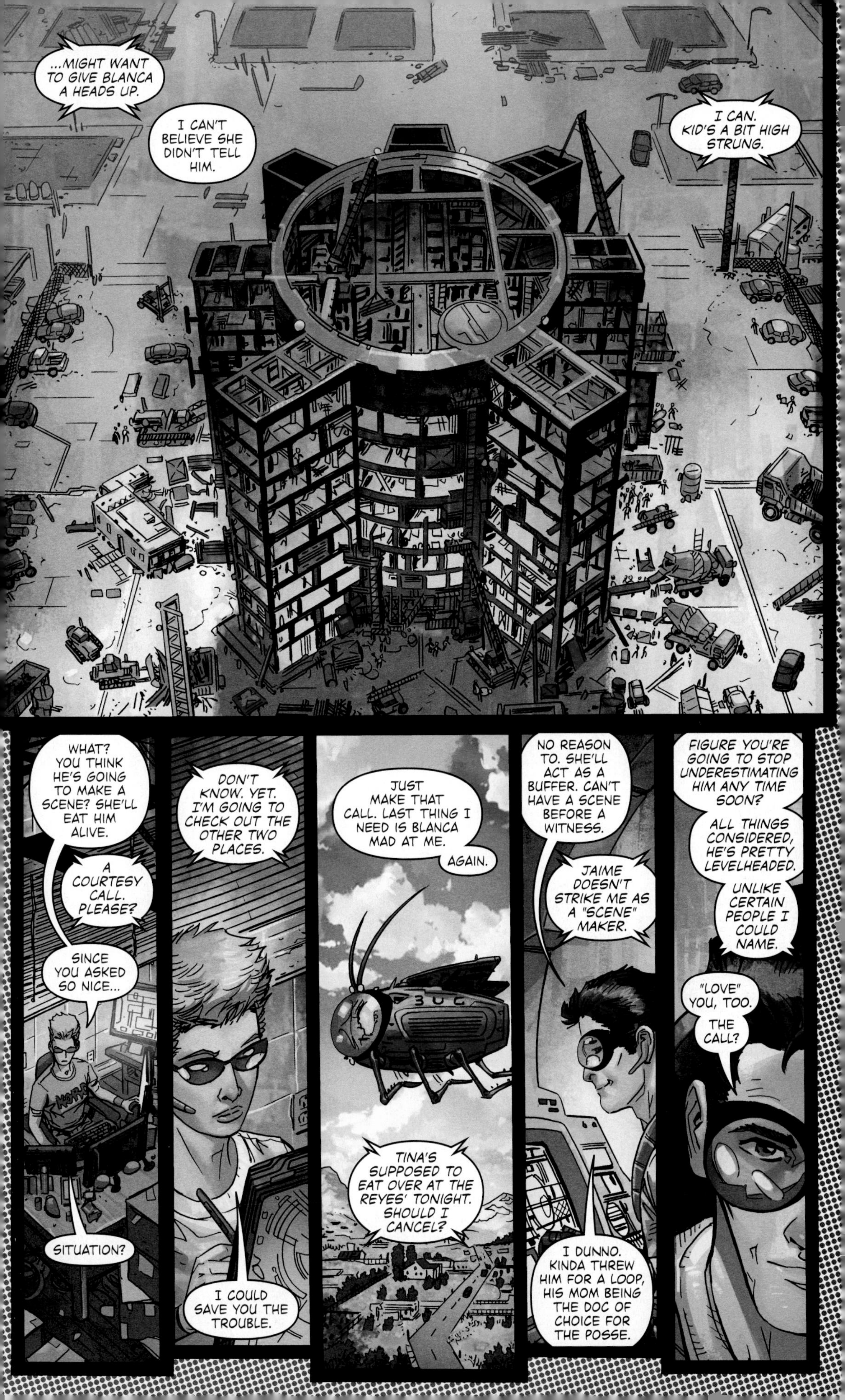
...MIGHT WANT TO GIVE BLANCA A HEADS UP.
I CAN'T BELIEVE SHE DIDN'T TELL HIM.
I CAN. KID'S A BIT HIGH STRUNG.
WHAT? YOU THINK HE'S GOING TO MAKE A SCENE? SHE'LL EAT HIM ALIVE.
A COURTESY CALL. PLEASE?
SINCE YOU ASKED SO NICE...
SITUATION?
DON'T KNOW. YET. I'M GOING TO CHECK OUT THE OTHER TWO PLACES.
I COULD SAVE YOU THE TROUBLE.
JUST MAKE THAT CALL. LAST THING I NEED IS BLANCA MAD AT ME.
AGAIN.
TINA'S SUPPOSED TO EAT OVER AT THE REYES' TONIGHT. SHOULD I CANCEL?
NO REASON TO. SHE'LL ACT AS A BUFFER. CAN'T HAVE A SCENE BEFORE A WITNESS.
JAIME DOESN'T STRIKE ME AS A "SCENE" MAKER.
I DUNNO. KINDA THREW HIM FOR A LOOP, HIS MOM BEING THE DOC OF CHOICE FOR THE POSSE.
FIGURE YOU'RE GOING TO STOP UNDERESTIMATING HIM ANY TIME SOON?
ALL THINGS CONSIDERED, HE'S PRETTY LEVELHEADED.
UNLIKE CERTAIN PEOPLE I COULD NAME.
"LOVE" YOU, TOO.
THE CALL?

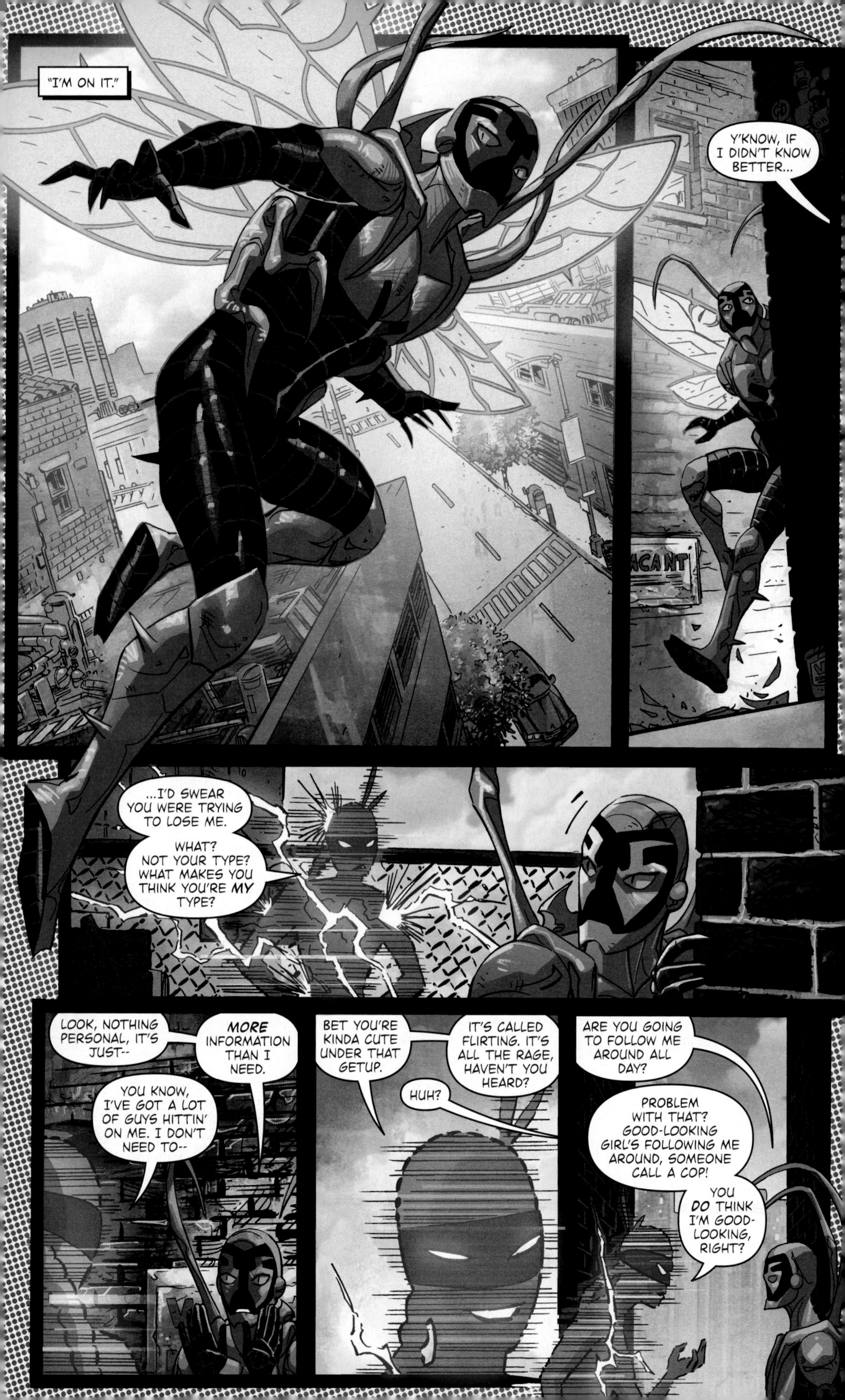
"I'M ON IT."
Y'KNOW, IF I DIDN'T KNOW BETTER...
VACANT
...I'D SWEAR YOU WERE TRYING TO LOSE ME.
WHAT? NOT YOUR TYPE? WHAT MAKES YOU THINK YOU'RE **MY** TYPE?
LOOK, NOTHING PERSONAL, IT'S JUST--
MORE INFORMATION THAN I NEED.
YOU KNOW, I'VE GOT A LOT OF GUYS HITTIN' ON ME. I DON'T NEED TO--
BET YOU'RE KINDA CUTE UNDER THAT GETUP.
IT'S CALLED FLIRTING. IT'S ALL THE RAGE, HAVEN'T YOU HEARD?
HUH?
ARE YOU GOING TO FOLLOW ME AROUND ALL DAY?
PROBLEM WITH THAT? GOOD-LOOKING GIRL'S FOLLOWING ME AROUND, SOMEONE CALL A COP!
YOU **DO** THINK I'M GOOD-LOOKING, RIGHT?

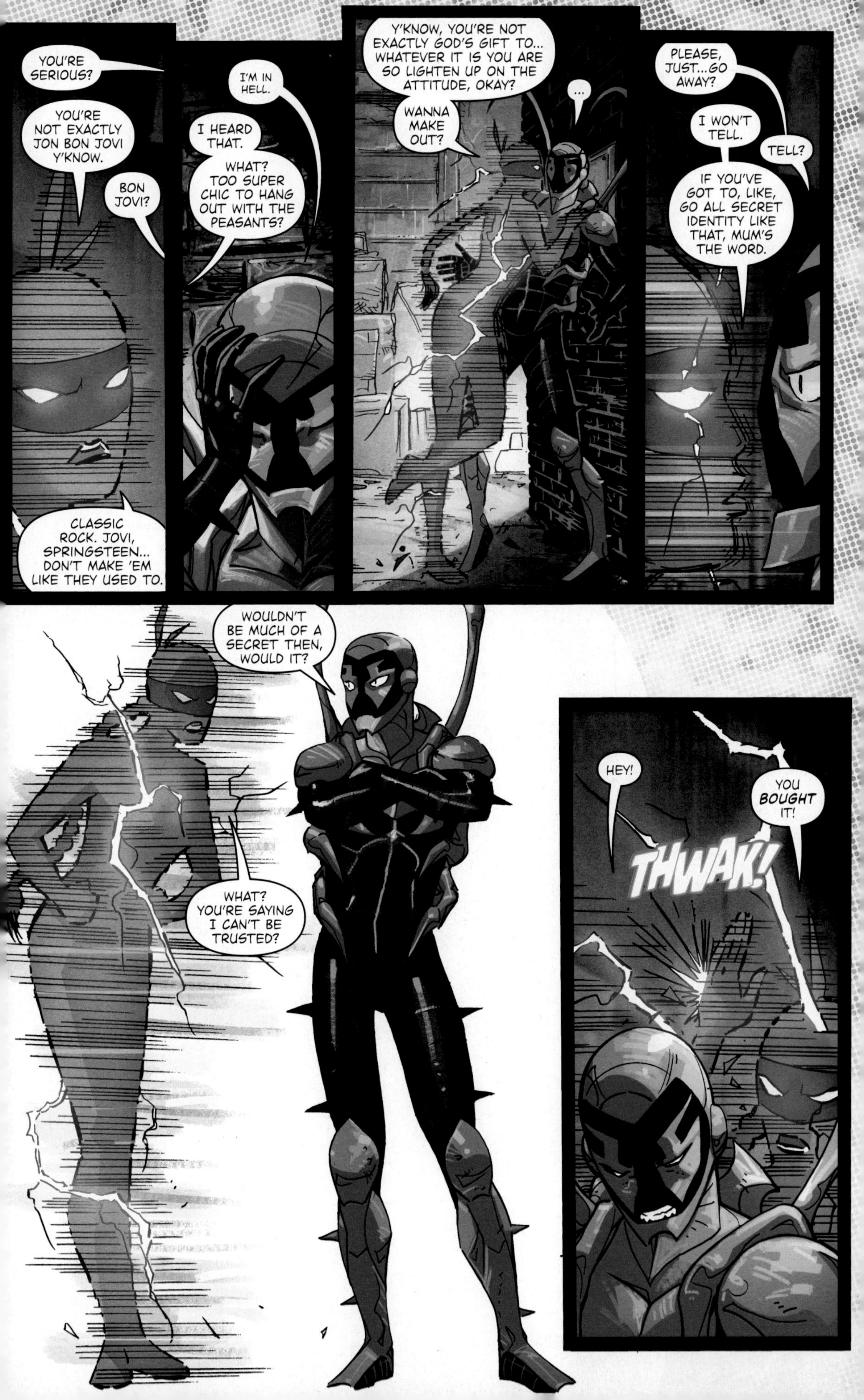
YOU'RE SERIOUS?
YOU'RE NOT EXACTLY JON BON JOVI Y'KNOW.
BON JOVI?
CLASSIC ROCK. JOVI, SPRINGSTEEN... DON'T MAKE 'EM LIKE THEY USED TO.
I'M IN HELL.
I HEARD THAT.
WHAT? TOO SUPER CHIC TO HANG OUT WITH THE PEASANTS?
Y'KNOW, YOU'RE NOT EXACTLY GOD'S GIFT TO... WHATEVER IT IS YOU ARE SO LIGHTEN UP ON THE ATTITUDE, OKAY?
WANNA MAKE OUT?
...
PLEASE, JUST...GO AWAY?
I WON'T TELL.
TELL?
IF YOU'VE GOT TO, LIKE, GO ALL SECRET IDENTITY LIKE THAT, MUM'S THE WORD.
WOULDN'T BE MUCH OF A SECRET THEN, WOULD IT?
WHAT? YOU'RE SAYING I CAN'T BE TRUSTED?
HEY!
YOU BOUGHT IT!
THWAK!

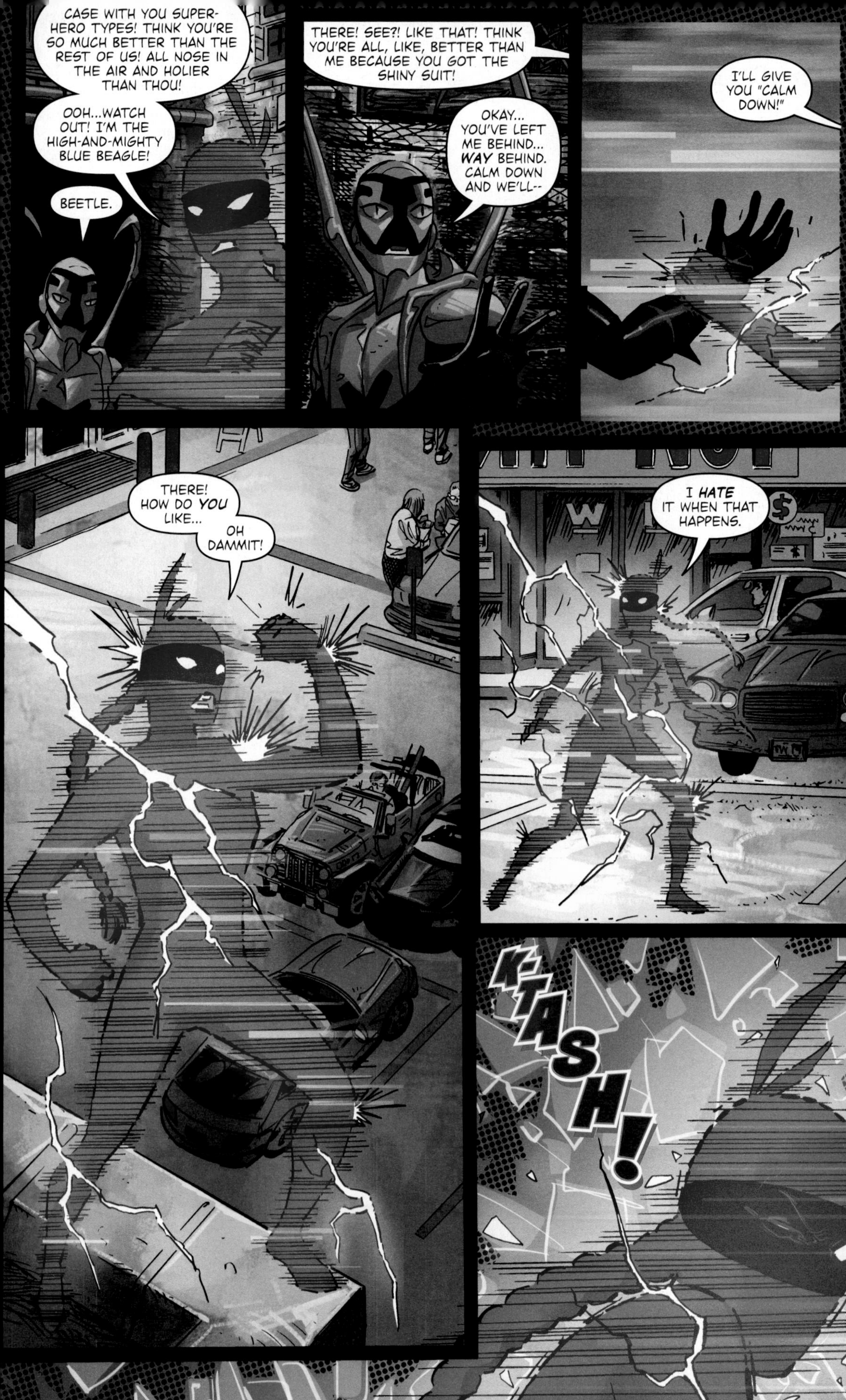

CASE WITH YOU SUPER-HERO TYPES! THINK YOU'RE SO MUCH BETTER THAN THE REST OF US! ALL NOSE IN THE AIR AND HOLIER THAN THOU!
OOH...WATCH OUT! I'M THE HIGH-AND-MIGHTY BLUE BEAGLE!
BEETLE.
THERE! SEE?! LIKE THAT! THINK YOU'RE ALL, LIKE, BETTER THAN ME BECAUSE YOU GOT THE SHINY SUIT!
OKAY... YOU'VE LEFT ME BEHIND... **WAY** BEHIND. CALM DOWN AND WE'LL--
I'LL GIVE YOU "CALM DOWN!"
THERE! HOW DO **YOU** LIKE...
OH DAMMIT!
I **HATE** IT WHEN THAT HAPPENS.
K-TASH!

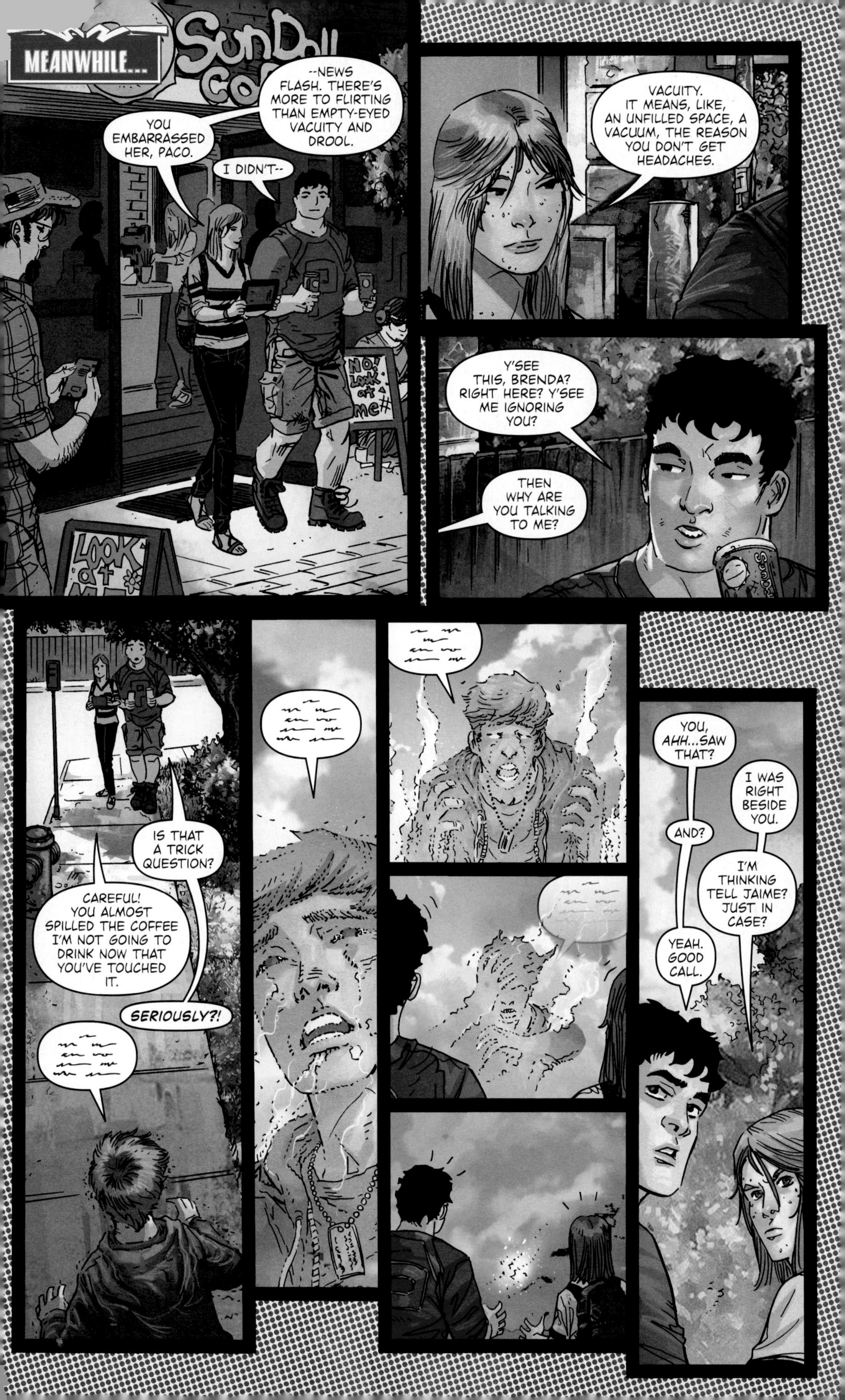
MEANWHILE...
SunDoll Co
YOU EMBARRASSED HER, PACO.
I DIDN'T--
--NEWS FLASH. THERE'S MORE TO FLIRTING THAN EMPTY-EYED VACUITY AND DROOL.
NO! Look at me#
LOOK at ME
VACUITY. IT MEANS, LIKE, AN UNFILLED SPACE, A VACUUM, THE REASON YOU DON'T GET HEADACHES.
Y'SEE THIS, BRENDA? RIGHT HERE? Y'SEE ME IGNORING YOU?
THEN WHY ARE YOU TALKING TO ME?
IS THAT A TRICK QUESTION?
CAREFUL! YOU ALMOST SPILLED THE COFFEE I'M NOT GOING TO DRINK NOW THAT YOU'VE TOUCHED IT.
SERIOUSLY?!
YOU, AHH...SAW THAT?
I WAS RIGHT BESIDE YOU.
AND?
I'M THINKING TELL JAIME? JUST IN CASE?
YEAH. GOOD CALL.

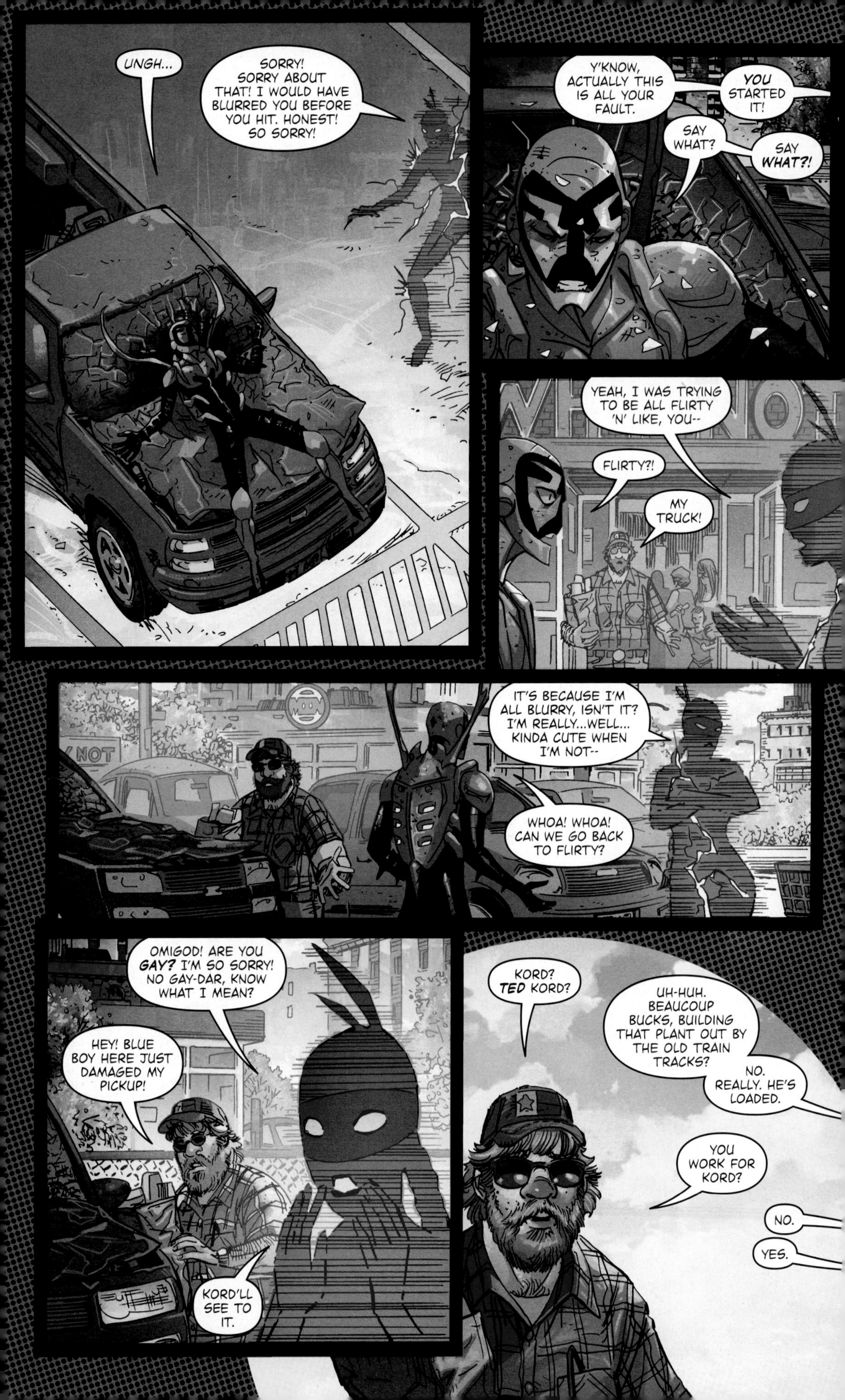
UNGH...
SORRY! SORRY ABOUT THAT! I WOULD HAVE BLURRED YOU BEFORE YOU HIT. HONEST! SO SORRY!
Y'KNOW, ACTUALLY THIS IS ALL YOUR FAULT.
YOU STARTED IT!
SAY WHAT?
SAY WHAT?!
YEAH, I WAS TRYING TO BE ALL FLIRTY 'N' LIKE, YOU--
FLIRTY?!
MY TRUCK!
IT'S BECAUSE I'M ALL BLURRY, ISN'T IT? I'M REALLY...WELL... KINDA CUTE WHEN I'M NOT--
WHOA! WHOA! CAN WE GO BACK TO FLIRTY?
OMIGOD! ARE YOU GAY? I'M SO SORRY! NO GAY-DAR, KNOW WHAT I MEAN?
HEY! BLUE BOY HERE JUST DAMAGED MY PICKUP!
KORD'LL SEE TO IT.
KORD? TED KORD?
UH-HUH. BEAUCOUP BUCKS, BUILDING THAT PLANT OUT BY THE OLD TRAIN TRACKS?
NO. REALLY. HE'S LOADED.
YOU WORK FOR KORD?
NO.
YES.

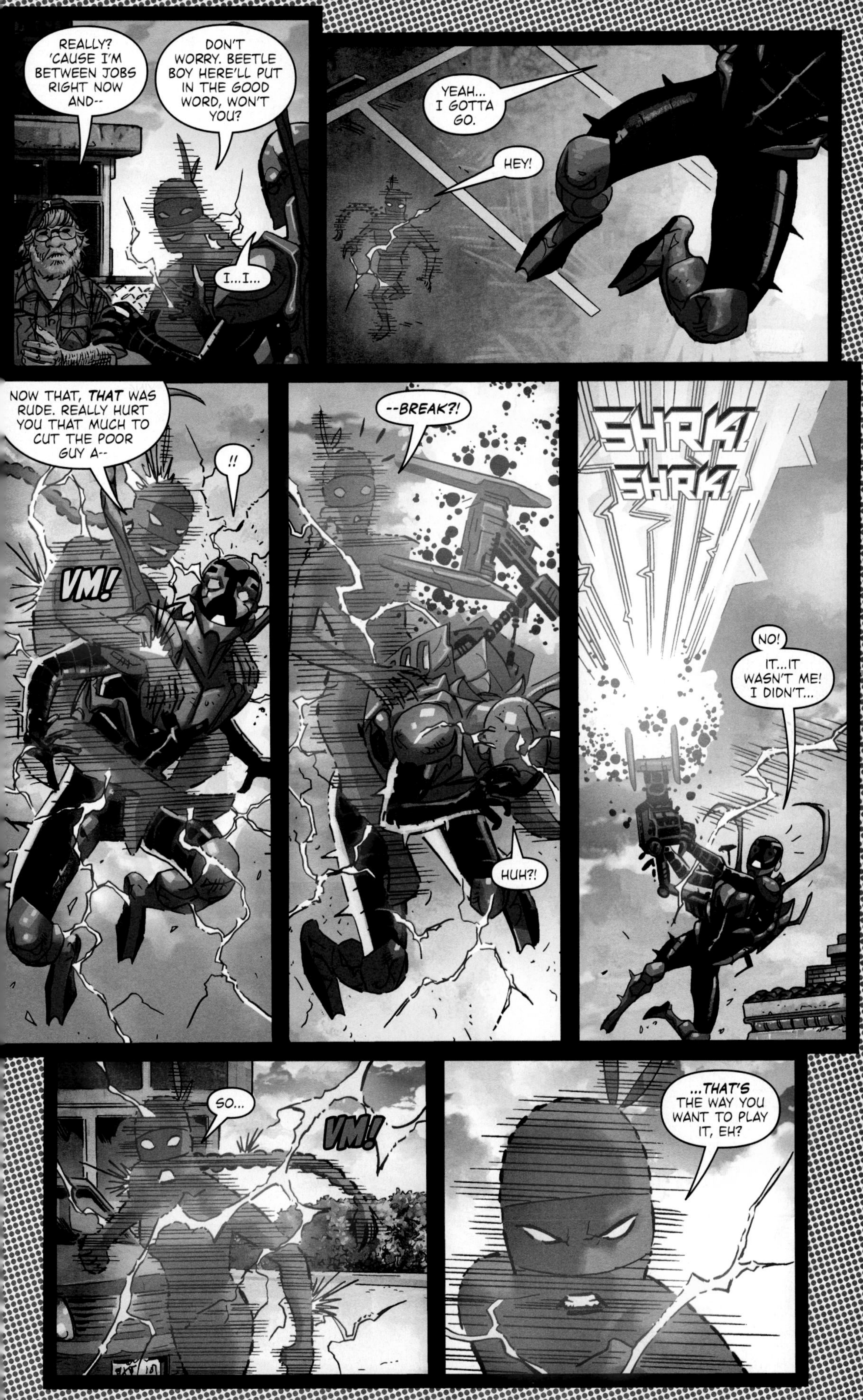
REALLY? 'CAUSE I'M BETWEEN JOBS RIGHT NOW AND--
DON'T WORRY. BEETLE BOY HERE'LL PUT IN THE GOOD WORD, WON'T YOU?
I...I...
YEAH... I GOTTA GO.
HEY!
NOW THAT, THAT WAS RUDE. REALLY HURT YOU THAT MUCH TO CUT THE POOR GUY A--
!!
VM!
--BREAK?!
HUH?!
SHRK! SHRK!
NO!
IT...IT WASN'T ME! I DIDN'T...
SO...
VM!
...THAT'S THE WAY YOU WANT TO PLAY IT, EH?

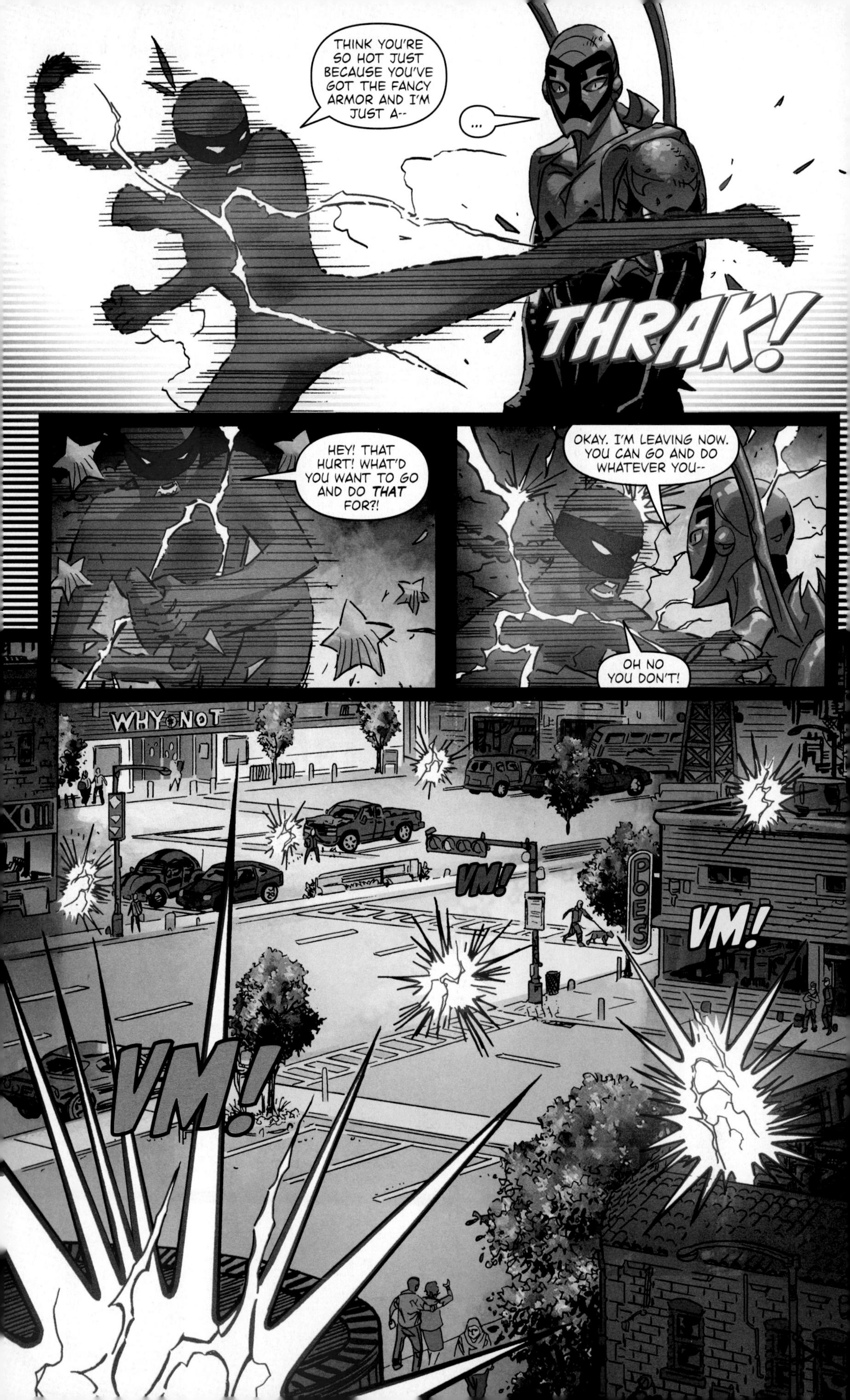
THINK YOU'RE SO HOT JUST BECAUSE YOU'VE GOT THE FANCY ARMOR AND I'M JUST A--
...
THRAK!
HEY! THAT HURT! WHAT'D YOU WANT TO GO AND DO **THAT** FOR?!
OKAY. I'M LEAVING NOW. YOU CAN GO AND DO WHATEVER YOU--
OH NO YOU DON'T!
WHY NOT
POES
VM!
VM!
VM!

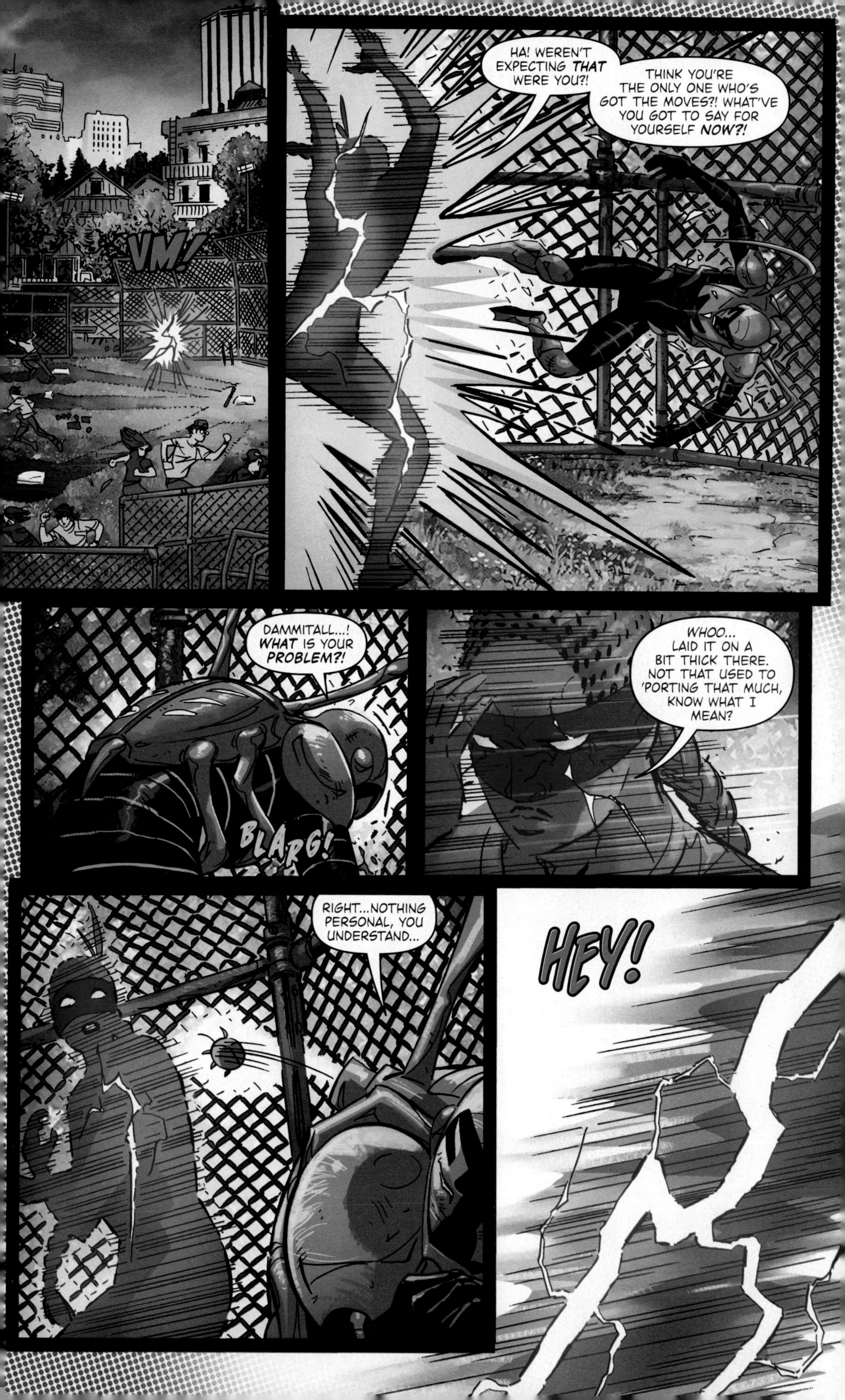
VM!
HA! WEREN'T EXPECTING THAT WERE YOU?!
THINK YOU'RE THE ONLY ONE WHO'S GOT THE MOVES?! WHAT'VE YOU GOT TO SAY FOR YOURSELF NOW?!
DAMMITALL...! WHAT IS YOUR PROBLEM?!
BLARG!
WHOO... LAID IT ON A BIT THICK THERE. NOT THAT USED TO 'PORTING THAT MUCH, KNOW WHAT I MEAN?
RIGHT...NOTHING PERSONAL, YOU UNDERSTAND...
HEY!

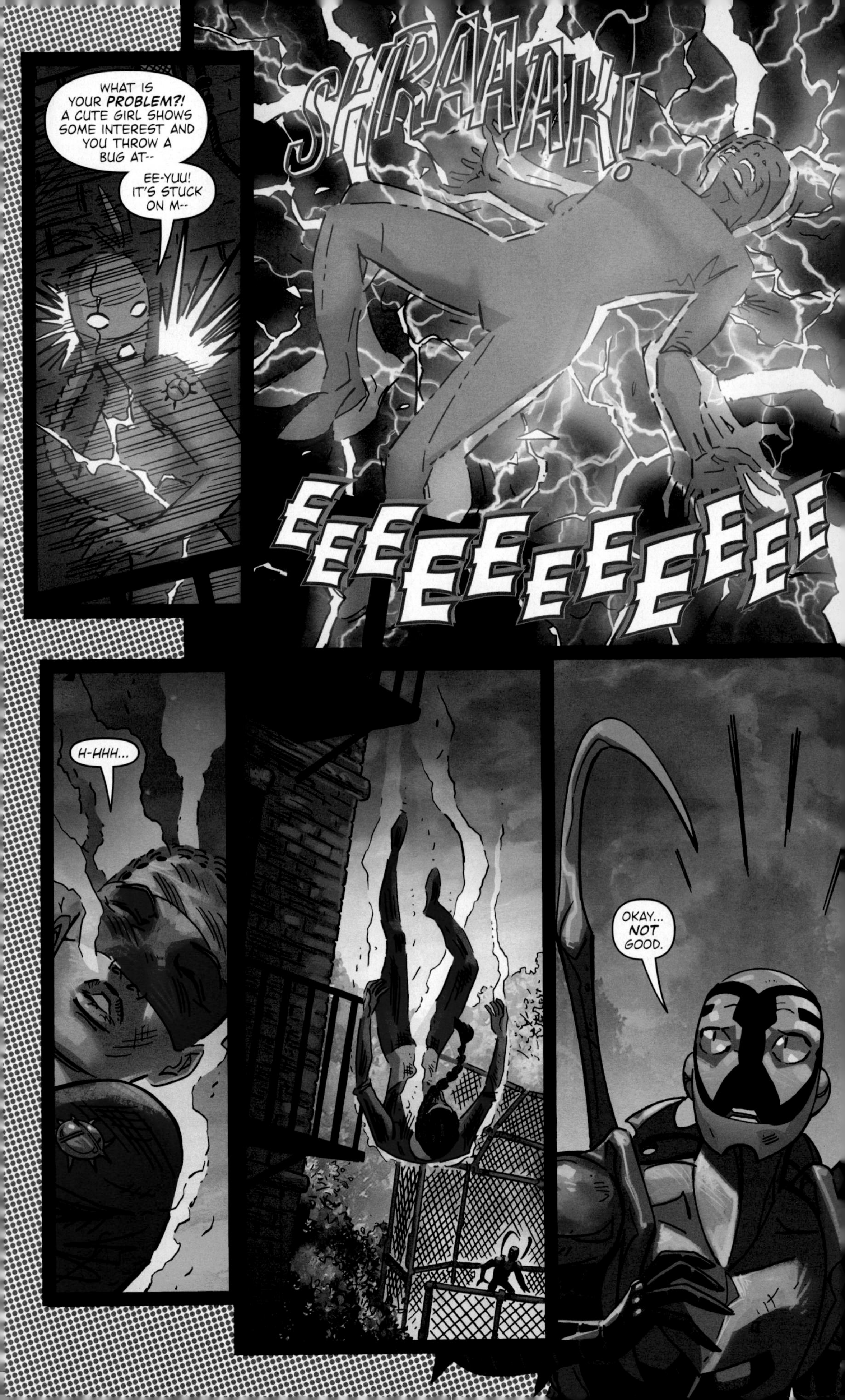
WHAT IS YOUR **PROBLEM?!** A CUTE GIRL SHOWS SOME INTEREST AND YOU THROW A BUG AT--
EE-YUU! IT'S STUCK ON M--
SHRAAAAK!
EEEEEEEEEEEEEE
H-HHH...
OKAY... **NOT** GOOD.

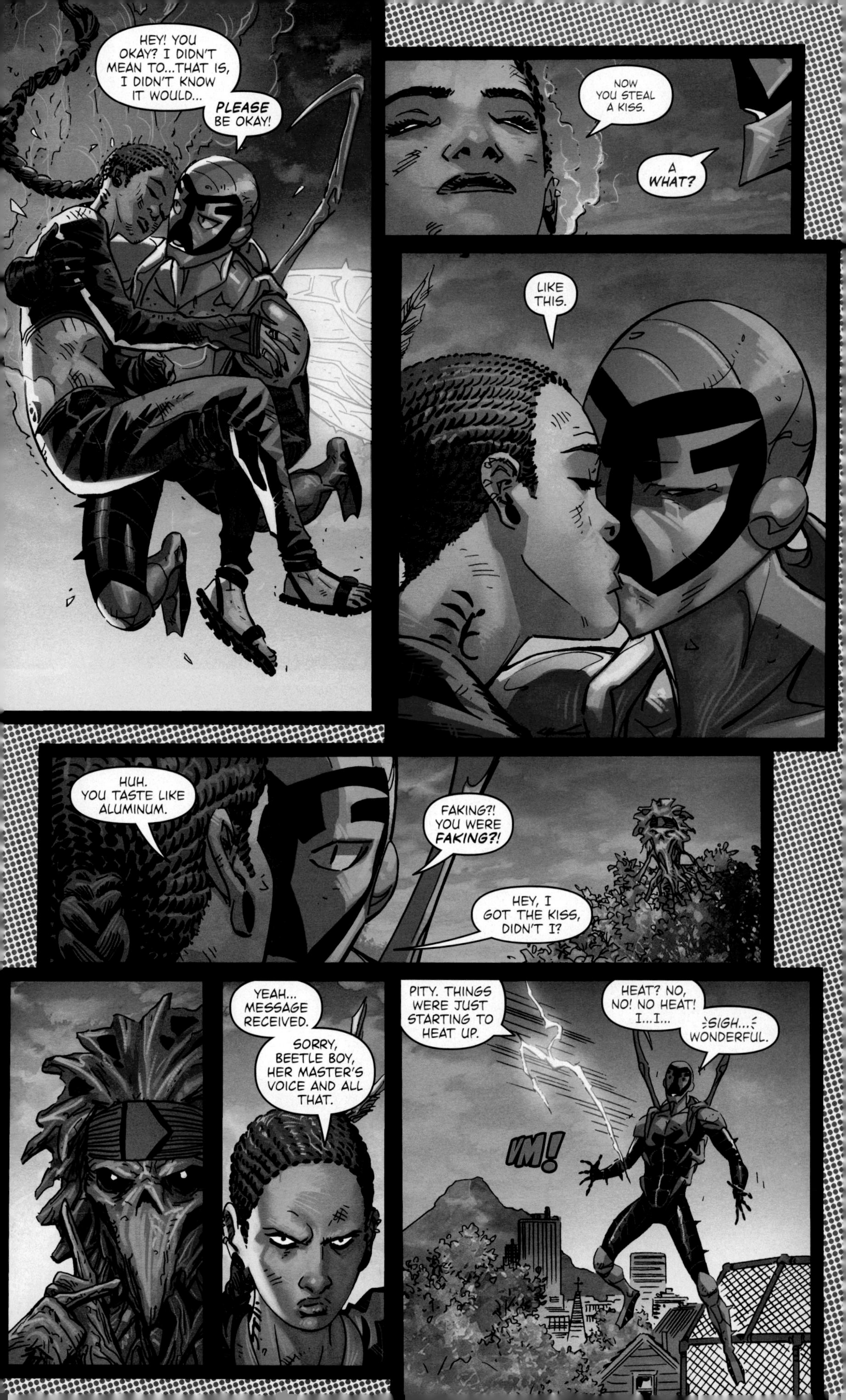

HEY! YOU OKAY? I DIDN'T MEAN TO...THAT IS, I DIDN'T KNOW IT WOULD... PLEASE BE OKAY!
NOW YOU STEAL A KISS.
A WHAT?
LIKE THIS.
HUH. YOU TASTE LIKE ALUMINUM.
FAKING?! YOU WERE FAKING?!
HEY, I GOT THE KISS, DIDN'T I?
YEAH... MESSAGE RECEIVED.
SORRY, BEETLE BOY, HER MASTER'S VOICE AND ALL THAT.
PITY. THINGS WERE JUST STARTING TO HEAT UP.
HEAT? NO, NO! NO HEAT! I...I...
SIGH... WONDERFUL.
VM!

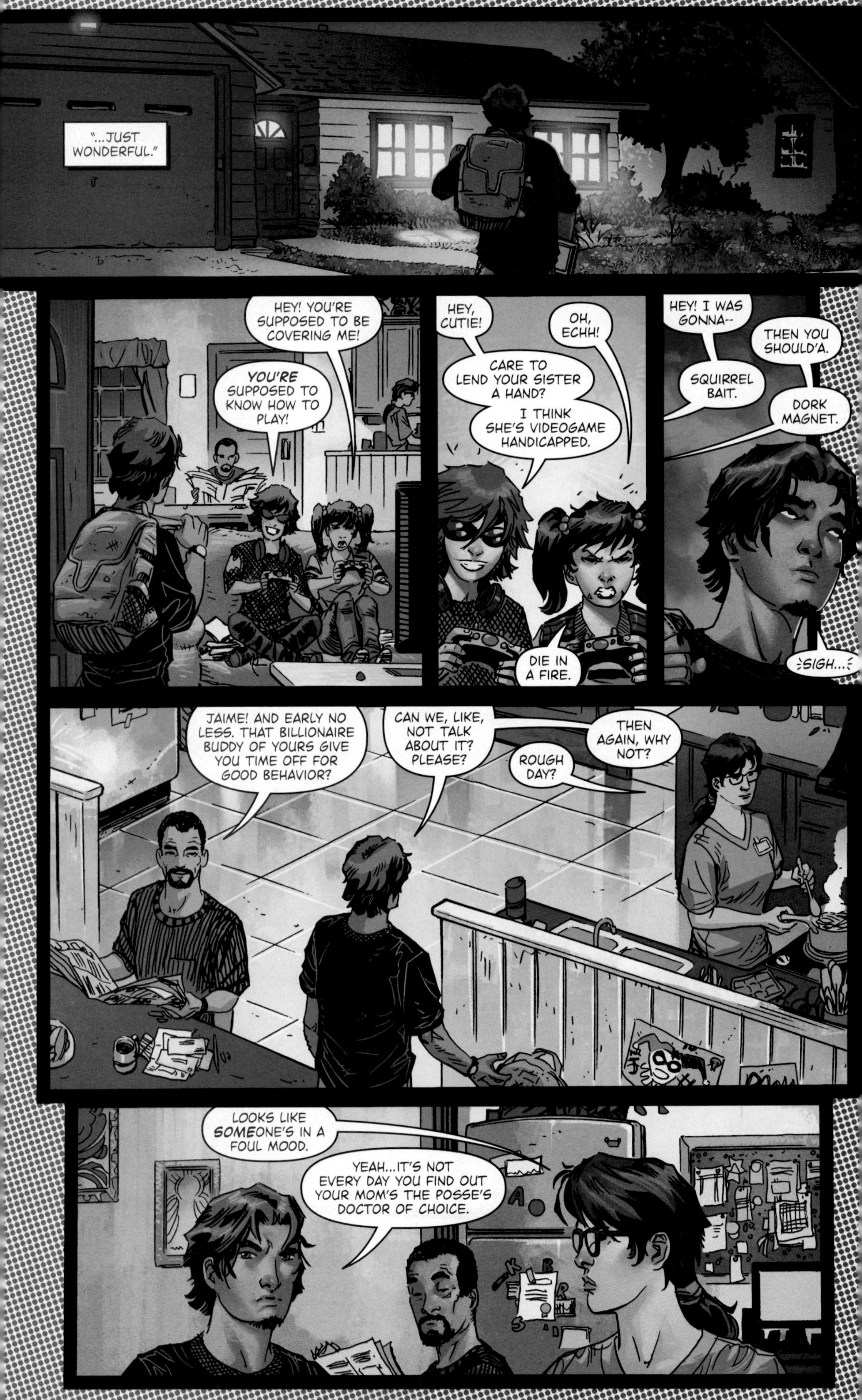
"...JUST WONDERFUL."
HEY! YOU'RE SUPPOSED TO BE COVERING ME!
YOU'RE SUPPOSED TO KNOW HOW TO PLAY!
HEY, CUTIE!
CARE TO LEND YOUR SISTER A HAND?
I THINK SHE'S VIDEOGAME HANDICAPPED.
OH, ECHH!
DIE IN A FIRE.
HEY! I WAS GONNA--
SQUIRREL BAIT.
THEN YOU SHOULD'A.
DORK MAGNET.
SIGH...
JAIME! AND EARLY NO LESS. THAT BILLIONAIRE BUDDY OF YOURS GIVE YOU TIME OFF FOR GOOD BEHAVIOR?
CAN WE, LIKE, NOT TALK ABOUT IT? PLEASE?
ROUGH DAY?
THEN AGAIN, WHY NOT?
LOOKS LIKE SOMEONE'S IN A FOUL MOOD.
YEAH...IT'S NOT EVERY DAY YOU FIND OUT YOUR MOM'S THE POSSE'S DOCTOR OF CHOICE.

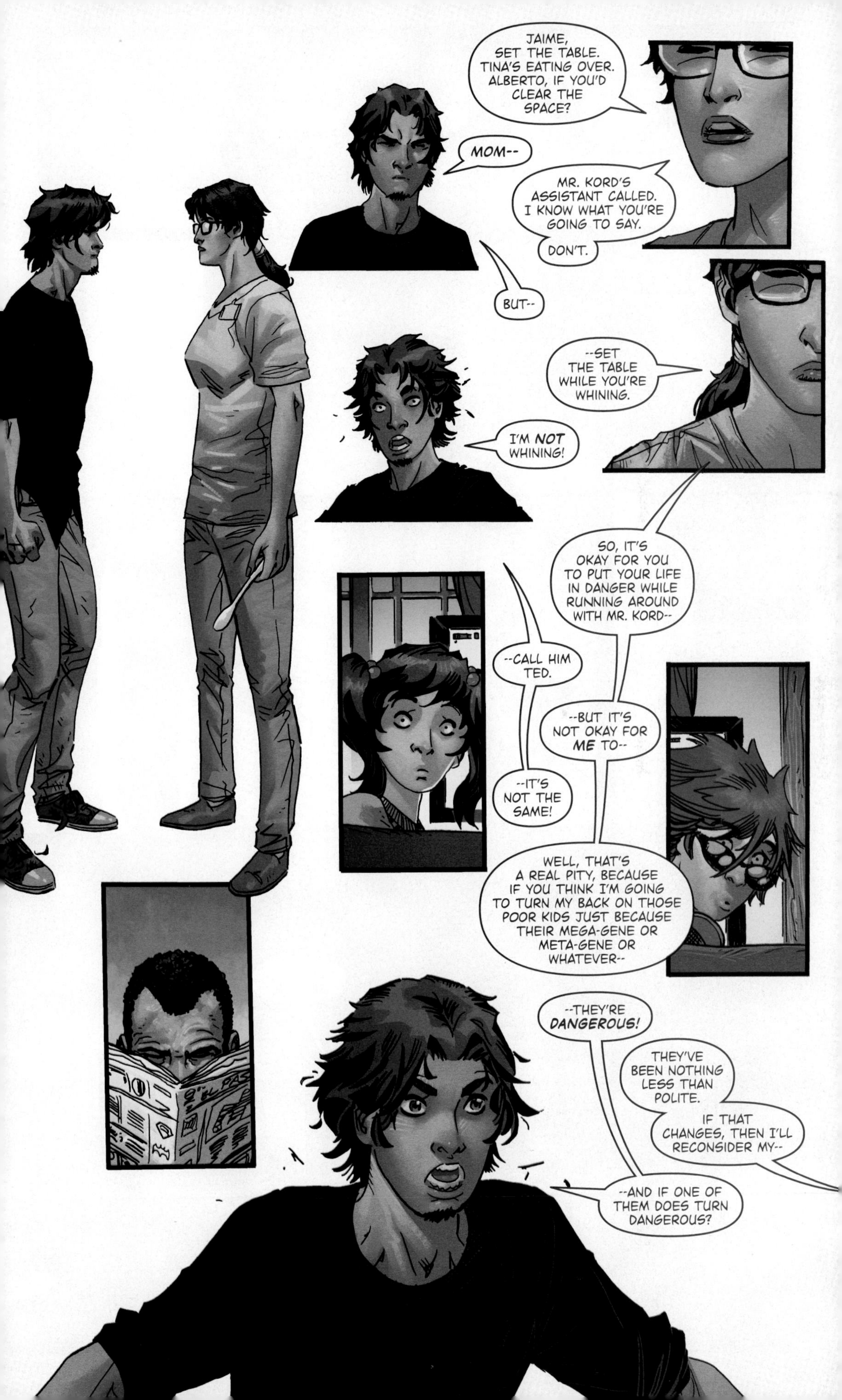
JAIME, SET THE TABLE. TINA'S EATING OVER. ALBERTO, IF YOU'D CLEAR THE SPACE?
MOM--
MR. KORD'S ASSISTANT CALLED. I KNOW WHAT YOU'RE GOING TO SAY.
DON'T.
BUT--
--SET THE TABLE WHILE YOU'RE WHINING.
I'M NOT WHINING!
SO, IT'S OKAY FOR YOU TO PUT YOUR LIFE IN DANGER WHILE RUNNING AROUND WITH MR. KORD--
--CALL HIM TED.
--BUT IT'S NOT OKAY FOR ME TO--
--IT'S NOT THE SAME!
WELL, THAT'S A REAL PITY, BECAUSE IF YOU THINK I'M GOING TO TURN MY BACK ON THOSE POOR KIDS JUST BECAUSE THEIR MEGA-GENE OR META-GENE OR WHATEVER--
--THEY'RE DANGEROUS!
THEY'VE BEEN NOTHING LESS THAN POLITE.
IF THAT CHANGES, THEN I'LL RECONSIDER MY--
--AND IF ONE OF THEM DOES TURN DANGEROUS?

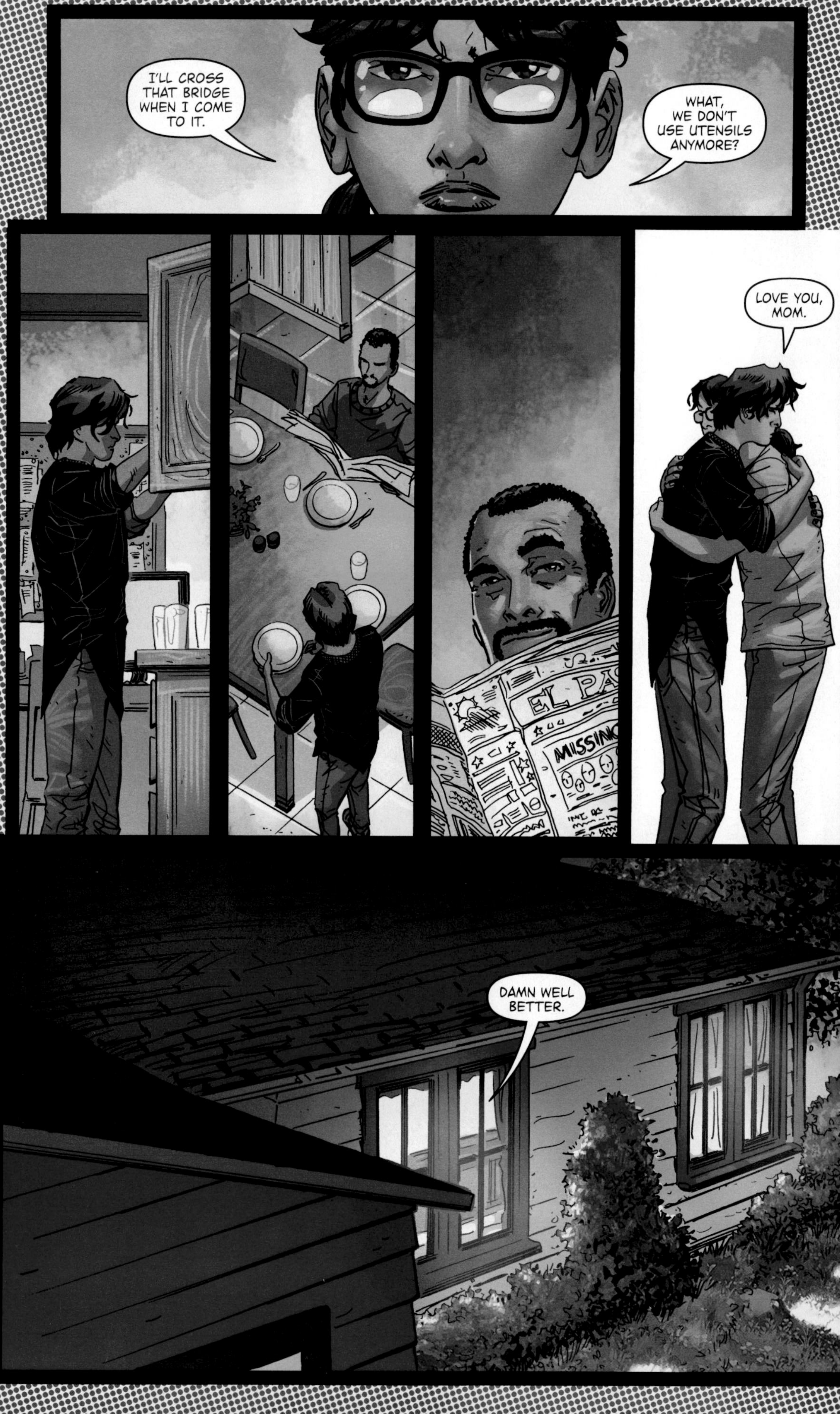
I'LL CROSS THAT BRIDGE WHEN I COME TO IT.
WHAT, WE DON'T USE UTENSILS ANYMORE?
EL PA
MISSING
LOVE YOU, MOM.
DAMN WELL BETTER.

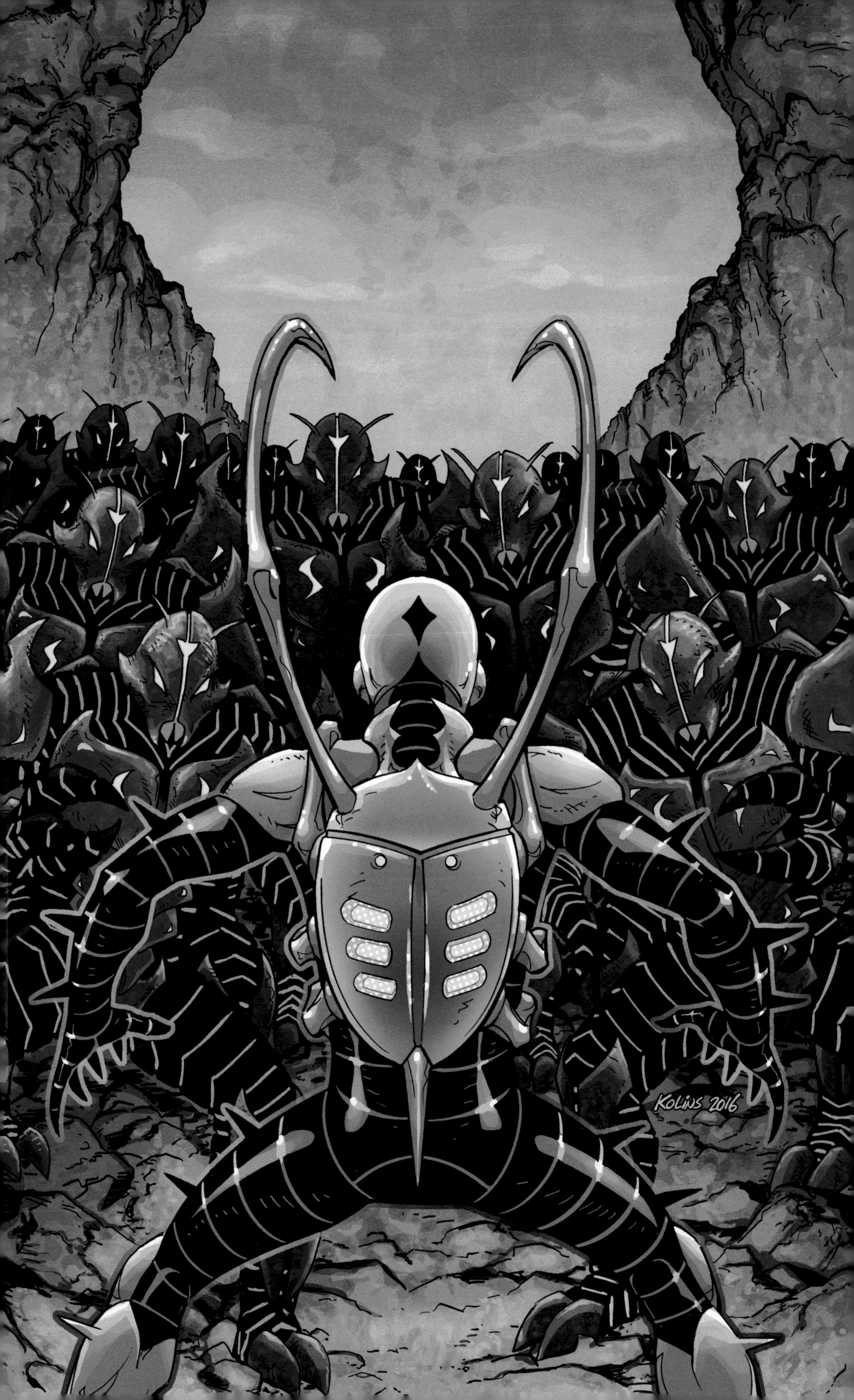
KOLINS 2016

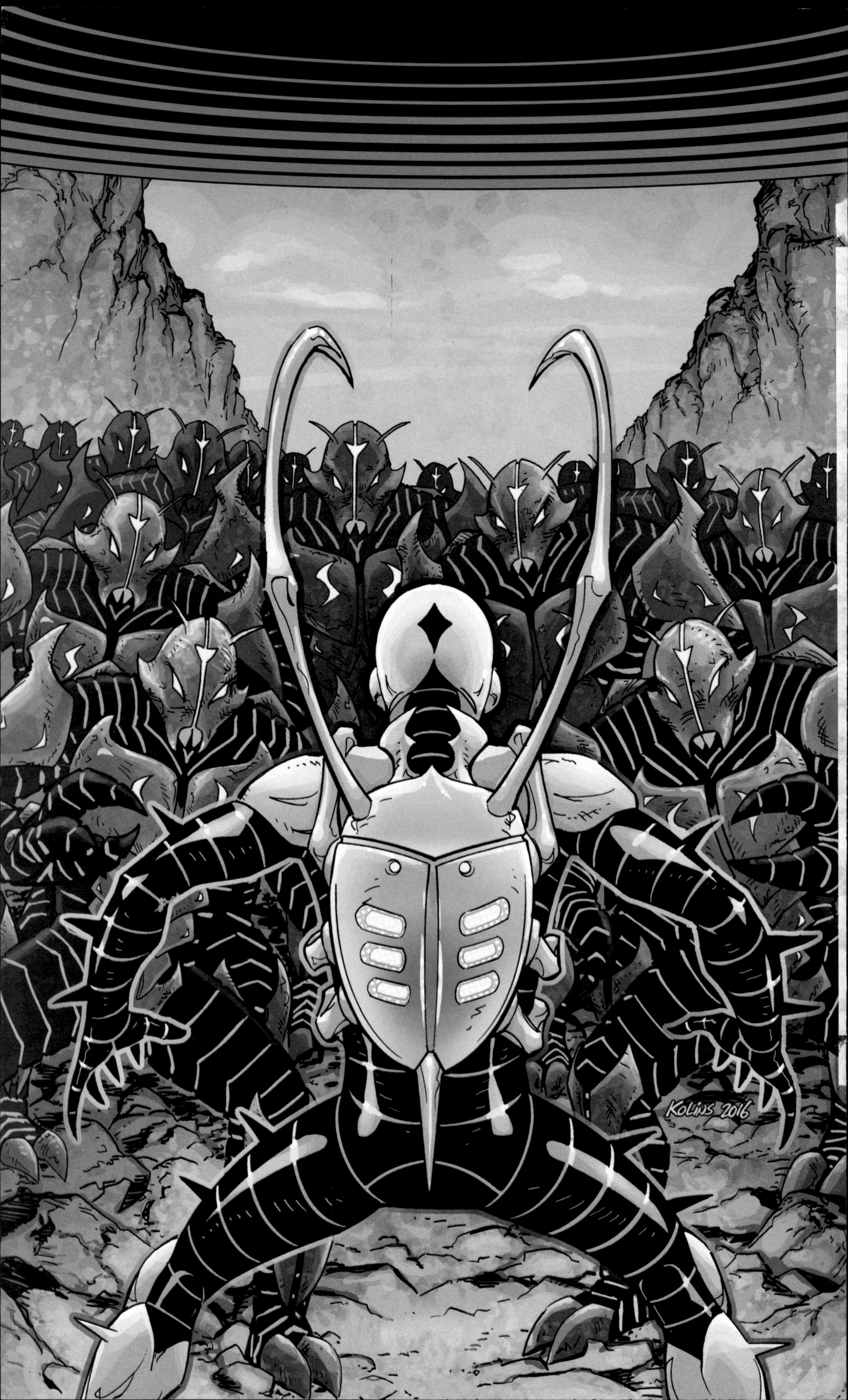
KOLINS 2016

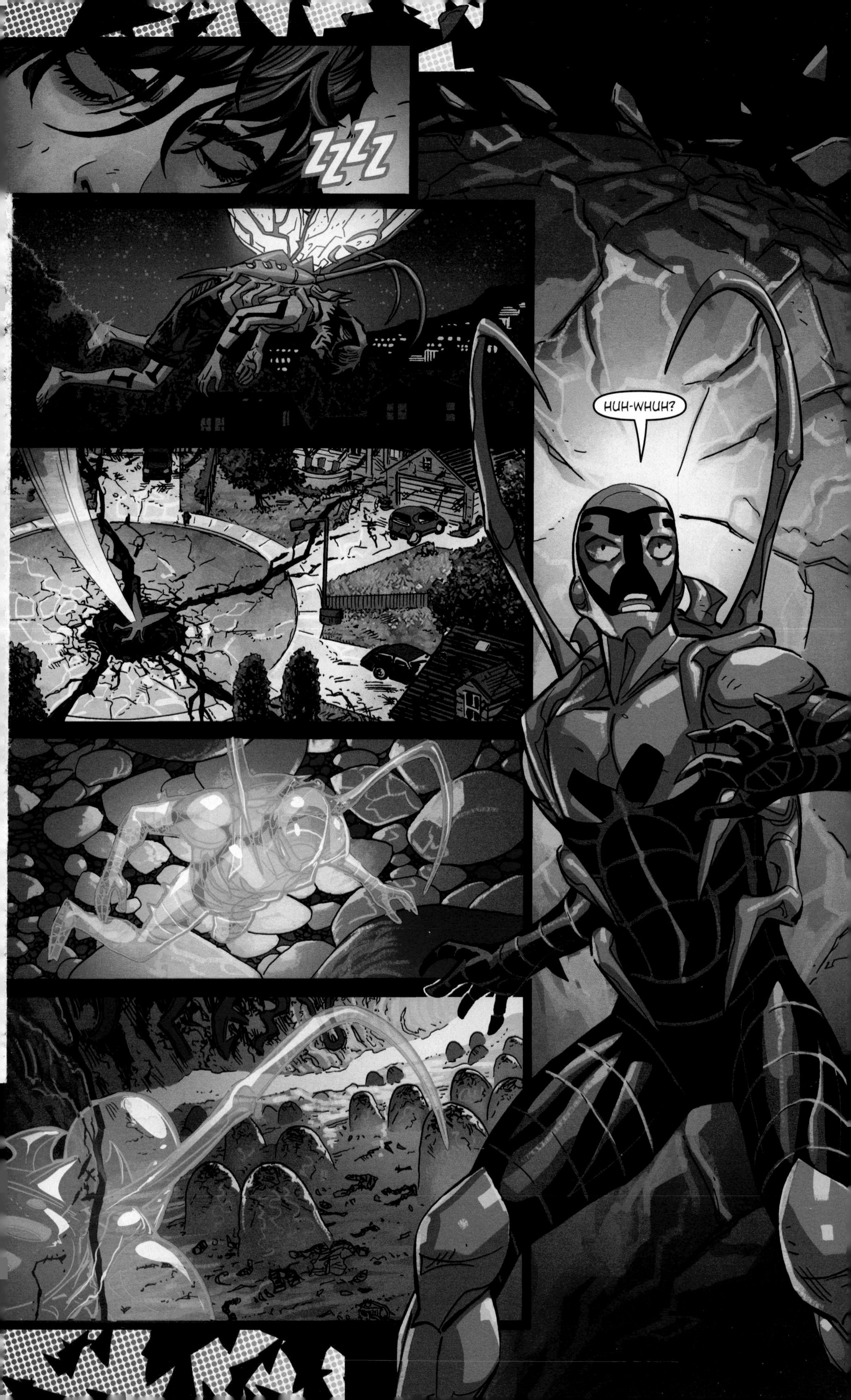
ZZZZ
HUH-WHUH?

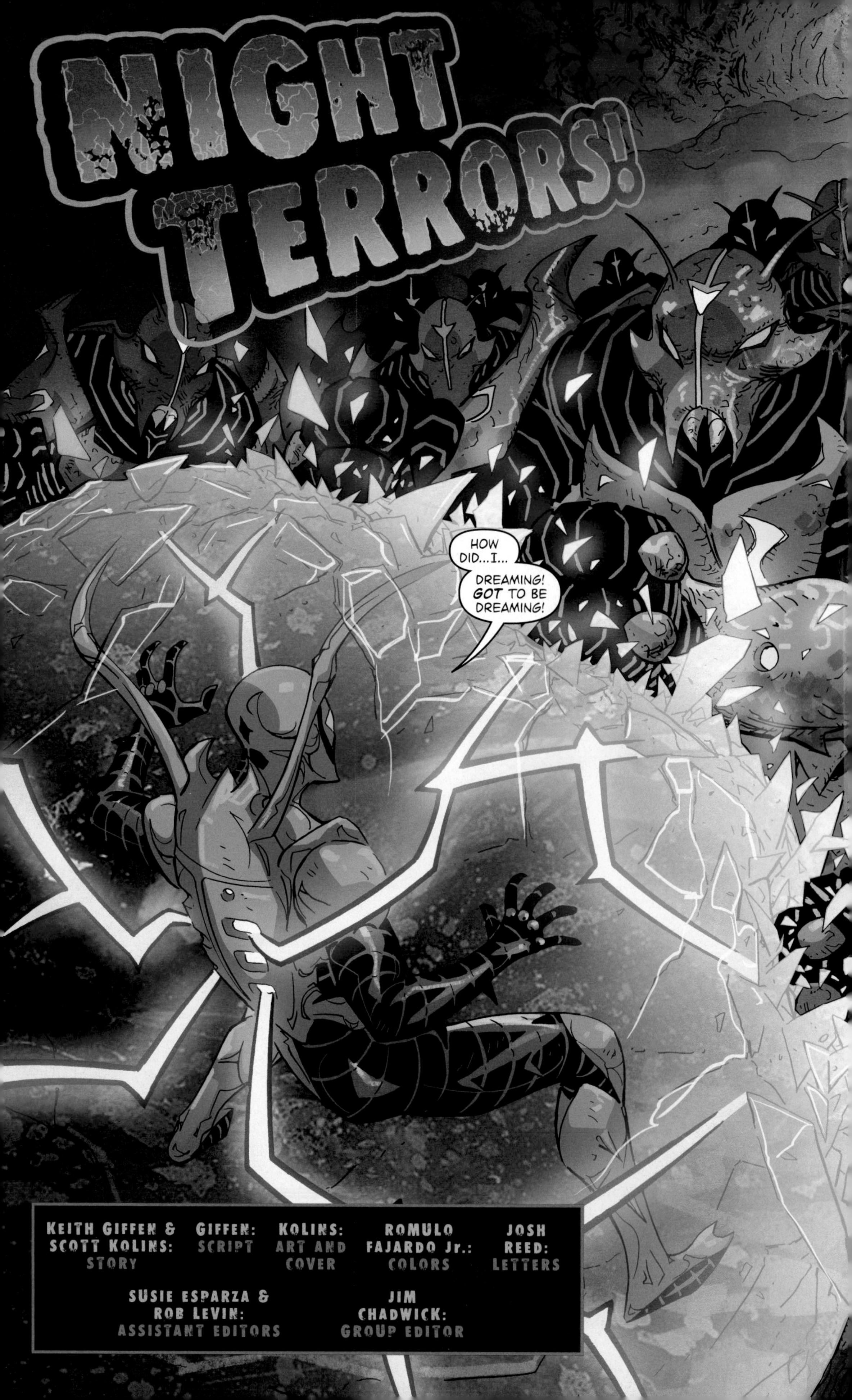
NIGHT TERRORS!
HOW DID...I...
DREAMING! GOT TO BE DREAMING!
KEITH GIFFEN & SCOTT KOLINS: STORY
GIFFEN: SCRIPT
KOLINS: ART AND COVER
ROMULO FAJARDO Jr.: COLORS
JOSH REED: LETTERS
SUSIE ESPARZA & ROB LEVIN: ASSISTANT EDITORS
JIM CHADWICK: GROUP EDITOR

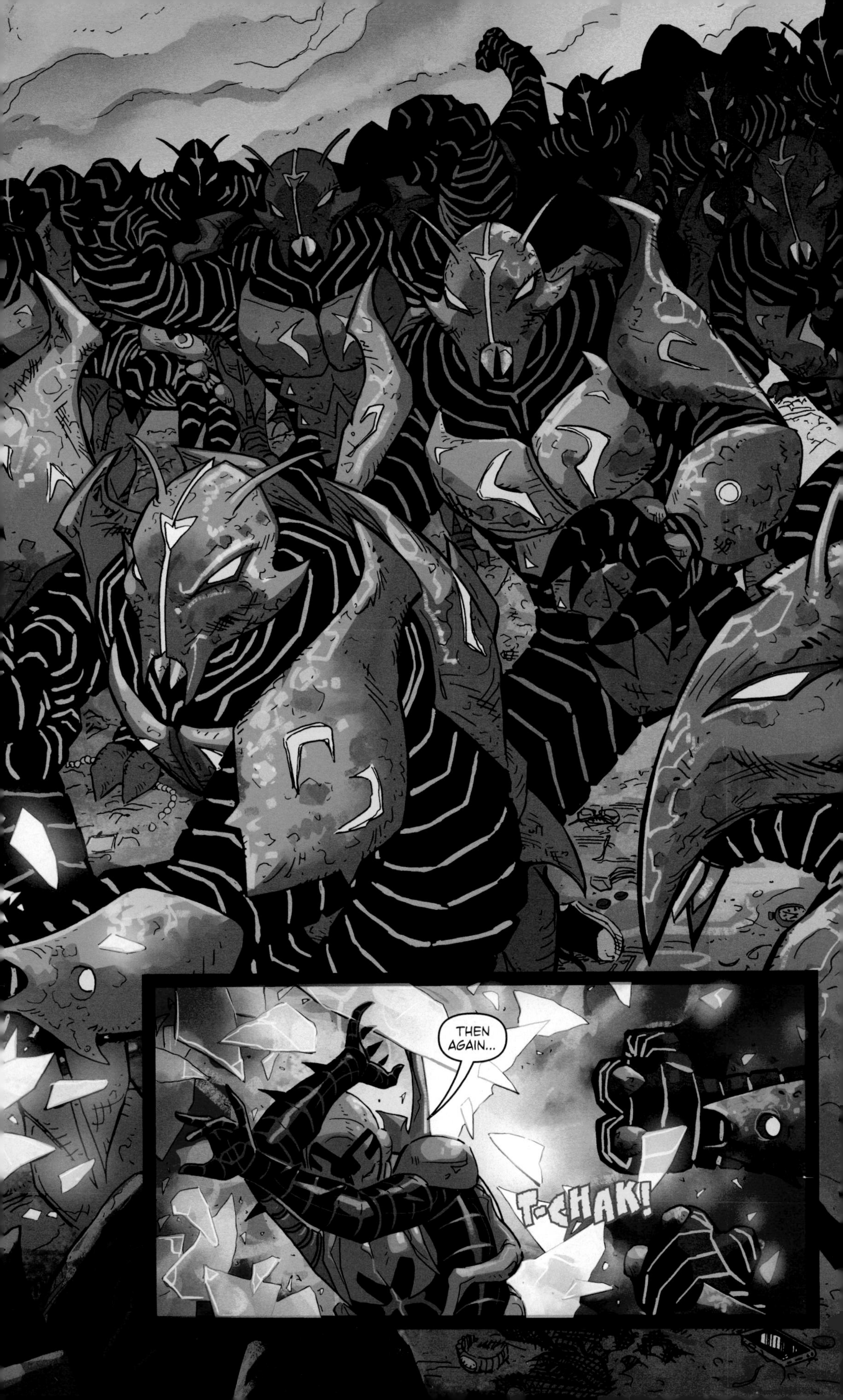
THEN AGAIN...
T-CHAK!

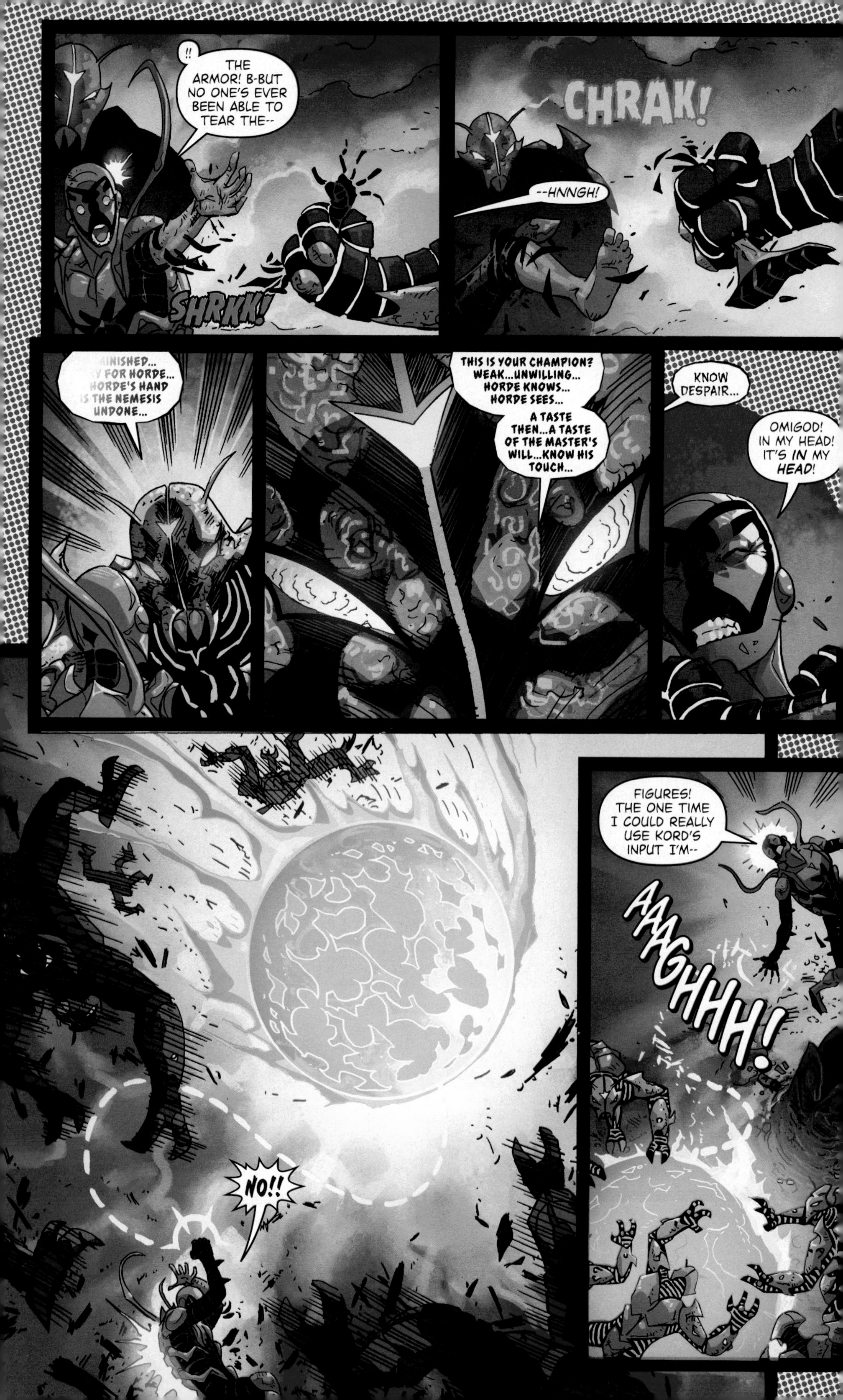
!!
THE ARMOR! B-BUT NO ONE'S EVER BEEN ABLE TO TEAR THE--
SHRKK!
CHRAK!
--HNNGH!
INISHED... FOR HORDE... HORDE'S HAND IS THE NEMESIS UNDONE...
THIS IS YOUR CHAMPION? WEAK...UNWILLING... HORDE KNOWS... HORDE SEES...
A TASTE THEN...A TASTE OF THE MASTER'S WILL...KNOW HIS TOUCH...
KNOW DESPAIR...
OMIGOD! IN MY HEAD! IT'S IN MY HEAD!
NO!!
FIGURES! THE ONE TIME I COULD REALLY USE KORD'S INPUT I'M--
AAAGHHHH!

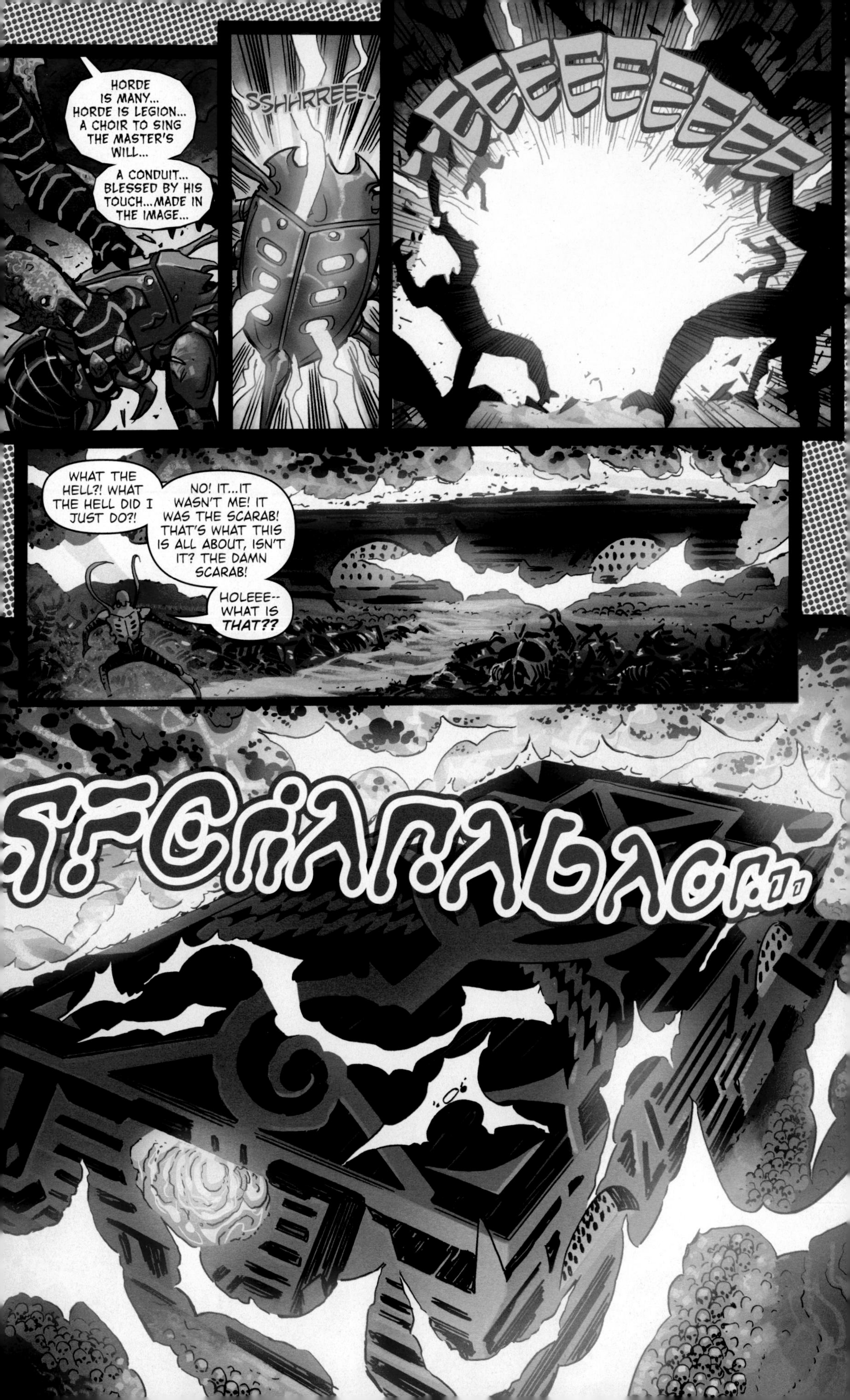
HORDE IS MANY... HORDE IS LEGION... A CHOIR TO SING THE MASTER'S WILL...
A CONDUIT... BLESSED BY HIS TOUCH...MADE IN THE IMAGE...
SSHHRREE--
EEEEEEEEE
WHAT THE HELL?! WHAT THE HELL DID I JUST DO?!
NO! IT...IT WASN'T ME! IT WAS THE SCARAB! THAT'S WHAT THIS IS ALL ABOUT, ISN'T IT? THE DAMN SCARAB!
HOLEEE-- WHAT IS THAT??

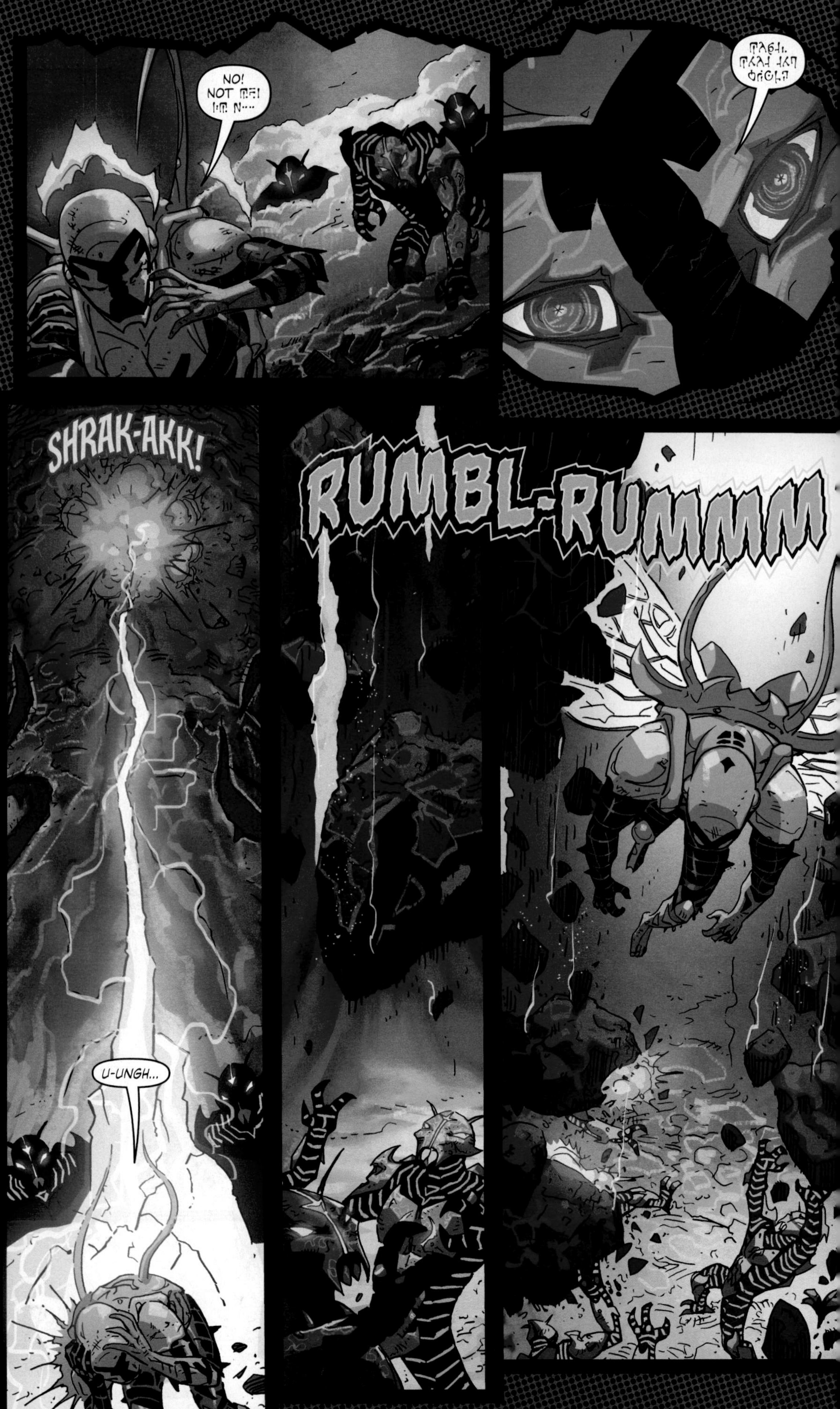
NO!
NOT
SHRAK-AKK!
U-UNGH...
RUMBL-RUMMM

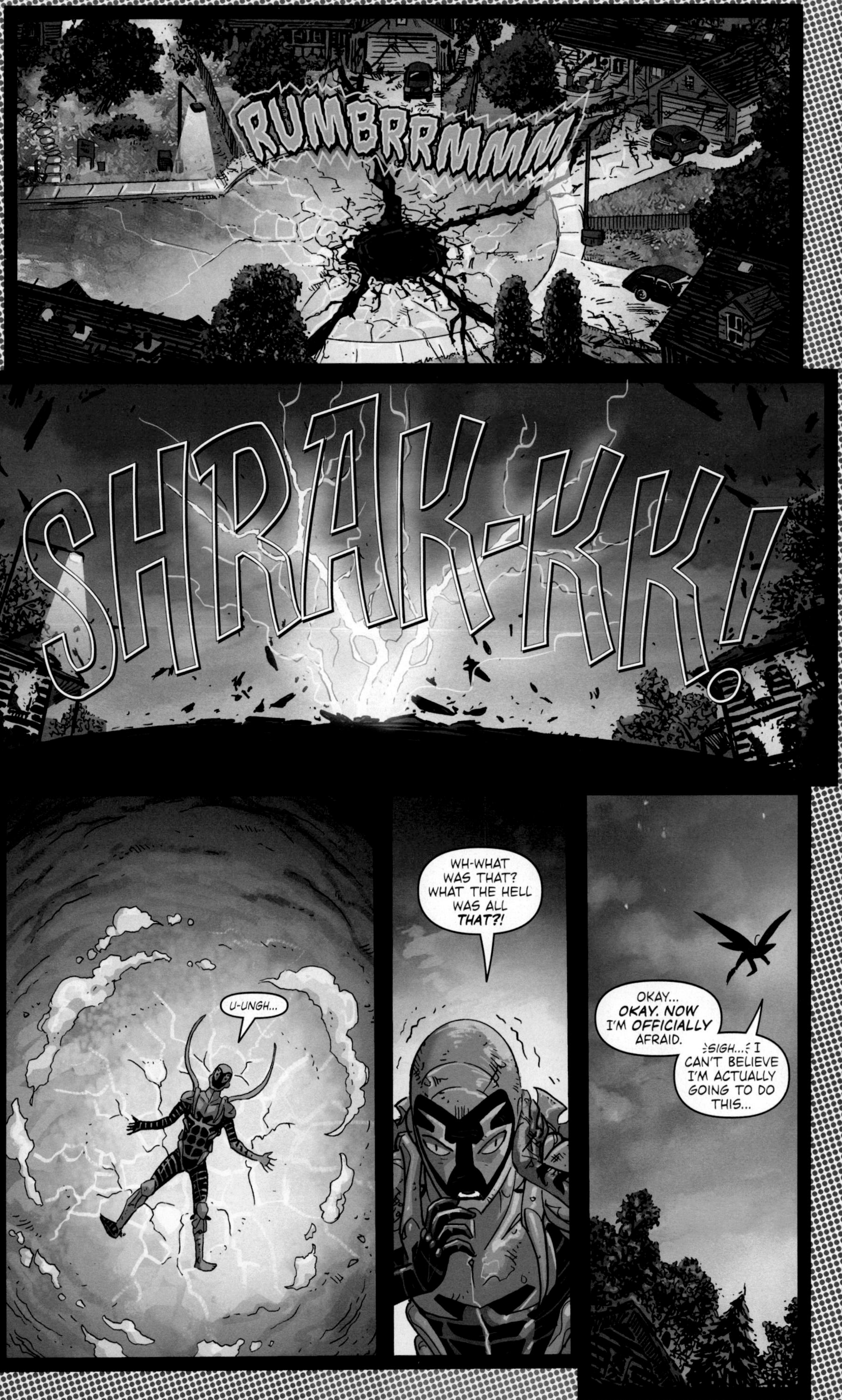
RUMBRRMMM
SHRAK-KK!
U-UNGH...
WH-WHAT WAS THAT? WHAT THE HELL WAS ALL THAT?!
OKAY... OKAY. NOW I'M OFFICIALLY AFRAID.
SIGH... I CAN'T BELIEVE I'M ACTUALLY GOING TO DO THIS...

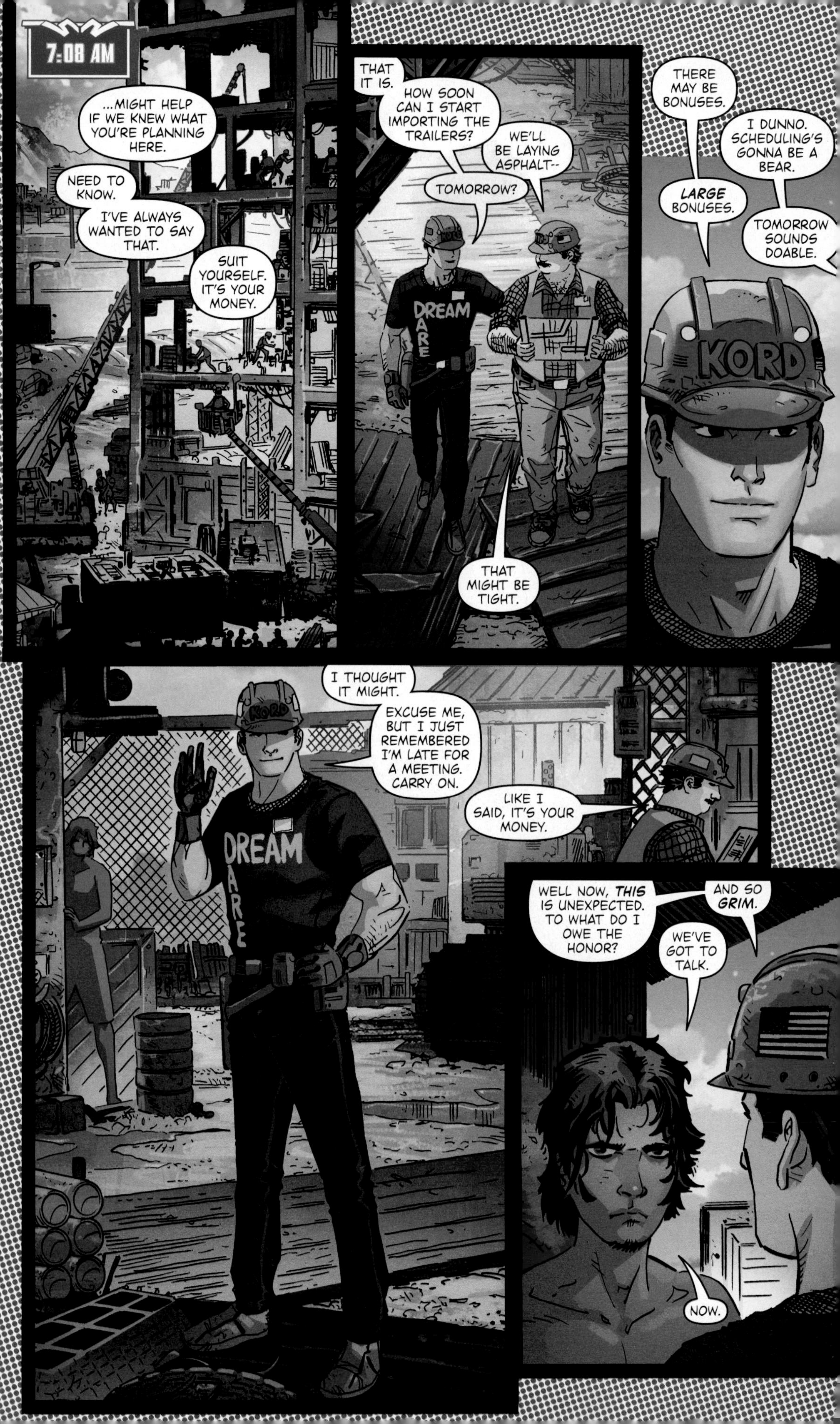
7:08 AM
...MIGHT HELP IF WE KNEW WHAT YOU'RE PLANNING HERE.
NEED TO KNOW.
I'VE ALWAYS WANTED TO SAY THAT.
SUIT YOURSELF. IT'S YOUR MONEY.
THAT IT IS.
HOW SOON CAN I START IMPORTING THE TRAILERS?
WE'LL BE LAYING ASPHALT--
TOMORROW?
THAT MIGHT BE TIGHT.
THERE MAY BE BONUSES.
LARGE BONUSES.
I DUNNO. SCHEDULING'S GONNA BE A BEAR.
TOMORROW SOUNDS DOABLE.
KORD
I THOUGHT IT MIGHT.
EXCUSE ME, BUT I JUST REMEMBERED I'M LATE FOR A MEETING. CARRY ON.
LIKE I SAID, IT'S YOUR MONEY.
DREAM
WELL NOW, THIS IS UNEXPECTED. TO WHAT DO I OWE THE HONOR?
AND SO GRIM.
WE'VE GOT TO TALK.
NOW.

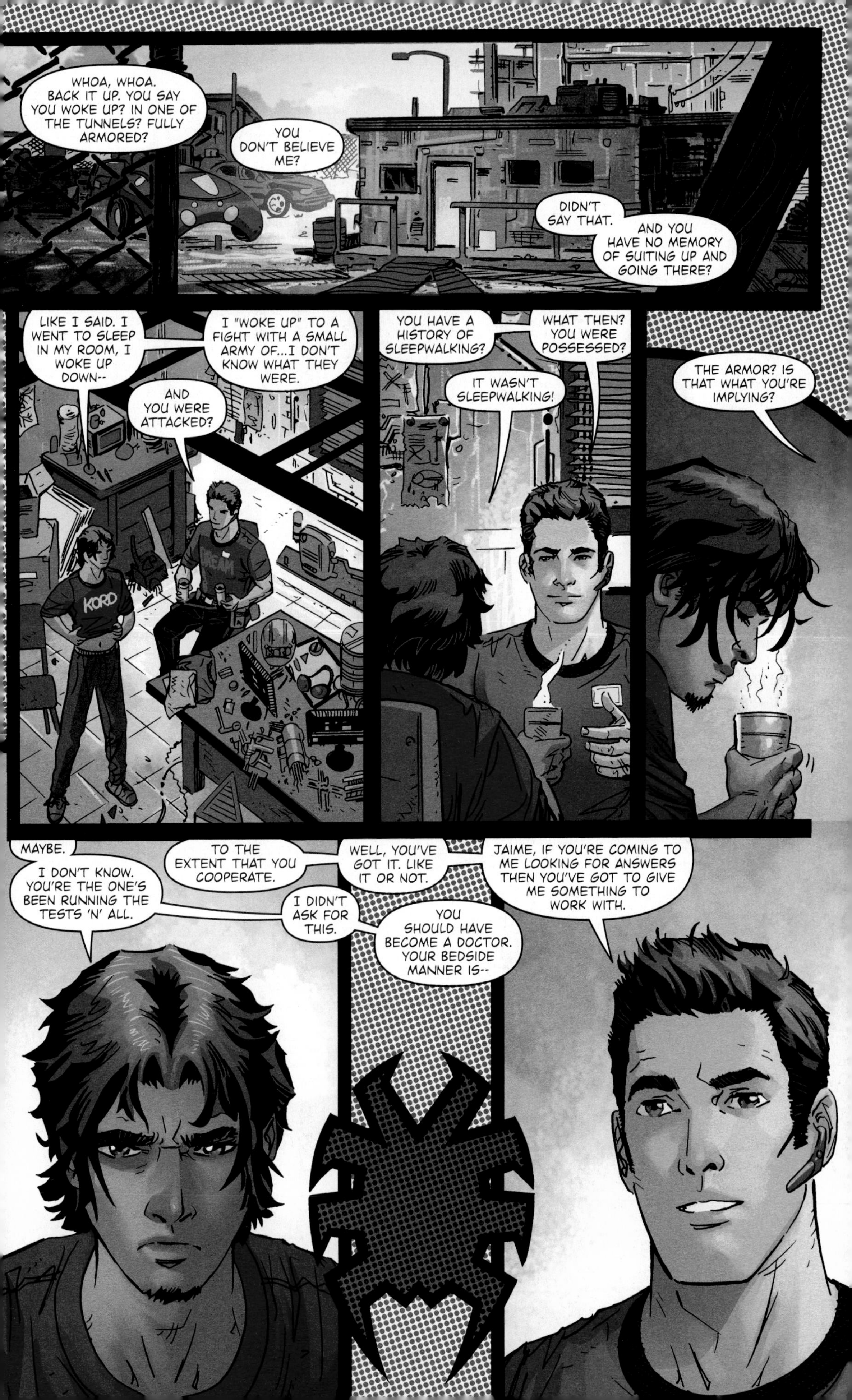
WHOA, WHOA. BACK IT UP. YOU SAY YOU WOKE UP? IN ONE OF THE TUNNELS? FULLY ARMORED?
YOU DON'T BELIEVE ME?
DIDN'T SAY THAT.
AND YOU HAVE NO MEMORY OF SUITING UP AND GOING THERE?
LIKE I SAID. I WENT TO SLEEP IN MY ROOM, I WOKE UP DOWN--
I "WOKE UP" TO A FIGHT WITH A SMALL ARMY OF...I DON'T KNOW WHAT THEY WERE.
AND YOU WERE ATTACKED?
KORD
DREAM
YOU HAVE A HISTORY OF SLEEPWALKING?
IT WASN'T SLEEPWALKING!
WHAT THEN? YOU WERE POSSESSED?
THE ARMOR? IS THAT WHAT YOU'RE IMPLYING?
MAYBE.
I DON'T KNOW. YOU'RE THE ONE'S BEEN RUNNING THE TESTS 'N' ALL.
TO THE EXTENT THAT YOU COOPERATE.
I DIDN'T ASK FOR THIS.
WELL, YOU'VE GOT IT. LIKE IT OR NOT.
YOU SHOULD HAVE BECOME A DOCTOR. YOUR BEDSIDE MANNER IS--
JAIME, IF YOU'RE COMING TO ME LOOKING FOR ANSWERS THEN YOU'VE GOT TO GIVE ME SOMETHING TO WORK WITH.

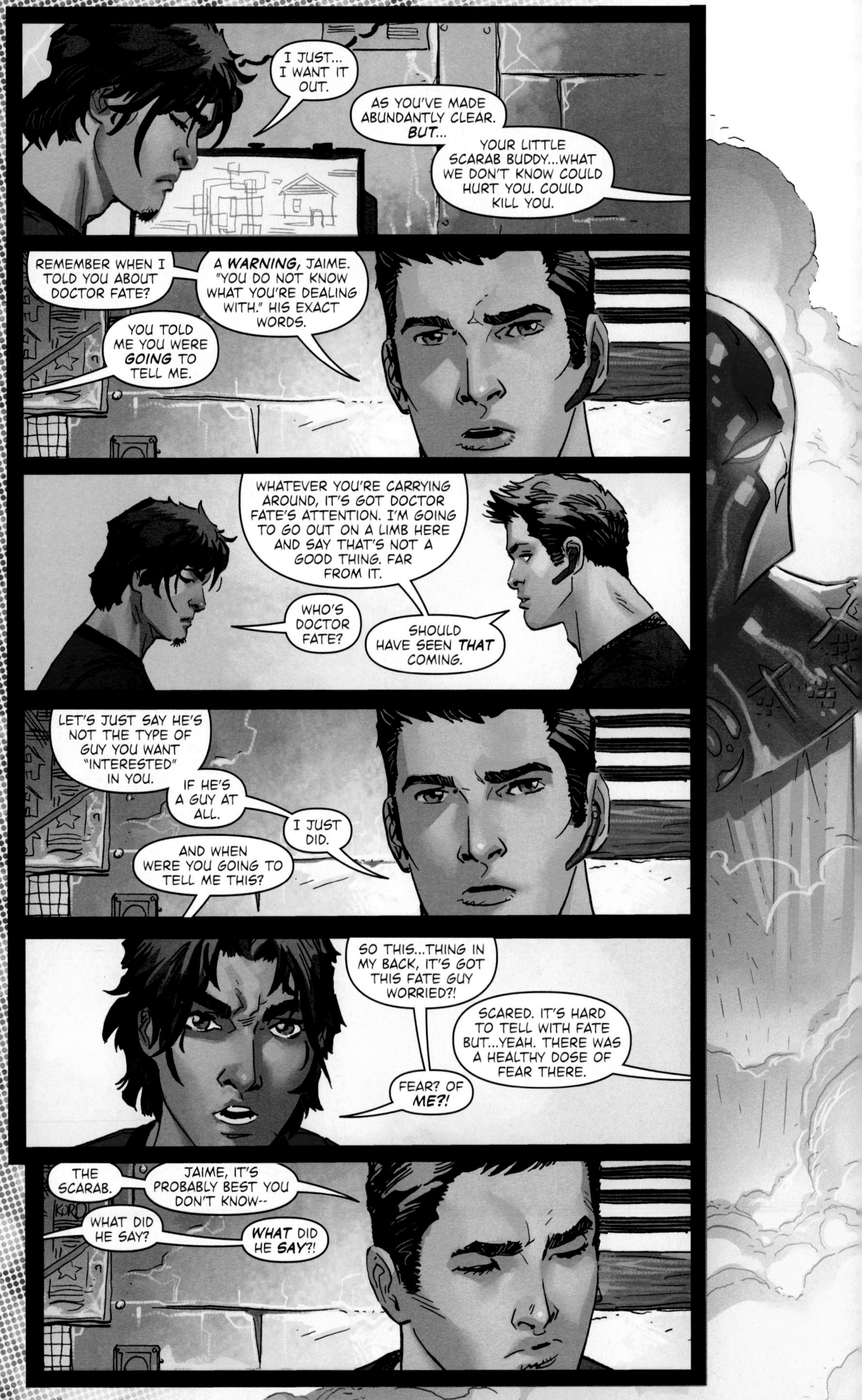

I JUST... I WANT IT OUT.
AS YOU'VE MADE ABUNDANTLY CLEAR. BUT...
YOUR LITTLE SCARAB BUDDY...WHAT WE DON'T KNOW COULD HURT YOU. COULD KILL YOU.
REMEMBER WHEN I TOLD YOU ABOUT DOCTOR FATE?
A WARNING, JAIME. "YOU DO NOT KNOW WHAT YOU'RE DEALING WITH." HIS EXACT WORDS.
YOU TOLD ME YOU WERE GOING TO TELL ME.
WHATEVER YOU'RE CARRYING AROUND, IT'S GOT DOCTOR FATE'S ATTENTION. I'M GOING TO GO OUT ON A LIMB HERE AND SAY THAT'S NOT A GOOD THING. FAR FROM IT.
WHO'S DOCTOR FATE?
SHOULD HAVE SEEN THAT COMING.
LET'S JUST SAY HE'S NOT THE TYPE OF GUY YOU WANT "INTERESTED" IN YOU.
IF HE'S A GUY AT ALL.
AND WHEN WERE YOU GOING TO TELL ME THIS?
I JUST DID.
SO THIS...THING IN MY BACK, IT'S GOT THIS FATE GUY WORRIED?!
SCARED. IT'S HARD TO TELL WITH FATE BUT...YEAH. THERE WAS A HEALTHY DOSE OF FEAR THERE.
FEAR? OF ME?!
THE SCARAB.
JAIME, IT'S PROBABLY BEST YOU DON'T KNOW--
WHAT DID HE SAY?
WHAT DID HE SAY?!

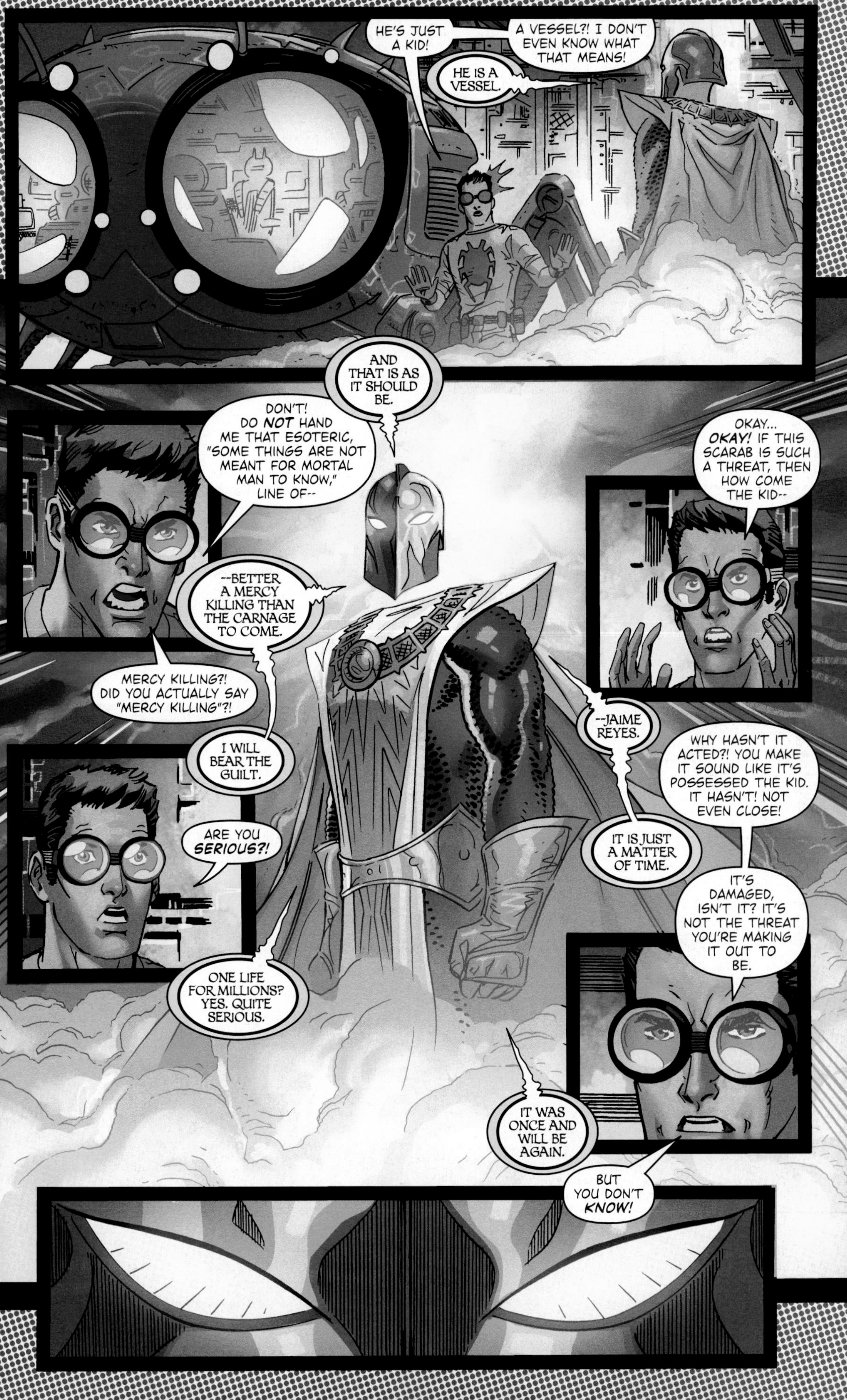
HE'S JUST A KID!
A VESSEL?! I DON'T EVEN KNOW WHAT THAT MEANS!
HE IS A VESSEL.
AND THAT IS AS IT SHOULD BE.
DON'T! DO NOT HAND ME THAT ESOTERIC, "SOME THINGS ARE NOT MEANT FOR MORTAL MAN TO KNOW," LINE OF--
--BETTER A MERCY KILLING THAN THE CARNAGE TO COME.
MERCY KILLING?! DID YOU ACTUALLY SAY "MERCY KILLING"?!
I WILL BEAR THE GUILT.
ARE YOU SERIOUS?!
ONE LIFE FOR MILLIONS? YES. QUITE SERIOUS.
OKAY... OKAY! IF THIS SCARAB IS SUCH A THREAT, THEN HOW COME THE KID--
--JAIME REYES.
WHY HASN'T IT ACTED?! YOU MAKE IT SOUND LIKE IT'S POSSESSED THE KID. IT HASN'T! NOT EVEN CLOSE!
IT IS JUST A MATTER OF TIME.
IT'S DAMAGED, ISN'T IT? IT'S NOT THE THREAT YOU'RE MAKING IT OUT TO BE.
IT WAS ONCE AND WILL BE AGAIN.
BUT YOU DON'T KNOW!

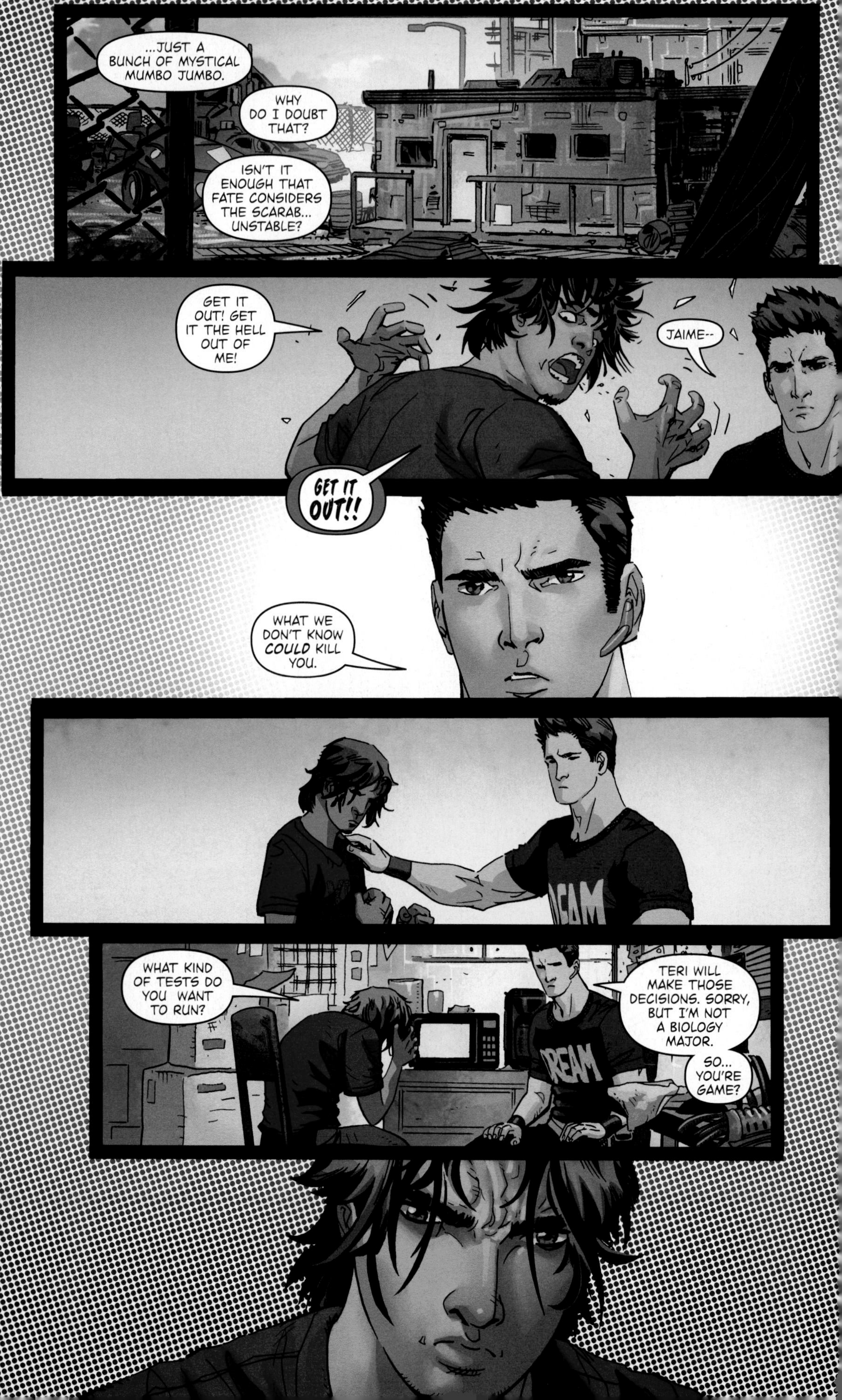
...JUST A BUNCH OF MYSTICAL MUMBO JUMBO.
WHY DO I DOUBT THAT?
ISN'T IT ENOUGH THAT FATE CONSIDERS THE SCARAB... UNSTABLE?
GET IT OUT! GET IT THE HELL OUT OF ME!
JAIME--
GET IT OUT!!
WHAT WE DON'T KNOW COULD KILL YOU.
DREAM
WHAT KIND OF TESTS DO YOU WANT TO RUN?
TERI WILL MAKE THOSE DECISIONS. SORRY, BUT I'M NOT A BIOLOGY MAJOR.
SO... YOU'RE GAME?
DREAM

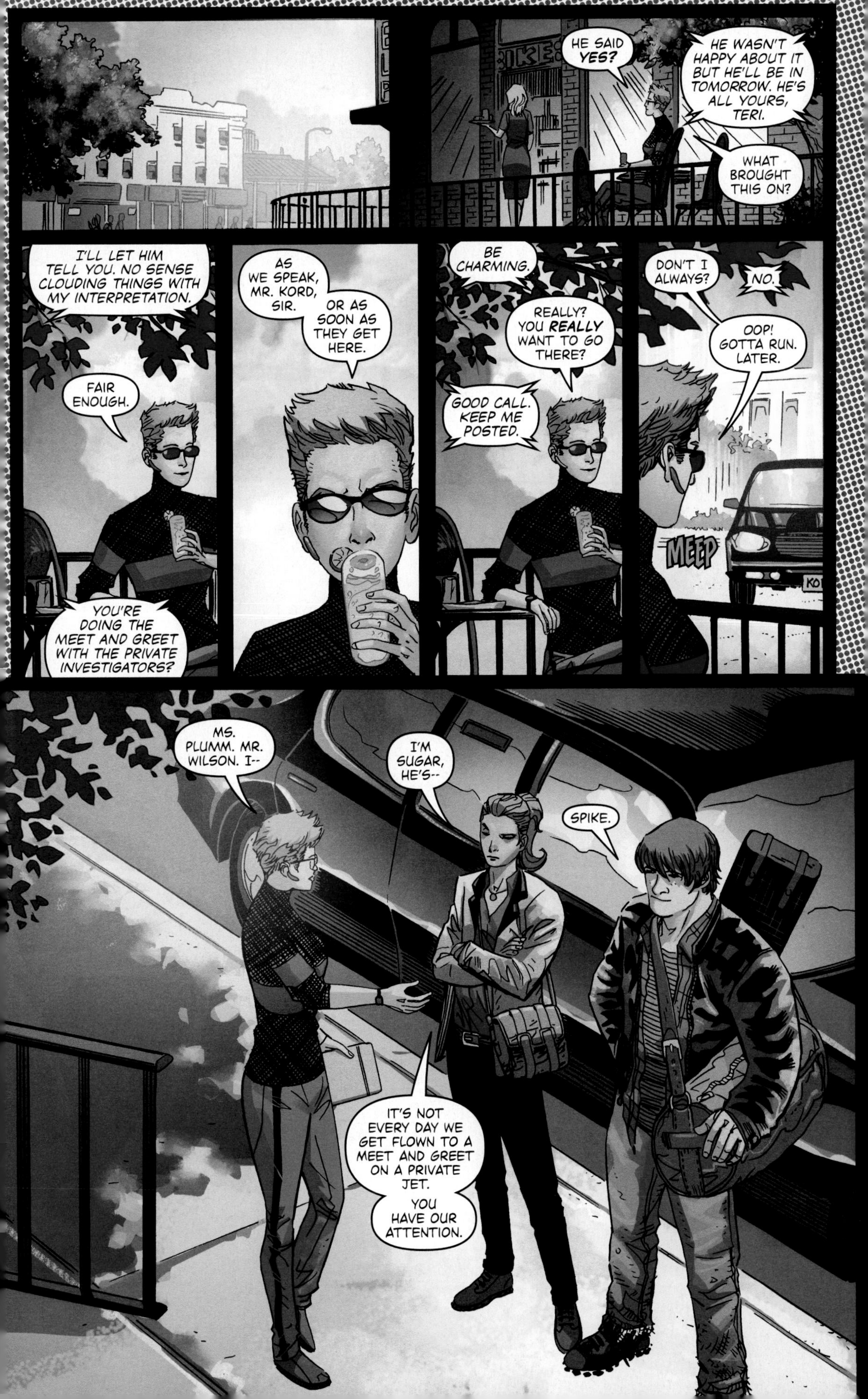
HE SAID **YES?**
HE WASN'T HAPPY ABOUT IT BUT HE'LL BE IN TOMORROW. HE'S ALL YOURS, TERI.
WHAT BROUGHT THIS ON?
I'LL LET HIM TELL YOU. NO SENSE CLOUDING THINGS WITH MY INTERPRETATION.
FAIR ENOUGH.
YOU'RE DOING THE MEET AND GREET WITH THE PRIVATE INVESTIGATORS?
AS WE SPEAK, MR. KORD, SIR.
OR AS SOON AS THEY GET HERE.
BE CHARMING.
REALLY? YOU **REALLY** WANT TO GO THERE?
GOOD CALL. KEEP ME POSTED.
DON'T I ALWAYS?
NO.
OOP! GOTTA RUN. LATER.
MEEP
MS. PLUMM. MR. WILSON. I--
I'M SUGAR, HE'S--
SPIKE.
IT'S NOT EVERY DAY WE GET FLOWN TO A MEET AND GREET ON A PRIVATE JET.
YOU HAVE OUR ATTENTION.

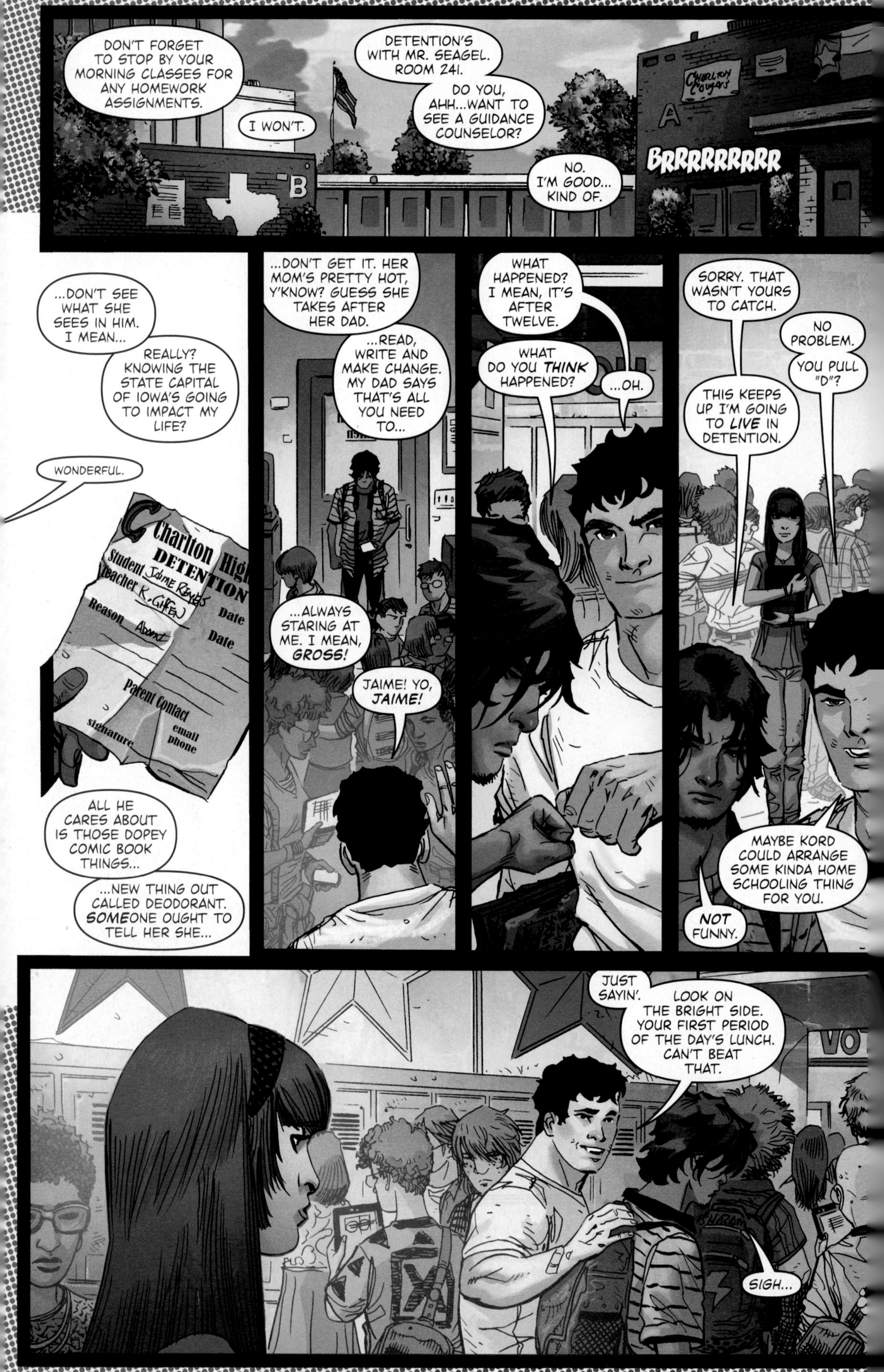
DON'T FORGET TO STOP BY YOUR MORNING CLASSES FOR ANY HOMEWORK ASSIGNMENTS.
I WON'T.
DETENTION'S WITH MR. SEAGEL. ROOM 241.
DO YOU, AHH...WANT TO SEE A GUIDANCE COUNSELOR?
NO. I'M GOOD... KIND OF.
BRRRRRRRRR
A
B
...DON'T SEE WHAT SHE SEES IN HIM. I MEAN...
REALLY? KNOWING THE STATE CAPITAL OF IOWA'S GOING TO IMPACT MY LIFE?
WONDERFUL.
Charlton High
DETENTION
Student Jaime Reyes
Teacher K. Giffen
Reason Absent
Date
Date
Parent Contact
email
phone
signature
ALL HE CARES ABOUT IS THOSE DOPEY COMIC BOOK THINGS...
...NEW THING OUT CALLED DEODORANT. SOMEONE OUGHT TO TELL HER SHE...
...DON'T GET IT. HER MOM'S PRETTY HOT, Y'KNOW? GUESS SHE TAKES AFTER HER DAD.
...READ, WRITE AND MAKE CHANGE. MY DAD SAYS THAT'S ALL YOU NEED TO...
...ALWAYS STARING AT ME. I MEAN, GROSS!
JAIME! YO, JAIME!
WHAT HAPPENED? I MEAN, IT'S AFTER TWELVE.
WHAT DO YOU THINK HAPPENED?
...OH.
SORRY. THAT WASN'T YOURS TO CATCH.
NO PROBLEM.
YOU PULL "D"?
THIS KEEPS UP I'M GOING TO LIVE IN DETENTION.
MAYBE KORD COULD ARRANGE SOME KINDA HOME SCHOOLING THING FOR YOU.
NOT FUNNY.
JUST SAYIN'.
LOOK ON THE BRIGHT SIDE. YOUR FIRST PERIOD OF THE DAY'S LUNCH. CAN'T BEAT THAT.
SIGH...

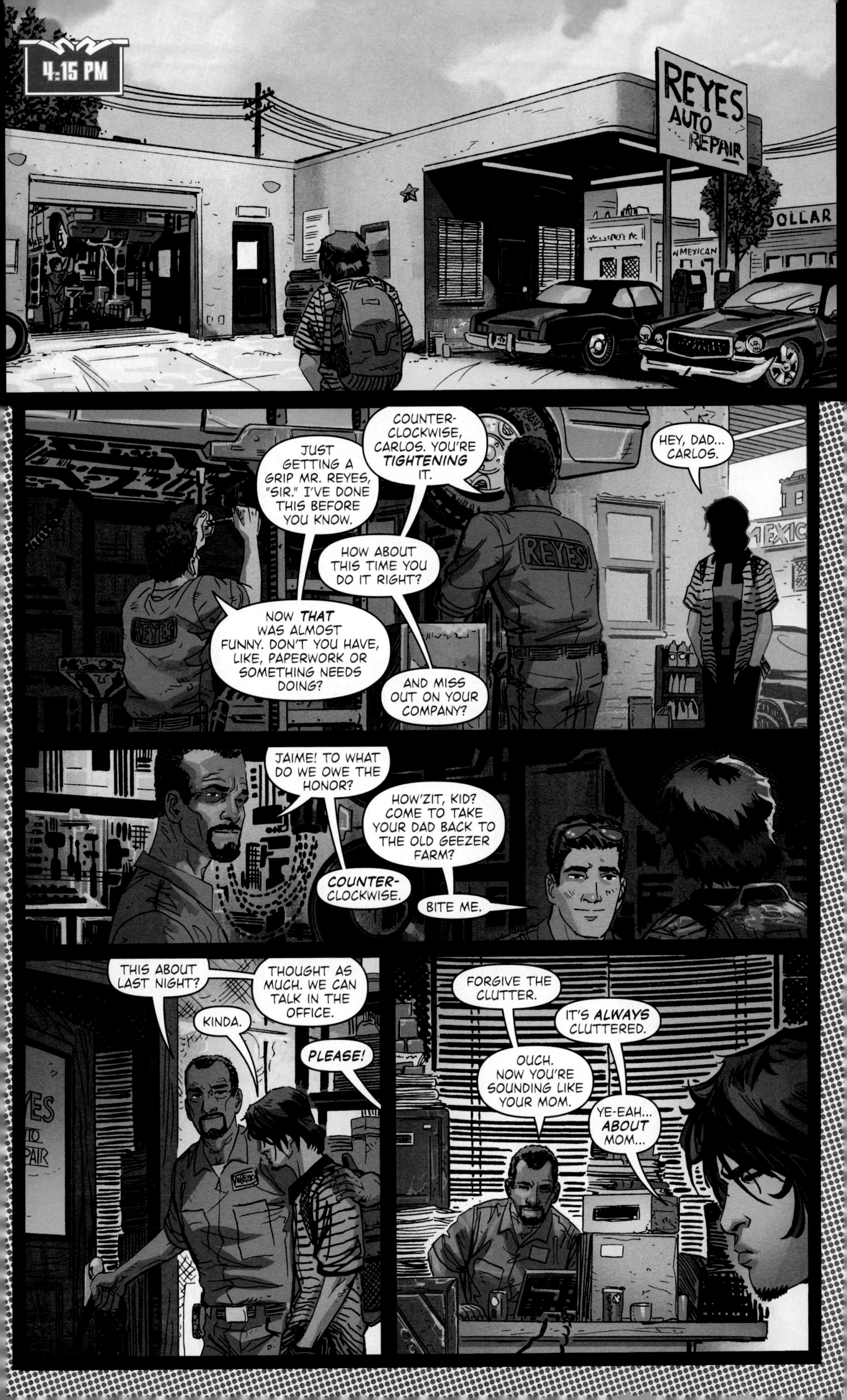
4:15 PM
REYES AUTO REPAIR
DOLLAR
MEXICAN
JUST GETTING A GRIP MR. REYES, "SIR." I'VE DONE THIS BEFORE YOU KNOW.
COUNTER-CLOCKWISE, CARLOS. YOU'RE TIGHTENING IT.
HOW ABOUT THIS TIME YOU DO IT RIGHT?
NOW THAT WAS ALMOST FUNNY. DON'T YOU HAVE, LIKE, PAPERWORK OR SOMETHING NEEDS DOING?
AND MISS OUT ON YOUR COMPANY?
HEY, DAD... CARLOS.
REYES
JAIME! TO WHAT DO WE OWE THE HONOR?
COUNTER-CLOCKWISE.
HOW'ZIT, KID? COME TO TAKE YOUR DAD BACK TO THE OLD GEEZER FARM?
BITE ME.
THIS ABOUT LAST NIGHT?
KINDA.
THOUGHT AS MUCH. WE CAN TALK IN THE OFFICE.
PLEASE!
FORGIVE THE CLUTTER.
IT'S ALWAYS CLUTTERED.
OUCH. NOW YOU'RE SOUNDING LIKE YOUR MOM.
YE-EAH... ABOUT MOM...

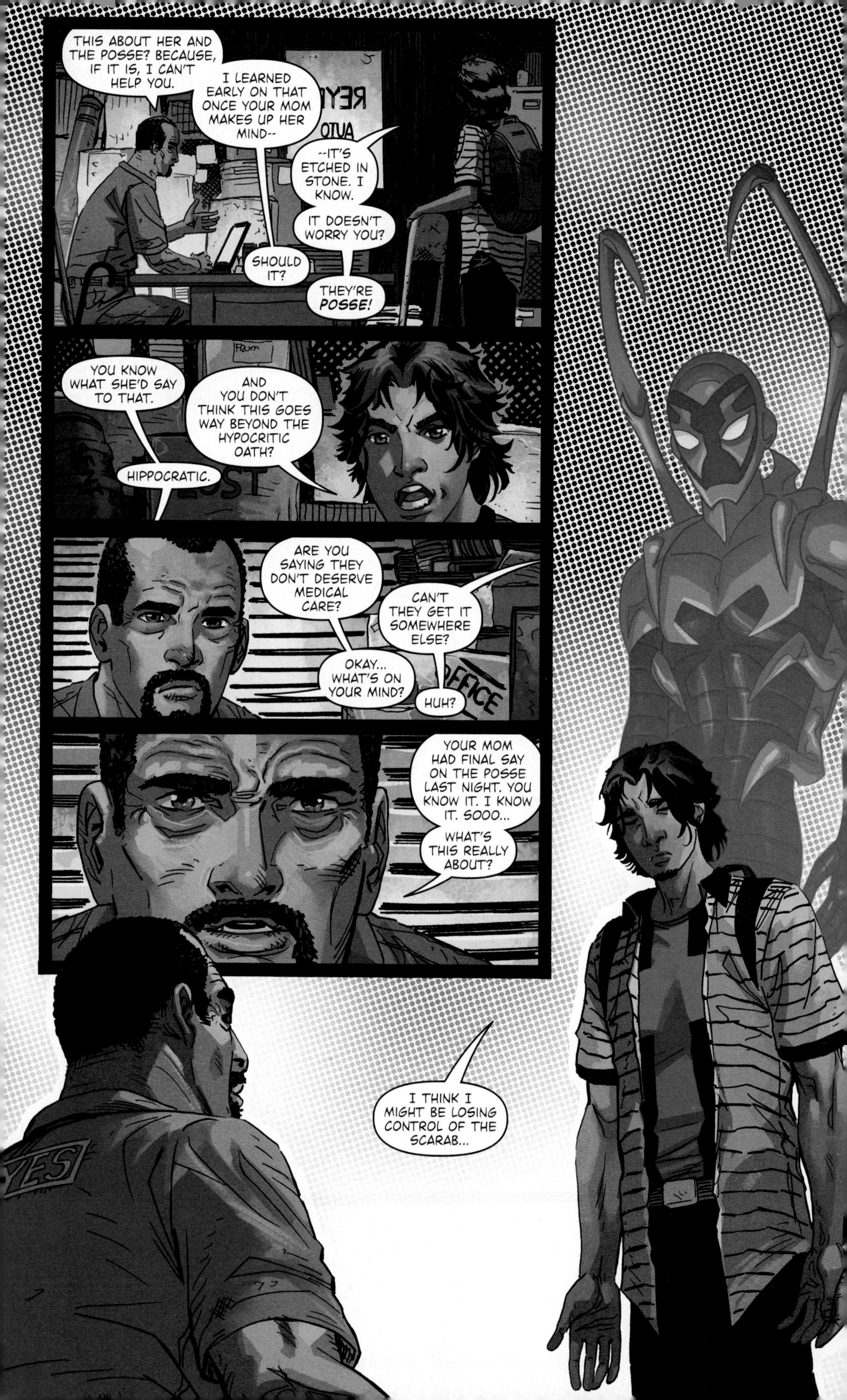
THIS ABOUT HER AND THE POSSE? BECAUSE, IF IT IS, I CAN'T HELP YOU.
I LEARNED EARLY ON THAT ONCE YOUR MOM MAKES UP HER MIND--
--IT'S ETCHED IN STONE. I KNOW.
IT DOESN'T WORRY YOU?
SHOULD IT?
THEY'RE POSSE!
YOU KNOW WHAT SHE'D SAY TO THAT.
AND YOU DON'T THINK THIS GOES WAY BEYOND THE HYPOCRITIC OATH?
HIPPOCRATIC.
ARE YOU SAYING THEY DON'T DESERVE MEDICAL CARE?
CAN'T THEY GET IT SOMEWHERE ELSE?
OKAY... WHAT'S ON YOUR MIND?
HUH?
YOUR MOM HAD FINAL SAY ON THE POSSE LAST NIGHT. YOU KNOW IT. I KNOW IT. SOOO...
WHAT'S THIS REALLY ABOUT?
I THINK I MIGHT BE LOSING CONTROL OF THE SCARAB...

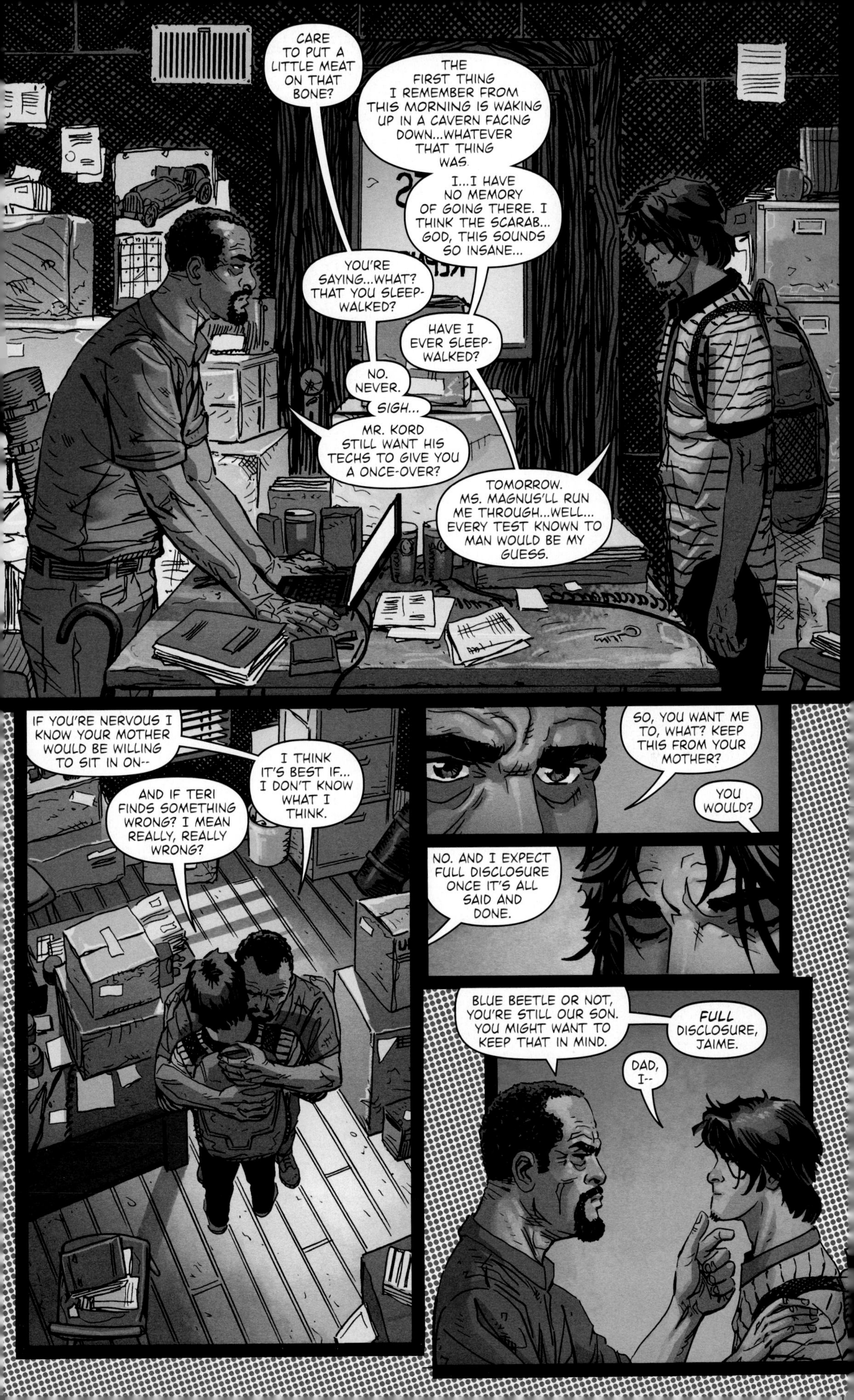
CARE TO PUT A LITTLE MEAT ON THAT BONE?
THE FIRST THING I REMEMBER FROM THIS MORNING IS WAKING UP IN A CAVERN FACING DOWN...WHATEVER THAT THING WAS.
I...I HAVE NO MEMORY OF GOING THERE. I THINK THE SCARAB... GOD, THIS SOUNDS SO INSANE...
YOU'RE SAYING...WHAT? THAT YOU SLEEP-WALKED?
HAVE I EVER SLEEP-WALKED?
NO. NEVER.
SIGH...
MR. KORD STILL WANT HIS TECHS TO GIVE YOU A ONCE-OVER?
TOMORROW. MS. MAGNUS'LL RUN ME THROUGH...WELL... EVERY TEST KNOWN TO MAN WOULD BE MY GUESS.
IF YOU'RE NERVOUS I KNOW YOUR MOTHER WOULD BE WILLING TO SIT IN ON--
I THINK IT'S BEST IF... I DON'T KNOW WHAT I THINK.
AND IF TERI FINDS SOMETHING WRONG? I MEAN REALLY, REALLY WRONG?
SO, YOU WANT ME TO, WHAT? KEEP THIS FROM YOUR MOTHER?
YOU WOULD?
NO. AND I EXPECT FULL DISCLOSURE ONCE IT'S ALL SAID AND DONE.
BLUE BEETLE OR NOT, YOU'RE STILL OUR SON. YOU MIGHT WANT TO KEEP THAT IN MIND.
FULL DISCLOSURE, JAIME.
DAD, I--

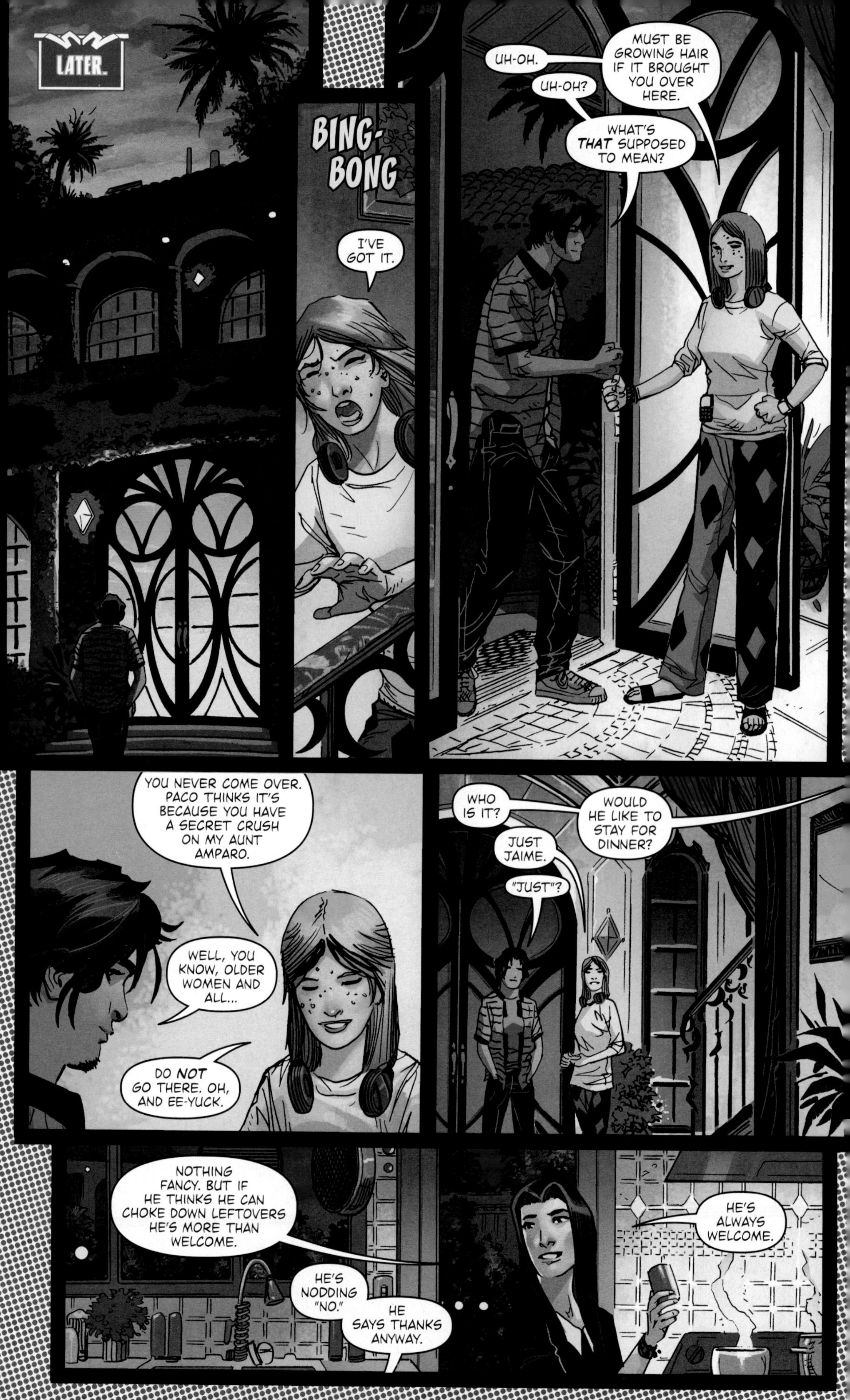
LATER.
BING-BONG
I'VE GOT IT.
UH-OH.
MUST BE GROWING HAIR IF IT BROUGHT YOU OVER HERE.
UH-OH?
WHAT'S THAT SUPPOSED TO MEAN?
YOU NEVER COME OVER. PACO THINKS IT'S BECAUSE YOU HAVE A SECRET CRUSH ON MY AUNT AMPARO.
WELL, YOU KNOW, OLDER WOMEN AND ALL...
DO NOT GO THERE. OH, AND EE-YUCK.
WHO IS IT?
WOULD HE LIKE TO STAY FOR DINNER?
JUST JAIME.
"JUST"?
NOTHING FANCY. BUT IF HE THINKS HE CAN CHOKE DOWN LEFTOVERS HE'S MORE THAN WELCOME.
HE'S NODDING "NO."
HE SAYS THANKS ANYWAY.
HE'S ALWAYS WELCOME.

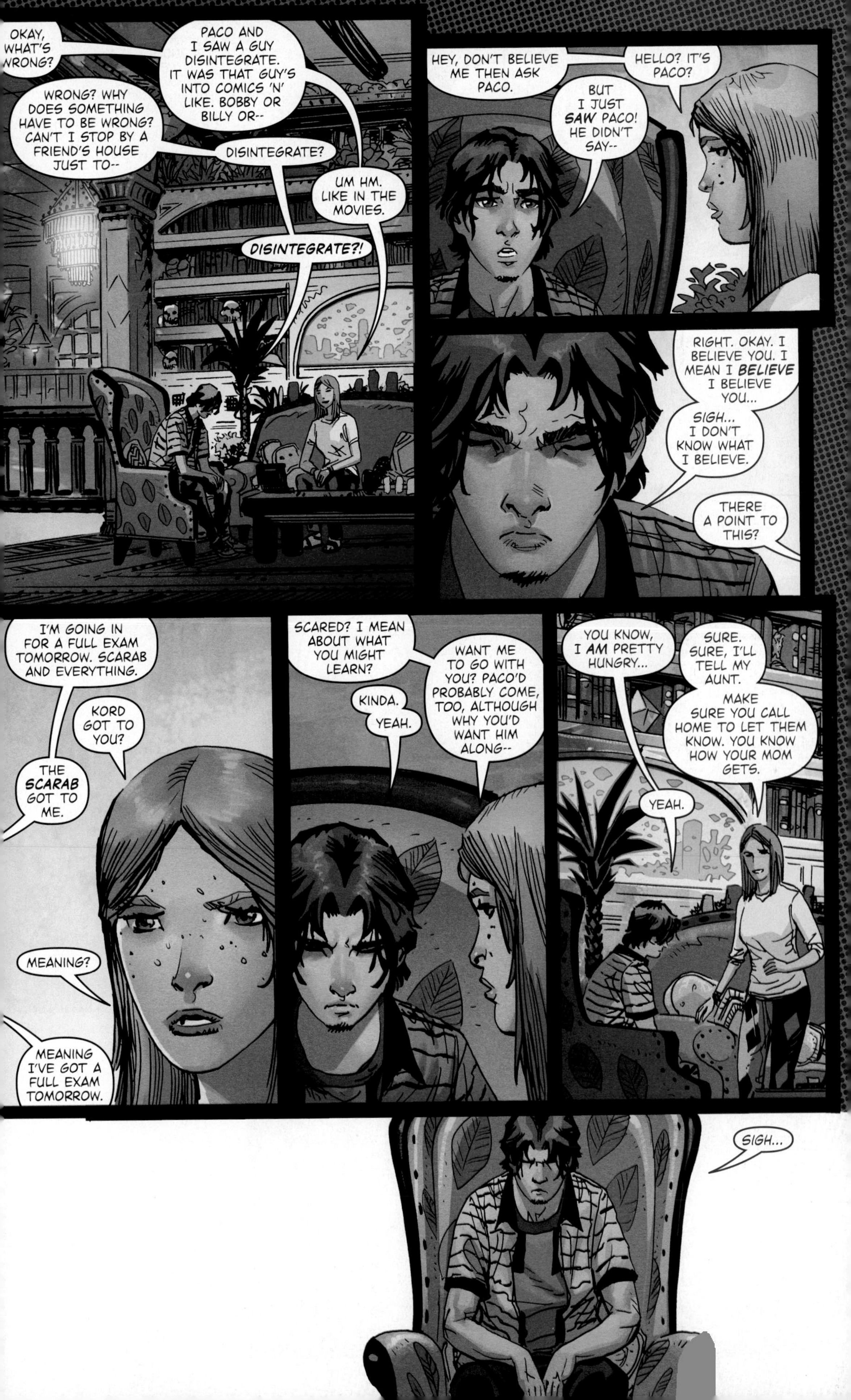
OKAY, WHAT'S WRONG?
PACO AND I SAW A GUY DISINTEGRATE. IT WAS THAT GUY'S INTO COMICS 'N' LIKE. BOBBY OR BILLY OR--
WRONG? WHY DOES SOMETHING HAVE TO BE WRONG? CAN'T I STOP BY A FRIEND'S HOUSE JUST TO--
DISINTEGRATE?
UM HM. LIKE IN THE MOVIES.
DISINTEGRATE?!
HEY, DON'T BELIEVE ME THEN ASK PACO.
HELLO? IT'S PACO?
BUT I JUST SAW PACO! HE DIDN'T SAY--
RIGHT. OKAY. I BELIEVE YOU. I MEAN I BELIEVE I BELIEVE YOU...
SIGH... I DON'T KNOW WHAT I BELIEVE.
THERE A POINT TO THIS?
I'M GOING IN FOR A FULL EXAM TOMORROW. SCARAB AND EVERYTHING.
KORD GOT TO YOU?
THE SCARAB GOT TO ME.
MEANING?
MEANING I'VE GOT A FULL EXAM TOMORROW.
SCARED? I MEAN ABOUT WHAT YOU MIGHT LEARN?
KINDA.
YEAH.
WANT ME TO GO WITH YOU? PACO'D PROBABLY COME, TOO, ALTHOUGH WHY YOU'D WANT HIM ALONG--
YOU KNOW, I AM PRETTY HUNGRY...
SURE. SURE, I'LL TELL MY AUNT.
MAKE SURE YOU CALL HOME TO LET THEM KNOW. YOU KNOW HOW YOUR MOM GETS.
YEAH.
SIGH...

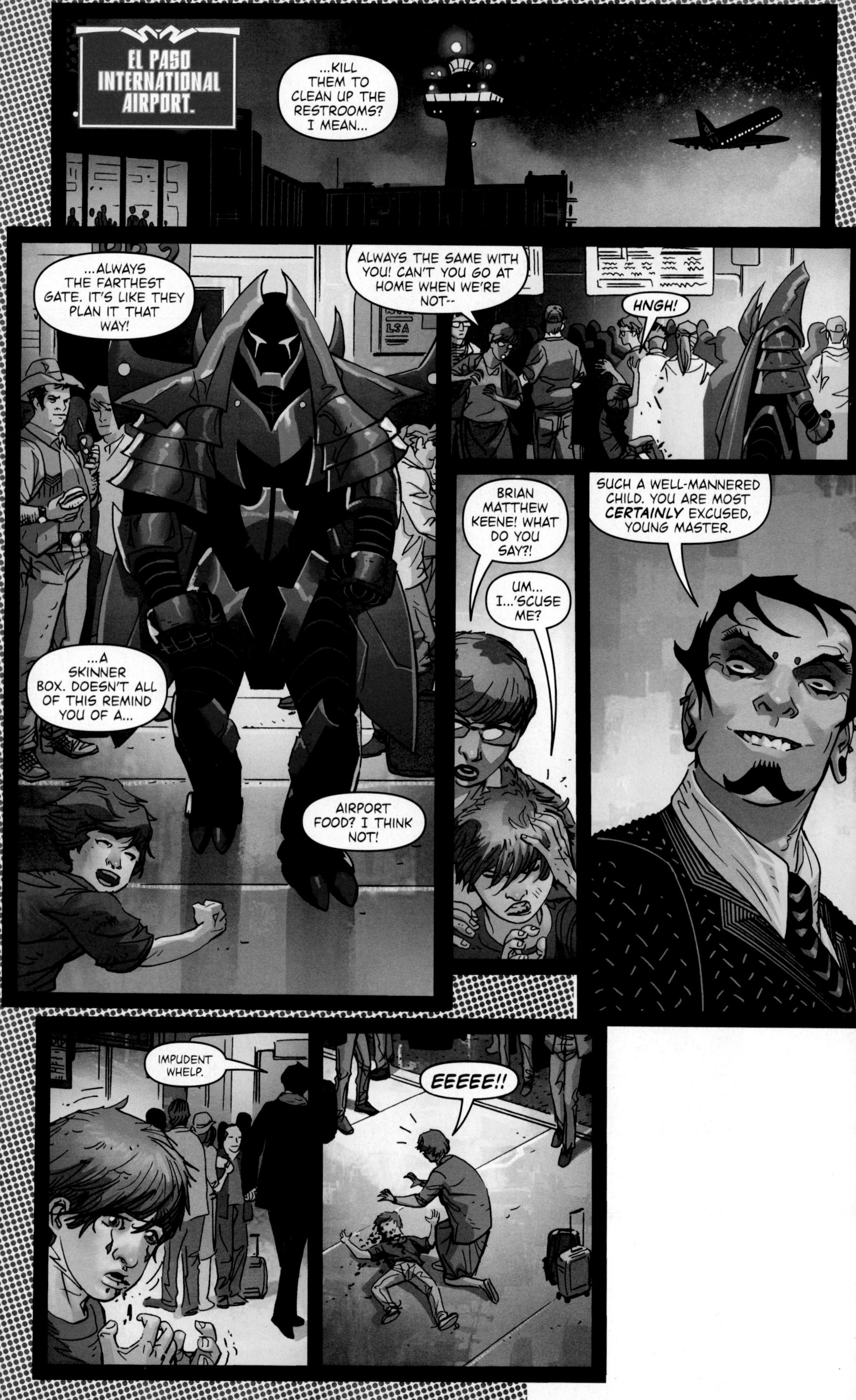
EL PASO INTERNATIONAL AIRPORT.
...KILL THEM TO CLEAN UP THE RESTROOMS? I MEAN...
...ALWAYS THE FARTHEST GATE. IT'S LIKE THEY PLAN IT THAT WAY!
...A SKINNER BOX. DOESN'T ALL OF THIS REMIND YOU OF A...
AIRPORT FOOD? I THINK NOT!
ALWAYS THE SAME WITH YOU! CAN'T YOU GO AT HOME WHEN WE'RE NOT--
HNGH!
BRIAN MATTHEW KEENE! WHAT DO YOU SAY?!
UM... I...'SCUSE ME?
SUCH A WELL-MANNERED CHILD. YOU ARE MOST CERTAINLY EXCUSED, YOUNG MASTER.
IMPUDENT WHELP.
EEEEE!!

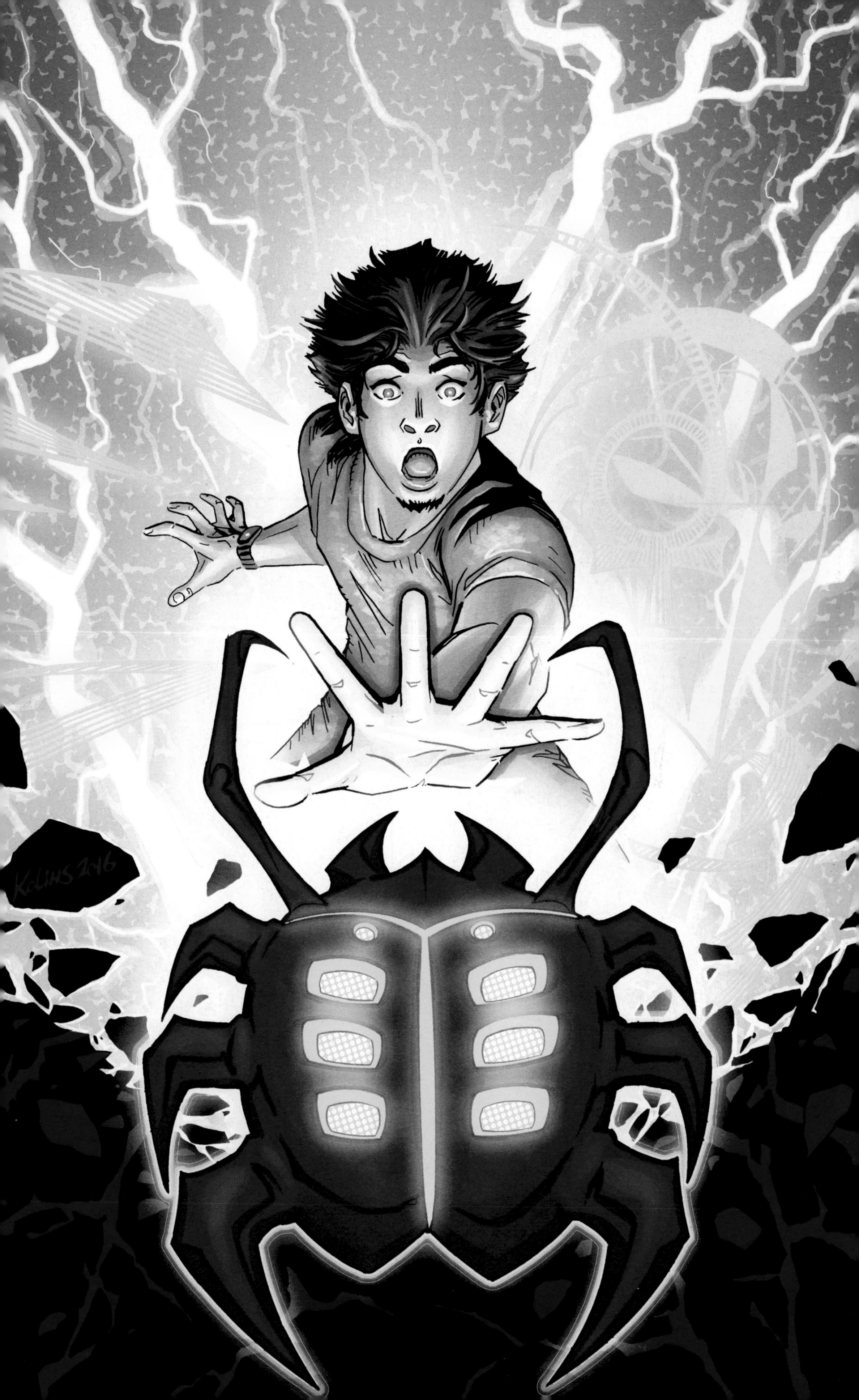

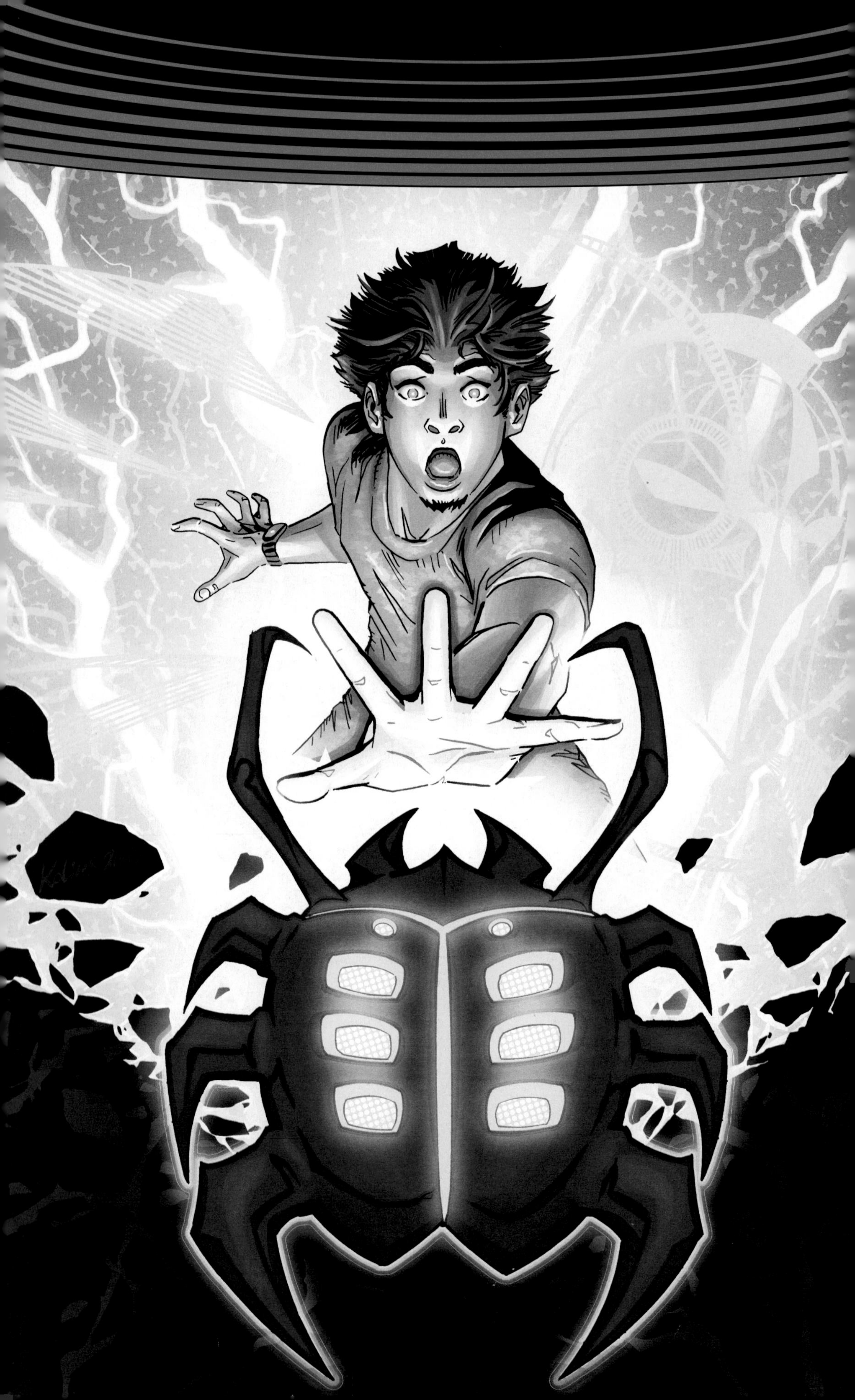

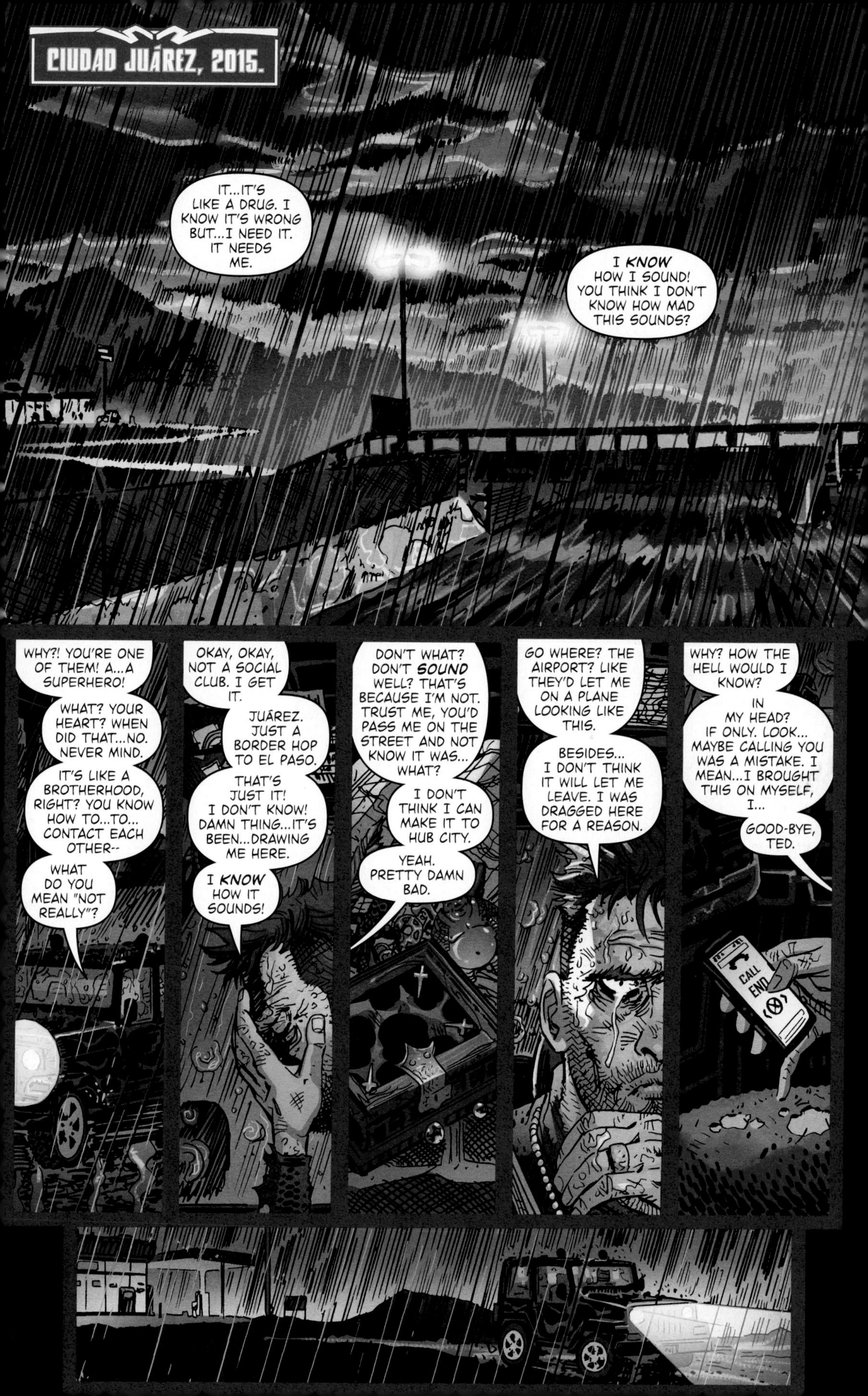
CIUDAD JUÁREZ, 2015.
IT...IT'S LIKE A DRUG. I KNOW IT'S WRONG BUT...I NEED IT. IT NEEDS ME.
I KNOW HOW I SOUND! YOU THINK I DON'T KNOW HOW MAD THIS SOUNDS?
WHY?! YOU'RE ONE OF THEM! A...A SUPERHERO!
WHAT? YOUR HEART? WHEN DID THAT...NO. NEVER MIND.
IT'S LIKE A BROTHERHOOD, RIGHT? YOU KNOW HOW TO...TO... CONTACT EACH OTHER--
WHAT DO YOU MEAN "NOT REALLY"?
OKAY, OKAY, NOT A SOCIAL CLUB. I GET IT.
JUÁREZ. JUST A BORDER HOP TO EL PASO.
THAT'S JUST IT! I DON'T KNOW! DAMN THING...IT'S BEEN...DRAWING ME HERE.
I KNOW HOW IT SOUNDS!
DON'T WHAT? DON'T SOUND WELL? THAT'S BECAUSE I'M NOT. TRUST ME, YOU'D PASS ME ON THE STREET AND NOT KNOW IT WAS... WHAT?
I DON'T THINK I CAN MAKE IT TO HUB CITY.
YEAH. PRETTY DAMN BAD.
GO WHERE? THE AIRPORT? LIKE THEY'D LET ME ON A PLANE LOOKING LIKE THIS.
BESIDES... I DON'T THINK IT WILL LET ME LEAVE. I WAS DRAGGED HERE FOR A REASON.
WHY? HOW THE HELL WOULD I KNOW?
IN MY HEAD? IF ONLY. LOOK... MAYBE CALLING YOU WAS A MISTAKE. I MEAN...I BROUGHT THIS ON MYSELF, I...
GOOD-BYE, TED.
CALL END

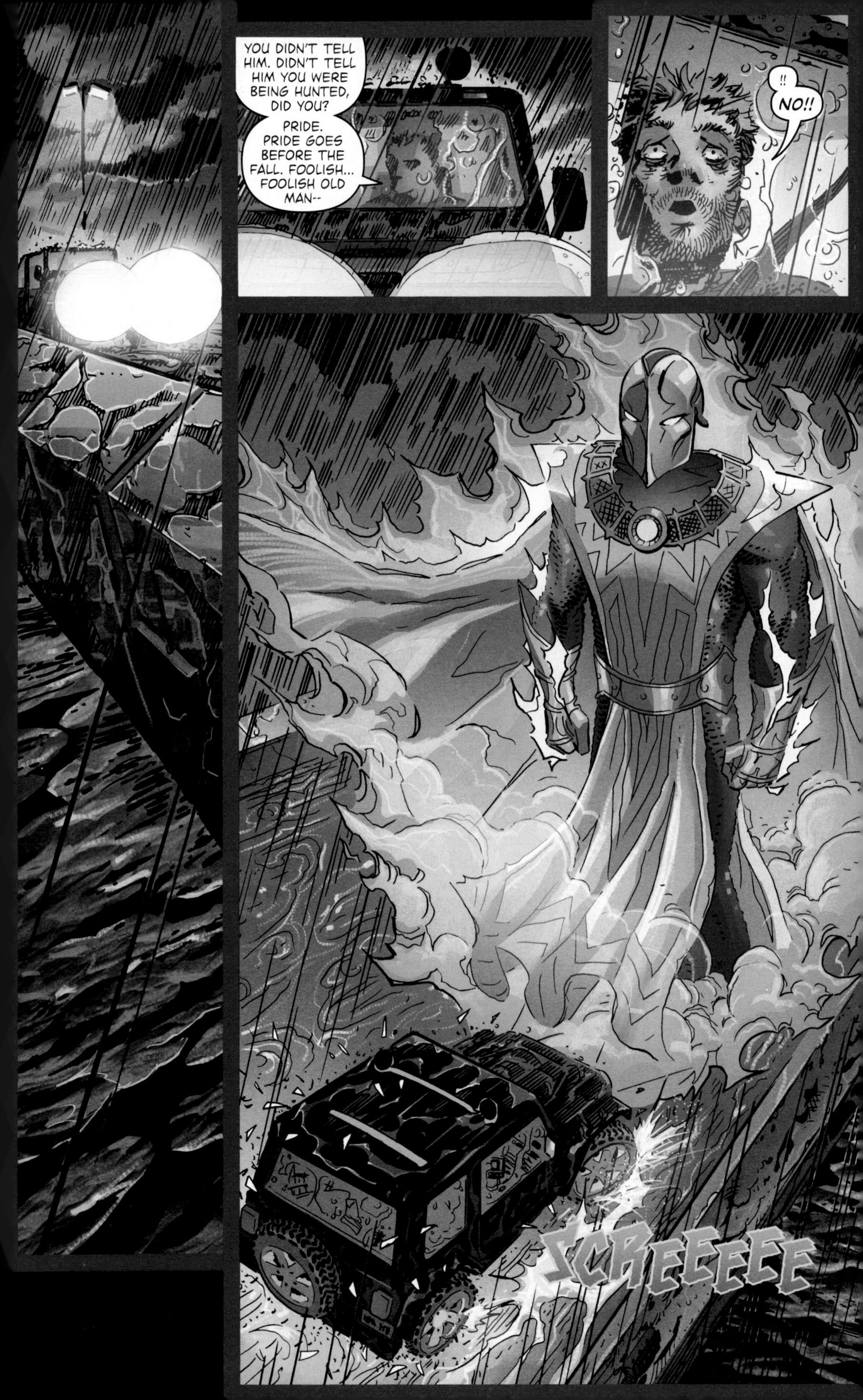
YOU DIDN'T TELL HIM. DIDN'T TELL HIM YOU WERE BEING HUNTED, DID YOU?
PRIDE. PRIDE GOES BEFORE THE FALL. FOOLISH... FOOLISH OLD MAN--
!!
NO!!
SCREEEEEE

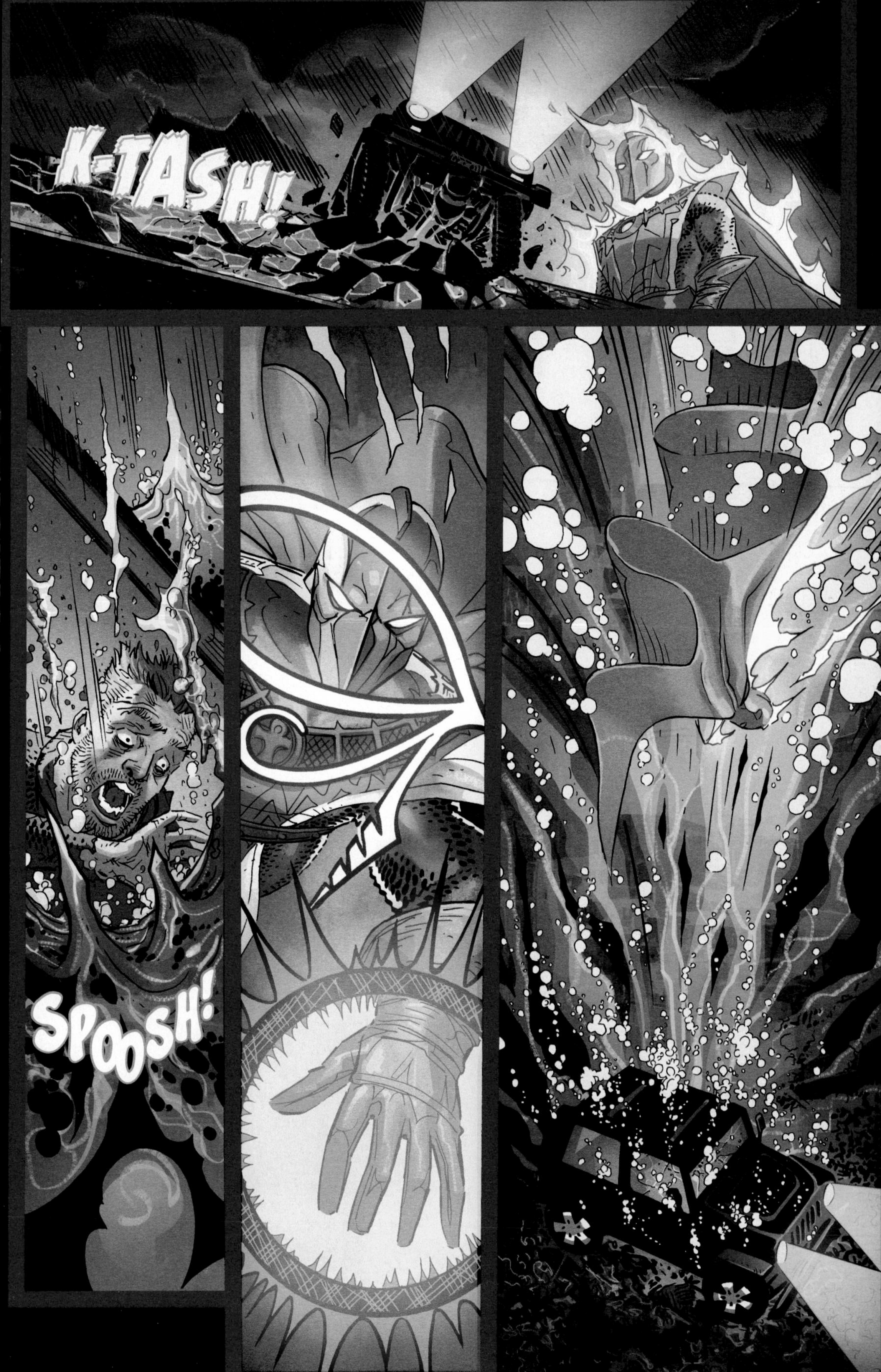
K-TASH!
SPOOSH!

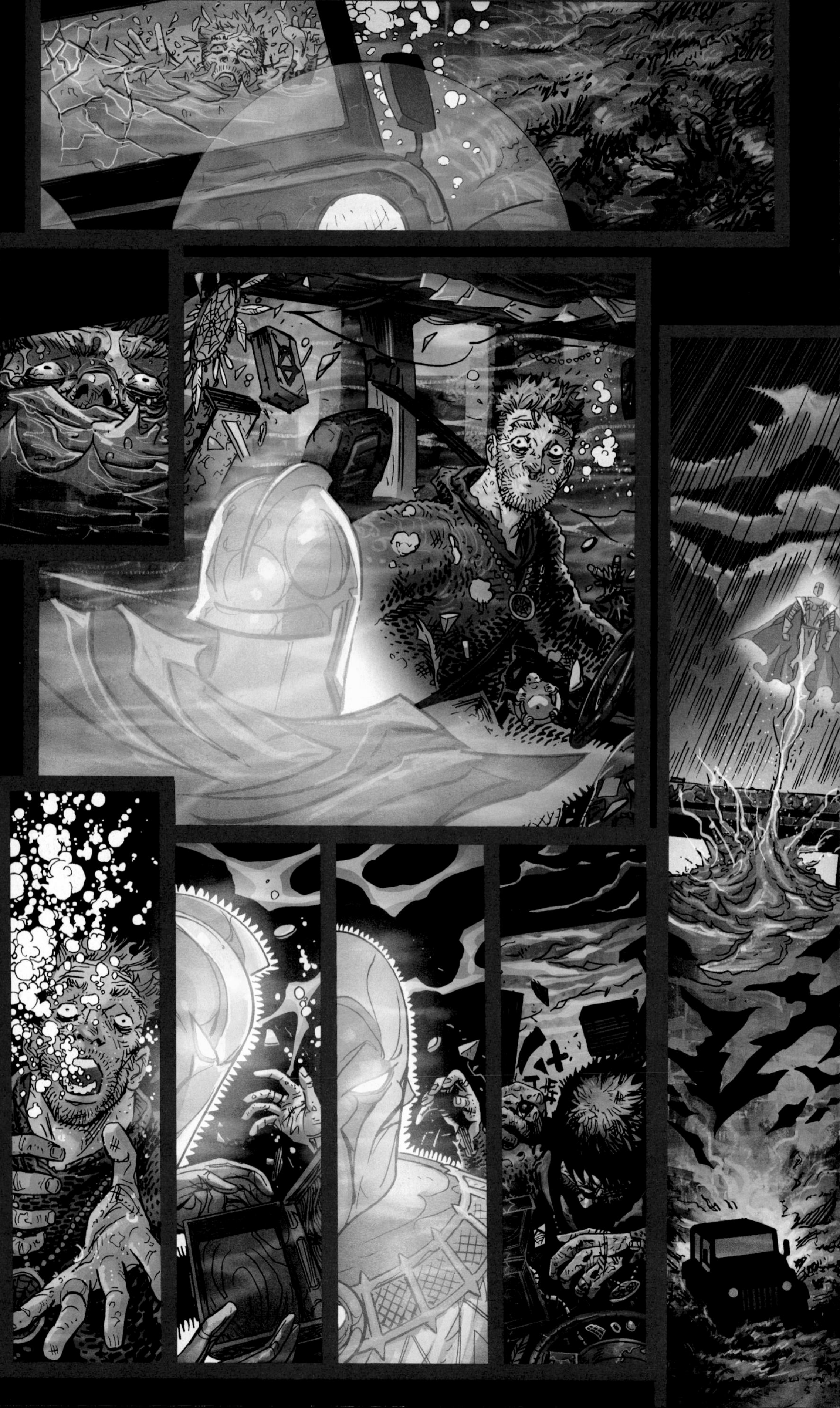

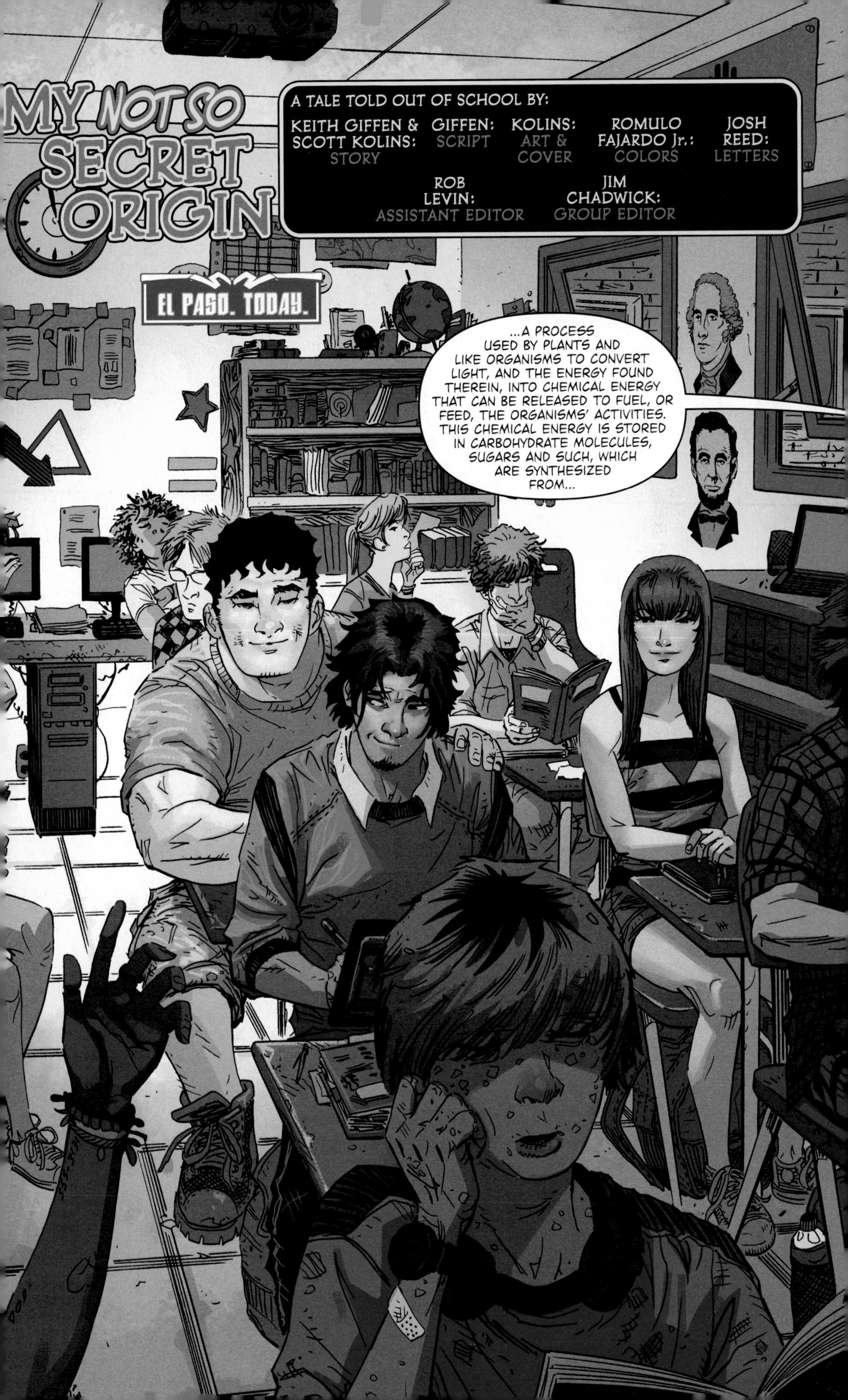
MY NOT SO SECRET ORIGIN
A TALE TOLD OUT OF SCHOOL BY:
KEITH GIFFEN & SCOTT KOLINS: STORY
GIFFEN: SCRIPT
KOLINS: ART & COVER
ROMULO FAJARDO Jr.: COLORS
JOSH REED: LETTERS
ROB LEVIN: ASSISTANT EDITOR
JIM CHADWICK: GROUP EDITOR
EL PASO. TODAY.
...A PROCESS USED BY PLANTS AND LIKE ORGANISMS TO CONVERT LIGHT, AND THE ENERGY FOUND THEREIN, INTO CHEMICAL ENERGY THAT CAN BE RELEASED TO FUEL, OR FEED, THE ORGANISMS' ACTIVITIES. THIS CHEMICAL ENERGY IS STORED IN CARBOHYDRATE MOLECULES, SUGARS AND SUCH, WHICH ARE SYNTHESIZED FROM...

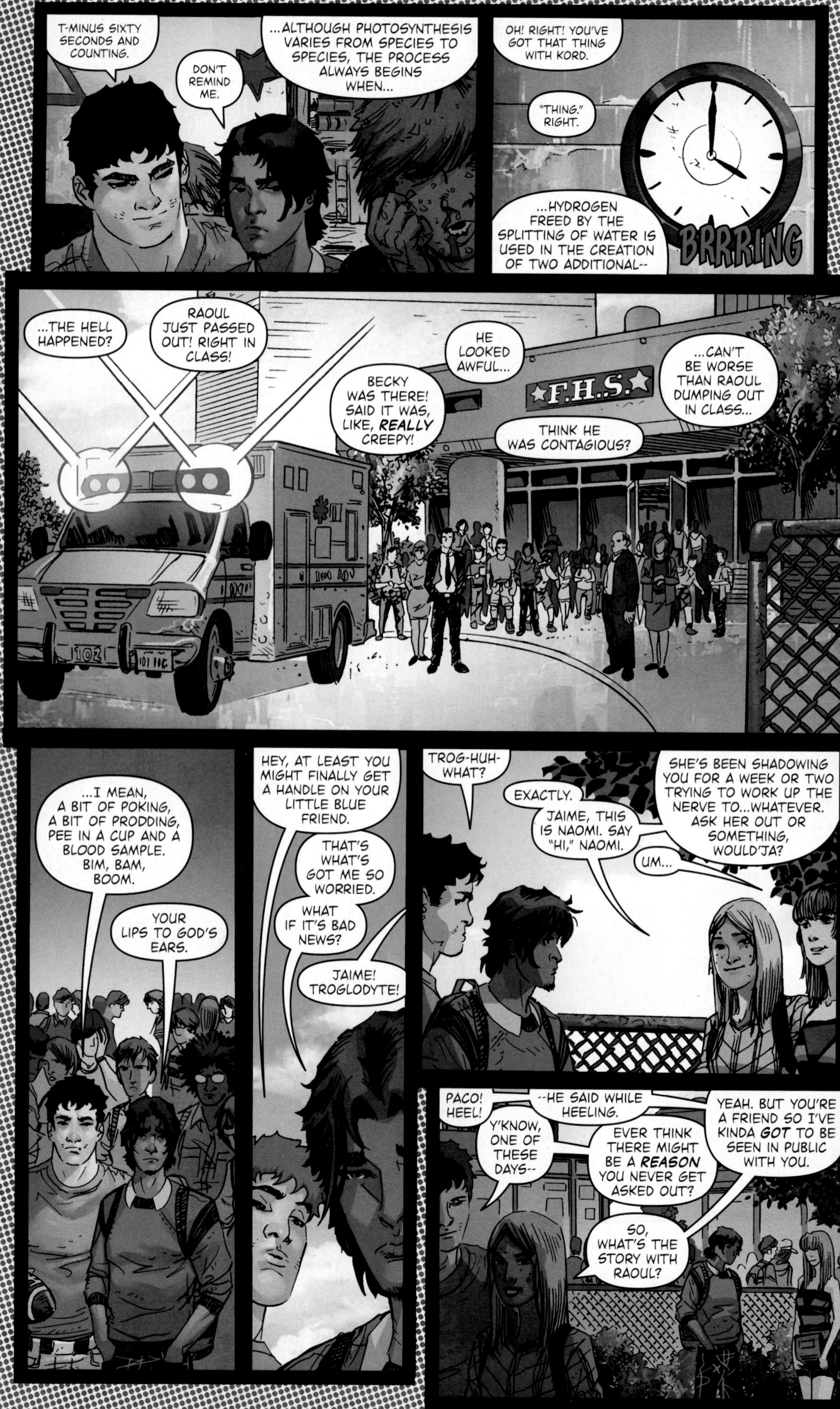
T-MINUS SIXTY SECONDS AND COUNTING.
DON'T REMIND ME.
...ALTHOUGH PHOTOSYNTHESIS VARIES FROM SPECIES TO SPECIES, THE PROCESS ALWAYS BEGINS WHEN...
OH! RIGHT! YOU'VE GOT THAT THING WITH KORD.
"THING." RIGHT.
...HYDROGEN FREED BY THE SPLITTING OF WATER IS USED IN THE CREATION OF TWO ADDITIONAL--
BRRRING
...THE HELL HAPPENED?
RAOUL JUST PASSED OUT! RIGHT IN CLASS!
BECKY WAS THERE! SAID IT WAS, LIKE, REALLY CREEPY!
HE LOOKED AWFUL...
F.H.S.
THINK HE WAS CONTAGIOUS?
...CAN'T BE WORSE THAN RAOUL DUMPING OUT IN CLASS...
102
...I MEAN, A BIT OF POKING, A BIT OF PRODDING, PEE IN A CUP AND A BLOOD SAMPLE. BIM, BAM, BOOM.
YOUR LIPS TO GOD'S EARS.
HEY, AT LEAST YOU MIGHT FINALLY GET A HANDLE ON YOUR LITTLE BLUE FRIEND.
THAT'S WHAT'S GOT ME SO WORRIED.
WHAT IF IT'S BAD NEWS?
JAIME! TROGLODYTE!
TROG-HUH-WHAT?
EXACTLY.
JAIME, THIS IS NAOMI. SAY "HI," NAOMI.
SHE'S BEEN SHADOWING YOU FOR A WEEK OR TWO TRYING TO WORK UP THE NERVE TO...WHATEVER. ASK HER OUT OR SOMETHING, WOULD'JA?
UM...
PACO! HEEL!
--HE SAID WHILE HEELING.
Y'KNOW, ONE OF THESE DAYS--
EVER THINK THERE MIGHT BE A REASON YOU NEVER GET ASKED OUT?
YEAH. BUT YOU'RE A FRIEND SO I'VE KINDA GOT TO BE SEEN IN PUBLIC WITH YOU.
SO, WHAT'S THE STORY WITH RAOUL?

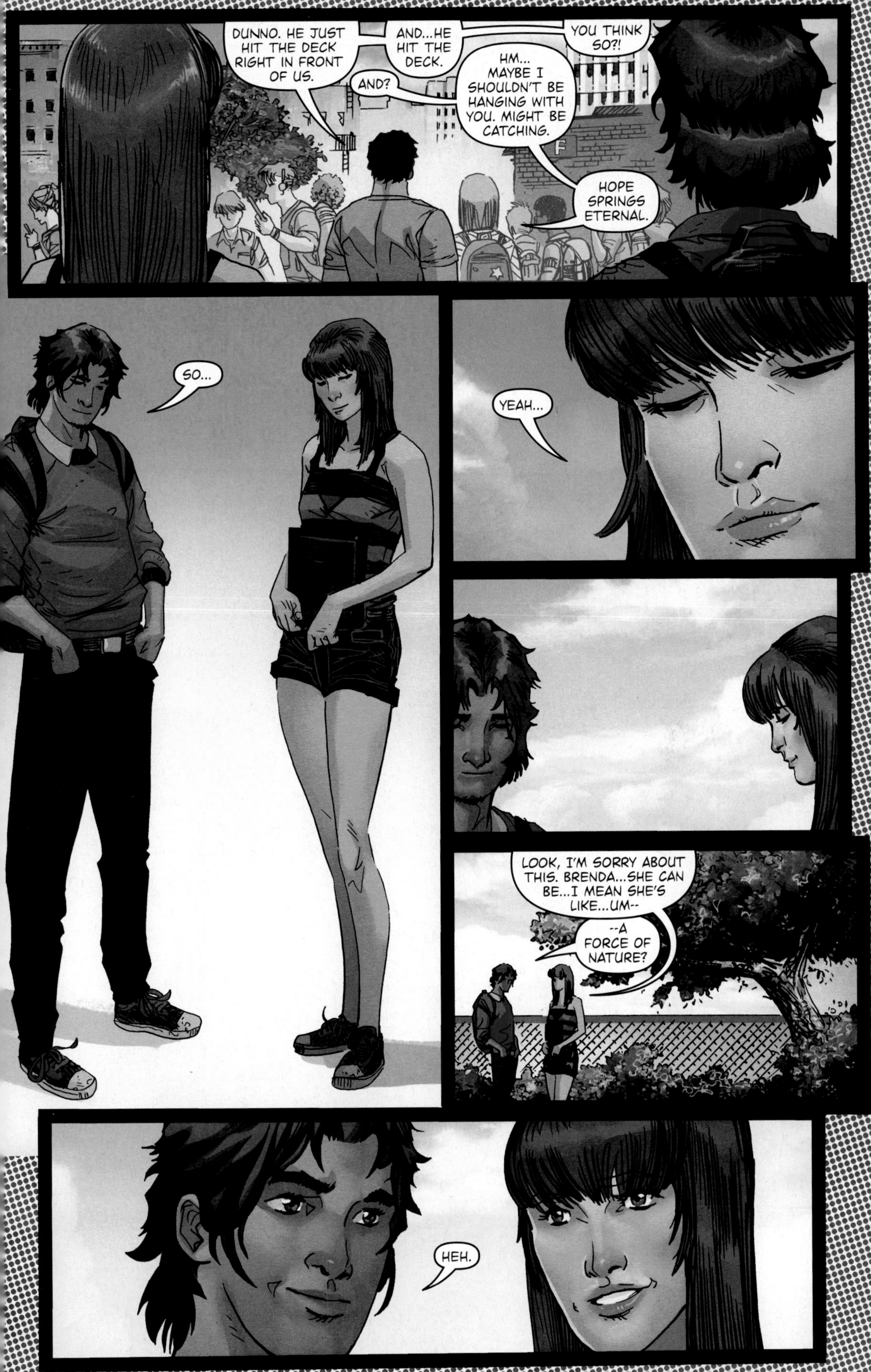
DUNNO. HE JUST HIT THE DECK RIGHT IN FRONT OF US.
AND...HE HIT THE DECK.
YOU THINK SO?!
AND?
HM... MAYBE I SHOULDN'T BE HANGING WITH YOU. MIGHT BE CATCHING.
HOPE SPRINGS ETERNAL.
SO...
YEAH...
LOOK, I'M SORRY ABOUT THIS. BRENDA...SHE CAN BE...I MEAN SHE'S LIKE...UM--
--A FORCE OF NATURE?
HEH.

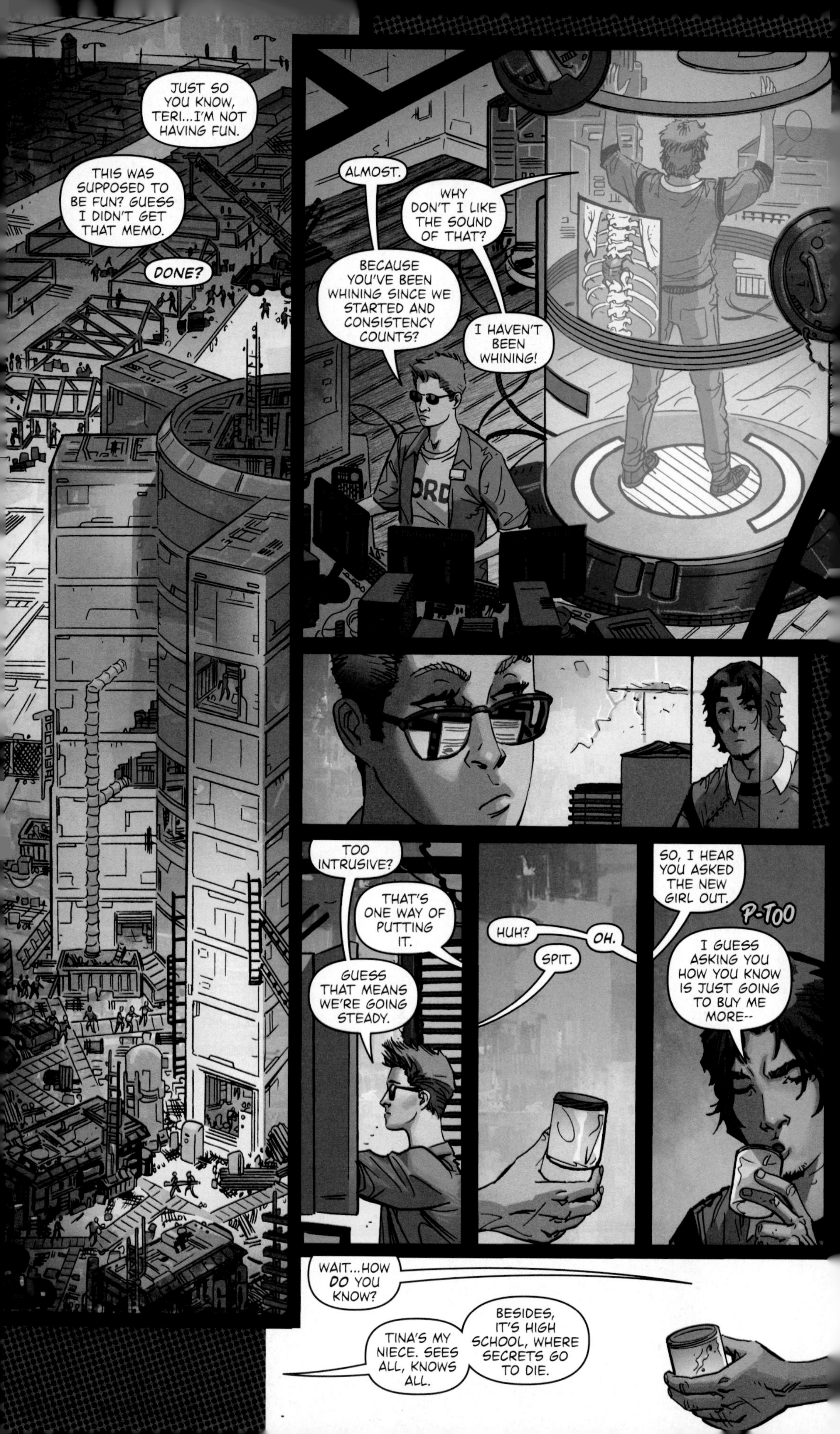
JUST SO YOU KNOW, TERI...I'M NOT HAVING FUN.
THIS WAS SUPPOSED TO BE FUN? GUESS I DIDN'T GET THAT MEMO.
DONE?
ALMOST.
WHY DON'T I LIKE THE SOUND OF THAT?
BECAUSE YOU'VE BEEN WHINING SINCE WE STARTED AND CONSISTENCY COUNTS?
I HAVEN'T BEEN WHINING!
TOO INTRUSIVE?
THAT'S ONE WAY OF PUTTING IT.
GUESS THAT MEANS WE'RE GOING STEADY.
HUH?
OH.
SPIT.
SO, I HEAR YOU ASKED THE NEW GIRL OUT.
P-TOO
I GUESS ASKING YOU HOW YOU KNOW IS JUST GOING TO BUY ME MORE--
WAIT...HOW *DO* YOU KNOW?
TINA'S MY NIECE. SEES ALL, KNOWS ALL.
BESIDES, IT'S HIGH SCHOOL, WHERE SECRETS GO TO DIE.

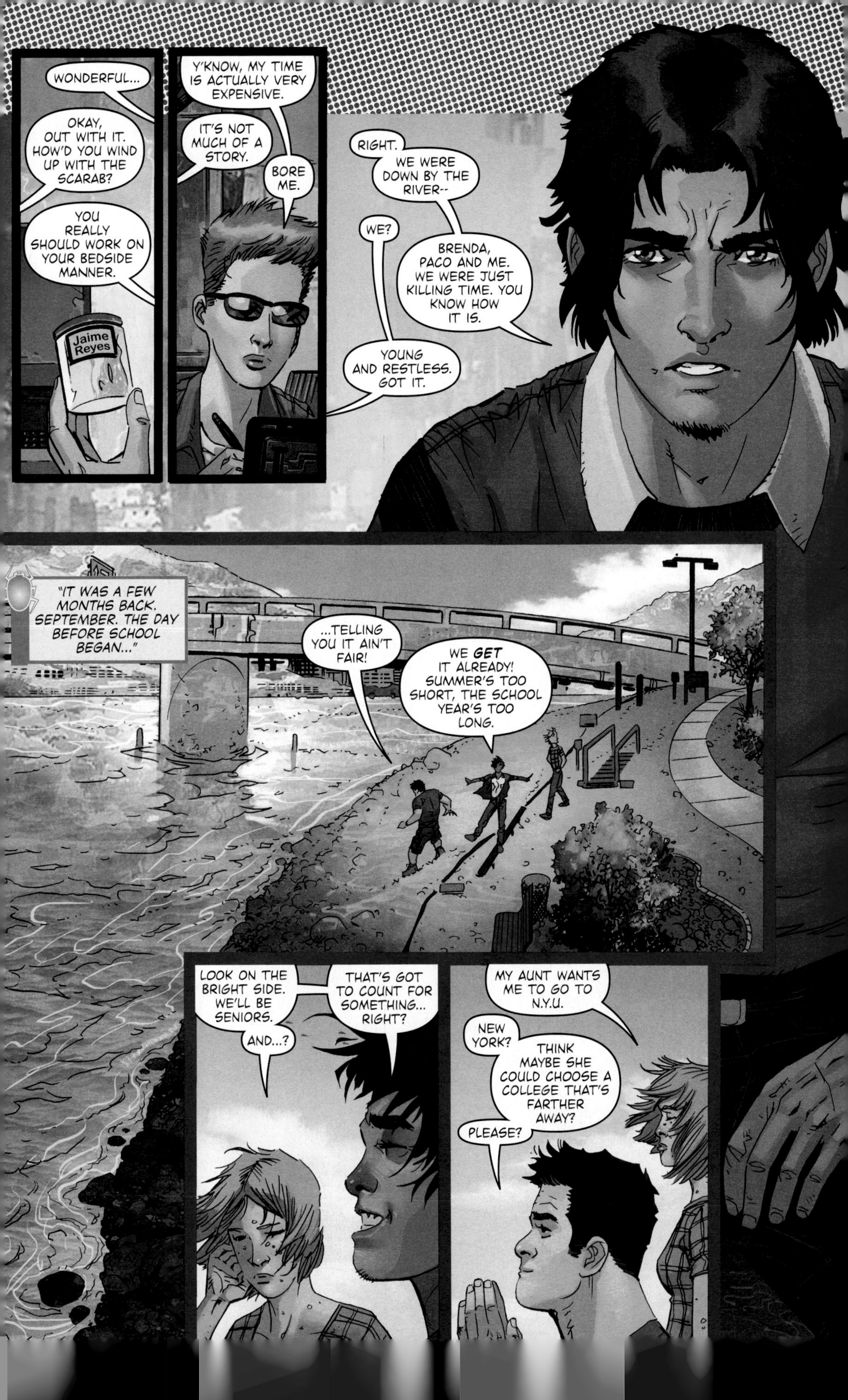
WONDERFUL...
OKAY, OUT WITH IT. HOW'D YOU WIND UP WITH THE SCARAB?
YOU REALLY SHOULD WORK ON YOUR BEDSIDE MANNER.
Jaime Reyes
Y'KNOW, MY TIME IS ACTUALLY VERY EXPENSIVE.
IT'S NOT MUCH OF A STORY.
BORE ME.
RIGHT. WE WERE DOWN BY THE RIVER--
WE?
BRENDA, PACO AND ME. WE WERE JUST KILLING TIME. YOU KNOW HOW IT IS.
YOUNG AND RESTLESS. GOT IT.
"IT WAS A FEW MONTHS BACK. SEPTEMBER. THE DAY BEFORE SCHOOL BEGAN..."
...TELLING YOU IT AIN'T FAIR!
WE **GET** IT ALREADY! SUMMER'S TOO SHORT, THE SCHOOL YEAR'S TOO LONG.
LOOK ON THE BRIGHT SIDE. WE'LL BE SENIORS.
AND...?
THAT'S GOT TO COUNT FOR SOMETHING... RIGHT?
MY AUNT WANTS ME TO GO TO N.Y.U.
NEW YORK?
THINK MAYBE SHE COULD CHOOSE A COLLEGE THAT'S FARTHER AWAY?
PLEASE?

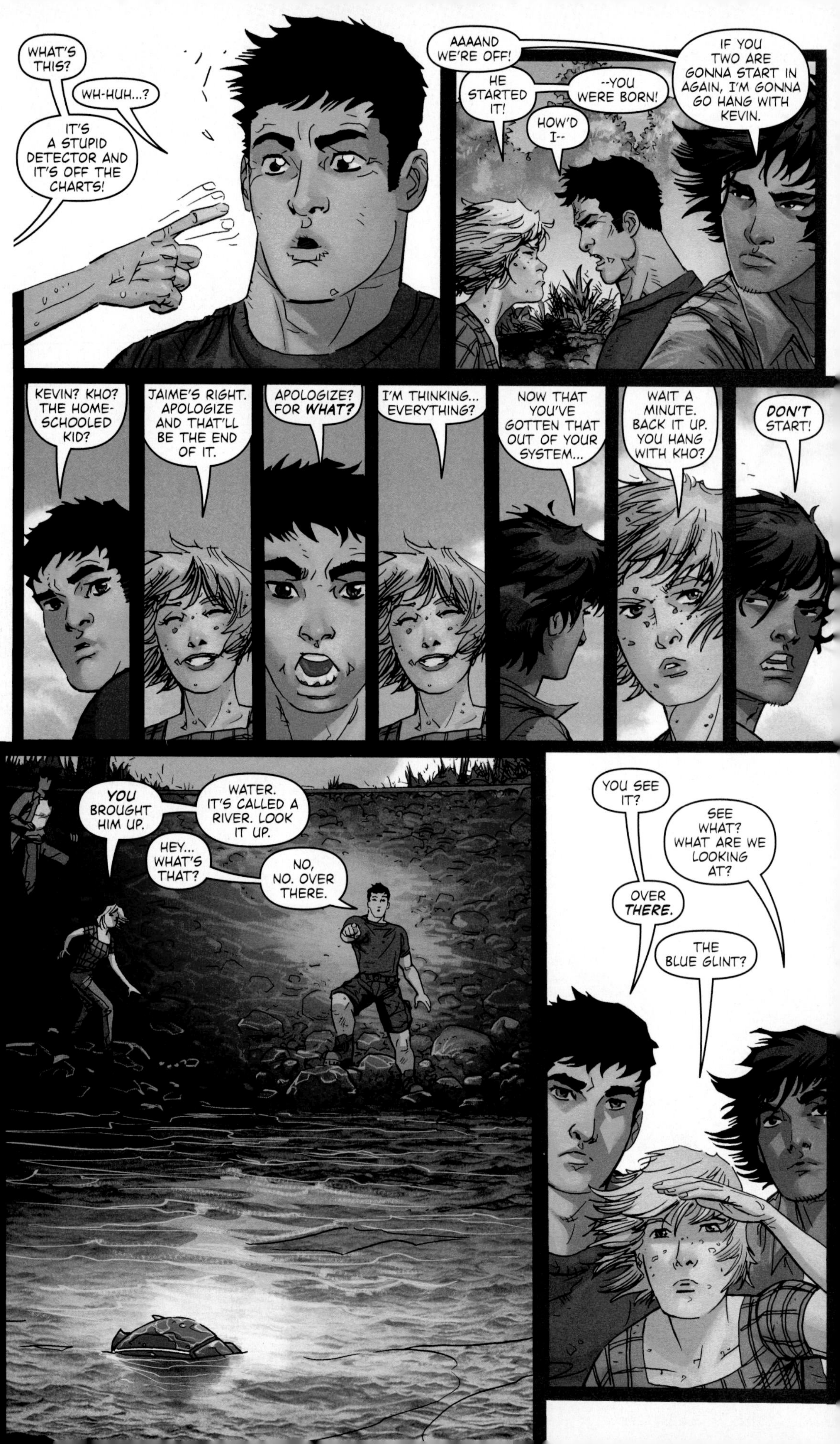
WHAT'S THIS?
WH-HUH...?
IT'S A STUPID DETECTOR AND IT'S OFF THE CHARTS!
AAAAND WE'RE OFF!
HE STARTED IT!
--YOU WERE BORN!
HOW'D I--
IF YOU TWO ARE GONNA START IN AGAIN, I'M GONNA GO HANG WITH KEVIN.
KEVIN? KHO? THE HOME-SCHOOLED KID?
JAIME'S RIGHT. APOLOGIZE AND THAT'LL BE THE END OF IT.
APOLOGIZE? FOR WHAT?
I'M THINKING... EVERYTHING?
NOW THAT YOU'VE GOTTEN THAT OUT OF YOUR SYSTEM...
WAIT A MINUTE. BACK IT UP. YOU HANG WITH KHO?
DON'T START!
YOU BROUGHT HIM UP.
WATER. IT'S CALLED A RIVER. LOOK IT UP.
HEY... WHAT'S THAT?
NO, NO. OVER THERE.
YOU SEE IT?
SEE WHAT? WHAT ARE WE LOOKING AT?
OVER THERE.
THE BLUE GLINT?

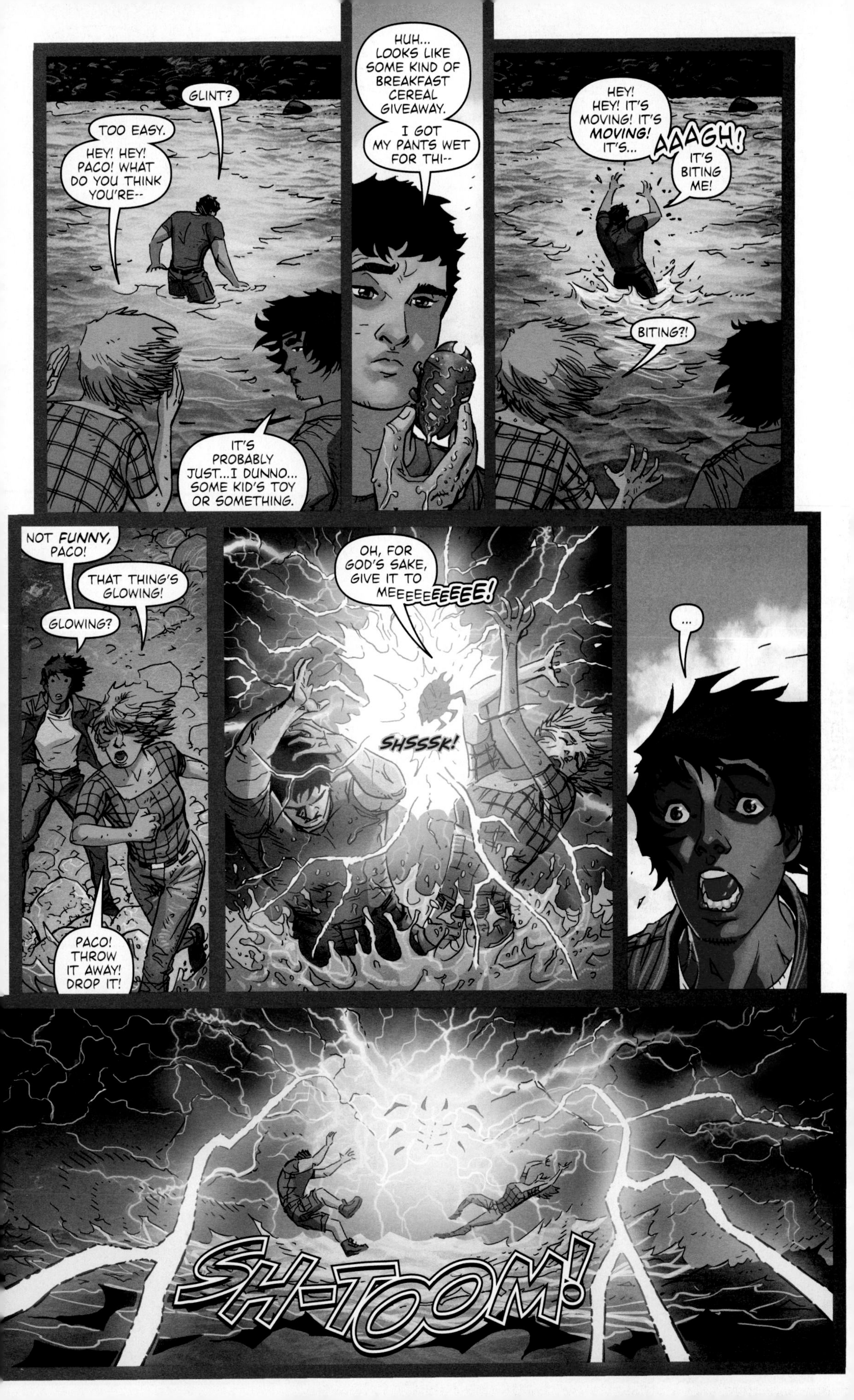
GLINT?
TOO EASY.
HEY! HEY! PACO! WHAT DO YOU THINK YOU'RE--
IT'S PROBABLY JUST...I DUNNO... SOME KID'S TOY OR SOMETHING.
HUH... LOOKS LIKE SOME KIND OF BREAKFAST CEREAL GIVEAWAY.
I GOT MY PANTS WET FOR THI--
HEY! HEY! IT'S MOVING! IT'S MOVING! IT'S...
AAAGH!
IT'S BITING ME!
BITING?!
NOT FUNNY, PACO!
THAT THING'S GLOWING!
GLOWING?
PACO! THROW IT AWAY! DROP IT!
OH, FOR GOD'S SAKE, GIVE IT TO MEEEEEEEEEE!
SHSSSK!
...
SH-TOOOM!

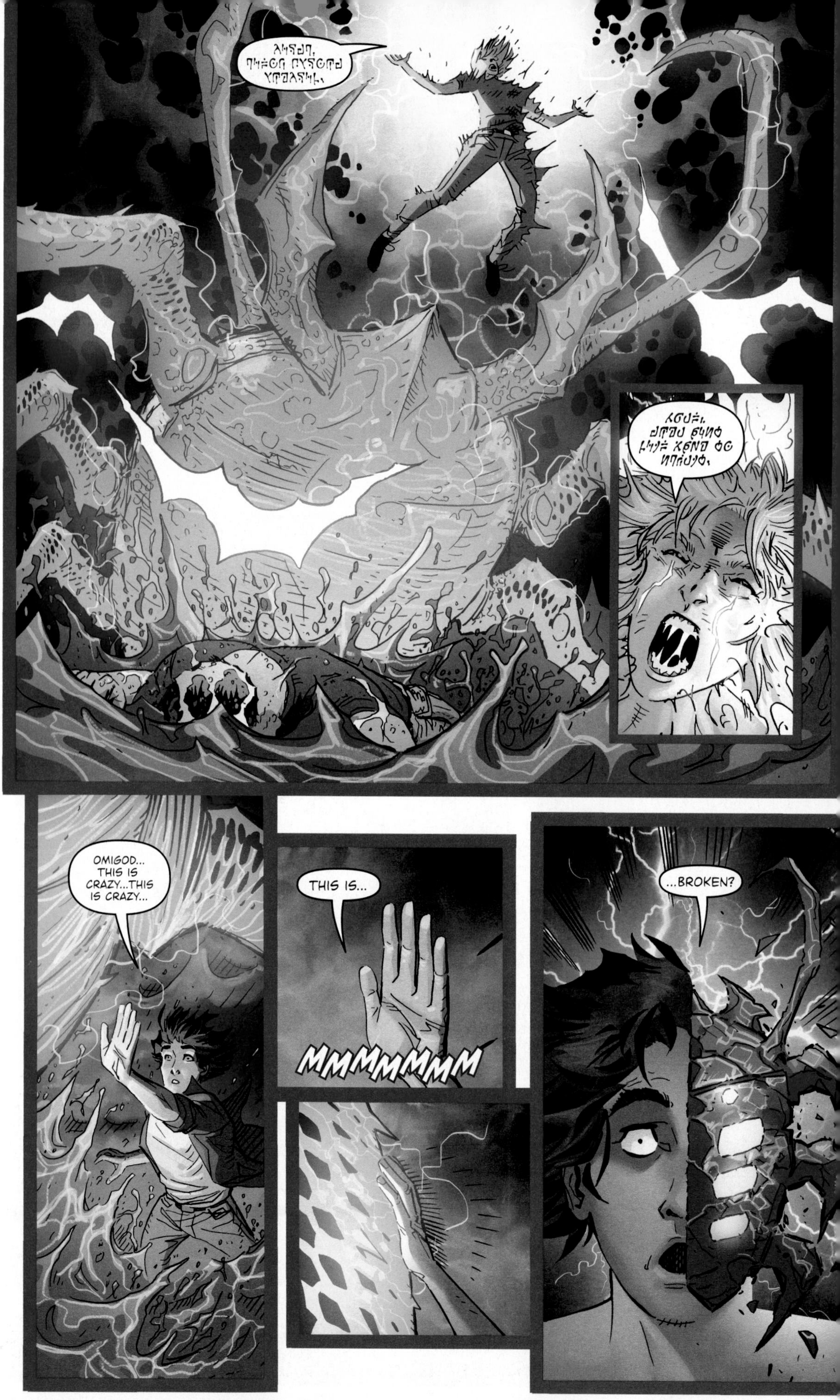
OMIGOD... THIS IS CRAZY...THIS IS CRAZY...
THIS IS...
MMMMMMMM
...BROKEN?

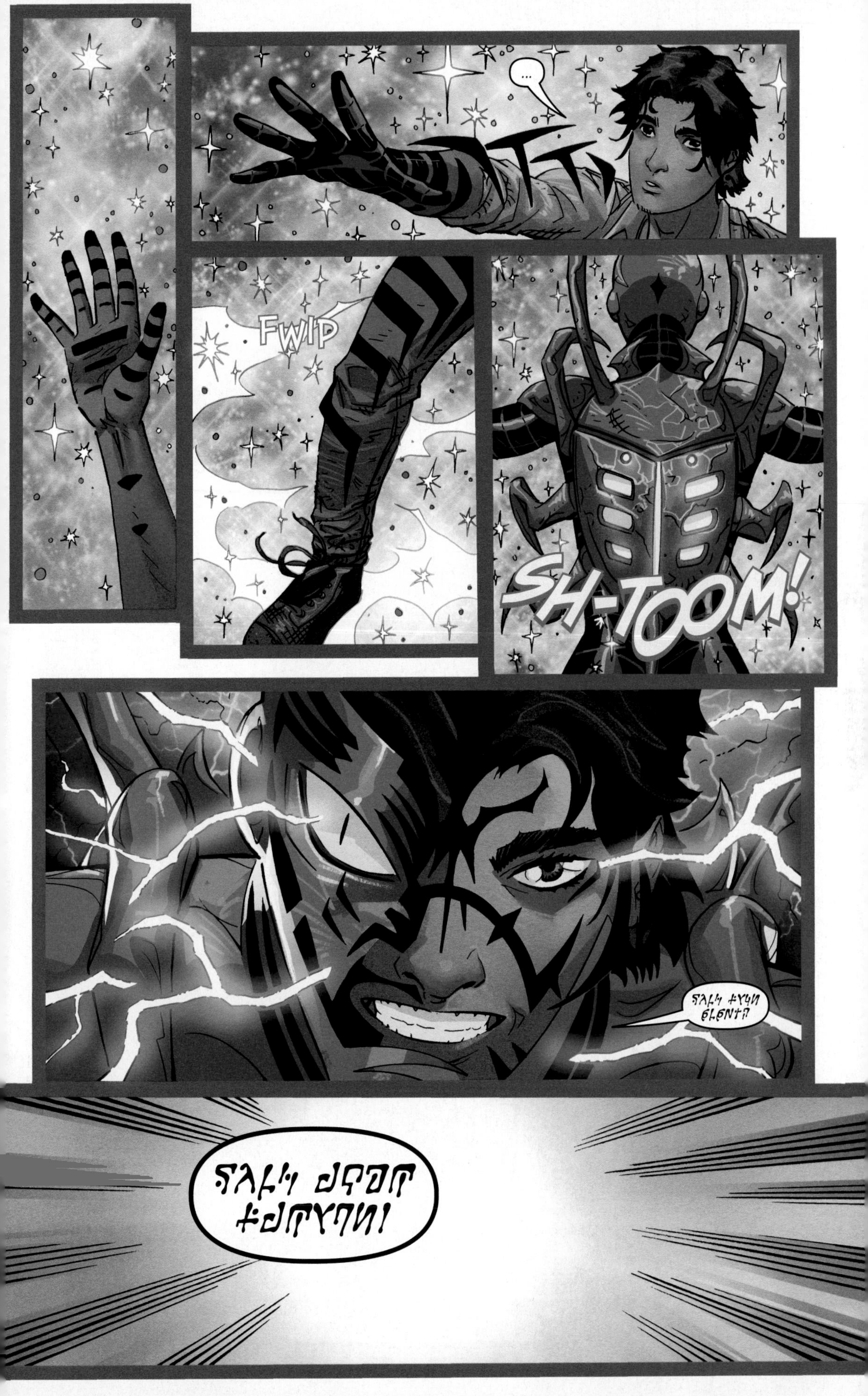
...
FWIP
SH-TOOM!

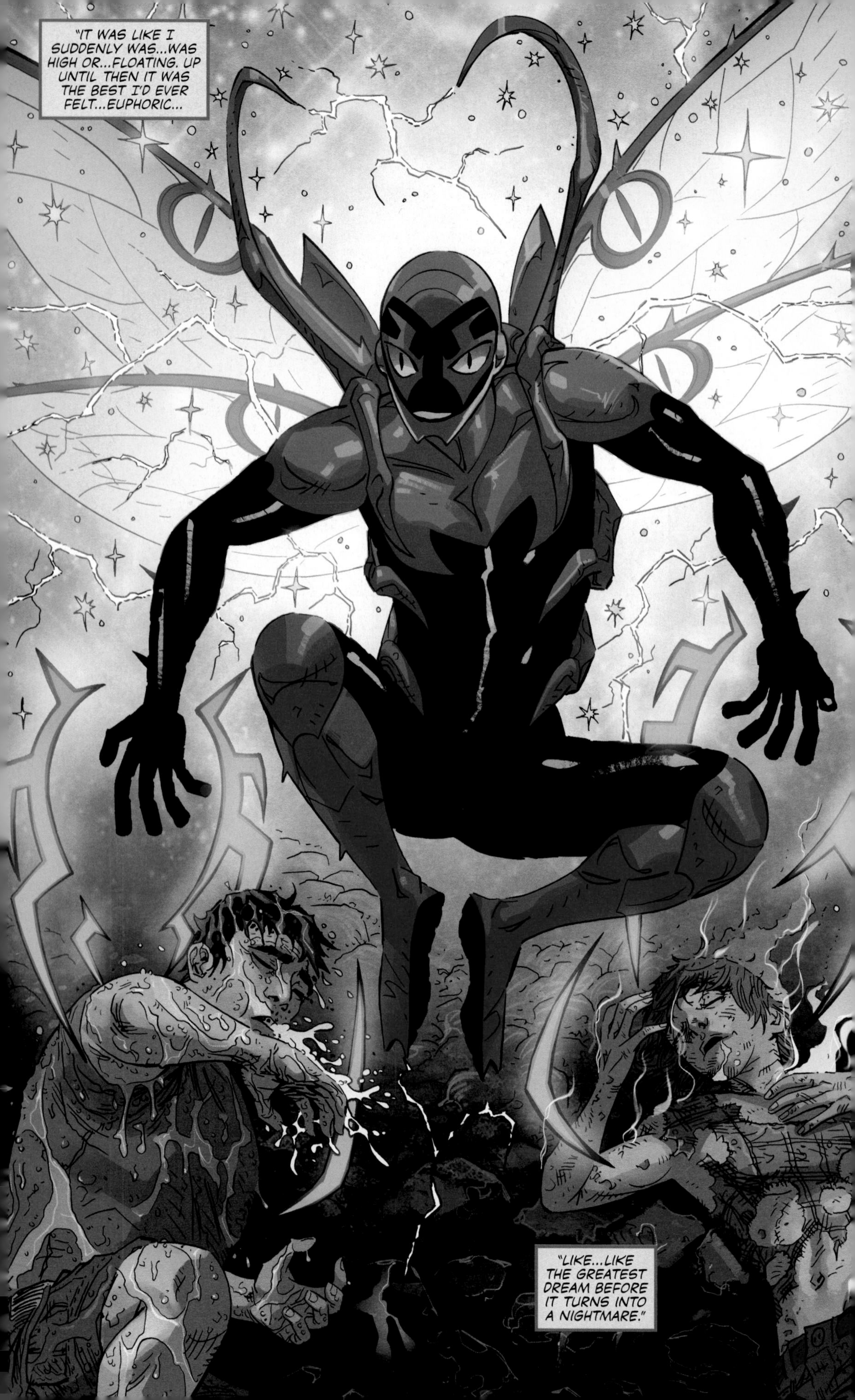
"IT WAS LIKE I SUDDENLY WAS...WAS HIGH OR...FLOATING. UP UNTIL THEN IT WAS THE BEST I'D EVER FELT...EUPHORIC...
"LIKE...LIKE THE GREATEST DREAM BEFORE IT TURNS INTO A NIGHTMARE."

SIGH...

THAT'S IT?

AS MUCH AS I CAN...REMEMBER. YOU KNOW THE REST. I'M FIGURING TED HAS A FILE ON ME.

YOU'VE READ IT, RIGHT?

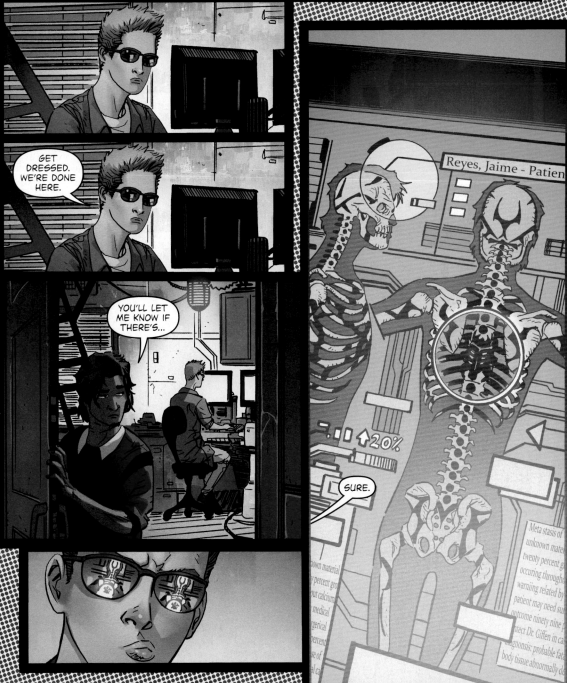

GET DRESSED. WE'RE DONE HERE.

YOU'LL LET ME KNOW IF THERE'S...

SURE.

Reyes, Jaime - Patien

↑20%

Meta stasis of
unknown mater
twenty percent g
occuring through
warning related by
patient may need su
outcome ninety nine p
tect Dr. Giffen in ca
diagnosis: probable fata
body tissue abnormally de

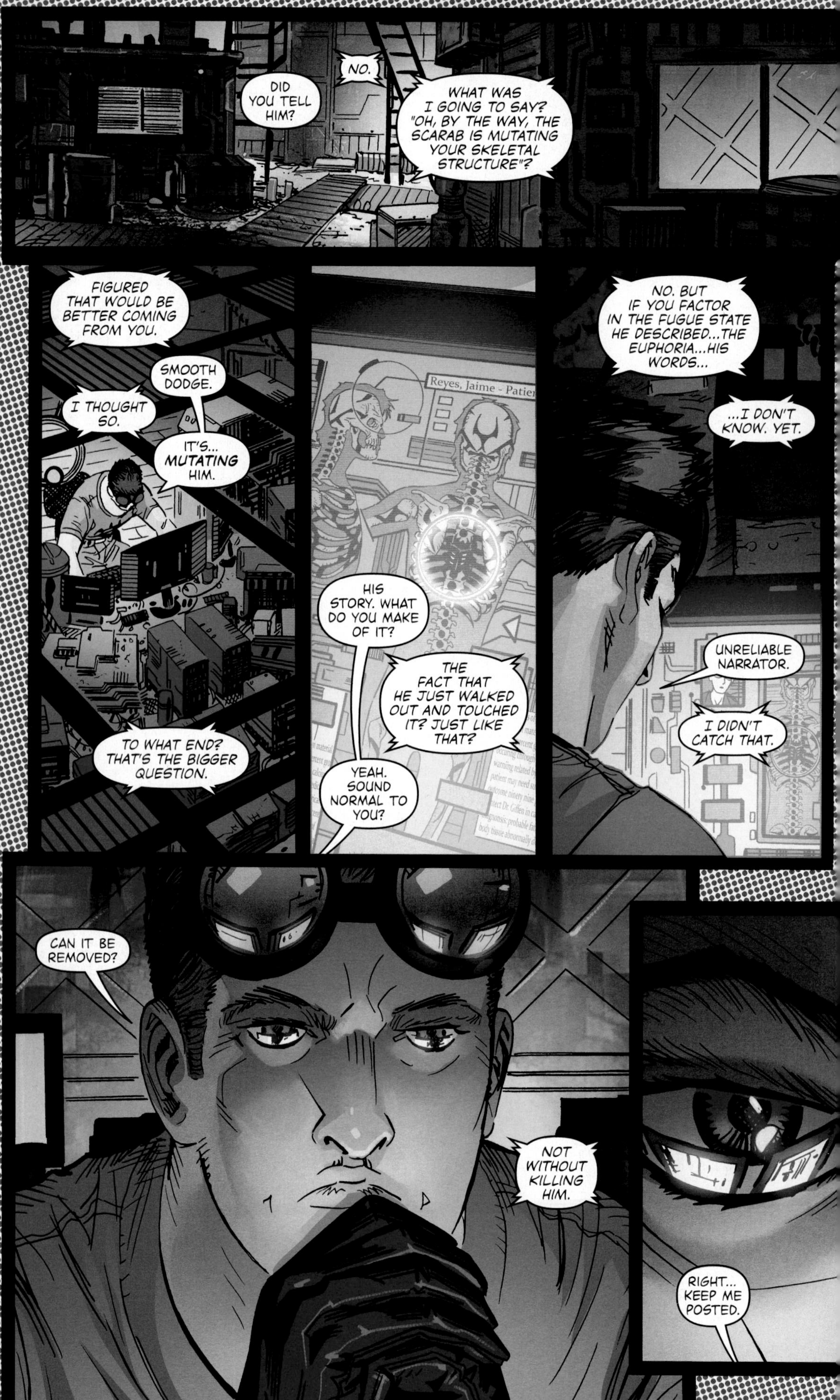
DID YOU TELL HIM?
NO.
WHAT WAS I GOING TO SAY? "OH, BY THE WAY, THE SCARAB IS MUTATING YOUR SKELETAL STRUCTURE"?
FIGURED THAT WOULD BE BETTER COMING FROM YOU.
SMOOTH DODGE.
I THOUGHT SO.
IT'S... MUTATING HIM.
TO WHAT END? THAT'S THE BIGGER QUESTION.
HIS STORY. WHAT DO YOU MAKE OF IT?
THE FACT THAT HE JUST WALKED OUT AND TOUCHED IT? JUST LIKE THAT?
YEAH. SOUND NORMAL TO YOU?
NO. BUT IF YOU FACTOR IN THE FUGUE STATE HE DESCRIBED...THE EUPHORIA...HIS WORDS...
...I DON'T KNOW. YET.
UNRELIABLE NARRATOR.
I DIDN'T CATCH THAT.
CAN IT BE REMOVED?
NOT WITHOUT KILLING HIM.
RIGHT... KEEP ME POSTED.

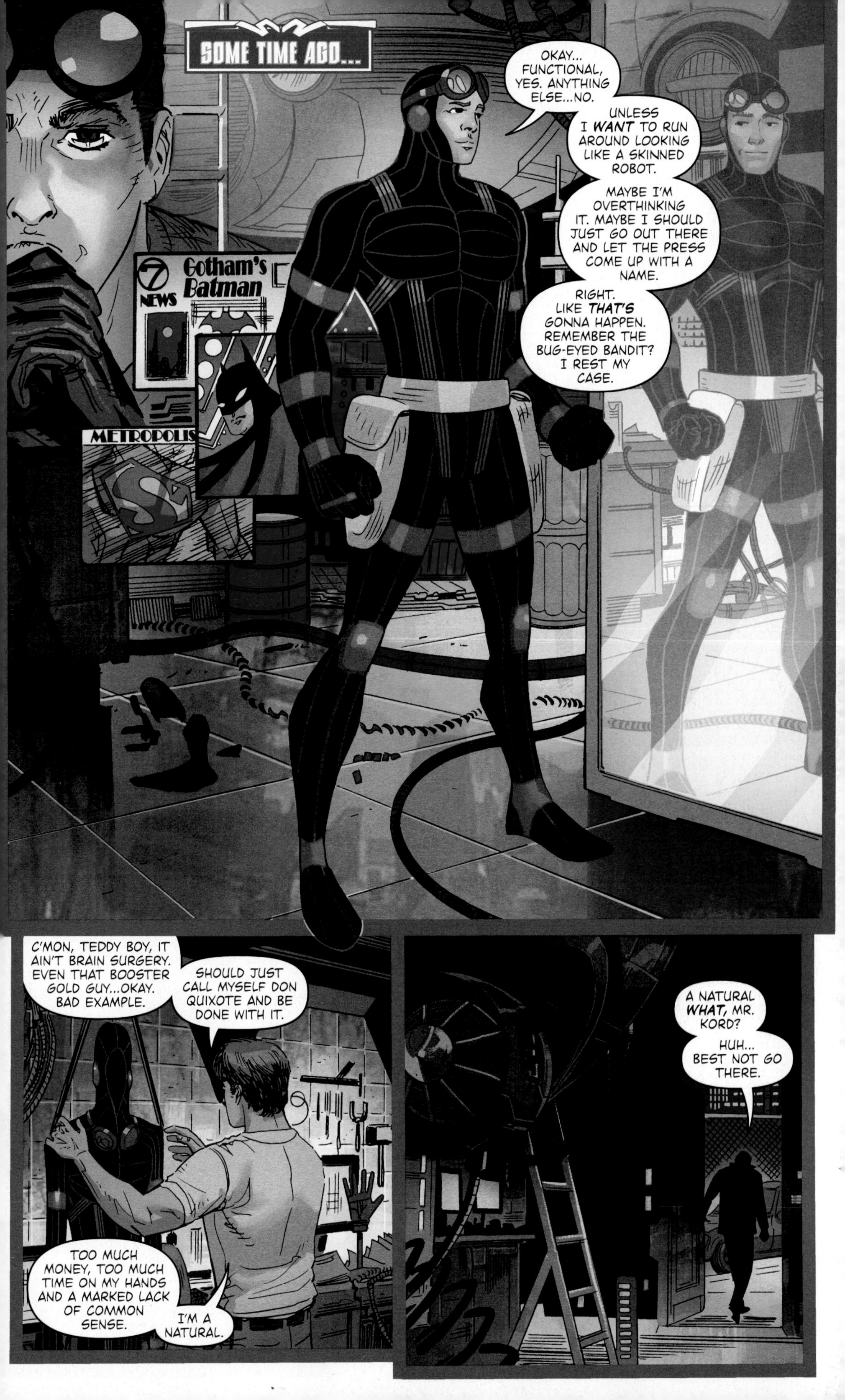

SOME TIME AGO...
OKAY... FUNCTIONAL, YES. ANYTHING ELSE...NO.
UNLESS I WANT TO RUN AROUND LOOKING LIKE A SKINNED ROBOT.
MAYBE I'M OVERTHINKING IT. MAYBE I SHOULD JUST GO OUT THERE AND LET THE PRESS COME UP WITH A NAME.
RIGHT. LIKE THAT'S GONNA HAPPEN. REMEMBER THE BUG-EYED BANDIT? I REST MY CASE.
7 NEWS
Gotham's Batman
METROPOLIS
C'MON, TEDDY BOY, IT AIN'T BRAIN SURGERY. EVEN THAT BOOSTER GOLD GUY...OKAY. BAD EXAMPLE.
SHOULD JUST CALL MYSELF DON QUIXOTE AND BE DONE WITH IT.
TOO MUCH MONEY, TOO MUCH TIME ON MY HANDS AND A MARKED LACK OF COMMON SENSE.
I'M A NATURAL.
A NATURAL WHAT, MR. KORD?
HUH... BEST NOT GO THERE.

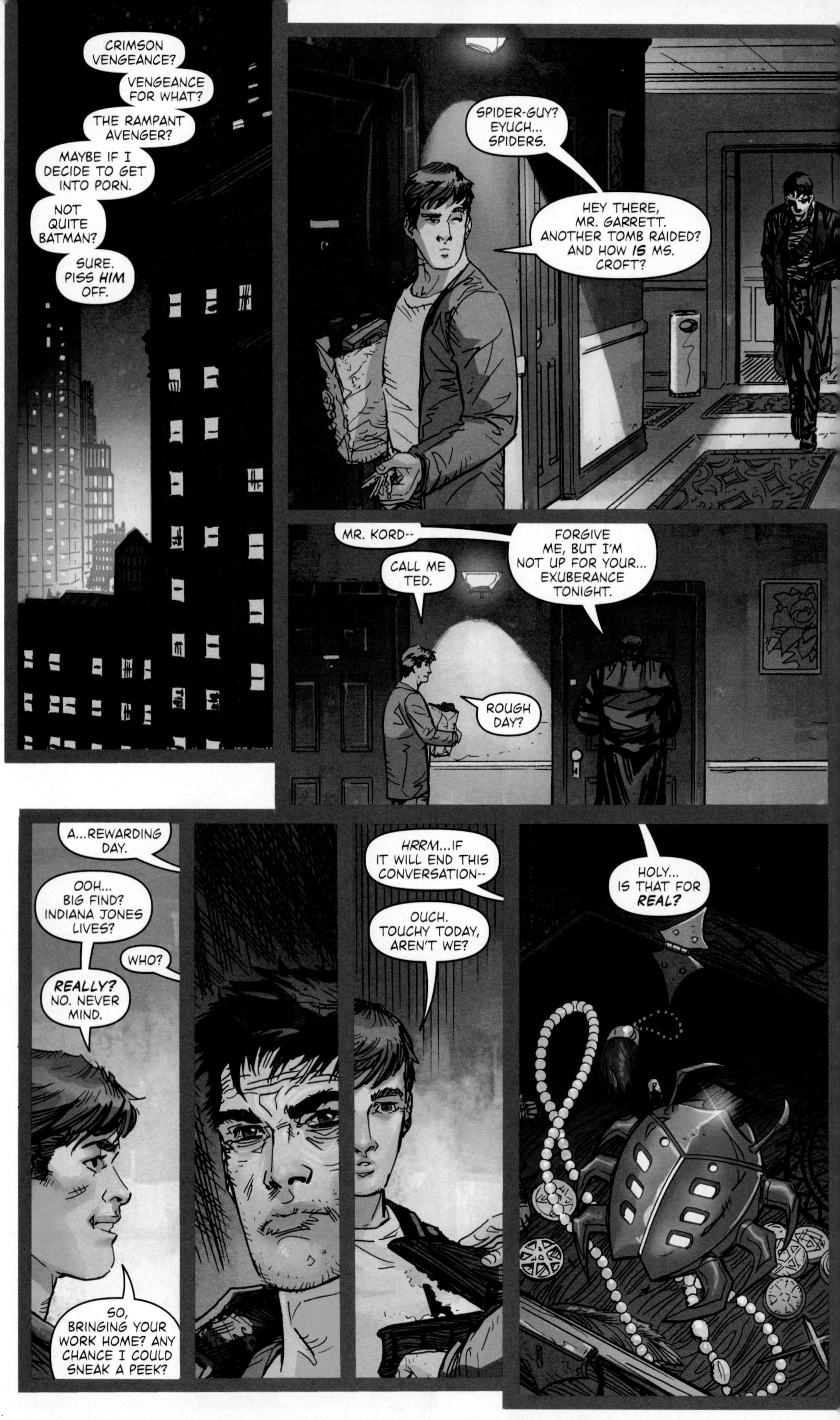
CRIMSON VENGEANCE?
VENGEANCE FOR WHAT?
THE RAMPANT AVENGER?
MAYBE IF I DECIDE TO GET INTO PORN.
NOT QUITE BATMAN?
SURE. PISS ***HIM*** OFF.
SPIDER-GUY? EYUCH... SPIDERS.
HEY THERE, MR. GARRETT. ANOTHER TOMB RAIDED? AND HOW ***IS*** MS. CROFT?
MR. KORD--
CALL ME TED.
FORGIVE ME, BUT I'M NOT UP FOR YOUR... EXUBERANCE TONIGHT.
ROUGH DAY?
A...REWARDING DAY.
OOH... BIG FIND? INDIANA JONES LIVES?
WHO?
REALLY? NO. NEVER MIND.
SO, BRINGING YOUR WORK HOME? ANY CHANCE I COULD SNEAK A PEEK?
HRRM...IF IT WILL END THIS CONVERSATION--
OUCH. TOUCHY TODAY, AREN'T WE?
HOLY... IS THAT FOR ***REAL?***

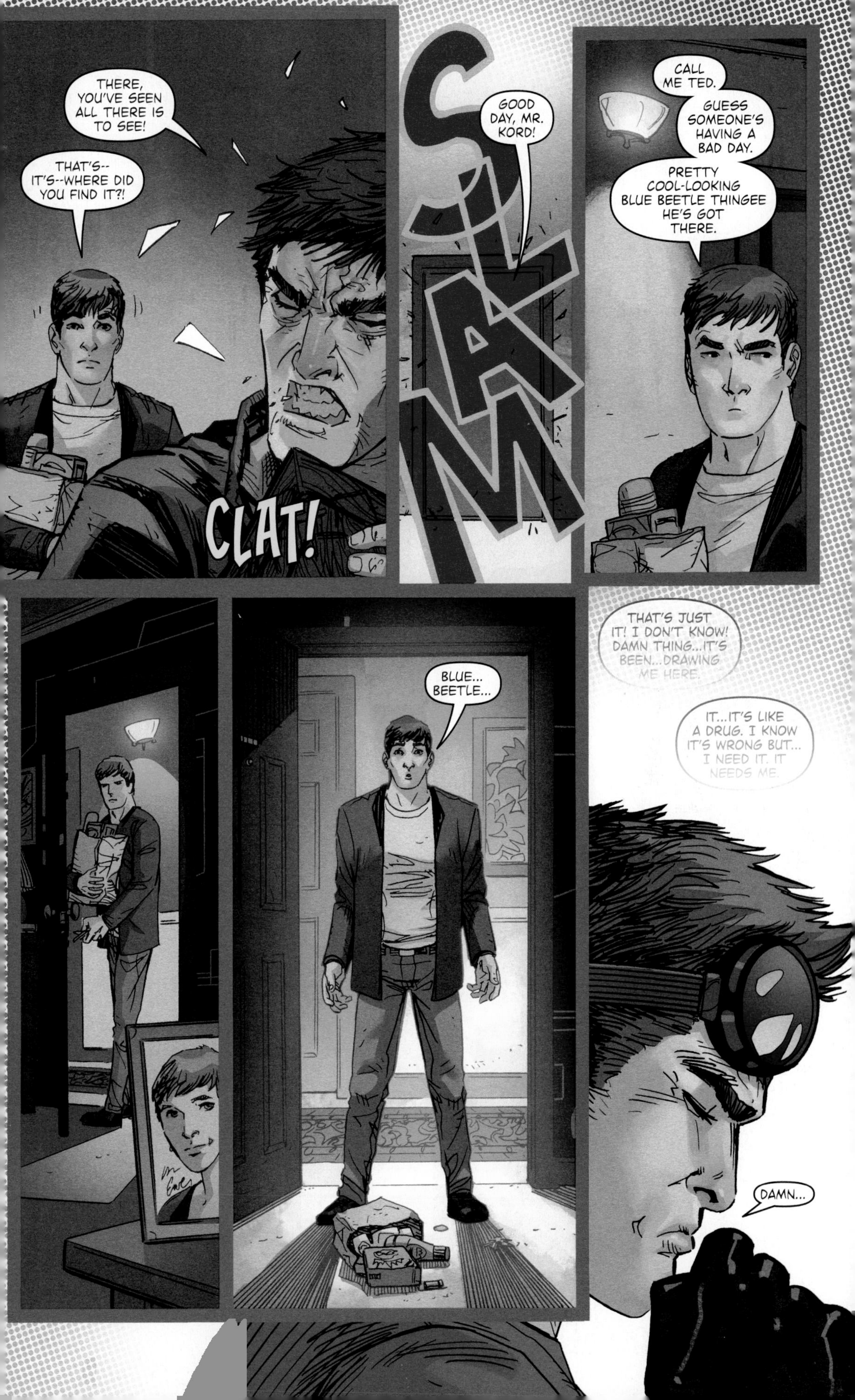

THERE, YOU'VE SEEN ALL THERE IS TO SEE!
THAT'S-- IT'S--WHERE DID YOU FIND IT?!
CLAT!
SLAM
GOOD DAY, MR. KORD!
CALL ME TED.
GUESS SOMEONE'S HAVING A BAD DAY.
PRETTY COOL-LOOKING BLUE BEETLE THINGEE HE'S GOT THERE.
BLUE... BEETLE...
THAT'S JUST IT! I DON'T KNOW! DAMN THING...IT'S BEEN...DRAWING ME HERE.
IT...IT'S LIKE A DRUG. I KNOW IT'S WRONG BUT... I NEED IT. IT NEEDS ME.
DAMN...

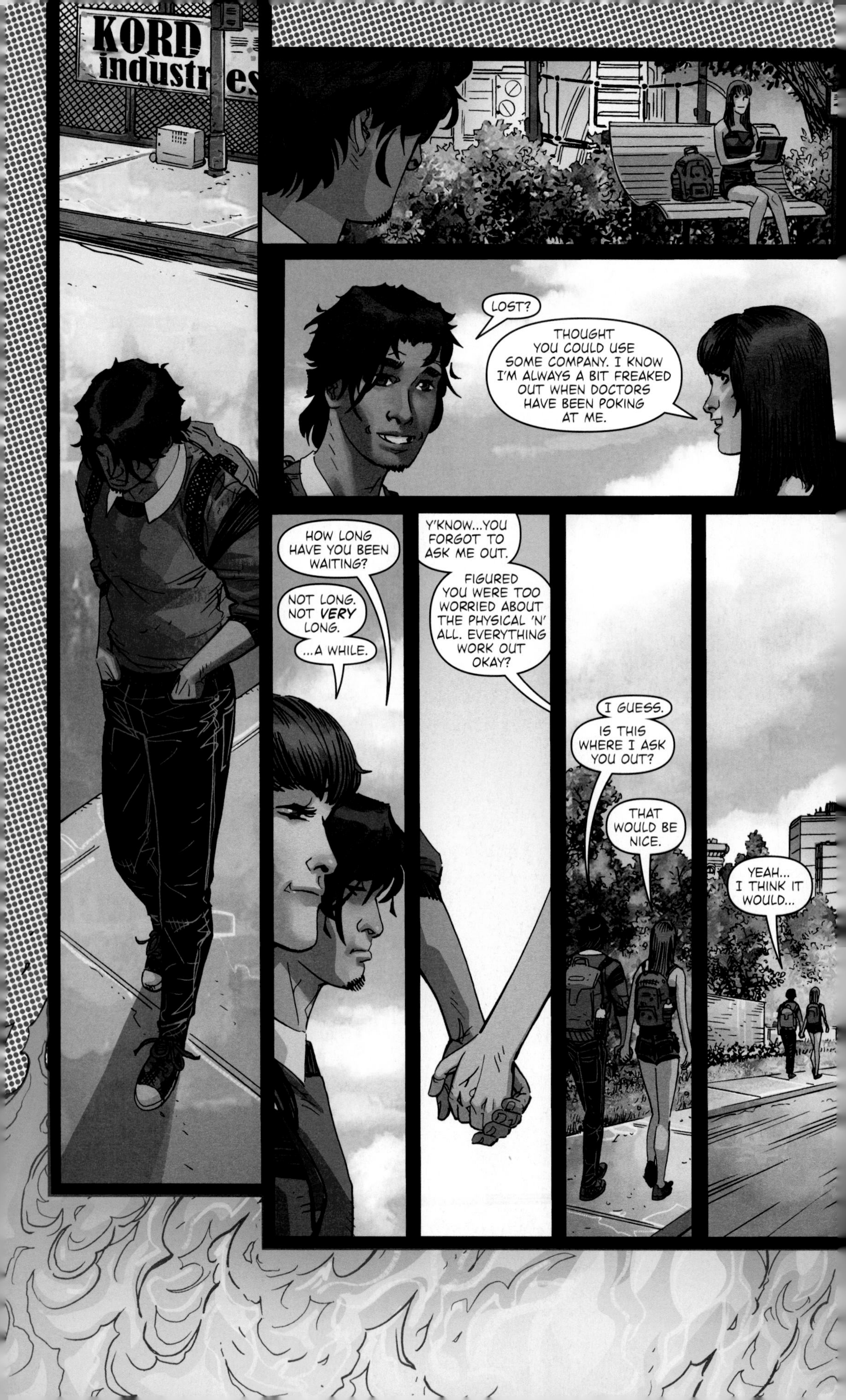
KORD industries
LOST?
THOUGHT YOU COULD USE SOME COMPANY. I KNOW I'M ALWAYS A BIT FREAKED OUT WHEN DOCTORS HAVE BEEN POKING AT ME.
HOW LONG HAVE YOU BEEN WAITING?
NOT LONG. NOT VERY LONG.
...A WHILE.
Y'KNOW...YOU FORGOT TO ASK ME OUT.
FIGURED YOU WERE TOO WORRIED ABOUT THE PHYSICAL 'N' ALL. EVERYTHING WORK OUT OKAY?
I GUESS.
IS THIS WHERE I ASK YOU OUT?
THAT WOULD BE NICE.
YEAH... I THINK IT WOULD...

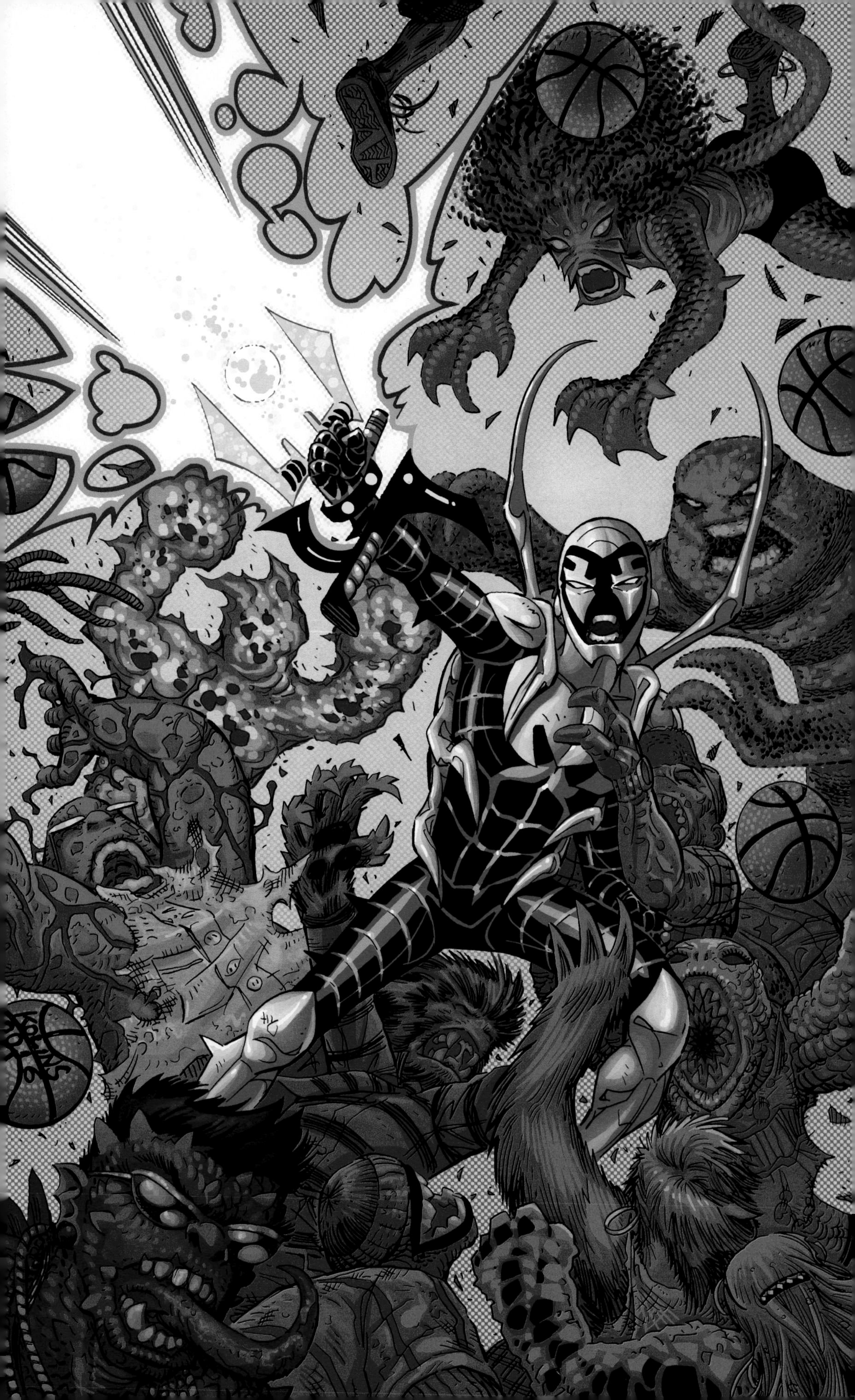

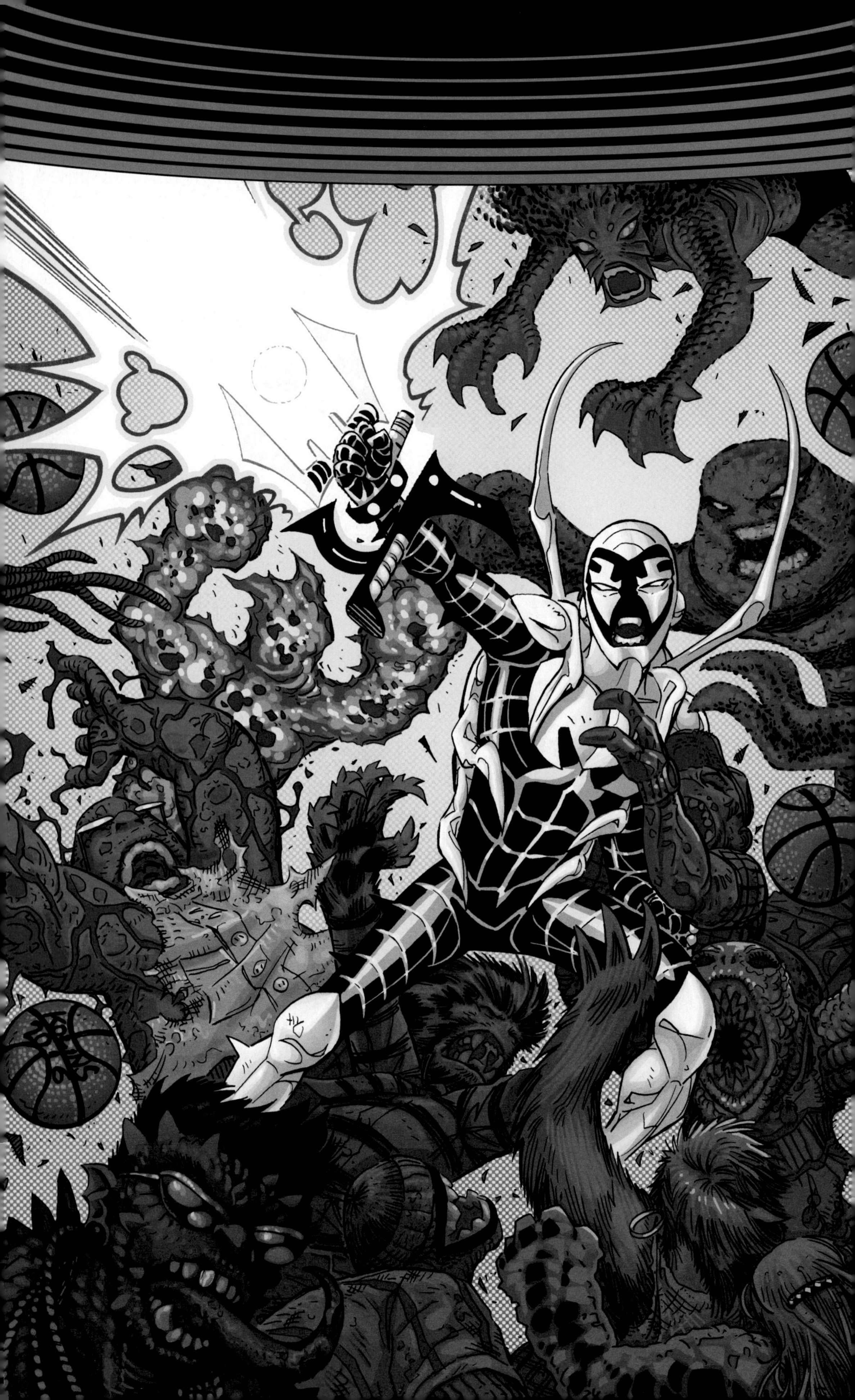

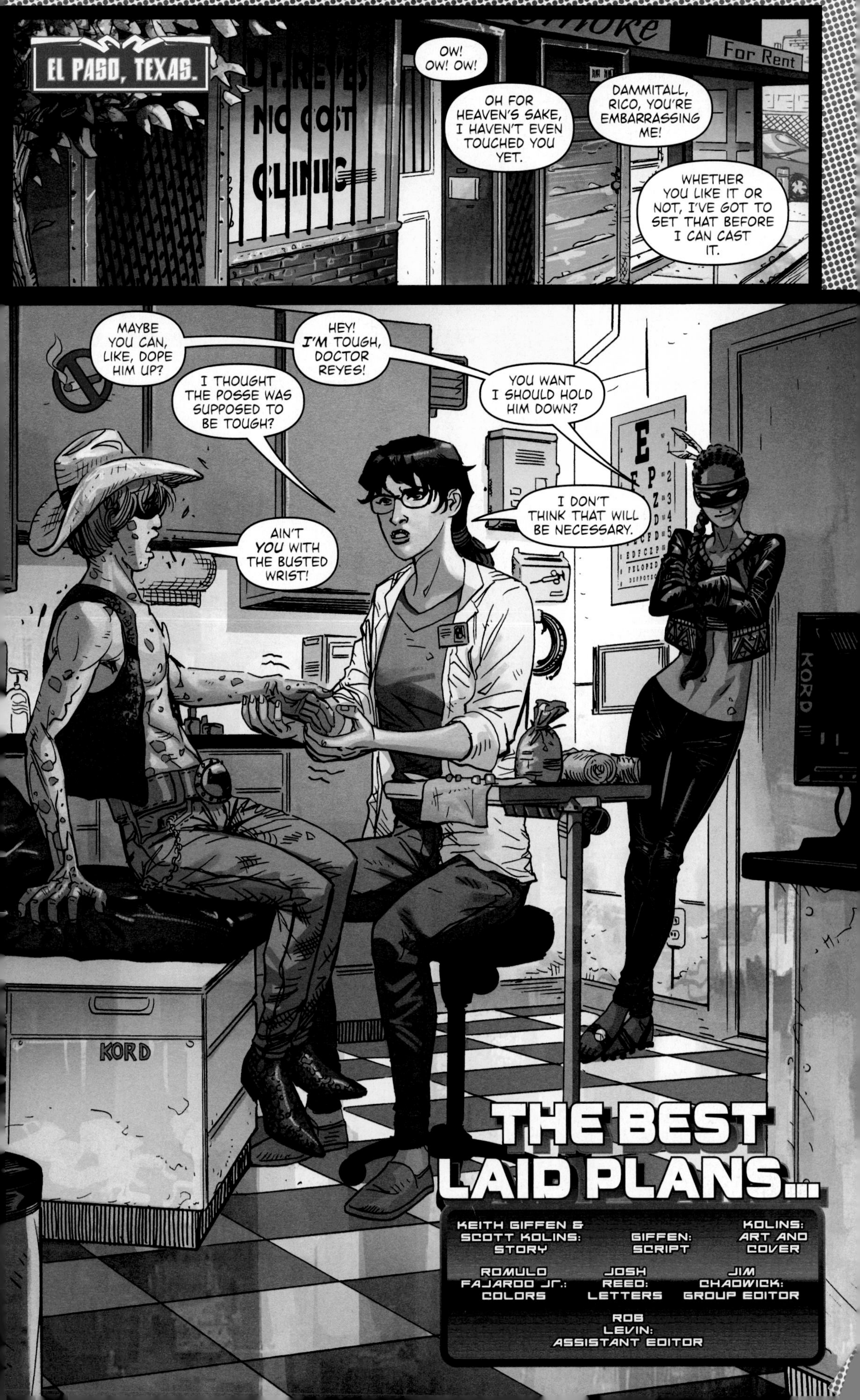
EL PASO, TEXAS.
NO COST
CLINIC
For Rent
OW! OW! OW!
OH FOR HEAVEN'S SAKE, I HAVEN'T EVEN TOUCHED YOU YET.
DAMMITALL, RICO, YOU'RE EMBARRASSING ME!
WHETHER YOU LIKE IT OR NOT, I'VE GOT TO SET THAT BEFORE I CAN CAST IT.
MAYBE YOU CAN, LIKE, DOPE HIM UP?
HEY! I'M TOUGH, DOCTOR REYES!
YOU WANT I SHOULD HOLD HIM DOWN?
I THOUGHT THE POSSE WAS SUPPOSED TO BE TOUGH?
AIN'T YOU WITH THE BUSTED WRIST!
I DON'T THINK THAT WILL BE NECESSARY.
KORD
KORD
THE BEST LAID PLANS...
KEITH GIFFEN & SCOTT KOLINS: STORY
GIFFEN: SCRIPT
KOLINS: ART AND COVER
ROMULO FAJARDO JR.: COLORS
JOSH REED: LETTERS
JIM CHADWICK: GROUP EDITOR
ROB LEVIN: ASSISTANT EDITOR

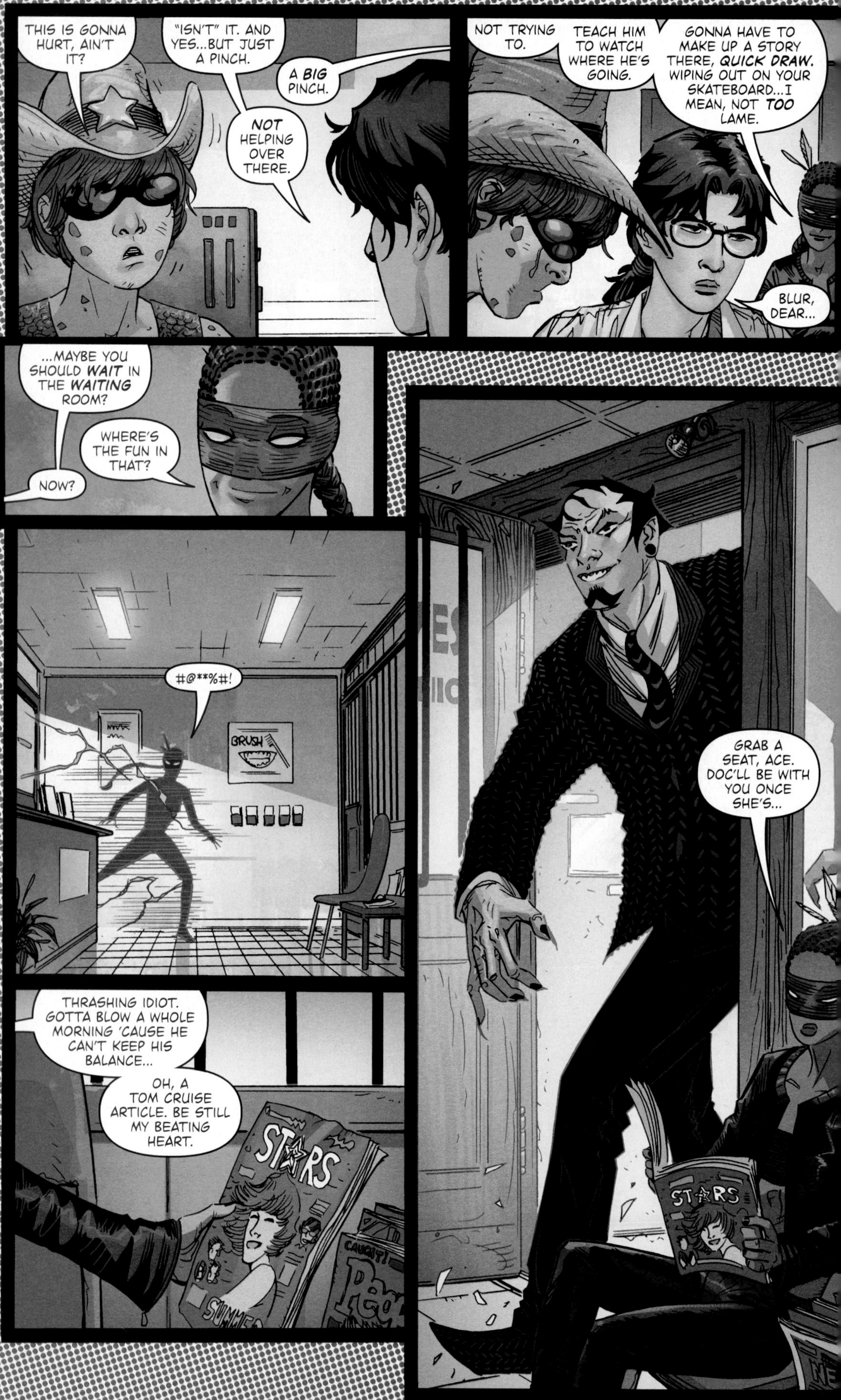
THIS IS GONNA HURT, AIN'T IT?
"ISN'T" IT. AND YES...BUT JUST A PINCH.
A BIG PINCH.
NOT HELPING OVER THERE.
NOT TRYING TO.
TEACH HIM TO WATCH WHERE HE'S GOING.
GONNA HAVE TO MAKE UP A STORY THERE, QUICK DRAW. WIPING OUT ON YOUR SKATEBOARD...I MEAN, NOT TOO LAME.
BLUR, DEAR...
...MAYBE YOU SHOULD WAIT IN THE WAITING ROOM?
NOW?
WHERE'S THE FUN IN THAT?
#@**%#!
BRUSH
THRASHING IDIOT. GOTTA BLOW A WHOLE MORNING 'CAUSE HE CAN'T KEEP HIS BALANCE...
OH, A TOM CRUISE ARTICLE. BE STILL MY BEATING HEART.
STARS
GRAB A SEAT, ACE. DOC'LL BE WITH YOU ONCE SHE'S...

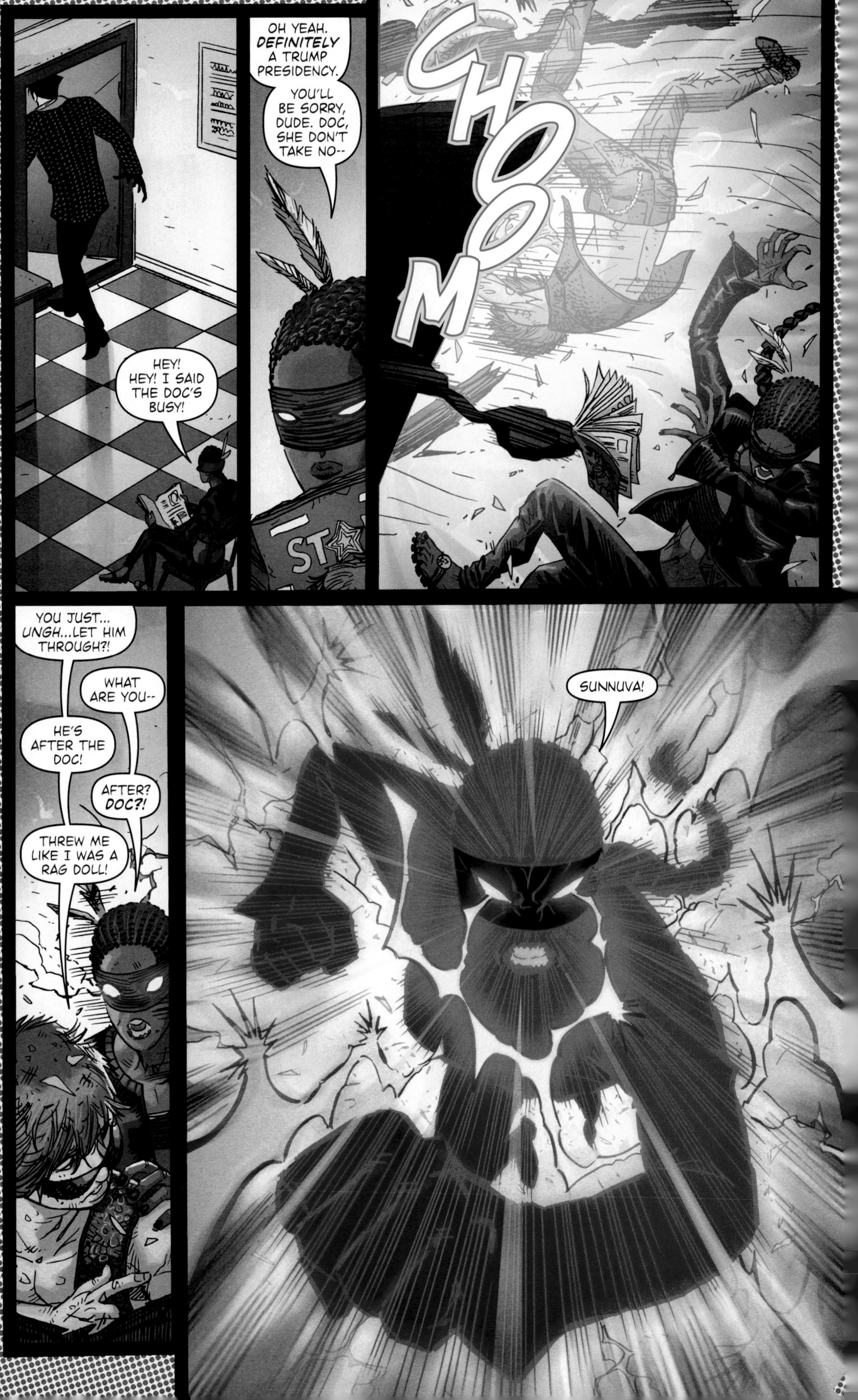
OH YEAH. DEFINITELY A TRUMP PRESIDENCY.
YOU'LL BE SORRY, DUDE. DOC, SHE DON'T TAKE NO--
HEY! HEY! I SAID THE DOC'S BUSY!
CHOOM
YOU JUST... UNGH...LET HIM THROUGH?!
WHAT ARE YOU--
HE'S AFTER THE DOC!
AFTER? DOC?!
THREW ME LIKE I WAS A RAG DOLL!
SUNNUVA!

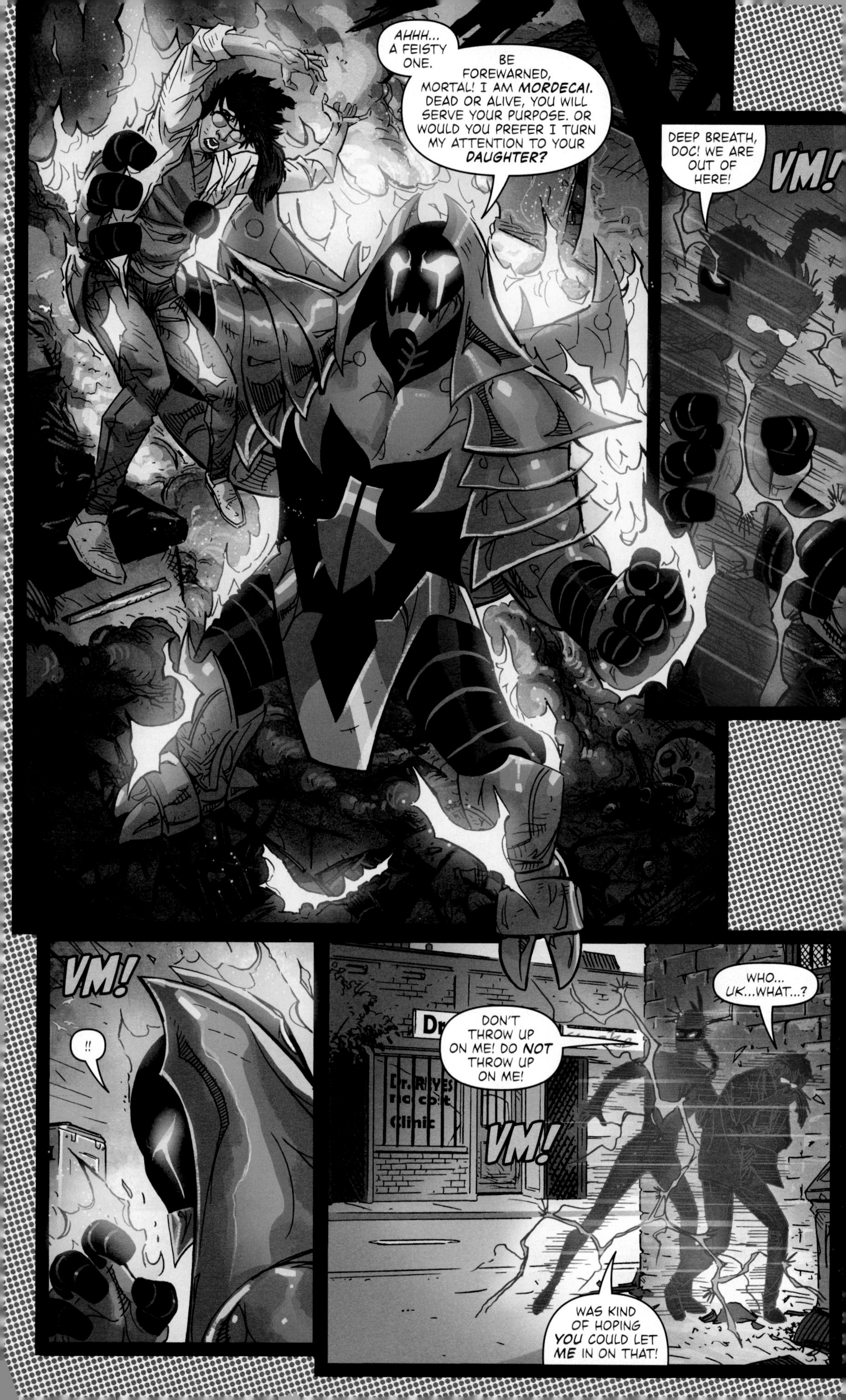
AHHH... A FEISTY ONE.
BE FOREWARNED, MORTAL! I AM MORDECAI. DEAD OR ALIVE, YOU WILL SERVE YOUR PURPOSE. OR WOULD YOU PREFER I TURN MY ATTENTION TO YOUR DAUGHTER?
DEEP BREATH, DOC! WE ARE OUT OF HERE!
VM!
VM!
!!
DON'T THROW UP ON ME! DO NOT THROW UP ON ME!
Dr. REYES
no cost
Clinic
VM!
WHO... UK...WHAT...?
WAS KIND OF HOPING YOU COULD LET ME IN ON THAT!

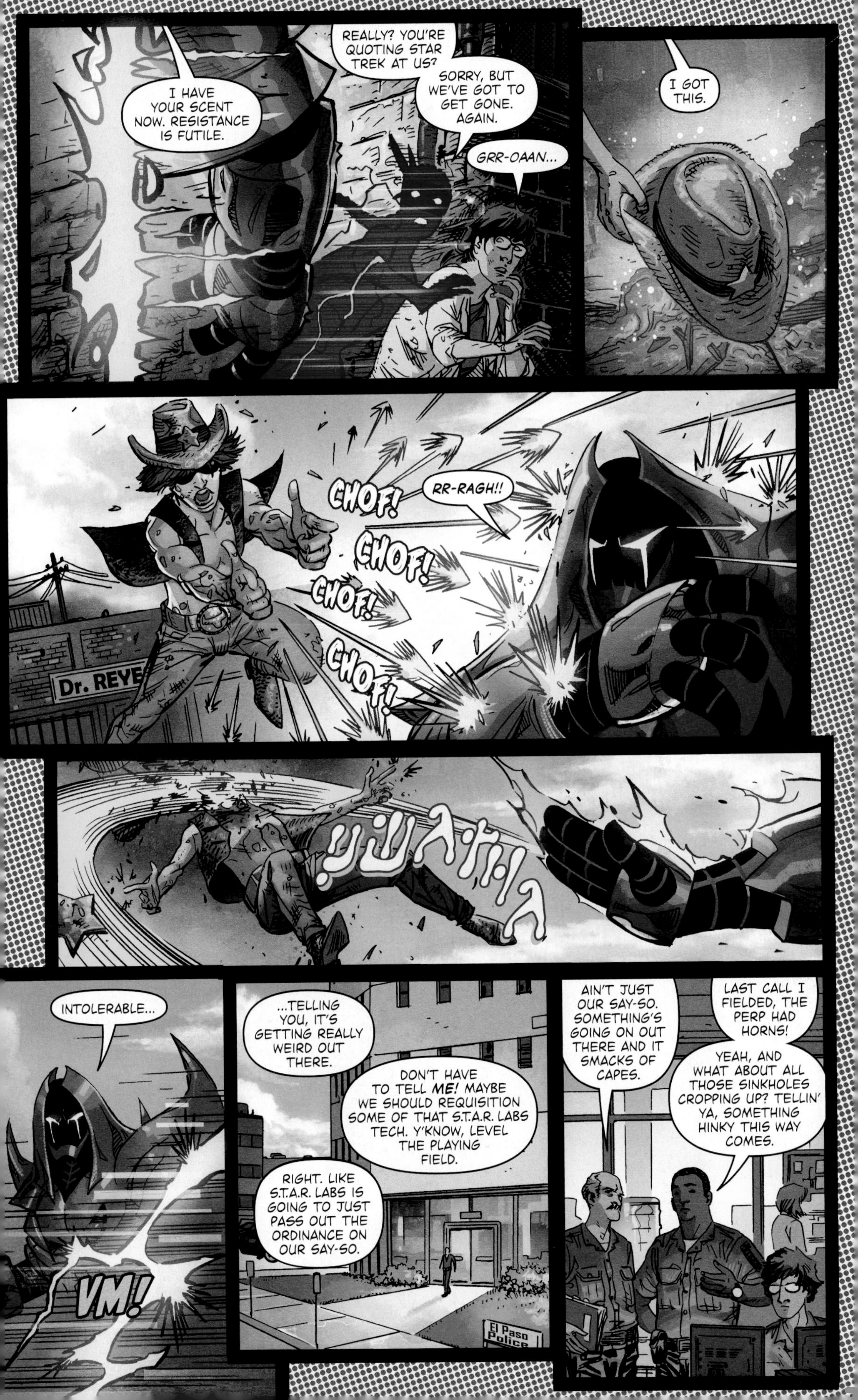
I HAVE YOUR SCENT NOW. RESISTANCE IS FUTILE.
REALLY? YOU'RE QUOTING STAR TREK AT US?
SORRY, BUT WE'VE GOT TO GET GONE. AGAIN.
GRR-OAAN...
I GOT THIS.
CHOF!
RR-RAGH!!
CHOF!
CHOF!
CHOF!
Dr. REYE
INTOLERABLE...
VM!
...TELLING YOU, IT'S GETTING REALLY WEIRD OUT THERE.
DON'T HAVE TO TELL *ME!* MAYBE WE SHOULD REQUISITION SOME OF THAT S.T.A.R. LABS TECH. Y'KNOW, LEVEL THE PLAYING FIELD.
RIGHT. LIKE S.T.A.R. LABS IS GOING TO JUST PASS OUT THE ORDINANCE ON OUR SAY-SO.
El Paso Police
AIN'T JUST OUR SAY-SO. SOMETHING'S GOING ON OUT THERE AND IT SMACKS OF CAPES.
LAST CALL I FIELDED, THE PERP HAD HORNS!
YEAH, AND WHAT ABOUT ALL THOSE SINKHOLES CROPPING UP? TELLIN' YA, SOMETHING HINKY THIS WAY COMES.

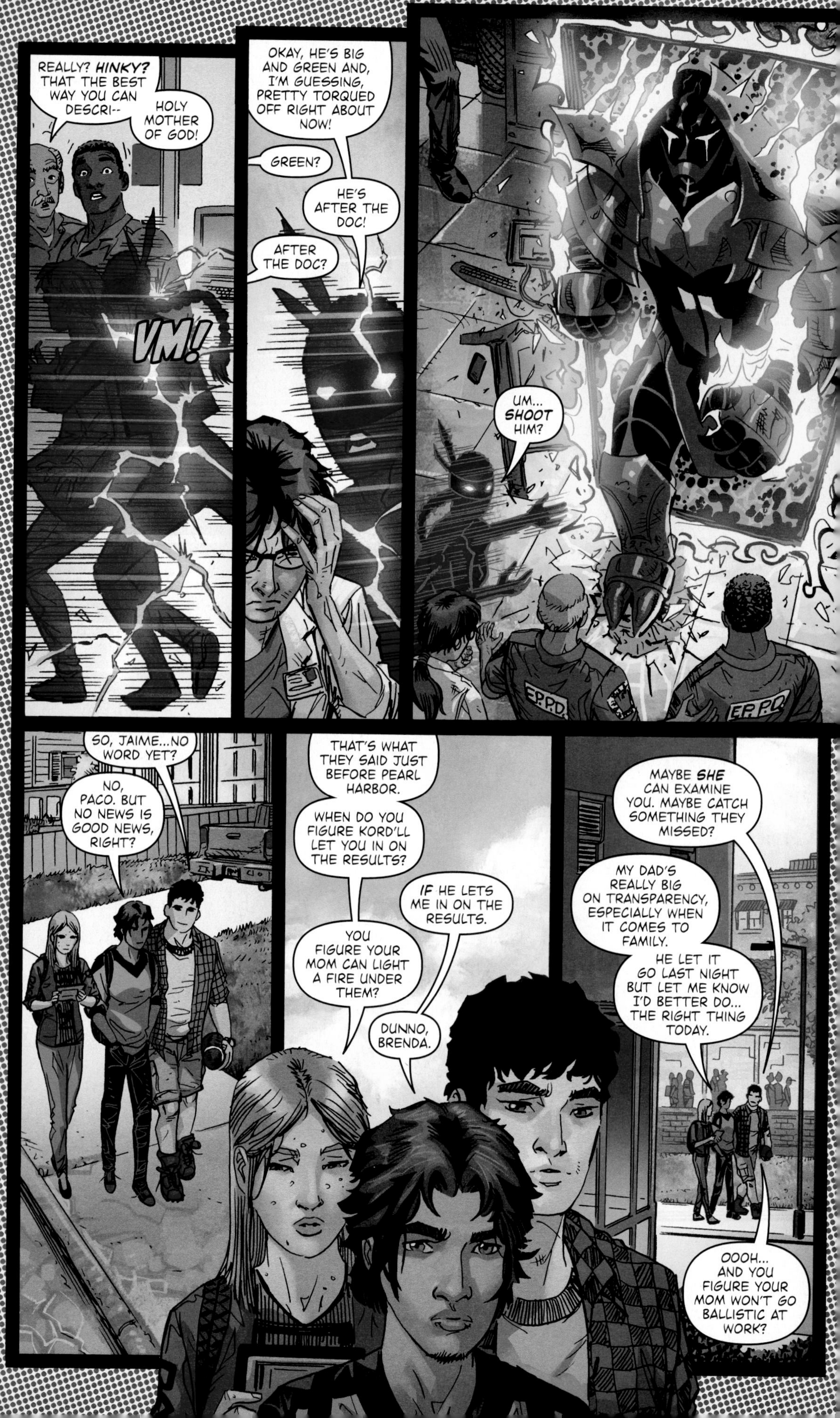
REALLY? HINKY? THAT THE BEST WAY YOU CAN DESCRI--
HOLY MOTHER OF GOD!
VM!
OKAY, HE'S BIG AND GREEN AND, I'M GUESSING, PRETTY TORQUED OFF RIGHT ABOUT NOW!
GREEN?
HE'S AFTER THE DOC!
AFTER THE DOC?
UM... SHOOT HIM?
E.P.P.D.
E.P.P.D.
SO, JAIME...NO WORD YET?
NO, PACO. BUT NO NEWS IS GOOD NEWS, RIGHT?
THAT'S WHAT THEY SAID JUST BEFORE PEARL HARBOR.
WHEN DO YOU FIGURE KORD'LL LET YOU IN ON THE RESULTS?
IF HE LETS ME IN ON THE RESULTS.
YOU FIGURE YOUR MOM CAN LIGHT A FIRE UNDER THEM?
DUNNO, BRENDA.
MAYBE SHE CAN EXAMINE YOU. MAYBE CATCH SOMETHING THEY MISSED?
MY DAD'S REALLY BIG ON TRANSPARENCY, ESPECIALLY WHEN IT COMES TO FAMILY.
HE LET IT GO LAST NIGHT BUT LET ME KNOW I'D BETTER DO... THE RIGHT THING TODAY.
OOOH... AND YOU FIGURE YOUR MOM WON'T GO BALLISTIC AT WORK?

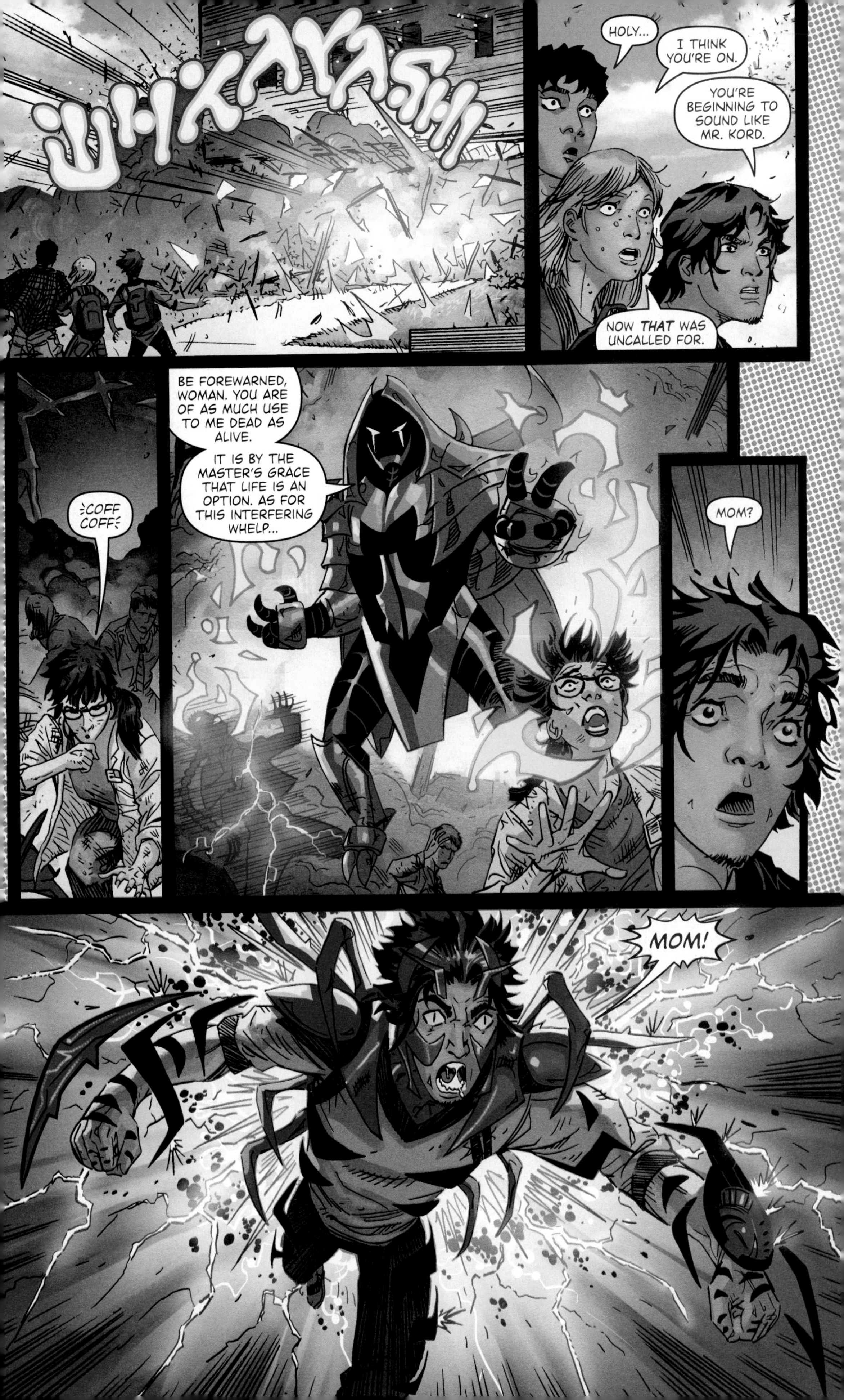

WHKAYAKASH!!
HOLY...
I THINK YOU'RE ON.
YOU'RE BEGINNING TO SOUND LIKE MR. KORD.
NOW THAT WAS UNCALLED FOR.
COFF COFF
BE FOREWARNED, WOMAN. YOU ARE OF AS MUCH USE TO ME DEAD AS ALIVE.
IT IS BY THE MASTER'S GRACE THAT LIFE IS AN OPTION. AS FOR THIS INTERFERING WHELP...
MOM?
MOM!

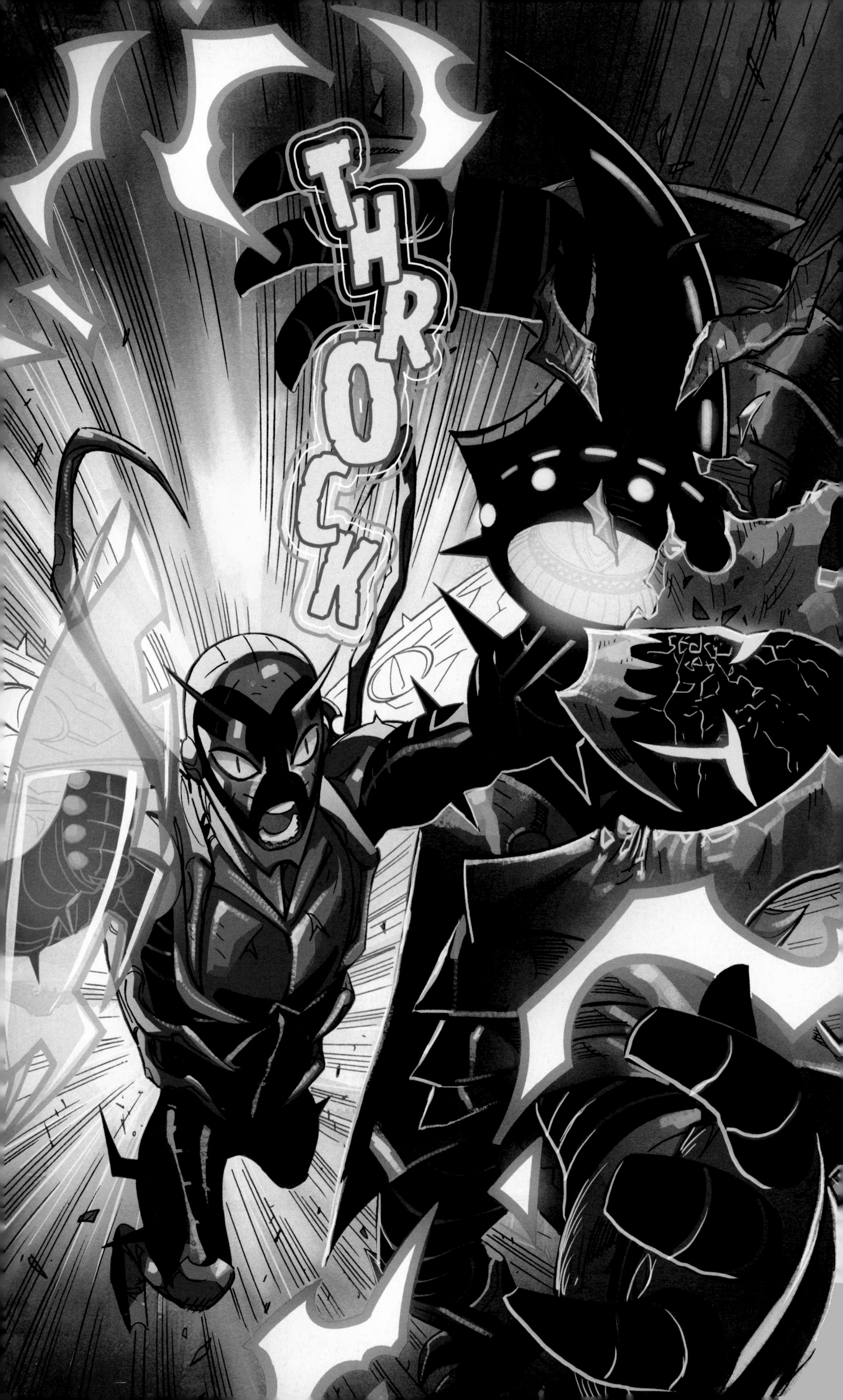
THROCK

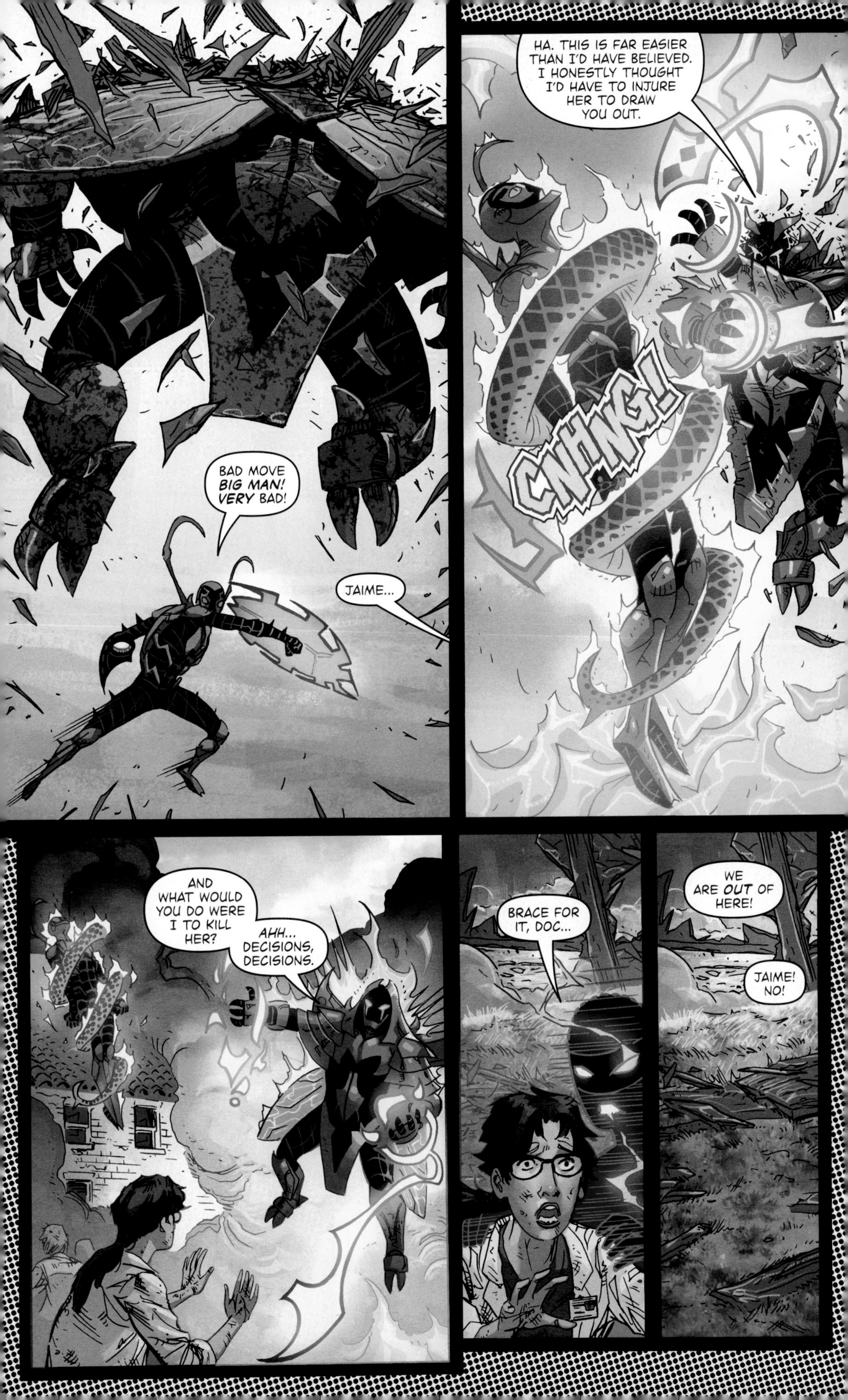
BAD MOVE *BIG MAN! VERY* BAD!
JAIME...
HA. THIS IS FAR EASIER THAN I'D HAVE BELIEVED. I HONESTLY THOUGHT I'D HAVE TO INJURE HER TO DRAW YOU OUT.
CNANG!
AND WHAT WOULD YOU DO WERE I TO KILL HER?
AHH... DECISIONS, DECISIONS.
BRACE FOR IT, DOC...
WE ARE *OUT* OF HERE!
JAIME! NO!

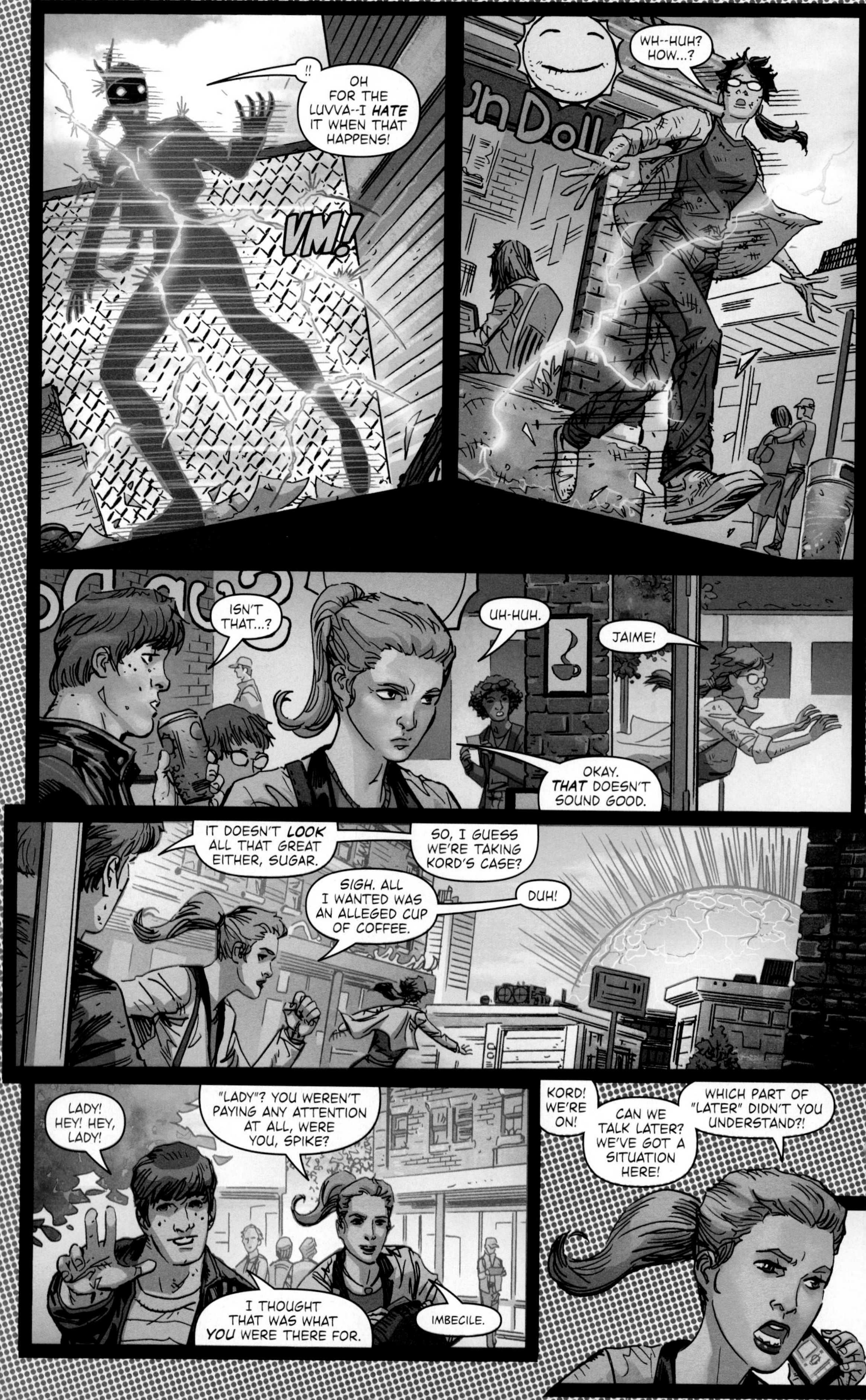
!!
OH FOR THE LUVVA--I HATE IT WHEN THAT HAPPENS!
VM!
WH--HUH? HOW...?
ISN'T THAT...?
UH-HUH.
JAIME!
OKAY. THAT DOESN'T SOUND GOOD.
IT DOESN'T LOOK ALL THAT GREAT EITHER, SUGAR.
SO, I GUESS WE'RE TAKING KORD'S CASE?
SIGH. ALL I WANTED WAS AN ALLEGED CUP OF COFFEE.
DUH!
LADY! HEY! HEY, LADY!
"LADY"? YOU WEREN'T PAYING ANY ATTENTION AT ALL, WERE YOU, SPIKE?
I THOUGHT THAT WAS WHAT YOU WERE THERE FOR.
IMBECILE.
KORD! WE'RE ON!
CAN WE TALK LATER? WE'VE GOT A SITUATION HERE!
WHICH PART OF "LATER" DIDN'T YOU UNDERSTAND?!

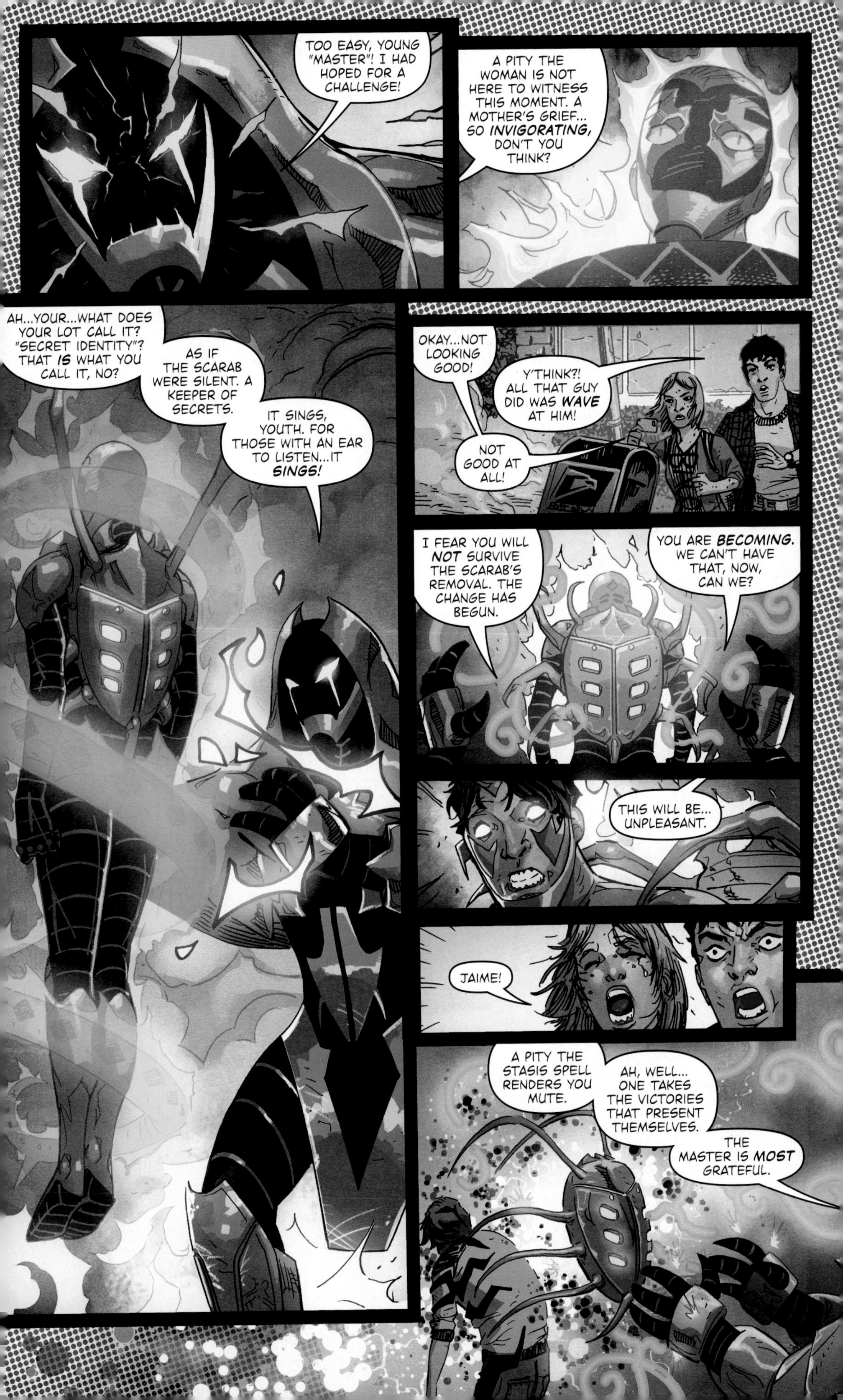

TOO EASY, YOUNG "MASTER"! I HAD HOPED FOR A CHALLENGE!
A PITY THE WOMAN IS NOT HERE TO WITNESS THIS MOMENT. A MOTHER'S GRIEF... SO INVIGORATING, DON'T YOU THINK?
AH...YOUR...WHAT DOES YOUR LOT CALL IT? "SECRET IDENTITY"? THAT IS WHAT YOU CALL IT, NO?
AS IF THE SCARAB WERE SILENT. A KEEPER OF SECRETS.
IT SINGS, YOUTH. FOR THOSE WITH AN EAR TO LISTEN...IT SINGS!
OKAY...NOT LOOKING GOOD!
Y'THINK?! ALL THAT GUY DID WAS WAVE AT HIM!
NOT GOOD AT ALL!
I FEAR YOU WILL NOT SURVIVE THE SCARAB'S REMOVAL. THE CHANGE HAS BEGUN.
YOU ARE BECOMING. WE CAN'T HAVE THAT, NOW, CAN WE?
THIS WILL BE... UNPLEASANT.
JAIME!
A PITY THE STASIS SPELL RENDERS YOU MUTE.
AH, WELL... ONE TAKES THE VICTORIES THAT PRESENT THEMSELVES.
THE MASTER IS MOST GRATEFUL.

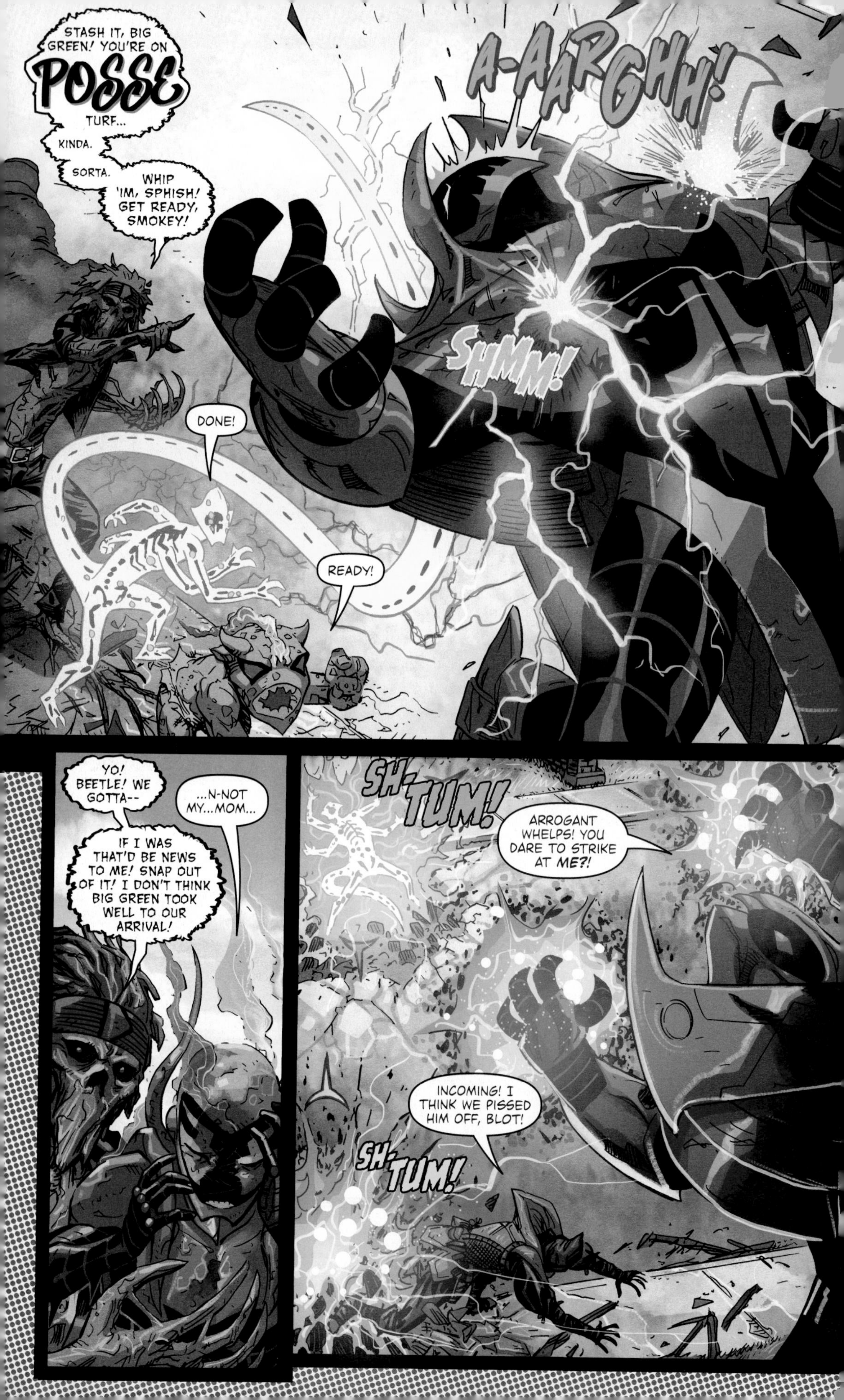

STASH IT, BIG GREEN! YOU'RE ON POSSE TURF...
KINDA.
SORTA.
WHIP 'IM, SPHISH! GET READY, SMOKEY!
A-AARGHH!
SHMM!
DONE!
READY!
YO! BEETLE! WE GOTTA--
...N-NOT MY...MOM...
IF I WAS THAT'D BE NEWS TO ME! SNAP OUT OF IT! I DON'T THINK BIG GREEN TOOK WELL TO OUR ARRIVAL!
SH-TUM!
ARROGANT WHELPS! YOU DARE TO STRIKE AT ME?!
INCOMING! I THINK WE PISSED HIM OFF, BLOT!
SH-TUM!

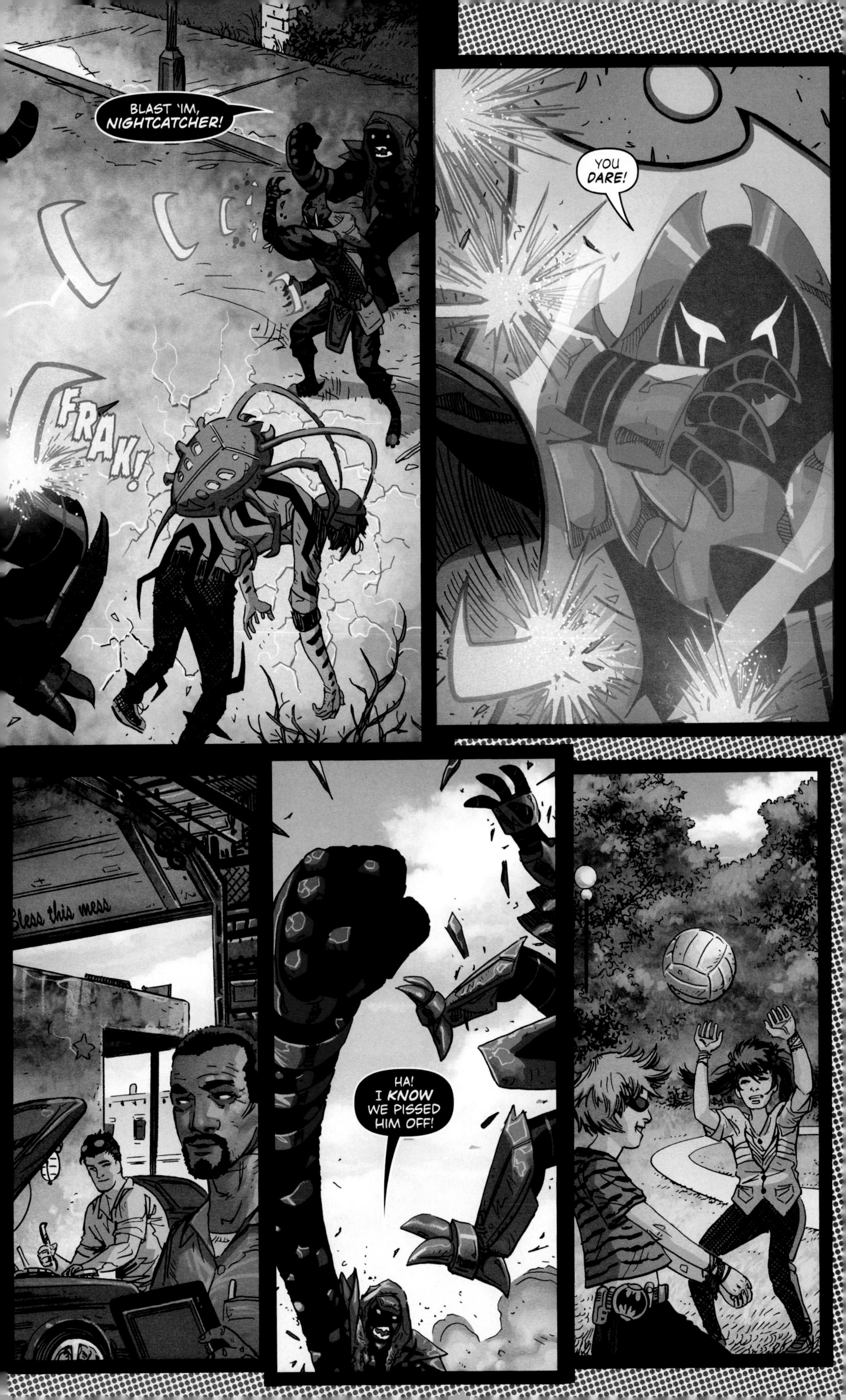
BLAST 'IM, NIGHTCATCHER!
FRAK!
YOU DARE!
Bless this mess
HA! I KNOW WE PISSED HIM OFF!

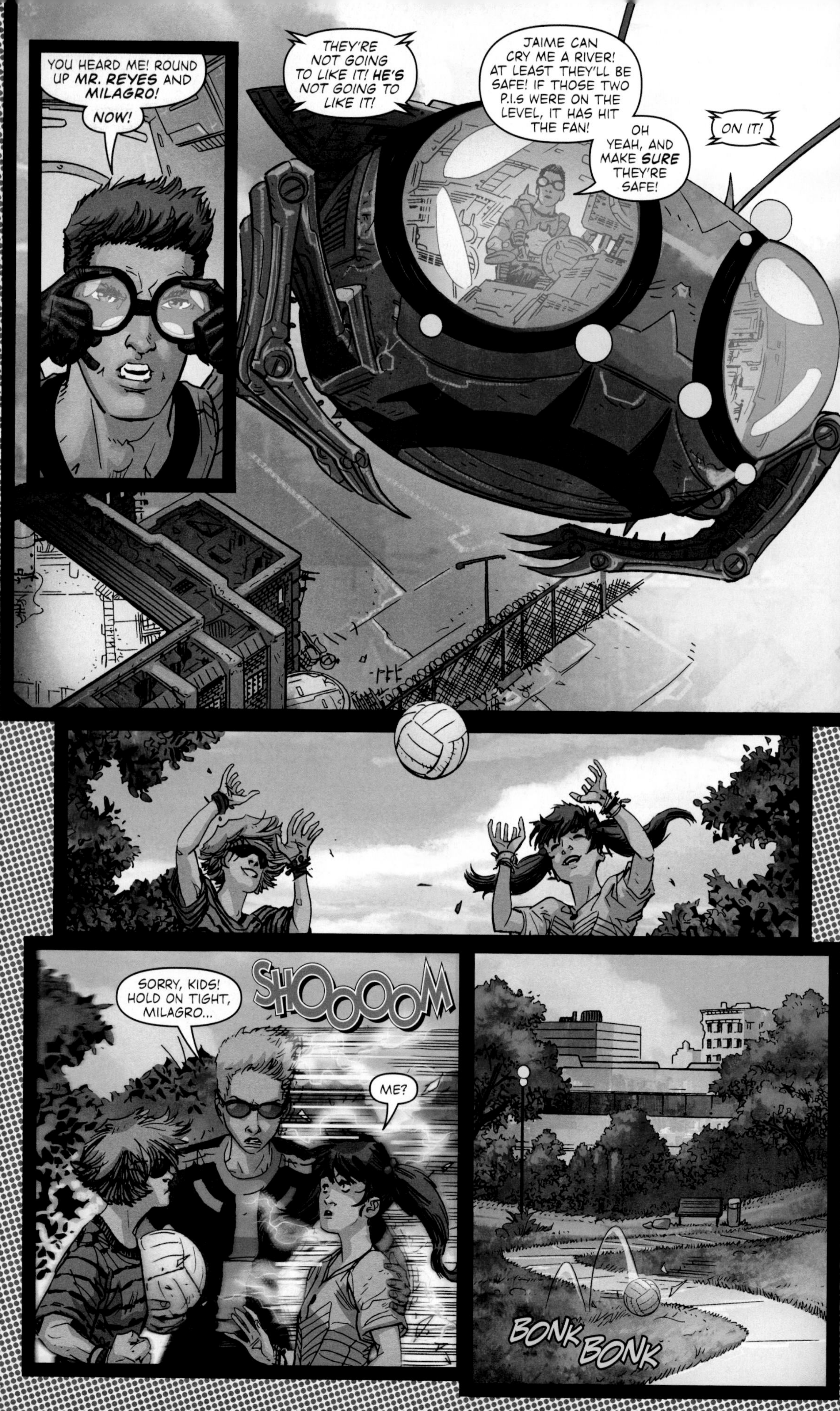
YOU HEARD ME! ROUND UP MR. REYES AND MILAGRO!
NOW!
THEY'RE NOT GOING TO LIKE IT! HE'S NOT GOING TO LIKE IT!
JAIME CAN CRY ME A RIVER! AT LEAST THEY'LL BE SAFE! IF THOSE TWO P.I.S WERE ON THE LEVEL, IT HAS HIT THE FAN!
OH YEAH, AND MAKE SURE THEY'RE SAFE!
ON IT!
SORRY, KIDS! HOLD ON TIGHT, MILAGRO...
SHOOOOOM
ME?
BONK BONK

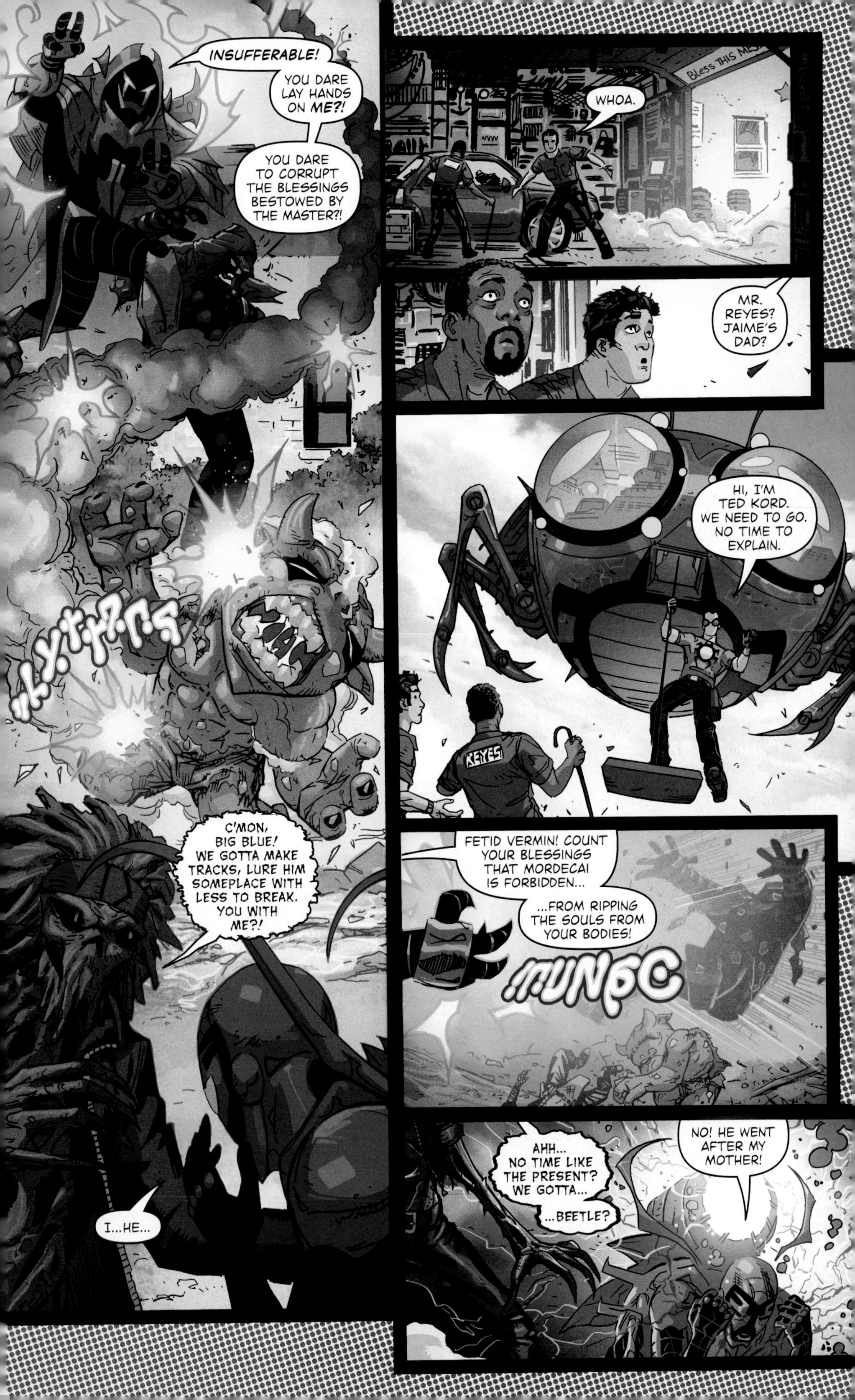
INSUFFERABLE!
YOU DARE LAY HANDS ON ME?!
YOU DARE TO CORRUPT THE BLESSINGS BESTOWED BY THE MASTER?!
C'MON, BIG BLUE! WE GOTTA MAKE TRACKS, LURE HIM SOMEPLACE WITH LESS TO BREAK. YOU WITH ME?!
I...HE...
WHOA.
MR. REYES? JAIME'S DAD?
HI, I'M TED KORD. WE NEED TO GO. NO TIME TO EXPLAIN.
REYES
FETID VERMIN! COUNT YOUR BLESSINGS THAT MORDECAI IS FORBIDDEN...
...FROM RIPPING THE SOULS FROM YOUR BODIES!
AHH... NO TIME LIKE THE PRESENT? WE GOTTA...
...BEETLE?
NO! HE WENT AFTER MY MOTHER!

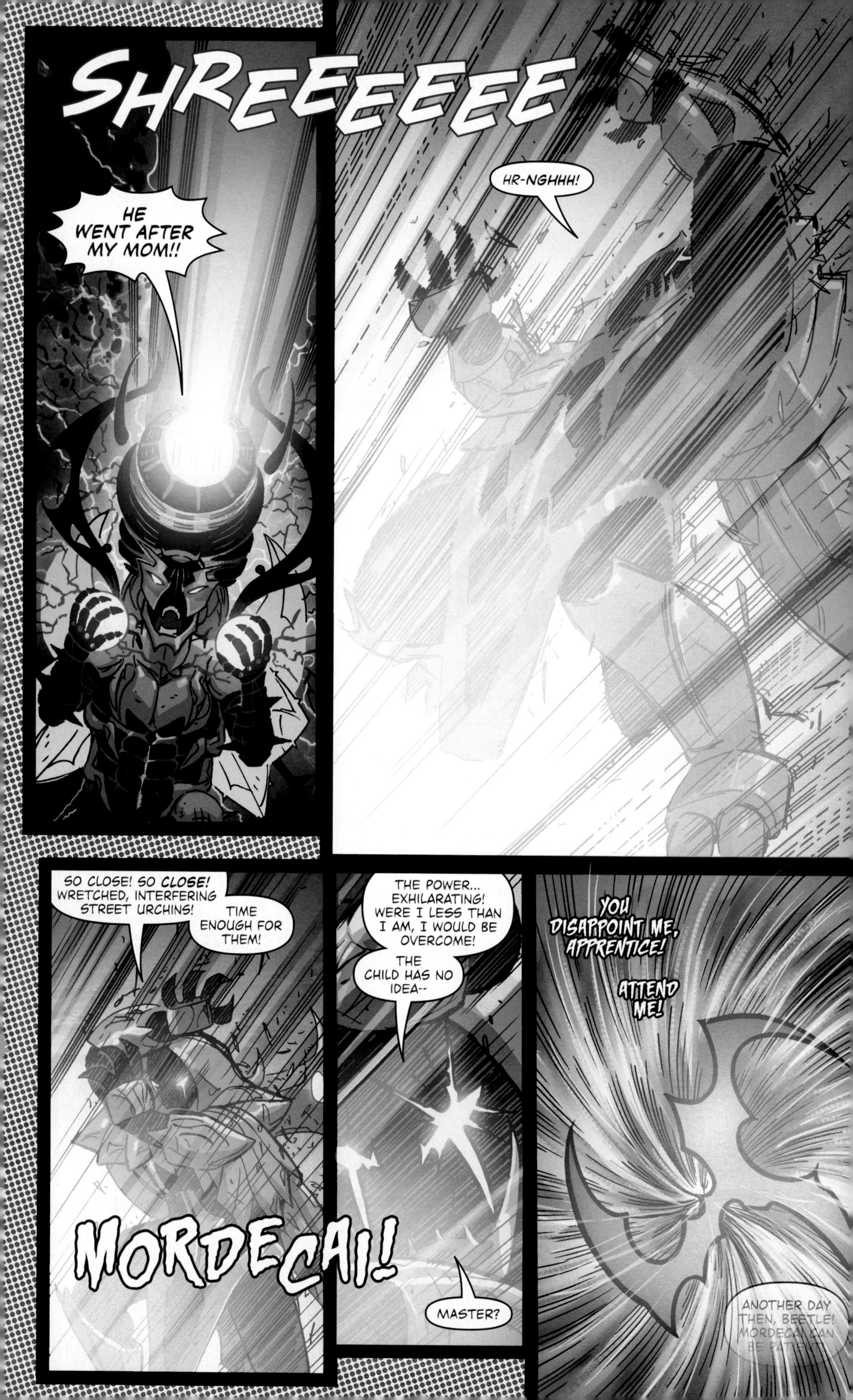
SHREEEEEEE
HE WENT AFTER MY MOM!!
HR-NGHHH!
SO CLOSE! SO CLOSE! WRETCHED, INTERFERING STREET URCHINS!
TIME ENOUGH FOR THEM!
THE POWER... EXHILARATING! WERE I LESS THAN I AM, I WOULD BE OVERCOME!
THE CHILD HAS NO IDEA--
MORDECAI!
MASTER?
YOU DISAPPOINT ME, APPRENTICE!
ATTEND ME!
ANOTHER DAY THEN, BEETLE! MORDECAI CAN

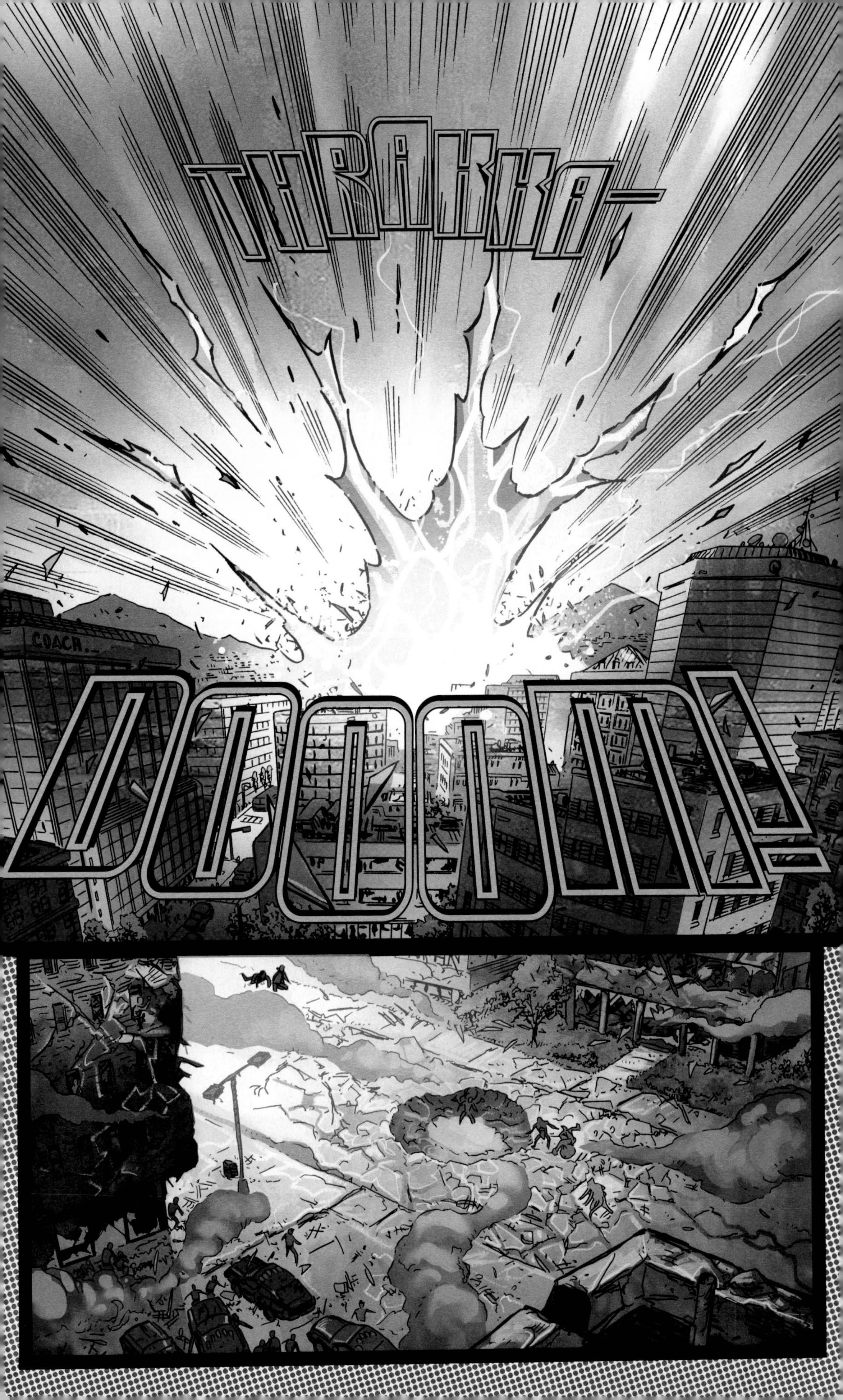
THRAKKA-
DOOOM!
COACH..

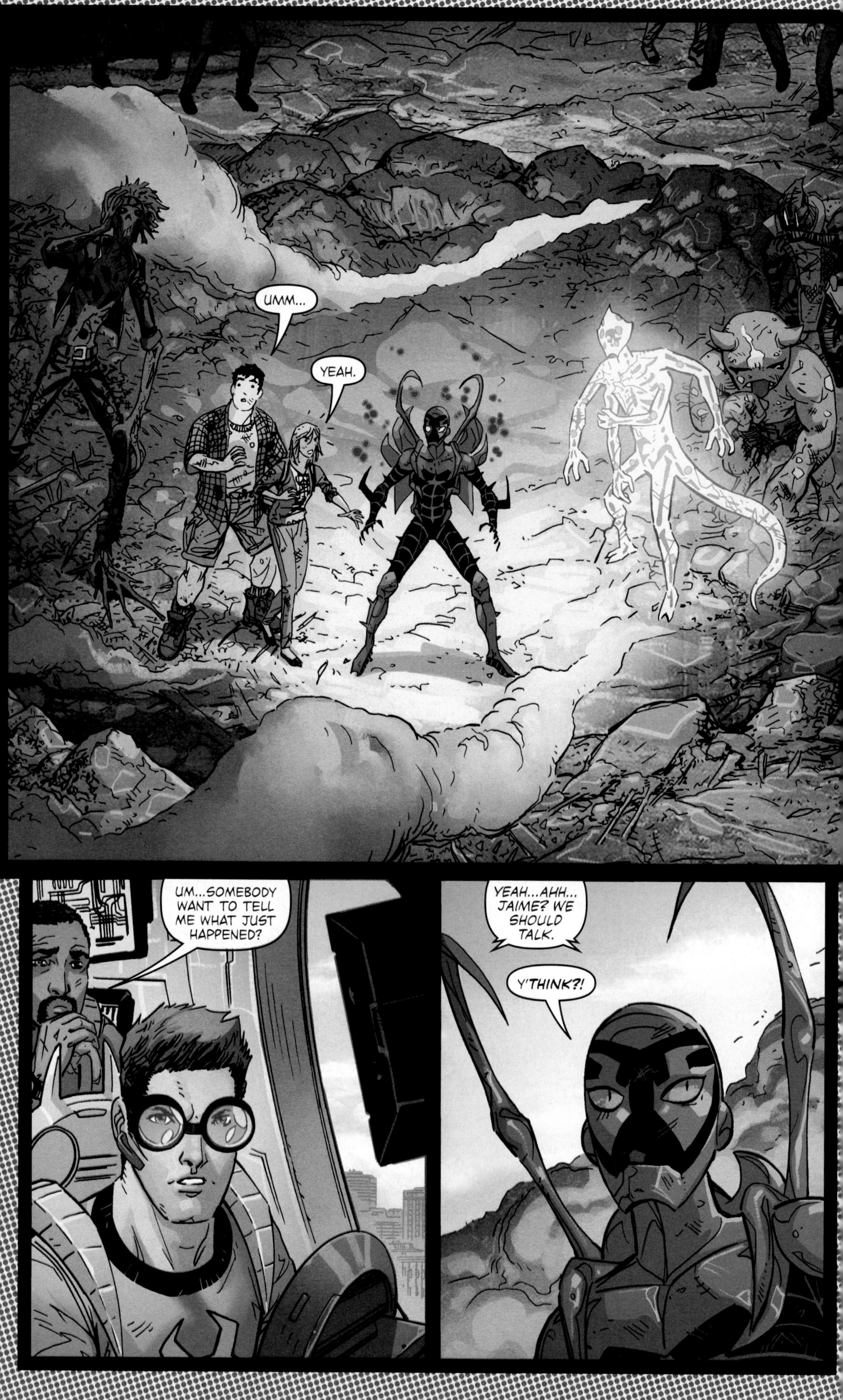
UMM...
YEAH.
UM...SOMEBODY WANT TO TELL ME WHAT JUST HAPPENED?
YEAH...AHH... JAIME? WE SHOULD TALK.
Y'THINK?!

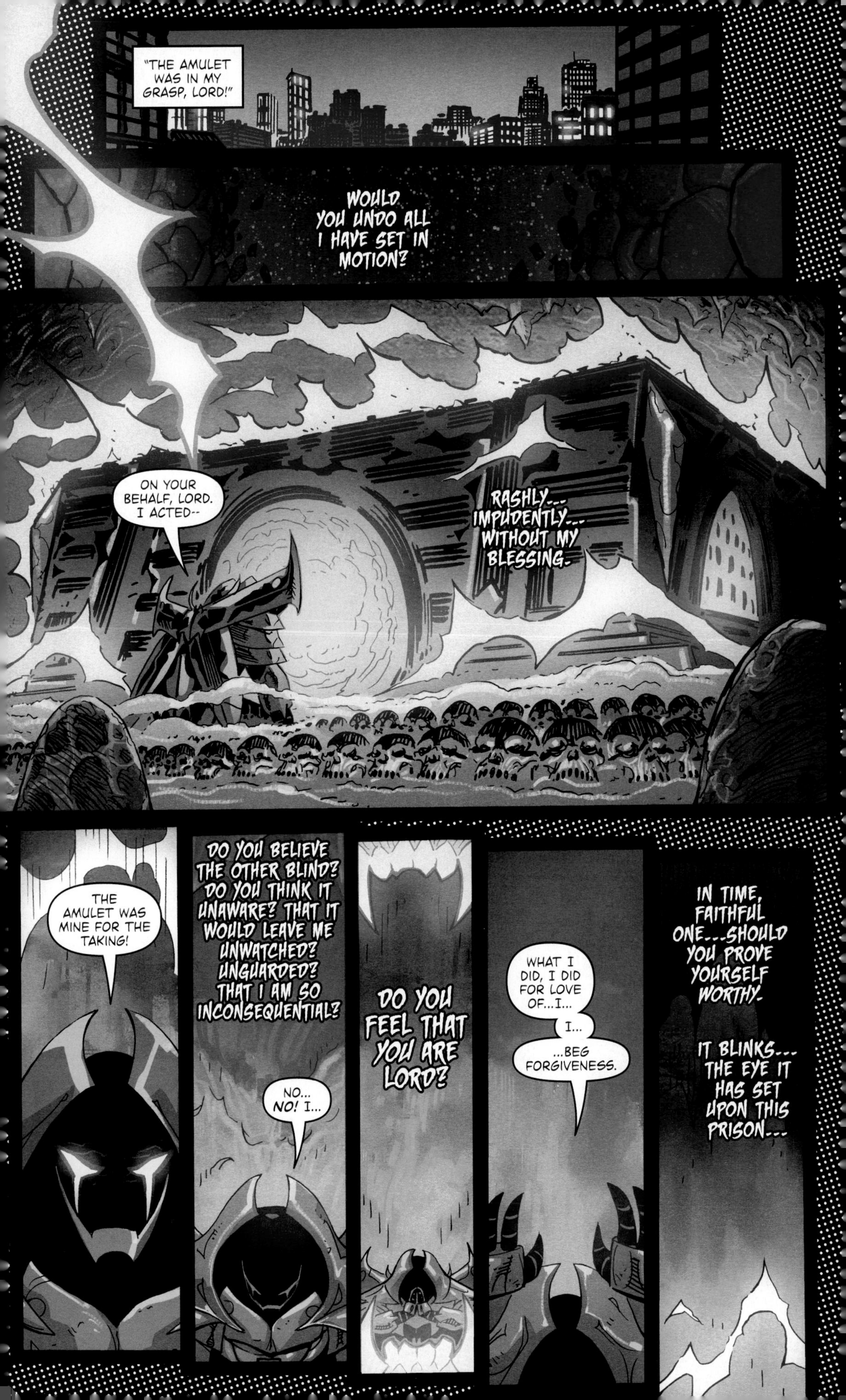
"THE AMULET WAS IN MY GRASP, LORD!"
WOULD YOU UNDO ALL I HAVE SET IN MOTION?
ON YOUR BEHALF, LORD. I ACTED--
RASHLY... IMPUDENTLY... WITHOUT MY BLESSING.
THE AMULET WAS MINE FOR THE TAKING!
DO YOU BELIEVE THE OTHER BLIND? DO YOU THINK IT UNAWARE? THAT IT WOULD LEAVE ME UNWATCHED? UNGUARDED? THAT I AM SO INCONSEQUENTIAL?
NO... NO! I...
DO YOU FEEL THAT YOU ARE LORD?
WHAT I DID, I DID FOR LOVE OF...I...
I...
...BEG FORGIVENESS.
IN TIME, FAITHFUL ONE...SHOULD YOU PROVE YOURSELF WORTHY.
IT BLINKS... THE EYE IT HAS SET UPON THIS PRISON...

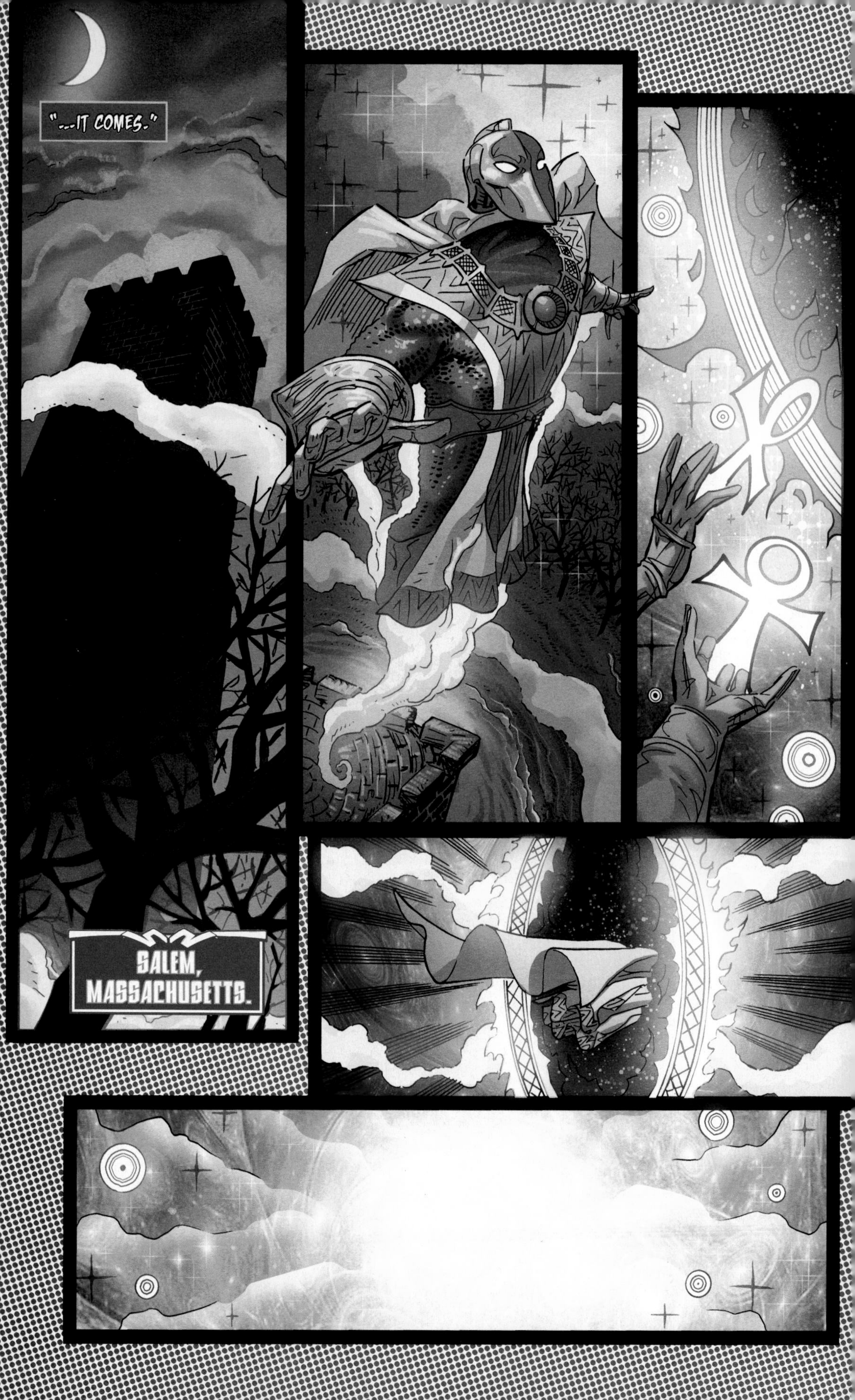
"...IT COMES."
SALEM, MASSACHUSETTS.

blue beetle

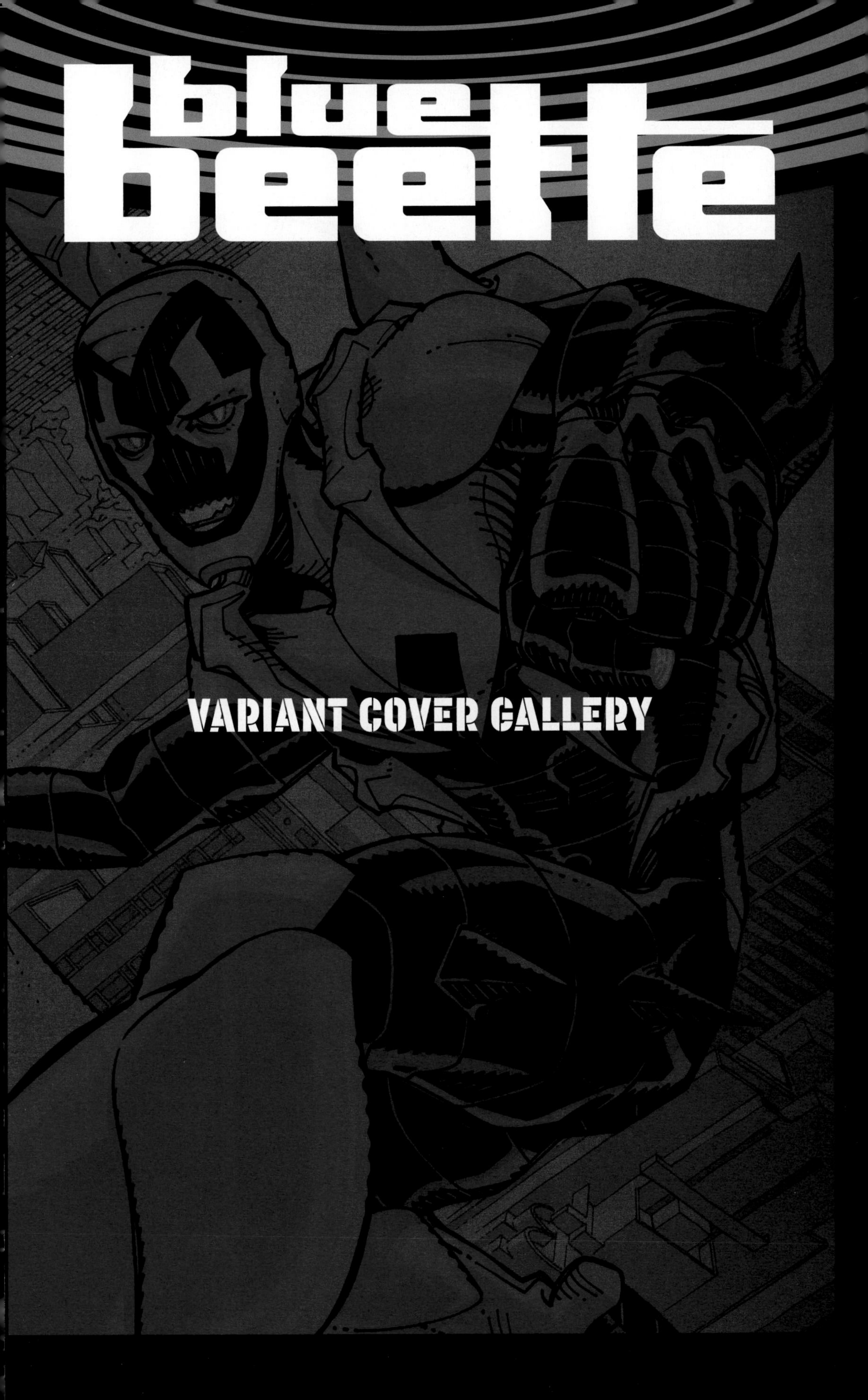

VARIANT COVER GALLERY

BLUE BEETLE: REBIRTH #1 variant cover by CULLY HAMNER

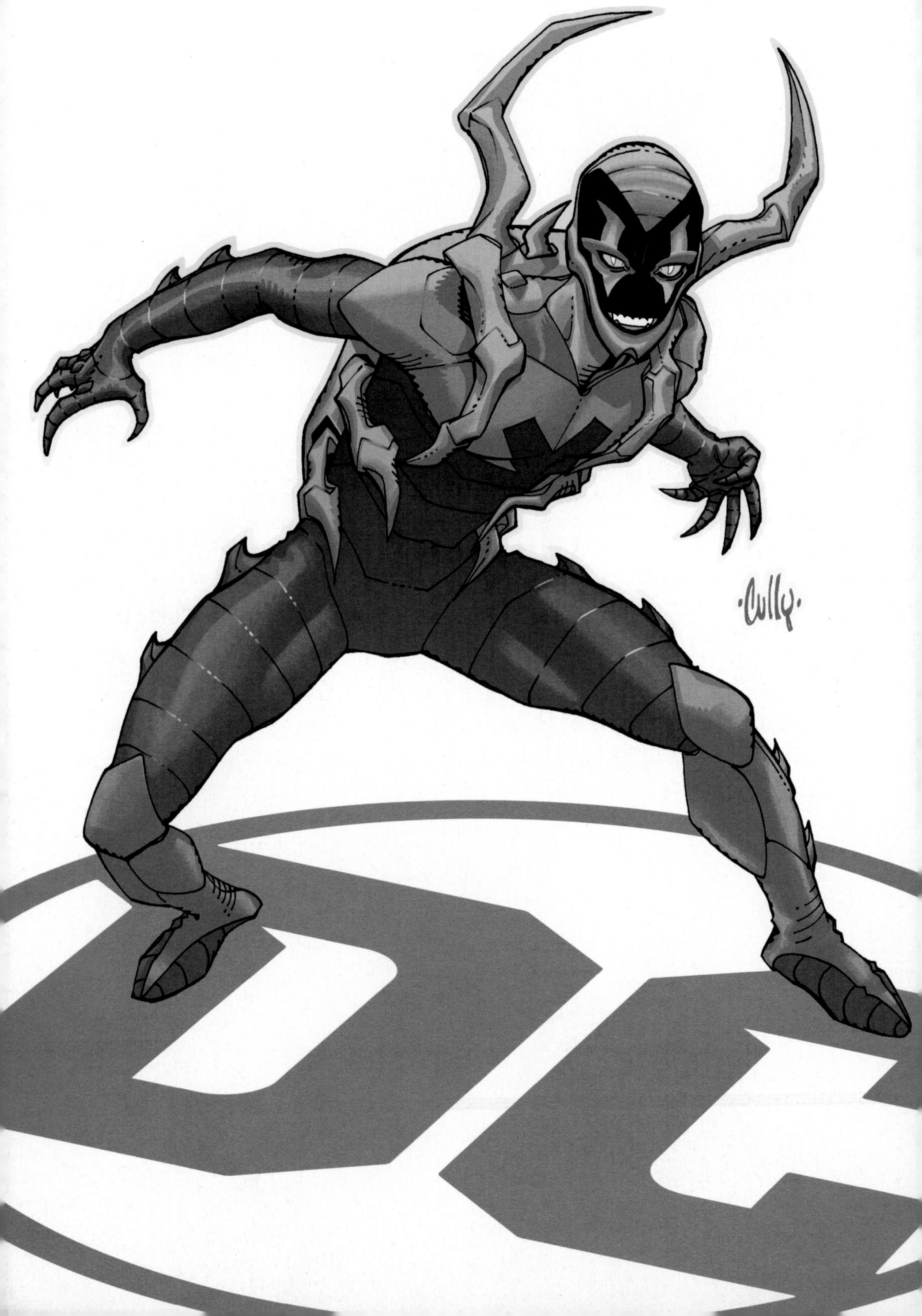
·Cully·

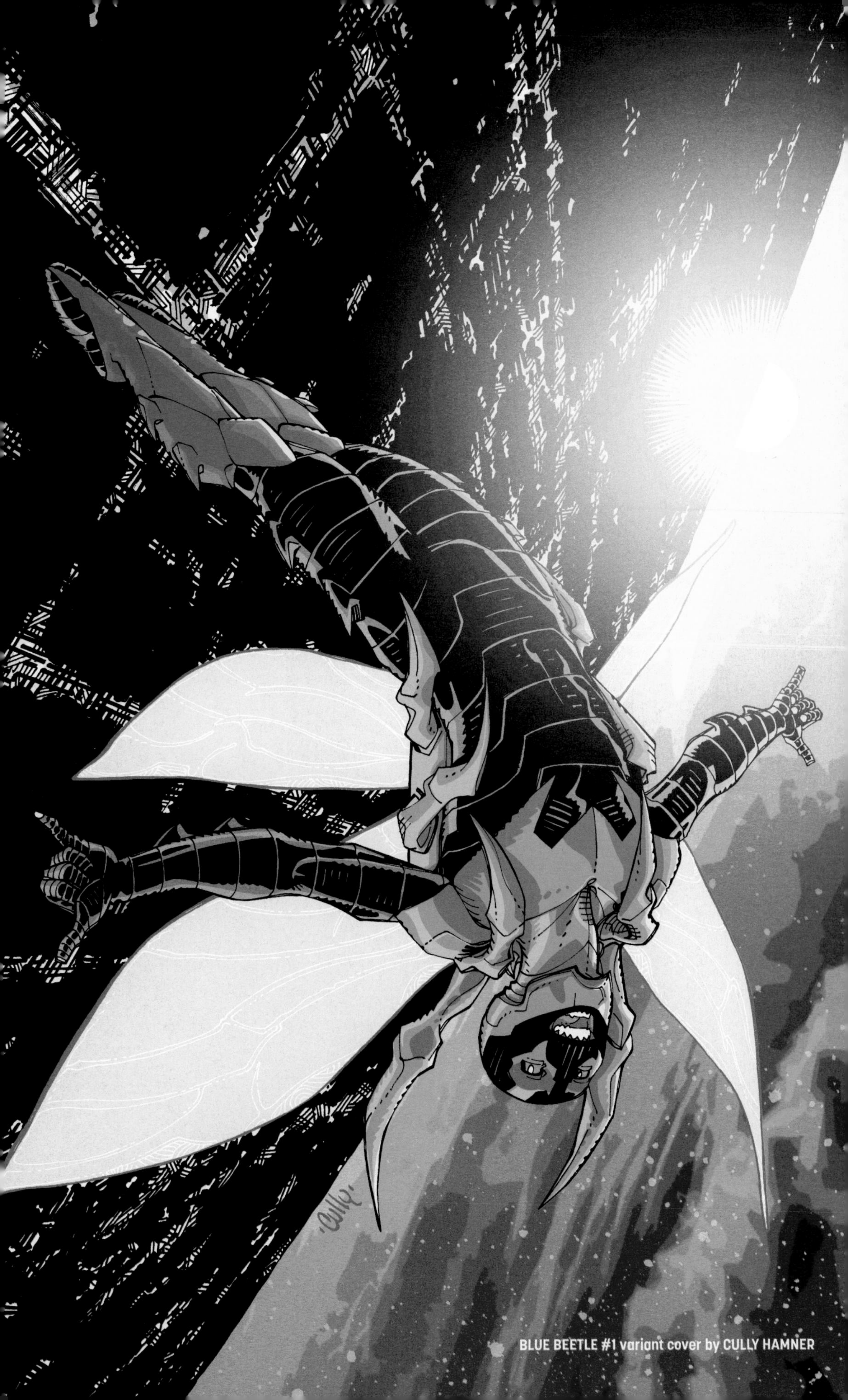

BLUE BEETLE #1 variant cover by CULLY HAMNER

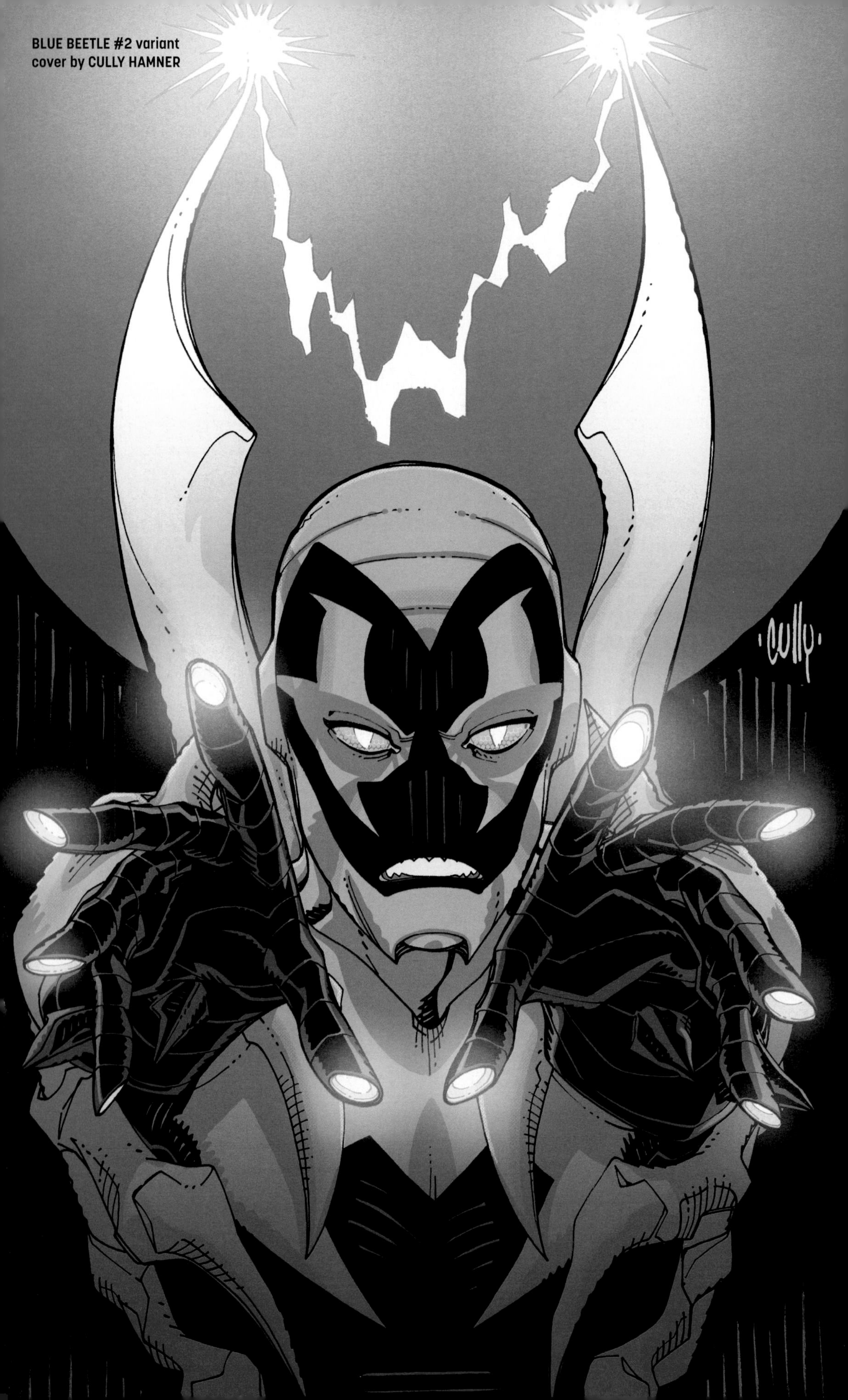
cully

BLUE BEETLE #2 variant
cover by CULLY HAMNER

BLUE BEETLE #3 variant cover by CULLY HAMNER

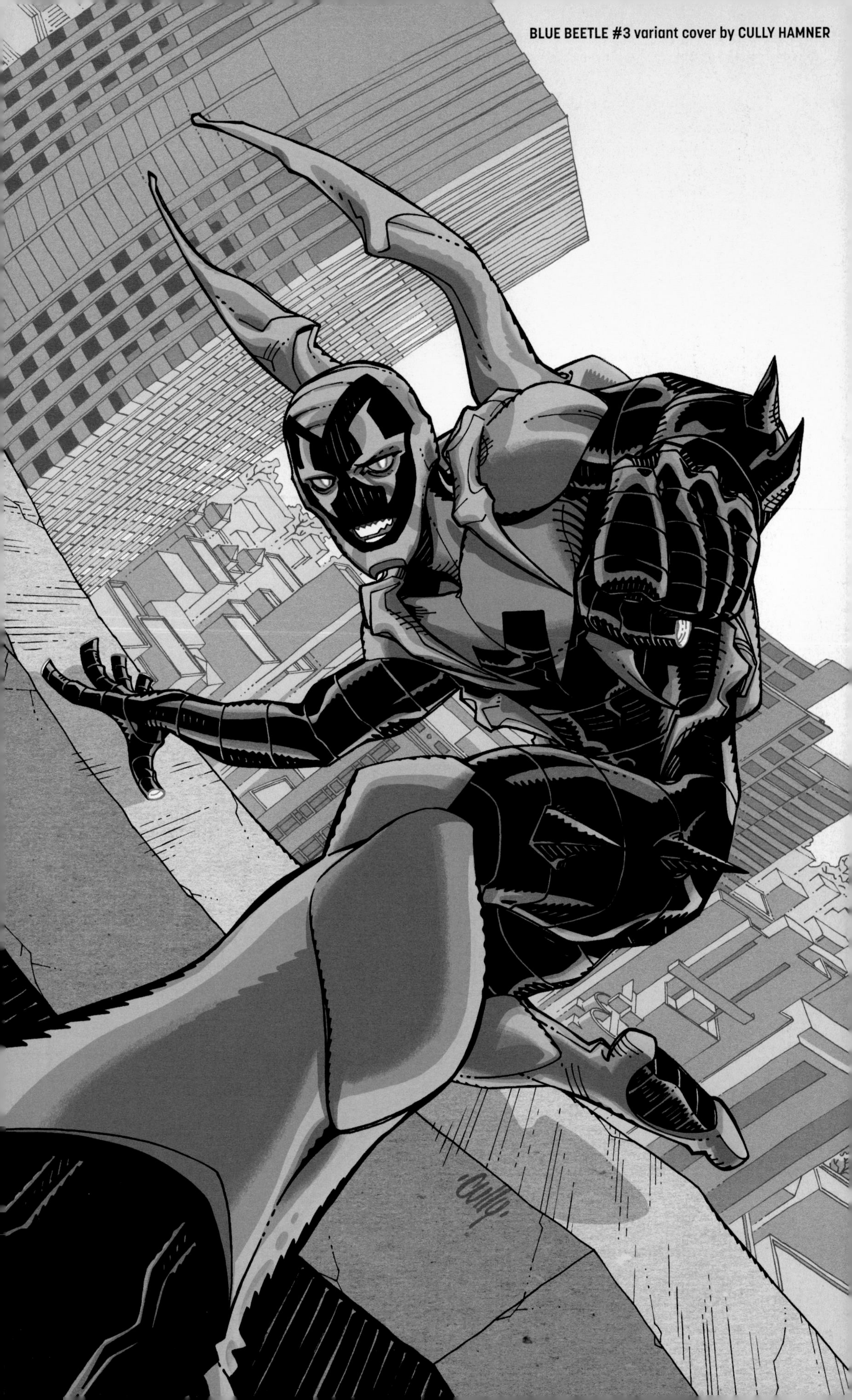
CULLY

BLUE BEETLE #4 variant cover by CULLY HAMNER

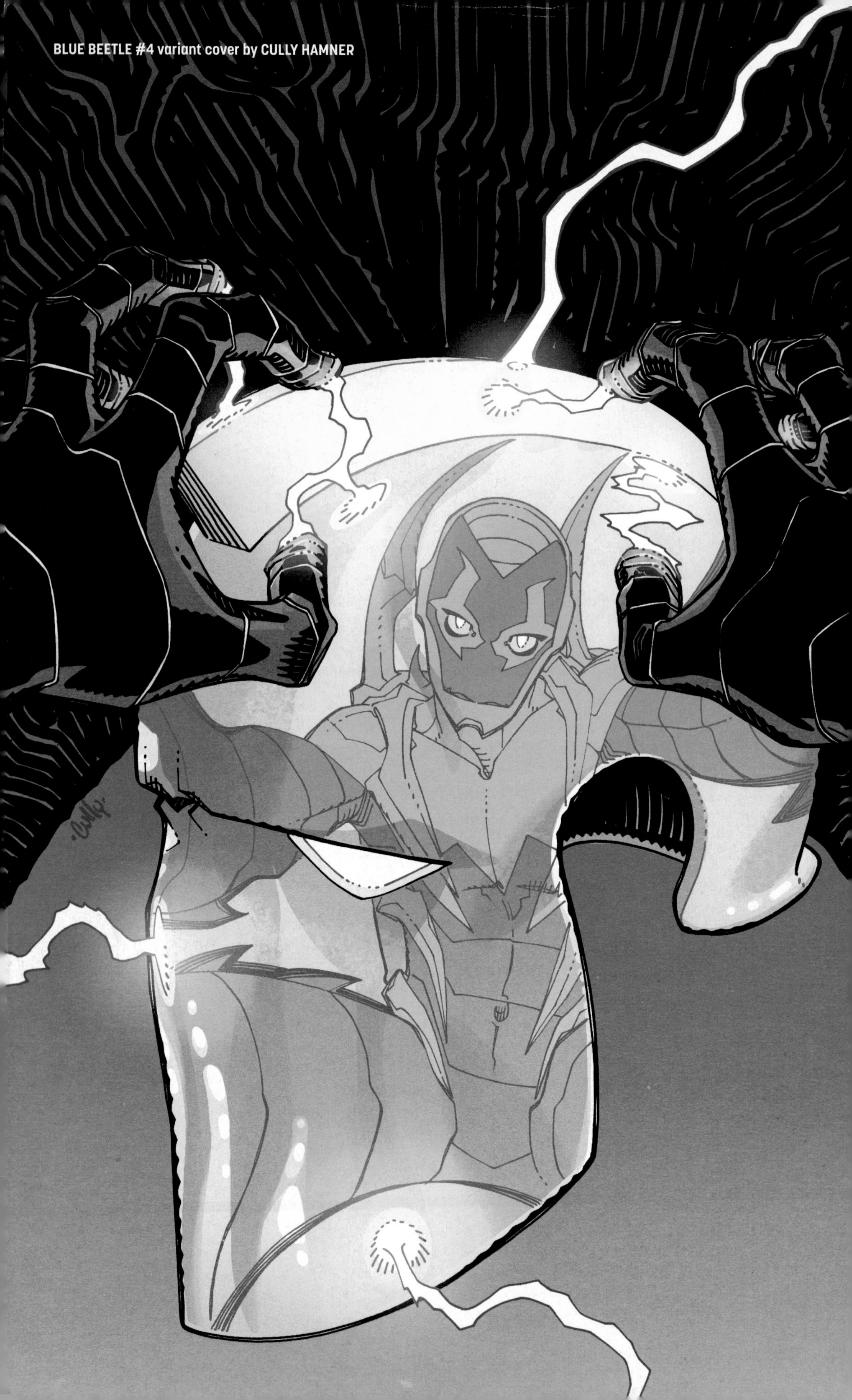

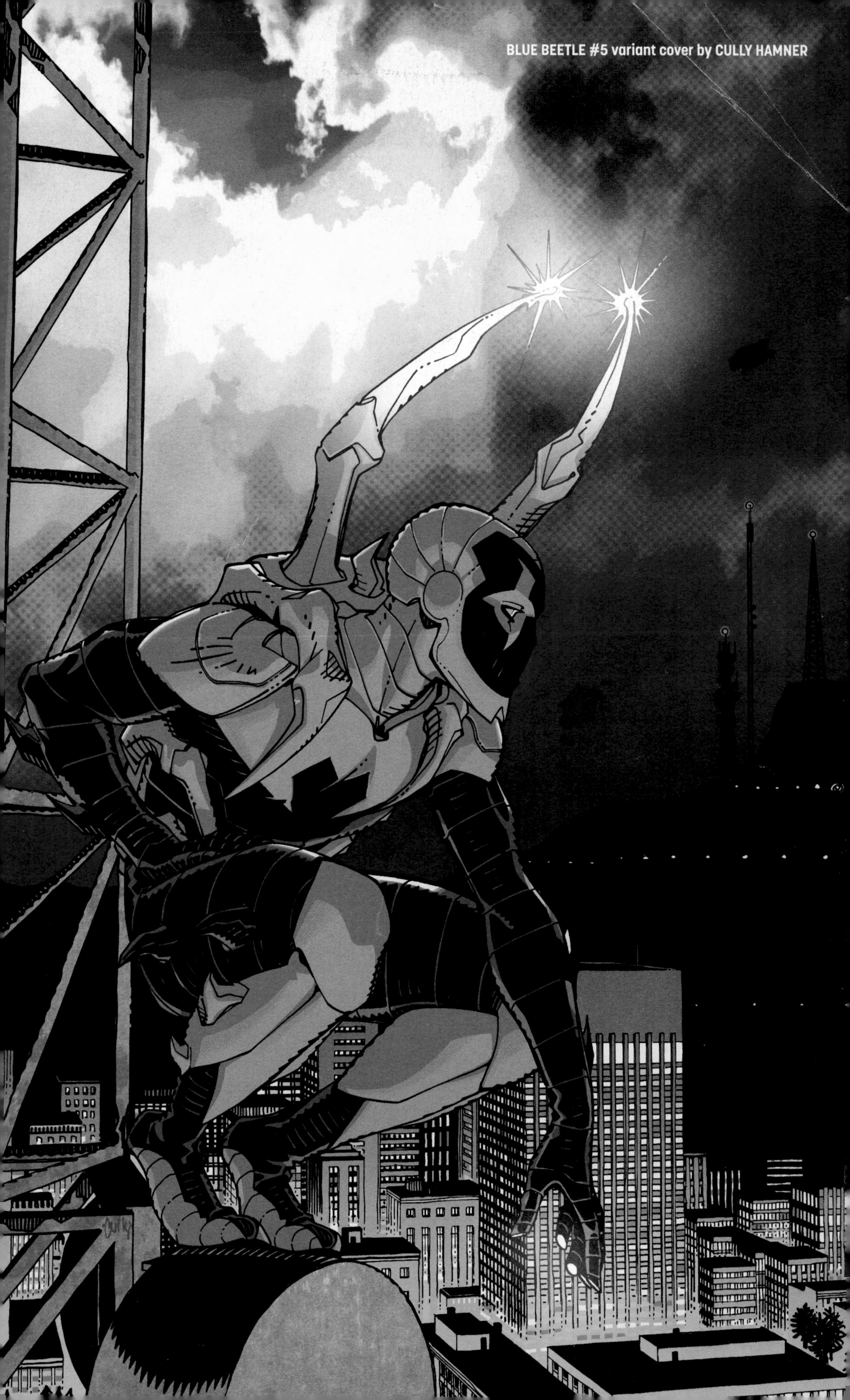

BLUE BEETLE #5 variant cover by CULLY HAMNER

CHARACTER CONCEPTS BY SCOTT KOLINS

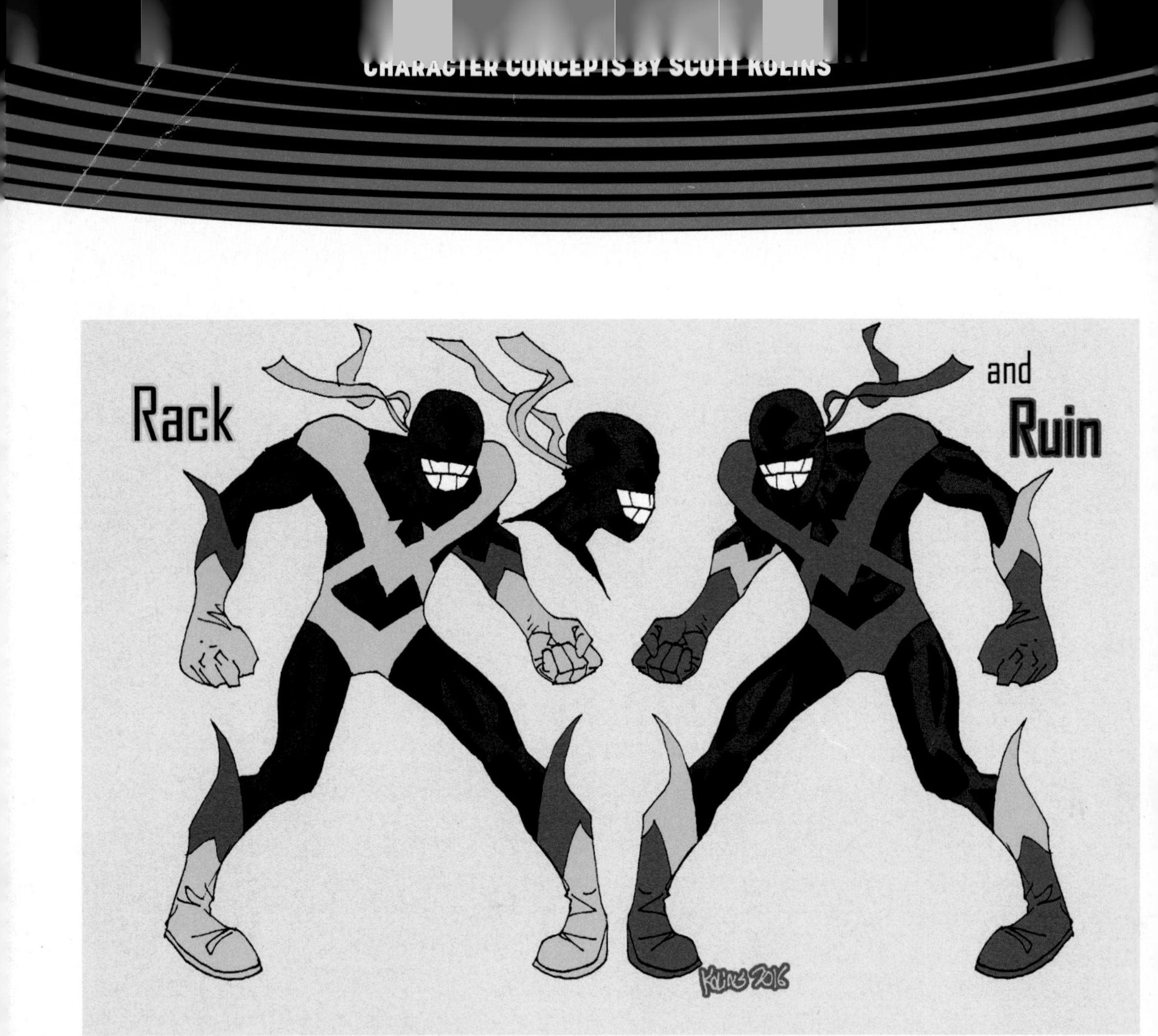
Rack
and
Ruin

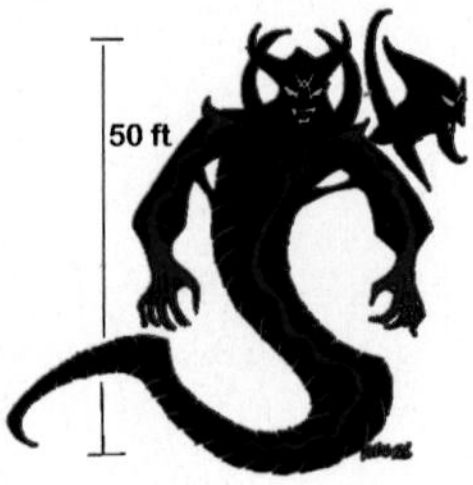
50 ft

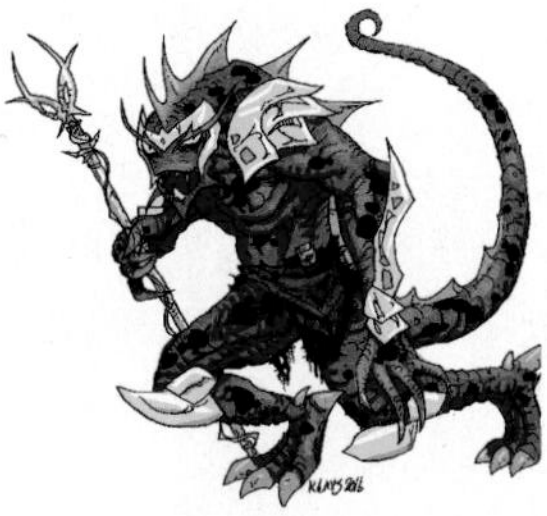

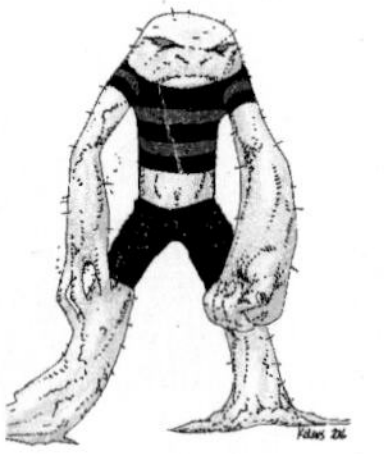

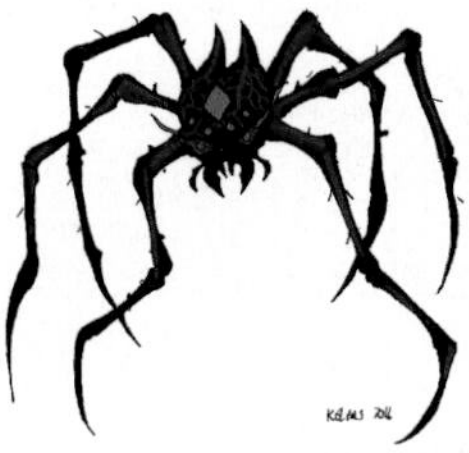

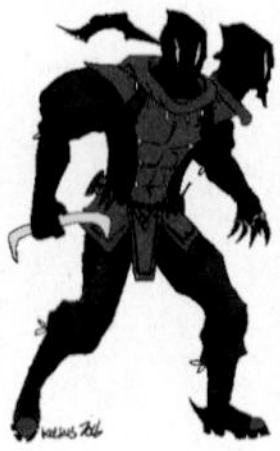

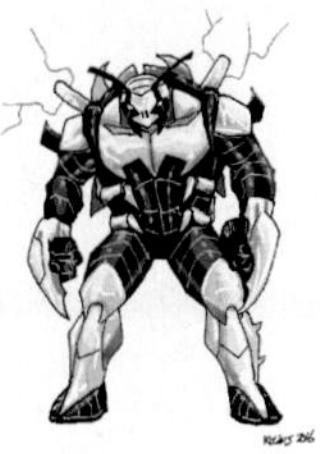

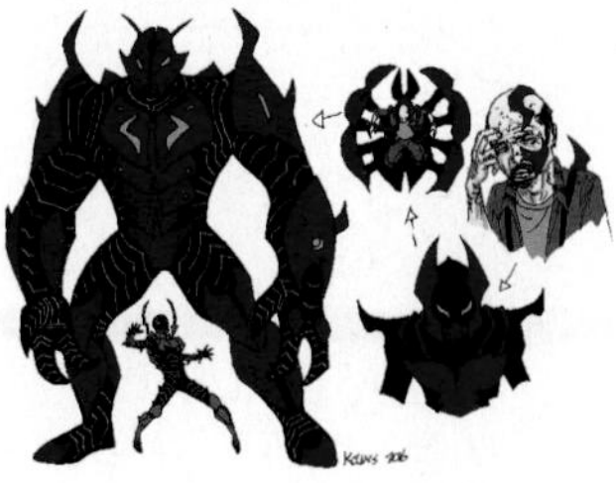

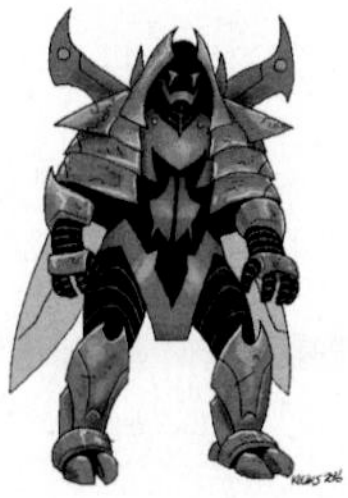

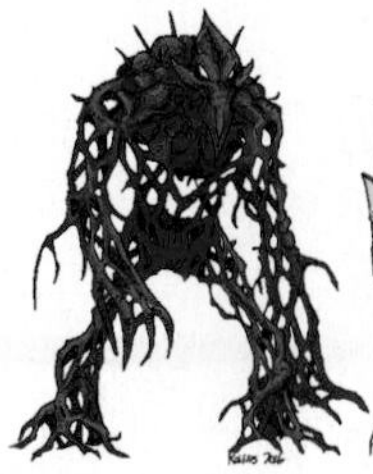

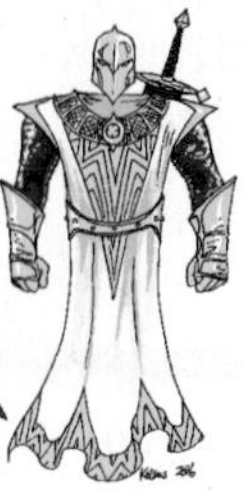